Additional Praise for
Principalities in Particular

"From the right, we now face conspiratorial theories of a 'deep state' that aims to undermine our social status quo. In contrast, this astonishing book is unmistakable evidence of a 'deep church,' in which the author is a passionate participant along with Karl Barth, Dietrich Bonhoeffer, Jacques Ellul, William Stringfellow, Walter Wink, and Daniel Berrigan, to name only its more prominent members, in whose orbit the author lives. Wylie-Kellermann, as a man of that 'deep church,' speaks in innocent seriousness concerning the radical claims of the gospel; he shows, moreover, how those claims impinge on public policy and summon to a life of glad serious obedience. This is an urgently required book just now because the contemporary church is so absorbed in accommodation to culture and worried about survival that it too often has only feeble words and acts in the world. Wylie-Kellermann shows that there is decisive news to be performed around our most vexing concrete public issues. Every page of this book is an invitation to obedient imagination that leads beyond despair, fatigue, and cynicism."
—**Walter Brueggemann, professor emeritus, Columbia Theological Seminary**

"Stringfellow rightly said that the drama of history unfolds between God, humanity, and the powers and principalities. We still need ministry resources that deepen our biblical, theological, and spiritual understanding of the powers. Bill Wylie-Kellermann unmasks and engages the powers through historical moments, mentors, biblical analysis, and his own call as pastor, teacher, and activist. The result is not only informative, but transformative as well."
—**Yvonne V. Delk, founding director, Center for African American Theological Studies, Chicago**

Principalities in Particular

Principalities in Particular

A Practical Theology of the Powers That Be

Bill Wylie-Kellermann

With a Foreword by Rose Marie Berger

PRINCIPALITIES IN PARTICULAR

A Practical Theology of the Powers That Be

Copyright © 2017 Fortress Press. All rights reserved. Except for brief quotations in critical articles or reviews, no part of this book may be reproduced in any manner without prior written permission from the publisher. Email copyright@fortresspress.com or write to Permissions, Fortress Press, PO Box 1209, Minneapolis, MN 55440-1209.

Cover design: Rob Dewey

Print ISBN: 978-1-5064-3168-0

eBook ISBN: 978-1-5064-3824-5

For Isaac, Cedar, and Ira
with
Word and World, Roots and Spirit

Learning the Word in the Shell of the World
4/28/12

it is
new as an egg nested high in the cleft of a rock
teeming precariously, with life,
and ancient, even as the rock itself

fresh as manna glistening the ground
of a wilderness camp
convened in the company of ungulates, angels,
and wild beasts.
we travel light, learning this day
our daily bread – and nothing more

it is living and lucid in the school of Isaiah
harboring for decades, their mentor's edgy
and sighted poems
read, reimagined, rewrit, performed as news
of imperial collapse at the turn of history's hope
and healing.

all as we stumble, hastening to keep up
shook by parables afoot, spun over shoulder
by a rabbi (this image of God) schooling us in the Way
by walking it
barely sitting to teach
till in the occupied temple court
with spies and cops hovering

practically the spot where Paul was busted
student of Gamaliel and Stephen
organizing a movement
one road, one household, one city at a time
tell me what *ekklesia* looks like
this is what *ekklesia* looks like

and so it looked to hermits and monks of invention
trekking off again to desert huts
jumping ship from empire's smooth
and bellicose arrangement
there to gather wry stories and sayings,
to ponder the sparest in a cup

what would claire or francis,
(gone begging in mendicancy) say?
taught by birds and sister moon to pray.

wending their way to Gandhi's ashram
clinging like warriors in a circle to truth
the deep thing worth dying for

Bonhoeffer had an appointment there
to relearn the Sermon on the Mount
from a Hindu pilgrim with
salt of the earth and sea in hand.

but he was waylaid by events
necessitating a seminary underground
where he set the needle on a 78
of Negro Spirituals from Abyssinian
and translated them, guttural thick and precise,
as a stick in the spokes of a wheel—

find the cost of freedom schools buried in the ground

how does it all come 'round again? rise again and live?

it is in the silence broken by Audre, by Martin,
it's there in Daniel's poem telling Phil's hammer stroke,
or in Dorothy's little way
and Peter's agronomic university
the Alleluia of Bill's ashes buried

it is in the soil, the fallen grain,
the hospitable loaf passed, teeming and ancient,
hand to hand to hand

in all we have, and all we are
being enough,
it is

                                                                                bwk

Contents

	Foreword	xv
	Acknowledgments and Thanks	xxiii
	Introduction: From Moment to Moment	xxix

Part I. A Theological Introduction

1.	William Stringfellow: A Story of This Theological Conversation	3
2.	A Personal and Activist Appreciation: The Life and Legacy of Walter Wink (2016)	29
3.	Death Shall Have No Dominion: Daniel Berrigan of the Resurrection (2017)	37
4.	From the Beginning: Two Creation Liturgies	45

Part II. Particular Powers

5.	Barbed Wire and Beyond: The Freedom to Unmake Nuclear Weapons (1983)	71
6.	Discerning the Angel of Detroit: The Spirits and Powers at Work in One City (1989)	85
7.	Fallen: The Law and the State (1991)	99

8.	The Machinery of War: Technology and the Powers That Indwell (1991)	105
9.	Confronting the Drug Powers; Freeing the Captives (1992)	111
10.	Family: Icon and Principality (1994)	125
11.	Spiritual Warfare and Economic Justice (1994)	135
12.	The Powers in Healing and Hospital Ministry (1996)	143
13.	Death Has Its Day: The BP Oil Spill (2010)	149
14.	Readers before Profits: The Detroit Newspaper Strike (1996)	151
15.	Labor Unions and the Principalities (1998)	157
16.	Exorcising an American Demon: Racism Is a Principality (1998)	165
17.	The Fall in Play: Sports as a Principality (1998)	173
18.	Global Economy: False Gods and the Power of Love (2003)	185
19.	Unholy Alliance: John Wesley and Global Powers of Slavery (2003)	193
20.	Be Not Awed: The War in Iraq (2003)	199
21.	Katrina and the Wrath to Come (2005)	205
22.	Surveillance and Impeachment (2007)	209
23.	Lest Death Prevail: Harry Potter and the Principalities (2011)	217
24.	Coming to a City Near You: Emergency Management (2014)	221

25.	The Dismantling of Public Education: Separate and Unequal (2014)	*229*
26.	Her Name Was Charity: The Detroit Water Struggle (2014)	*239*
27.	Church and the Powers (Church as a Power) (2016)	*245*
28.	Trump Powers: Principalities and the President (2017)	*259*
	Appendix I: Thinking Biblically and Theologically about a Particular Power: An Inventory of Provoking Questions	*289*
	Appendix II: Theological Exegesis of the Neighborhood	*291*
	Appendix III: The Angel of a Congregation: Possible Elements of a Continuing Discernment Process (After the work of Walter Wink)	*293*
	Appendix IV	*297*
	Index of Names and Subjects	*299*

Foreword

Many Christian ministers claim to defend scripture. Few have done so in a court of law.

In Benton Harbor, Michigan, in 2009, there unfolded the strange legal case of *The People of Michigan v. Edward Pinkney*.

The Rev. Edward Pinkney, a Missionary Baptist pastor and civil rights leader, had been in a long fight with the "powers that be" in Benton Harbor to defend the African American community there against corporate overreach. While Pinkney was on parole for a previous political conviction, he wrote an opinion piece in the local *People's Tribune* in which he called down biblical curses on the sentencing judge. In King James cadences, Pinkney wrote, "The Lord shall smite thee with consumption and with a fever and with an inflammation and with extreme burning. They the demons shall pursue thee until thou [perish]."[1] His parole officer deemed this a violation. Pinkney was hauled back into court, charged with the serious crime of making threats against or attempting to intimidate a judge.

The Rev. William Wylie-Kellermann, a United Methodist minister from nearby Detroit, was called in as an expert witness for the defense. Court documents reveal, "Reverend Kellermann testified that he recognized the passage in Rev. Pinkney's article as derived from the Book of Deuteronomy," which describes the covenant between human beings and God "and the blessings and curses which flow from that covenant.

---

1. Edward Pinkney, "Corrupt judge denies new jury trial in Pinkney case," *The People's Tribune*, November/December 2007; http://www.peoplestribune.org/PT.2007.11/PT.2007.11.18.html (accessed April 30, 2017). (The text is an allusion to Deuteronomy 28:22, which is, however, misquoted in the *Tribune* story, reading "persist" instead of "perish.") See also Bill Wylie-Kellermann, "A True Threat: Rev. Pinkney and the Book of Deuteronomy," posted on Benton Harbor Black Autonomy Network Community Organization blog on August 14, 2008; http://www.bhbanco.org/2008/08/true-threat-rev-pinkney-and-book-of.html (accessed April 26, 2017).

Reverend Kellermann further explained that according to the Bible, the curses described in Deuteronomy are visited upon [humans] by God," not by other human beings.[2]

Despite this argument, Judge Dennis Wiley sentenced the Rev. Pinkney to three to ten years in state prison for spouting Deuteronomy. The court ruled that Pinkney's Deuteronomical curses constituted a "true threat" against a judicial colleague.

The book you now hold engages the question: What is the particular nature of the "powers and principalities" at work in American Empire in the twentieth and twenty-first century—and what constitutes a true spiritual threat to life?

In the first century, convict Paul wrote about the particular "powers and principalities" of the Roman Empire. From central lock-up, Paul declared, "For our struggle is not against enemies of blood and flesh, but against the rulers, against the authorities, against the cosmic powers of this present darkness, against the spiritual forces of evil in the heavenly places" (Eph 6:12).

Paul moves seamlessly between material and spiritual powers, as William Stringfellow reminds us, "in which political authority encompasses and conjoins the angelic powers and incumbent rulers."[3] The concept of angels as God's messengers is not foreign to scripture. The description of "fallen angels" is less familiar, but also native to the New Testament. Both 2 Peter 2:4 and Jude 1:6 refer to angels who have sinned against God and await punishment on the day of judgment. These are "the angels that did not keep their own position, but left their proper dwelling" (Jude 1:6), because they no longer served God.

***

I am neither theologian nor biblical scholar. I am a poet. But I am also one acquainted with angels. Early in life, I was aware of the sort of angel that has "kept to its own position," in particular, an angel of annunciation. On a bright day in 1966, at age four, I lay down for my afternoon nap. My grandmother was visiting, in anticipation of my sister's birth. As I lay in bed, my window suddenly filled to the frame with an angel. In her arms, she carried my baby sister to her birth. This angel flashed like sunlight on water. Behind her, sycamore trees

---

2. *People of the State of Michigan v. Edward Pinkney* (July 14, 2009), http://www.aclumich.org/sites/default/files/file/pinkneydecision.pdf (accessed April 24, 2017).
3. William Stringfellow, *Conscience and Obedience* (Waco, TX: Word, 1977), 48.

whipped in the December wind. I ran to tell my grandmother the good news that I had a baby sister. Within the hour, my father called to confirm the birth. My experience is as vivid to me now as it was then. This was an angelic power going about her work, serving life.

But soon enough, I learned to recognize the other sort, angels who had abandoned their "own position," had "fallen," and had taken up service to the Angel of Death. In 1986, I moved to Washington, DC, to join the community of Christians at Sojourners and *Sojourners* magazine (where many of the writings of Bill Wylie-Kellermann, William Stringfellow, Daniel Berrigan, and Walter Wink first appeared). At that time, my adopted city was called the "murder capital of the world," gripped by crack cocaine. DC then (and now) was a disenfranchised second-class client government with limited self-rule. Ronald Reagan was resident president.

The Angel of DC was riddled with an addiction to death and power. In my neighborhood, overdose deaths skyrocketed and "drug-related violence" was a daily occurrence. Two miles south, the Reagan administration was involved in a "dark alliance" of covert operations that involved the CIA using gangs in California to smuggle guns and drugs in order to finance the terrorist effort to overthrow the Nicaraguan government. The Iran-Contra Affair was no different from the local crack-and-Glock economy, except by scale.[4]

I lived in the epicenter of overlapping principalities of city and nation. The angels struggled over our heads in spiritual battle. The powers had lost their vocation to serve life and instead served death by domination.

I saw these "dark angels," as I named them, in my dreams, prayers, and waking visions. They slipped up through manhole covers with the gangrenous stench of a subterranean world that flowed with rot, from the White House and down the alleys of my neighborhood—and into the bloodstreams of my neighbors.

"When the drug powers invade a city neighborhood they are attended by a palpable spirit," writes Wylie-Kellermann. "It is truly predatory and invasive, bearing along the true presence of death."[5]

---

4. Gary Webb, *Dark Alliance: The CIA, the Contras, and the Crack Cocaine Explosion* (New York: Seven Stories, 1998).
5. See chapter 9, below.

This was never more true than when third-grader Donte Manning was shot in drug-deal crossfire around the corner from my house on Holy Thursday in 2005. A few days later, the Manning family asked friend Jacqueline Ponders to make their first public statement. "The family is praying that the person who is responsible for this crime, that God will convict their heart, that they will come forth and turn themselves in." I heard the echoes of Cain and Abel, and of God who asks Cain, "Where is your brother?"[6]

This is what the struggle "against the cosmic powers of this present darkness" looked like *in particular* in those days.

Whether fasting on Capitol Hill to end the weapons trade or walking through drug deals on the way to the corner store, I learned these spirits are best engaged with the Jesus Prayer: "Lord Jesus Christ, Son of God, have mercy on me, a sinner." (The Orthodox call this ancient appeal an "arrow prayer" for its ability to penetrate the thick veil between earthly and spiritual principalities.) I learned to keep my quiver full.

***

How are we to understand the spiritual battles of our own time, in our particular social location?

German Jewish philosopher Walter Benjamin turned to Jewish mysticism "for a model of praxis in dark times," as Margaret Cohen described it.[7] Benjamin saw a great spiritual battle taking place in his context of 1930s Europe. It was a battle for the "angel of history." Benjamin saw this angel depicted in Paul Klee's drawing *Angelus Novus*. As Benjamin described him, the angel is "looking as though he is about to move away from something he is fixedly contemplating. His eyes are staring, his mouth is open, his wings are spread. . . . His face is turned toward the past. Where we perceive a chain of events, he sees one single catastrophe which keeps piling wreckage upon wreckage and hurls it in front of his feet. The angel would like to stay, awaken the dead, and make whole what has been smashed. But a storm is blowing from Paradise; it has got caught in his wings with such violence that the angel can no longer close them."[8]

---

6. Rose Marie Berger, *Who Killed Donte Manning? The Story of an American Neighborhood* (Baltimore: Apprentice House, 2010).
7. Margaret Cohen, "Benjamin's Phantasmagoria: The Arcades Project," *The Cambridge Companion to Walter Benjamin*, ed. David S. Ferris (Cambridge: Cambridge University Press, 2004), 210.
8. Walter Benjamin, "Theses on the Philosophy of History," *Illuminations*, introduction by Hannah

Wylie-Kellermann names in the following pages the angels of our particular history who have "fallen" or failed at their station: the American demon of white supremacy; the fallen angel of barbed wire (which marks trespass, bars hospitality: As Polish poet Czeslaw Milosz wrote, "The extermination camps became a central fact of the century and barbed wire its emblem");[9] the twin demons of secrecy and surveillance that accompany the security state; the church itself as power, both fallen and saved. Wylie-Kellermann catches that violent wind pinning the angel's wings wide open.

This talk of spirits and principalities and powers bears wisdom for the Christ-bearing diaspora today. It is difficult in a post-Christian era (which Stringfellow rightly argues was conceived in the fourth century, with the Constantinian arrangement) for disciples to remember Jesus's Beloved Community. It is a struggle to hold the "image of the world, still timidly developing . . . in which the miraculous has a legitimate place."[10]

***

It is not only Christians who engage the powers for the sake of survival. In 1990, the (Fourteenth) Dalai Lama invited Jewish leaders to Dharamsala, India, home to Tibetan Buddhists who had been driven out by China's imperial reach. His question to his Jewish guests: "Can you tell us the secret of Jewish spiritual survival in exile?" Rabbi Zalman Schachter, Hasidic mystic and animator of modern Jewish renewal, addressed the Dalai Lama by speaking of angels. In Jewish cosmology, angels are a way of describing "how divine energy comes into this world or creation and how energy goes back up," writes poet Rodger Kamenetz, who describes the exchange in *The Jew in the Lotus*. "Sometimes it's the image of Jacob's ladder, the angels climbing down and then back up. It's about how we move from the material to the spiritual world."[11]

Arendt (New York: Schocken, 1969), 257. http://pages.ucsd.edu/~rfrank/class_web/ES-200A/Week 2/benjamin_ps.pdf.
9. Czeslaw Milosz, "The Witness of Poetry," *The Charles Eliot Norton Lectures*, Book 38 (Cambridge, MA: Harvard University Press, 1984), 51.
10. Ibid., 53.
11. Rodger Kamenetz, "Rodger Kamenetz presents on The Jew in the Lotus," online at https://bodhitree.com/journal_archive/rodger-kamenetz-presents-his-book-the-jew-in-the-lotus (accessed May 1, 2017).

Schachter provided the Dalai Lama with a detailed map of the principalities and powers in the Jewish and Tibetan worlds, both earthly and heavenly. Then Schachter said, "There's an angel for each city and for each one of the peoples of this earth." The Dalai Lama became animated. This kind of mapping of spiritual powers to their earthly principalities made perfect sense to him. He grasped it as key for spiritual survival in exile over generations, across the rise and fall of civilizations.

Wylie-Kellermann offers here a similar spiritual mapping of divine powers, with similar value for the diaspora of Jesus-followers. (It is as practical, in particular, as the way tenant organizers in my neighborhood map power relationships and discern which are generative and which enslave.)

Walter Benjamin wrote, "[T]he Messiah arrives not merely as the Redeemer; he also arrives as the vanquisher of the Anti-Christ. The only writer of history with the gift of setting alight the sparks of hope in the past, is the one who is convinced of this: that not even the dead will be safe from the enemy, if he is victorious. And this enemy has not ceased to be victorious."[12] This is a book from one who believes in "setting alight the sparks of hope" found in the past to serve the vanquishing of the forces of death in our present and shared future.

Bill Wylie-Kellermann and his mentors—Stringfellow, Wink, Bonhoeffer, Berrigan, and the prophets of Detroit—understand the danger of the enemy. Yet Wylie-Kellermann writes for those who resist conformation to imperial faith and ecclesial "management" and who seek to be baptized (and to baptize future generations) to resist the same.

With baptism comes an oath to "renounce the devil and all his works, the vain pomp and glory of the world, with all covetous desires of the same, and the carnal desires of the flesh, so that thou wilt not follow nor be led by them."[13] Baptism is a vow to live free; to become an adept in the discerning of spirits—familial, ecclesial, political; and to praise God and serve life.

With this baptismal practice, one confesses that "death shall have no dominion." Even until today, this constitutes a "true threat" to the powers.

---

12. Walter Benjamin, "Theses on the Philosophy of History," *Illuminations*, introduction by Hannah Arendt (New York: Schocken, 1969), 255. http://pages.ucsd.edu/~rfrank/class_web/ES-200A/Week 2/benjamin_ps.pdf.
13. "Publick Baptism of Infants," *The 1662 Book of Common Prayer* as printed by John Baskerville in 1762 (accessed April 30, 2017); http://justus.anglican.org/resources/bcp/1662/baptism.pdf.

FOREWORD

You hold now an unsettling text. It deals with the spiritual consequences of events. It unsettles because it mirrors the mortality of civilizations (including, always, our own) and the stubborn endurance of life, should we choose it.

—Rose Marie Berger
Feast of St. Jutta in the third week of Easter

Rose Marie Berger, a senior associate editor of Sojourners magazine, *is a Catholic peace activist and poet. She lives in the Anacostia River watershed in Washington, DC.*

Acknowledgments and Thanks

Thank you, dear friends: To you, the co-conspirators, resurrection witnesses, practical theologians, street liturgists, wordsmiths and editors, institutional friends: the community who, in one or another way, helped in the practicing and the writing of this book:

Circles and their representatives: Liturgical resisters of the Powers-That-Be (with most of whom I've been arrested once or more), among them:

- the barbed-wire breakers at Wurtsmith AFB: Mary West, Tom Lumpkin, Gordon Judd, Bob Bossie, Larry Rosebaugh, Jerry Ebner;
- before them, Great Lakes Life Community: Ginger Hentz, Bob Randels, Chris and Jack Payden-Travers, Steve and Phyllis Senesi, Jasiu Milanowski, Eddie Gersh, Kate Byrne, Peter Weber;
- Michigan Faith and Resistance: Peter Dougherty, Liz Walters and the Abrahamics, Ardeth Platte, Carol Gilbert, Sheila Ganey, Barb Beasley, Joe and Jean Gump, Ron and Sigrid Dale, Marge Munger;
- Atlantic Life Community: John Bach, Bill Hartman, Philip Berrigan, Liz McAlister, John Schuchardt, Ladon Sheets, Steve Kelley, Louie DeBenedette, Artie Laffin, Kathy Boylan, Tom Lewis, Mitch Snyder;
- the Detroit Peace Community: Jeanie Wylie, John Zettner, Deb Choly, Marietta Jaeger, Susan Johnson, Connie Supan, Ray and Vivienne Kell, Ken Grunow, Joel Nigg;
- Pacific Life Community: Ched Myers, Jim and Shelley Douglass, Robert Aldridge;
- Lenten Desert Experience: Annie Bucher, Louis Vitale, John Dear;

- Peace Pentecost: Pio Celestino, Rose Berger, Jim Wallis, Yvonne Delk, Maurice McCrackin;
- Readers United: Grace Lee Boggs, Ernie Goodman, Mike Zelinski, Maryann Mahaffey, Robert Smith, Bishop Tom Gumbleton, Bishop H. Coleman McGeehee, Ed Rowe, Bob King, Norm Thomas, Rudi and Roseanne Simons;
- Save Our Sons and Daughters (SOSAD): Clementine Barfield, Thomas Lumpkin;
- Anti-Crack Marchers: Jimmy Boggs, Shea Howell, Richard Feldman;
- Bankruptcy and Emergency Management resisters: Elena Herrada, Luke Matteson, Antonio Cosme;
- Water Warriors: Charity Hicks, Mary Ellen Howard, Denise Griebler, Agnes Hitchcock, Terry Kelley, Elena Herrada;
- The Homrich Nine: Marian Kramer, Baxter Jones, Joan Smith, Jim Perkinson, Hans Barbe, David Olson, Marianne McGuire, Kim Redigan;
- and that is but the short list, representing and evoking;

St Peter's Episcopal Church, place, base, sanctuary, beloved community, hospitaliters, water distributers, and ministry makers, who have allowed me to bend their hearts and ears, preaching on my mentors and the powers;

Favorite among the wordwrights, Foreword writer of kind and careful thought: Rose Marie Berger;

Editors of these articles various: Jeanie Wylie-Kellermann (sweetest of them all), Julie Wortman, Dee Dee Risher, Jim Wallis, Karen Latea, Rose Berger, Jim Rice, Julie Polter, Jeff Dietrich, Joanne Kennedy, Lydia Wylie-Kellermann, Fred Vitale, Tom Stephens, Robert Ellsberg, and above all, Neil Elliott at Fortress Press, who summoned this proposal, then jumped at it, thoughtfully shaping the whole of this project down to the punctual detail—all of whom, every one, have encouraged me with a pretty free hand;

Beloved partner in Stringfellow research, Andrew "Uncas" McThenia, and another like, Anthony Dancer, plus Robert Boak Slocum and Paul West;

Intimate editor of Walter Wink, his partner in all things, even biblical and artistic and, yes, encourager of this project, June Keener Wink;

ACKNOWLEDGMENTS AND THANKS

Critical readers of this book or its parts, and its lavish endorsers: Frida Berrigan, Obrey Hendricks, Yvonne Delk, Laurel Dykstra, Walter Brueggemann, Ched Myers, Elaine Enns, Nelson Johnson, Jeanie Wylie-Kellermann, Denise Griebler, Jim Perkinson, Lily Mendoza, Elena Herrada, Gloria House: Bless you each;

For a Grant on "Principalities and Pastoral (Self) Care" that enabled in part a rereading of the Stringfellow corpus, the Louisville Institute;

For the vision to found and run, some forty years, an urban ministry training center in Chicago, the Seminary Consortium for Urban Pastoral Education, where, in its days of life, virtually all of this material was taught: Dave Frenchak (+ May 15, 2016 +) and Carol Ann McGibbon;

For other institutions and para-institutions with contextual pedagogies where the content of this book has also been welcomed: Whitaker School of Theology (EDOMI), Ecumenical Theological Seminary, Word and World, and Marygrove College (Masters in Social Justice);

For the notorious mentors themselves, attended herein, Daniel Berrigan, Walter Wink, William Stringfellow: gone to God in fullness, who, for love of the Word, engaged principalities and powers with their bodies, hearts, and minds: May this book honor them in a practical call to others, that they likewise be and do: Thanks be to God.

Further thanks to the publications that have first honored these words with print:

Sojourners Magazine, www.sojo.net, for the following, reprinted with permission:
"Discerning the Angel of Detroit," cover essay, October 1989
"Harry and the Principalities: Review of *Deathly Hallows 2*," November 2011
"Death Has Its Day: Guilty Bystanders to Planetary Destruction," August 2010
"False Gods and the Power of Love: Principalities of Global Economy," November 2003
"The Power of Alliance: Why the Church and the Labor Movement Belong Together," September/October 1998
"Exorcising an American Demon," cover essay, March/April 1998
"Readers before Profits," January/February, 1996
"Drugs: Shadow, Mirror, Mime," cover essay, June 1992

"The Machinery of War: Technology and the Powers That Indwell," June 1992
"Before Courts Human and Divine," from *Who Is My Neighbor?* (1994)

The Witness, for the following, used with permission:
"Genesis as Resistance," October 1992
"Spiritual Warfare and Economic Justice," May 1994
"Family: Icon and Principality," December 1994
"The Powers in Hospital Ministry," June 1996
"Renewing the Place of Play," and "The Fall in Play: Sports as a Principality," Jan/Feb 1998
"In One Another's Light: Reading Stringfellow and King," April 2005

CrossCurrents, used with author's licensed rights:
"Death Shall Have No Dominion: Daniel Berrigan of the Resurrection," September 2016, pp. 312–20

Center and Library for the Bible and Social Justice for the following, used with permission:
"Walter Wink: A Personal and Activist Appreciation," a talk given October 21, 2016, at the first Walter Wink Symposium, on the occasion of his library being there donated

Christian Social Action, for the following, used with permission:
"John Wesley and the Global Principality of Slavery," July/August 2003

Orbis Books, Maryknoll, New York, for the following, under the author's copyright, used with permission:
"Introduction," pp. xix–xxvi, and "Fallen the Law and the State," pp. 81–84, from *Seasons of Faith and Conscience: Kairos, Confession, Liturgy* (1991)

LA Catholic Worker, for the following, published under the author's rights and not copyrighted, but used with permission nevertheless:
"Be Not Awed," *Catholic Agitator*, April 2003

Detroit Catholic Worker, for the following, published under the author's rights and not copyrighted, but used with permission nevertheless:
"Be Not Awed," *On the Edge*, April 2003
"Surveillance and Impeachment," *On the Edge*, Summer 2007
"Sixty Years Later. The End of Brown. The Dismantling of Public Education: Separate and Unequal"

Catholic Worker, New York City, for the following, published under the author's rights and not copyrighted, but used with permission nevertheless:
"Detroit—Coming to a City Near You: Emergency Management," *Catholic Worker*, January–February 2014
"Her Name Was Charity: The Detroit Water Struggle," *Catholic Worker*, October–November 2014

Wipf and Stock Publishers (www.wipfandstock.com) for the following chapters from *Where the Water Goes Around* (2017), used by permission:
"Discerning the Angel of Detroit" (1989)
"Reading the Building: Seeing the Powers" (1995)
"Readers before Profits" (1996)
"Detroit: Is Your City Next?"; "Her Name Was Charity: The Detroit Water Struggle"; and "Sixty Years Later: In Detroit, the End of Brown" (2014)

Introduction: From Moment to Moment

For the sake of the present moment, I am looking at five decades past.

The fiftieth anniversary of Martin Luther King's speech breaking his silence on the war in Vietnam and naming the reigning "triplets," the dominating powers, of U.S. culture—racism, militarism, and extreme materialism—is upon us (April 4, 1967). And so it will shortly be fifty years since his assassination in Memphis, exactly one year later.

It will be fifty years since William Stringfellow lay in a hospital bed, preparing for radical and life-threatening surgery, while simultaneously contemplating the principalities. He'd been put onto them by the people of East Harlem. Crediting his neighbors' discernment and, even more, their resurrection witness, he would survive to write about and expose the powers for the next decade and a half. Second birthday indeed.[1]

Also at hand is the fiftieth anniversary of the Catonsville Nine action, wherein Daniel Berrigan, his brother Phil, and seven others entered the Maryland draft board to remove 1A files and to burn them with homemade napalm in a political exorcism of the Pentagon principalities and the power of death.[2] In priestly collars, the brothers subsequently graced the cover of *Time* magazine, implicating the church.

Fifty years ago, Karl Barth crossed over to the communion of saints (December 10, 1968), having named the angelic powers of the nation, so to speak, or the demonic, in addressing Nazism and the church struggle against it. Before his death, he came to the States and encouraged William Stringfellow in the theological pursuit of the powers.

Jacques Ellul's *Presence of the Kingdom* was republished in English fifty

---

1. William Stringfellow's *A Second Birthday* (New York: Doubleday, 1970) is his account of that illness.
2. Daniel Berrigan, *The Trial of the Catonsville Nine* (Boston: Beacon, 1970).

years ago, with an introduction by William Stringfellow.³ Ever since his time in the resistance in Vichy France, Ellul had been systematically unpacking, as theologian, lawyer, and social historian, such principalities as technology, political power, law, propaganda, and more. His *Presence* was the seminal postwar work laying out that biblical and social agenda, already being fulfilled.

Exactly five decades past, Walter Wink came to teach at Union Seminary in NYC (in September 1967). He would eventually be my New Testament instructor there. An activist in both racial justice and antiwar work, he had already written a review of Stringfellow's published first pass at a theology of the powers. Though the academic principalities would see fit to turn him out institutionally, his course had been seeded to write volume upon volume of biblical work naming, exposing, and engaging the powers.

Myself? Fifty years ago, I stood, a high school student in northwest Detroit, looking toward downtown and seeing the smoke of the '67 rebellion rising from the city. I had read King's speech and even had a first taste of Stringfellow. My vocation—place-based, pastoral, and political—passes through that moment. I did not yet understand that it marked a wider theological watershed that would play out in my own life and thinking, as for many others, in the decades to follow.

Put simply, if only in part, that watershed tells the reclamation of biblical language—of the "principalities and powers," integrally embedded in the New Testament, but long banished from the realm of social ethics by hermeneutical accommodation and convenience. In the last fifty years, that terminology has been reclaimed and made accessible to social activists and ministers of the gospel. For at least four of those decades, I have been writing, teaching, organizing, and acting—work framed theologically by this renewed recognition and language.

This book raises a series of questions: Can an understanding of the principalities and powers serve concretely the work of ministry and movement ethics? Can such a reading of the biblical text edify our political engagements—or even vice versa? Can it help us see the invisible dimension of power that forms us and drags us along, often helpless, in its spiritual wake? Can such a reading of the times and the text enable a resistance that is informed, discerning, and effectively

---

3. Jacques Ellul, *The Presence of the Kingdom* (New York: Seabury, 1967).

faithful? Could it facilitate transformation in ourselves and even this bizarrely wayward world? I practically pray, yes.

In fact, this book is a lived exploration of those questions and that prayer. It gathers up, each in its historical moment, some of my own published articles naming diverse principalities and the struggles to resist, rebuke, and transform them.

Mentors in the Communion

As a high school student, I could not have imagined that among the handful of activist commentators set to bring the powers back onto the biblical map, three of them would be personal mentors to me. *Principalities in Particular* begins with essays on each of them, William Stringfellow, Walter Wink, and Daniel Berrigan, all now of blessed memory and interceding for us among the communion of ancestors and saints. The chapter on Stringfellow briefly traces his conversation with others who have revived interest in the powers as a biblical way into social ethics, and so introduces the other two as well. The essay on Wink is a talk given last year on the occasion of his personal book collection being donated to the Center and Library for the Bible and Social Justice. It, in turn, reflects the love and appreciation of a eulogy I gave at his funeral. Because the focused reminiscence on Daniel Berrigan concerns the resurrection, I'd thought originally to conclude the book with it. But my judicious editor has convinced me that resurrection is not so much the place to end as the place to begin and that all that follows reflects a theology not only of the cross and the powers, but of resurrection as resistance to the power of death itself.

I am mindful that my mentors, like myself, are white, male, European. Yet, I have experimented with their insights, substantially rooted in a black-majority city, in movements, if not churches, most often led by women of color. That is a saving grace I name.

Following the mentor essays is a biblical study of two creation liturgical texts, one from the Hebrew Bible and the other from the New Testament, to illuminate particularly the theologies of Wink and Stringfellow and some of their practical implication. Included there is an exhausting, if not exhaustive, list of principalities spun by Stringfellow to illustrate their scope and significance for human community. In his own writing, he elaborated on a number of them.[4]

---

4. See the collected section on "Particular Powers" in *A Keeper of the Word: Selected Writings of William Stringfellow*, ed. Bill Wylie-Kellermann (Grand Rapids: Eerdmans, 1992), 223–93.

It is worth considering the present volume as a companion to two others that this one variously reflects. Most recent is my *Where the Water Goes 'Round*,[5] a collection specifically on struggles in Detroit where the essays are likewise each summoned by a particular movement moment and where a biblical analysis of the powers is just below the surface, if not outright and explicit. The other, the earlier of the two, is my *Seasons of Faith and Conscience*,[6] which treats the arms race and the faith-based anti-nuclear resistance to it as a particular instance of struggle viewed through the lens of the principalities. The latter was my own first foray into action and analysis predicated on engaging the powers.

Incarnation and the Powers

This matter of writing theology incarnationally, within a given historical moment, is itself an honoring of William Stringfellow's method. Most all of his books were tracts rooted in the sequence not only of anti-racist and anti-war struggle, but in a succession of U.S. political regimes and administrations. Something similar can be pointed to in Wink's work: He wrote in the context of the South African anti-apartheid struggle or the global nonviolent miracle of 1989. And it is certainly true of Daniel Berrigan, who was poet of the Word incarnate, knowing what time it was.

For these very reasons, I have organized ensuing chapters chronologically as published. I hope this furthers their contextualization, even as it exposes the weaknesses of my own development in thought. I have selected them in a way that minimizes duplication. However, in writing article-length treatments of the powers, it becomes necessary to reiterate the framing theology one way or another each time. I trust the reader to bear with me in this process.

I compile them convinced they are examples, even where clumsy ones, of a theological and analytical practice for which the present era calls out. In a time of global climate collapse, oil and water wars, drone strikes, emergency management of entire municipalities, secret and voluntary digital surveillance, corporate rule, racialized police lynchings, and continued nuclear proliferation, just to name a short list, I

---

5. Bill Wylie-Kellermann, *Where the Water Goes 'Round* (Eugene, OR: Cascade, 2017).
6. Bill Wylie-Kellermann, *Seasons of Faith and Conscience* (Maryknoll, NY: Orbis, 1992; republished Eugene, OR: Wipf & Stock, 2008).

want to hope that a collection such as this can be edifying and useful to folk in the seminary, the sanctuary, and the streets.

The first essay articulates liturgical direct action as an essential tactic of resistance to the principalities of nuclearism and is my personal entrée into this method of discernment. Others follow, which develop the politics and technology of death, specifically in the Wars of the Gulf and Iraq.

Around that same period in Detroit, we began each Good Friday undertaking a "stations of the cross" liturgy, walking the streets of the city to mark and meditate on where the Rulers of this World are crucifying Christ today. The impetus of that ritual was certainly rooted in the violence of militarism, but it quickly broadened to see the whole array of principalities. Virtually all of those named and chronicled in this table of contents have been stops or stations on that way of the cross.

This period also coincides with a broadening of my own nonviolent direct action to include urban and corporate powers. So, in these chapters the city itself is recognized as a principality, as is General Motors in its effort to level an entire neighborhood to build a Cadillac plant, or the drug powers, engaged at street level in crack marches, or the powers addressed by the Detroit newspaper strike, or the financial industry and Emergency Management opposed in the struggle for local democracy and education.

A number of essays touch on the environmental injustice of powerly assaults to the planet. Notice the reflections on the wrath of Hurricane Katrina, the BP oil spill in the Gulf, or, locally, the struggle for safe, affordable water in Michigan.

Several of these pieces arose as an attempt to develop and explore principalities that Stringfellow might allude to in an oblique or intuitive aside, or that he might include in a list of powers, but never further expand upon. Sports as a principality would be one example of this. The family would be another. Both might seem quaint or petty renditions, but exploring the implications of comprehending in them structural, spiritual realities, each with a life of their own, has genuinely deepened my own understanding and demonstrated again the practical value of this sort of analysis.

Another topic that might seem quaint or superficial is the consideration given to the Harry Potter films. I identify the books as beloved in our family, but the power of corporate media to render and reappropriate narratives as the "myth of redemptive violence" (Wink's term) is serious business, with deadly consequences in the culture.

Issues Pastoral and Spiritual

One of the most striking and useful lessons of a principalities theology of ministry is how often and fully they are implicated in pastoral issues. Family systems are one theoretical bridge for this insight. So, pastoral implications may be found most obviously in the essays on the drug system, the family, and explicitly in the connection between healing and the powers in the chapter on hospital ministry. But this is true so much more broadly. The stress of economic injustice plays out, for example, in addiction or domestic abuse. A captivity to social media can stunt personal growth and identity. The futurelessness projected by nuclear weaponry or the cascading consequences of environmental assault, even the pending destruction of an urban neighborhood, affect the long-term commitments of marriage, family, relationship, and community.

Perhaps the most significant offering of a fully developed theology of the principalities concerns the spiritual dimension of these material and structural realities. Marx and his movement kin, for contrary example, are inclined to see the dimension of spirit as a mystified masking of material relations, whereas this theological analysis stresses that the spiritual aspect is essential to the real power of the principalities. It is the spiritual dimension that must needs be unmasked, seen, and recognized if the principalities are to be fully engaged. It is not just a matter of having spiritual resources for the long-haul struggle, but of having spiritual tactics and resources for engaging what is, at least in part, a struggle of spirit. Our fight is not with flesh and blood, but with spiritual wickedness in high places. The essay on white racism, "Exorcising an American Demon," is emblematic of this approach to movement and transformation, but it may be seen in virtually every one of these essays.

It is certainly prominent in the concluding essay on the presidency and the powers. The Trump era has most immediately been characterized for its unleashing of a spirit of blind domination, be it street-level or global. That essay is one of those not collected and edited, but written specifically for this volume. In a chronological sequence that processed through the recent years of Detroit resistance, it seemed incumbent to land very present-tense on this political moment, particularly as read through the prescient notes and observations of Stringfellow, now fifty years in the testing. Landing there is also dicey, as the times seem more volatile and unpredictable than ever.

And, finally, there are the appendices. Though I make no great claims for them, their import should nevertheless not be underestimated. They collect teaching and training materials I have developed over the years and serve as practical resources for church and movement in thinking through the presence of the powers in our life and ministry. They reflect the very conviction of this book, that discerning the powers is possible for each of us in our community and moment. This is to say that from beginning to end, my heart's desire is not simply to honor my mentors (though that looms large and lovingly within me), but to serve the church as movement and the movement as church, both of which I name in Beloved Community.

Birthday of William Stringfellow, April 26, 2017

PART I

A Theological Introduction

1

William Stringfellow: A Story of This Theological Conversation

Proximate to the discernment of signs is the discernment of spirits. This gift enables the people of God to distinguish and recognize, identify and expose, report and rebuke the power of death incarnate in nations and institutions or other creatures, or possessing persons, while they also affirm the Word of God incarnate in all of life, exemplified preeminently in Jesus Christ. The discernment of spirits refers to the talent to recognize the Word of God in this world in principalities and persons despite the distortion of fallenness or transcending the moral reality of death permeating everything.

This is the gift which exposes and rebukes idolatry. This is the gift which confounds and undoes blasphemy. Similar to the discernment of signs, the discernment of spirits is inherently political while in practice it has specifically to do with pastoral care, with healing, with the nurture of human life, and with the fulfillment of all life.[1]

William Stringfellow was my mentor in the practical theology of principalities. I've spent the three decades since his death, if not thinking

---

1. William Stringfellow, *An Ethic for Christians and Other Aliens in a Strange Land* (Waco, TX: Word, 1973), 139; reprinted in Bill Wylie-Kellermann, ed., *A Keeper of the Word* (Grand Rapids, MI: Eerdmans, 1994), 302–3.

like he did, at least framing my work in the outlines of this thought on the powers.

In a certain sense, from his moving pulpit and podium, he summoned the attentive of a generation to this theology, bringing the principalities back into the light of day and onto the map of biblical social ethics. Many would know his work largely second-hand, through the deepening work of Walter Wink, whom he also nourished and mentored (and who also in turn mentored me). Yet others would know him not at all, since as a "lay theologian" he was tolerated as a guest in the academy, but never embraced, or honored, or even fully footnoted. My own students remain astonished: "How can we be about to graduate from seminary and we have never even heard of this guy?"

Stringfellow began writing about the principalities from the streets of East Harlem, where he had gone to serve as a neighborhood attorney. There he heard people speak of the cops, the mafia, the welfare bureaucracy, absentee realtors, even the foundations and nonprofits as predatory creatures arrayed against the community. If he worked out his theology in conversation with other theologians, to a large extent male and European, it never floated off into abstraction because of his street-level sources. As a way into my own theology, I want to begin with him and his theological conversation partners, but always with an eye to my own streets.

Political Exorcism

I have in my possession a little booklet, which belonged to Stringfellow, titled *Exorcism: The Report of a Commission Convened by the Bishop of Exeter*.[2] It introduced and published an ancient rite that he had acquired and first utilized to publicly exorcise President Richard Nixon on the eve of his second inauguration. (That administration, recall, shortly afterward succumbed to a public unraveling.) He employed it again with a small circle of friends at his home on Block Island to banish from the place of his household the presence of death after his beloved friend and partner, the poet Anthony Towne, had died in 1980.[3] Stringfellow considered these liturgical events neither spooky nor weird, but in fact enjoyed regarding them with deadly seriousness

---

2. Dom Robert Petitpierre, O.S.B., ed., *Exorcism: The Report of a Commission Convened by the Bishop of Exeter* (London: SPCK, 1972).
3. William Stringfellow, *A Simplicity of Faith* (Nashville: Abingdon, 1982), 54–58.

as inherently political, while in practice having specifically to do with pastoral care and healing.

Where the prayers name "the devil" or "the enemy," his copy of that text was altered by his own hand to consistently substitute "death" or "the power of death" (which he accounted a "living moral reality"). These are synonyms he would also likewise transpose back into his own baptismal vows, or anyone's, for that matter. Baptism specifically has about it elements of exorcism. Do you renounce the power of death and all its works? For William Stringfellow, this foundational rite of redemption and ministry celebrated freedom from the power of death—indeed from the principalities and powers of this world.

Stringfellow's first real dose of powers theology came at the World Conference of Christian Youth in Oslo, Norway, which he attended as a college sophomore in 1947.[4] Under the theme of the "Lordship of Christ," there was plenty of room for the triumphalism that characterized the expansive postwar American ecumenism in which Stringfellow was a participant. However, the speakers at that conference bore their good news out from the shadow of death. They spoke out of Christian resistance movements under Nazi occupation. They were chastened and sober. Among them were Martin Niemoeller of Germany, Bishop Belgrav of Norway, and Madeleine Barot of France.[5] Mme. Barot, for example, was particularly lucid in identifying the "chaos of order" in which humanity had fallen slave to its own systems, to its own production and discovery, and to its own propaganda, for which she saw the Babel story as emblematic.[6] In what is perhaps his most important book, *An Ethic for Christians and Other Aliens in a Strange Land*, Stringfellow alludes to that conference as the beginning of a conversation with those very people from whom he acknowledges learning two things: firstly, that in the overwhelming circumstance of Nazi possession and occupation, resistance (however symbolic, haphazard, and apparently futile) became the only way to live humanly, retaining sanity and conscience; and secondly, that recourse to the Bible in itself became a primary, practical, and essential tactic of resistance.[7] This confluence, a kind of sequence or circle really—Bible study, comprehension or dis-

---

4. See Bill Wylie-Kellermann, "WSCF Naming the Powers: William Stringfellow as Student and Theologian," *Student World* (Geneva) 63, no. 247 (Spring 2003): 24–35.
5. Their speeches are found in Paul Griswald Macy, ed., *The Report of the Second World Conference of Christian Youth* (Geneva: WCC, 1948). Other speakers included Reinhold Niebuhr, W. A. Visser't Hooft, Stephen Neill, and D. T. Niles.
6. "Confronting Moral Chaos," ibid., 153–65.
7. *An Ethic*, 117–20; reprinted in *Keeper*, 173–74.

cernment of the powers, and resistance for the sake of humanity—is hardly incidental. It was seminal to his life, to his method of biblical interpretation, to his thinking.

A Hermeneutical Exorcism

Stringfellow begins *An Ethic for Christians and Other Aliens in a Strange Land* by asserting that "the task is to treat the nation within the tradition of biblical politics—to understand America biblically—*not* the other way around, *not* (to put it in an appropriately awkward way) to construe the Bible Americanly."[8] Notice what is being said here. Within contemporary hermeneutics, the discipline of biblical interpretation, we might today point to this as acknowledgment of his contextual reading site, which is to say, of his own social location in imperial America. More, however, is suggested. Imperial America, its spirit and ethos, appears to assert itself as an active and aggressive agency in biblical interpretation, seeking to claim the text as its own.

Not only are the powers a question of hermeneutics. For William Stringfellow, hermeneutics are a question of the powers.

It is almost as though American empire, sensing its exposure in the biblical Word, engages a preemptive literary strike, claiming, possessing, and interpreting the Bible in its own guise, for its own convenience, justifying itself as the divinely favored nation. Stringfellow calls this violence, and it is a violence virtually synonymous with the Native American genocide or the racism of American chattel slavery or the nuclear arsenal or the shock and awe intended in the war against Iraq. In Detroit, we recognize it as one with the violence of expulsion by water shut-off and foreclosure under Emergency Management.

This powerly intervention is not a new or uniquely American process. In fact, for most of its history, the gods of this world have blinded the church to its own scriptures with respect to the "principalities and powers." In the history of hermeneutics, they have been excised, suppressed, and obscured. One analysis ties the effectual disappearance of the powers in Protestant theology to Luther and Calvin at the very beginning of the Reformation.[9] Stringfellow, however, locates that dissipation at an earlier juncture, with the "Constantinian

---

8. *An Ethic*, 13; reprinted in *Keeper*, 175. Acknowledging both its imprecision and chauvinism, I will continue here to use Stringfellow's term, "American."
9. See W. A. Visser 't Hooft *The Kingship of Christ* (New York: Harper & Brothers, 1948), 15–31. He argues that the significance of the victorious cosmic Christ was lost in their attenuated struggle with apocalyptic sects of the time.

Arrangement" of the fourth century. Beginning with that time, Christians had "forgotten or forsaken a worldview or, more precisely, doctrines of creation and fallen creation, similar to Paul's, in which political authority encompasses and conjoins the angelic powers and incumbent rulers."[10] Walter Wink subsequently concurred. The church, he writes,

> soon found itself the darling of Constantine. Called on to legitimate the empire, the church abandoned much of its social critique. The Powers were soon divorced from political affairs and made airy spirits who preyed only on individuals. The state was thus freed of one of the most powerful brakes against idolatry . . .[11]

Rome was effectively preempting its own exposure by and vulnerability in the Word of God. The New Testament was being read Romanly as it were, the substance of the powers written into the oblivion of spiritual individualism.

When Stringfellow first began to speak and write on the powers in the early sixties, he went on the road stumping in seminaries and universities. He identified the powers with institutions, images, and ideologies as creatures before God, having an independent life and integrity of their own, whose vocation is to praise God and serve human life. In the estate of the fall, however, they are seen to be demonic powers. Their vocation is lost and distorted, in fact inverted: Instead of praising God and serving human life, they pretend to the place of God and enslave human life.

This exposition, which became chapter three of *Free in Obedience* (1964), met a strange mix of fascination and rebuff. He loved to tell the story of an early presentation, in fact two of them, given in Boston. Scheduled for similar talks the same day at Harvard Business School and at the Divinity School, he debated with himself about excising, from the business school version, any explicit biblical reference or language, but decided in the end to let it stand intact. The business school students, it turned out, engaged him thoroughly, bending his ear long past the hour appointed, with numerous examples from their own experience of dominance and possession with respect to corpora-

---

10. William Stringfellow, *Conscience and Obedience* (Waco, TX: Word, 1977), 48.
11. Walter Wink, *Naming the Powers* (Philadelphia: Fortress Press, 1984), 113. The other volumes in his powers trilogy are *Unmasking the Powers* (Philadelphia: Fortress Press, 1986) and *Engaging the Powers* (Philadelphia: Fortress Press, 1992).

tions and the commercial powers. Their experiences verified his own observations.

Later at the seminary, however, with the identical speech, he was ridiculed and written off. Ruling authorities, principalities, world rulers of the present darkness! Come now! These were little more than Greco-Roman astralism, the incidental vestige of a quaint and archaic language, an esoteric parlance now obsolete, with no real meaning in history or human life.[12] Indeed.

At the seminary, not only did the consequences of the Constantinian comity reign, it was aided and abetted by yet another "power," in this case the tyranny of the historical-critical method. In Stringfellow's enumeration of the principalities, he came to include not simply all institutions and all images, but also all ideologies and all methods. Historical criticism entailed both. After imperial accommodation drove the majority of New Testament references to the powers off into long-standing spiritual abstraction, historical criticism, with its cosmological commitment to scientific rationalism and materialism, finished the job and wrote them off the New Testament map altogether. Wink has said an astonishing thing in precisely this regard. Commenting on the inability of several previous scholars working on the powers to confess their practical significance for a twentieth-century Christian ethic, he notes:

> They were themselves caught in the principality of New Testament criticism, which had become as dogmatic and stultified as the religious orthodoxy it had been invented to overthrow. Not surprisingly, as a New Testament scholar, I found it necessary to perform a public exorcism of myself, hermeneutically, by writing *The Bible in Human Transformation* . . .[13]

A hermeneutical exorcism! Wink's scholarly little tract[14] declared historical criticism bankrupt. It named the myth of objectivism, which fabricated an impassable gulf between text and reader, precluding commitment and engagement in either personal or social transformation. It exposed the idolatry of technique to which biblical studies had fallen prey. It identified the cult of expertise that severed scripture study from believing and worshiping communities. It got him

---

12. William Stringfellow, *Free in Obedience* (New York: Seabury, 1964), 51–52; reprinted in *A Keeper of the Word*, 192.
13. Walter Wink, "Stringfellow on the Powers," in *Radical Christian and Exemplary Lawyer*, ed. Andrew McThenia Jr. (Grand Rapids, MI: Eerdmans, 1995), 25.
14. Walter Wink, *The Bible in Human Transformation* (Philadelphia: Fortress Press, 1973). His sequel to it outlining a new paradigm was *Transforming Bible Study* (Nashville: Abingdon, 1980).

"blacklisted" in the scholarly guild and denied tenure at Union Seminary. And it freed him literally to write his remarkable trilogy on the powers.

The thirty-year theological odyssey of that principalities project was set in motion when Wink set out to review Stringfellow's *Free in Obedience* in 1964,[15] and beyond that, he has acknowledged the extent of his own indebtedness to the vitality of Stringfellow's thought.[16] The trilogy, in fact, has turned into at least seven books concerned with the powers.

Though there are several others, I would mention just one further way that Stringfellow seemed to regard the principalities as an agency aggressively intruding on Bible study. He contended that the single most important credential required for comprehending scripture was to give oneself in the vulnerability of listening to the Word. Yet in the present we are so assaulted by a profusion of what he termed "babel": verbal inflation and inversion, the distortions of doublespeak and overtalk, spin doctoring, sound bites, coded phrases, jargon, rhetorical wantonness, redundancy, exaggeration, incoherence, the chaos of voices, the violence of the repetitious lie.[17] He argues that this verbal overload and incapacitation has become virtually the main method of political rule. To have ears to hear, to listen conscientiously to the Bible, is itself, as he learned from participants in the confessing movements of World War II, to resist the assault of the powers.[18]

Barth: A Voice of Encouragement from the German Resistance

A striking omission from that list of European Christian resistance mentors in *An Ethic for Christians* is Karl Barth, the great Swiss biblical theologian. What to make of that? Jacques Ellul, his French counterpart, is listed as a subsequent conversant and there would be similar warrant for the inclusion of Barth as well.

It was virtually the gathering storm of World War II, a historical crisis, that urgently broke the European hermeneutical impasse with respect to the powers. As Dietrich Bonhoeffer wrote in 1932: "How can one close one's eyes at the fact that the demons themselves have taken over rule of the world, that it is the powers of darkness who have here made an awful conspiracy . . . ?"[19] Barth, of course, was an

---

15. Wink, "Stringfellow on the Powers," in McThenia Jr., *Radical Christian and Exemplary Lawyer*, 25.
16. Ibid., 25–26.
17. *An Ethic for Christians*, 97–107; reprinted in *Keeper*, 214–22.
18. "Listening Against Babel," in *Keeper*, 182–83.

active participant in the confessing church struggle—and he was a biblical spokesperson in the reclamation of powers theology. Moreover, his conversation with Stringfellow is notoriously public.

William Stringfellow was the only layperson, that is, the only nonacademic theologian, to question Barth in his sole visit to the United States in 1962. Stringfellow's questions were substantially concerned with the powers. They are telling for setting his own theological agenda for the decades to come.

> It appears to be widely believed, both within and, for that matter, outside the churches of the United States, that the history of redemption is encompassed merely by the saga of relationships in history between God and humanity. At the same time, it is in American Protestantism at least, commonplace to distinguish as nothing more than archaic imagery, the Biblical identification and discussion of the angelic powers present in the world. What there is of Protestant moral theology in America almost utterly ignores the attempt to account for, explicate, and relate one's self to the principalities and powers. Yet, empirically more and more, the principalities and powers seem to have an aggressive, indeed, possessive, ascendancy in American life—including, alas, the life of the American churches. Who are these principalities and powers? What is their significance in the creation and in the fall? What significance do they have with respect to merely human sin? What is their relation to the claim that Christ is the Lord of history? What is the relation of the power and presence of death in history to the principalities and powers, and therefore, practically speaking, what freedom does a Christian have from the dominion of all of these principalities and powers?[20]

Following these public queries, Barth whispered to him, "It's all in *Church and State*. It's all there."[21] Though Stringfellow is falsely accused of being a "Barthian," friends do attest that he read a volume of Barth's dogmatics and he certainly read *Church and State*,[22] wherein, among other things, Karl Barth specifically identifies the biblical view that both rulers and the angelic powers are conjoined in the state.

In the main, however, Barth's primary role in Stringfellow's developing theology was simply encouragement, emboldening him in an active

---

19. Quoted in Marva Dawn, *The Concept of "the Principalities and Powers" in the Works of Jacques Ellul* (PhD dissertation, University of Notre Dame, 1992), 12.
20. "Introduction to Theology: Conversation with Karl Barth," *A Keeper of the Word*, 190. As a measure of their significance, Stringfellow incorporated the questions into the text of *Free in Obedience* as an introit to his section on the Principalities.
21. The reference is to Karl Barth, *Church and State*, trans. G. Ronald Howe (London: SCM, 1939).
22. His copy of that text in marked and annotated. He cites it in *Conscience and Obedience*, 36.

pursuit of the principalities. He did it in two ways. First, by confirming Bill's articulation of the inquiry. It was simply on the basis of his questions that Barth said, "I like to hear you speak as you do" and "I think we agree," which then prompted him to turn and urge that audience, in an underscored aside, "Listen to this man!"[23] The other encouragement (and this is by no means incidental) was in conceiving of the principalities as a broader category than the state alone. Barth in his reply specifically mentioned ideology, sport, fashion, religion, and sex as examples.

Following their public exchange on the panel in Chicago, Barth visited "the notorious district of East Harlem, north of Manhattan" and was guided through it, as he aptly put it, "under the safe conduct"[24] of William Stringfellow. This was a momentous visitation, actually making the connection between the earlier crisis in Europe and one more current in the U.S. In the States, it was a different set of historical crises that broke open the powers biblically for reconsideration: not the context of National Socialism and World War II, but the racial crisis forced by the African American freedom struggle plus, one should add, the resistance movement fostered by war in southeast Asia.[25]

In Racial Crisis: Paradox as Method

The year following his public converse with Karl Barth, Stringfellow was back in Chicago in 1963 as a speaker at the first National Conference on Religion and Race, attended and addressed by Martin Luther King Jr. Stringfellow, for his part, created a small uproar by asserting that "racism is not an evil in human hearts or minds, racism is a prin-

---

23. From master tape-recording of the event held by Word Record and Music Group, Nashville, TN. Related to Stringfellow's "esteem" in the academy, it is telling that in the published transcript of that conversation, the University of Chicago Divinity School expunged both of those comments from the official record. See "Introduction to Theology," *Criterion* 2, no. 1 (Winter 1963): 22. In the forward to *Evangelical Theology: An Introduction* (Grand Rapids, MI: Eerdmans, 1963), the lectures Barth gave at the University of Chicago and Princeton University, he refers to "the conscientious and thoughtful New York attorney William Stringfellow who caught my attention more than any other person" (ix).
24. Eberhard Busch, *Karl Barth: His Life from Letters and Autobiographical Texts* (Grand Rapids, MI: Eerdmans, 1994), 460.
25. There are other theologians and biblical ethicists who in the crisis of history helped bring the Powers back into discussion. Among them was John Howard Yoder. Many, particularly in the Anabaptist and evangelical communities, would credit him almost entirely. His influential book, *The Politics of Jesus*, which did not appear until 1972, a decade after Stringfellow had been writing and speaking on the principalities, included a chapter on Jesus and Power, which drew heavily upon the work of Hendrik Berkhof. For a recent treatment of Yoder's theology of the powers see Jamie Pitts, *Principalities and Powers: Revising John Howard Yoder's Sociological Theology* (Eugene, OR: Pickwick, 2013).

cipality, a demonic power, a representative image, an embodiment of death, over which human beings have little or no control, but which works its awful influence in their lives."[26] At the height of the racial crisis, at the point where the churches (belatedly) were just stepping up to the struggle, Stringfellow had put his finger on the truth theologically. And in doing so, he also brought the principalities back further onto the map of American theological ethics. Though some present accounted this a word of despair, Stringfellow went on to say,

> This is the power with which Jesus Christ was confronted and which, at great and sufficient cost, he overcame. In other words, the issue here is not equality among human beings. The issue is not some common spiritual values, nor natural law, nor middle axioms. The issue is baptism. The issue is the unity of all humankind wrought by God in the life and work of Christ. Baptism is the sacrament of that unity of all humanity in God.[27]

This is an utterly remarkable confession of faith. Here, a modern principality is named as confronted by Christ. And racism, as a demonic power beyond desperate human control, is declared overcome and defeated in Christ. Moreover, the emblem of that freedom from bondage is the unity, not of all Christians, but the unity of all humankind witnessed in baptism. Stringfellow couldn't be clearer that this radical hope of reconciliation was predicated on the cross and upon tears yet to come, but it is a true hope and a true freedom rooted both in his realism about the principality and in his sacramental understanding of ethics.

Underscore this: Baptism is being named as a frontal assault upon the rule of the powers. That is true in the reconciled humanity to which it points. That is true in the allegiance to Christ that it asserts, obviating and mitigating every other claim or allegiance. And that is true in the freedom from death, literally the freedom to die, which it explicitly affirms.

It is worth making note here, if only in passing, of Stringfellow's theological method as reflected in the Chicago remarks. Observe how he holds apparent oppositions in tension: Racism is a power over which human beings have little or no control. Racism is the power confronted and overcome by Jesus Christ. Baptism signifies the unity and freedom

---

26. "Transcript" of his talk, published as "Care Enough to Weep," *The Witness*, February 21, 1963, 14. This version is from *A Keeper of the Word*. For more on racism as a principality, see chapter 13, "Exorcising an American Demon."
27. "Care Enough to Weep," 14–15.

that racism cannot undo.[28] It's worse than you think it is; you are freer than you know. The rigor of this paradoxical logic is astounding. And its practical consequence for an ethic of freedom is manifest. He lived that freedom himself.

When William Stringfellow wrote the story of his life in East Harlem, he subtitled it "an autobiographical polemic." That, too, is an evocative and paradoxical phrase. By it I believe he meant to suggest that not only is the Word inherent in our stories, but also that the "principalities and powers" are active characters in the drama of our lives. And this is so whether we acknowledge and resist them, or succumb to their wiles. Moreover, it seems Stringfellow saw the narrative of his own self-accounting as yet another engagement that carried the struggle a step further, affecting again the exposure of the powers.[29] This is biblically apropos. A gospel, for example, is the good news of Jesus's open confrontation with the rulers and authorities, which is itself—in the retelling of proclamation—a frontal assault on their rule.

The War Crisis: Death Fails

The other context that prompted a reawakened comprehension of the powers on the American scene was the war in southeast Asia. In Stringfellow's view, the war represented a grotesque example of the demonic, of death virtually as social purpose. It demonstrated the variety of concrete ways in which the military powers (particularly the Pentagon and the technocratic state) had passed out of human control, propagating the war largely by extra-constitutional authorities beyond the accountability of democratic restraint. Military technology was a driving force with a necessary logic all its own, from the think tanks of corporate research and development to the battlefield testing of firepower against human flesh.

At the height of the war in 1968, Stringfellow attended the trial of the Catonsville Nine. Dan and Phil Berrigan among others had burned

---

28. I am indebted the observation of Walter Wink who recognized this sort of syllogistic paradox in a passage from *Instead of Death*. See Wink, "Stringfellow on the Powers," 19–20.
29. In a certain sense, Stringfellow had begun applying to his own life something of the same hermeneutic he was developing with regard to the scriptures. Plainly put, he viewed the powers intervening and imposing themselves on the latter. He saw the Bible widely read in captivity to the principalities, read in the service of empire, read (as he put it) Americanly. The ethical task like the hermeneutical one involved breaking and transcending their spiritual grasp. See Bill Wylie-Kellermann, "Bill, the Bible, and the Seminary Underground," in McThenia Jr., ed., *Radical Christian and Exemplary Lawyer*, 56–72; also "Listening Against Babel," in *A Keeper of the Word*, 182–83, and Introduction to a previously unpublished Bible study guide, "Advent 1982: Preparing for the Coming of the Lord."

draft files with homemade napalm in a liturgical act of protest against the war in Vietnam. Bill would later refer to this as a "politically informed exorcism."[30] Concurrent with the trial there was a festival of hope: music, poetry, and words of encouragement to continued resistance were offered in the sanctuary of a Baltimore church. Stringfellow, who was about to undergo a risky life-threatening surgery to stem the deterioration of his health, could barely walk from pain. Summoned to the pulpit for a word, he offered an admonition, a benediction, an utterance of the gospel:

> Remember, now, that the State has only one power it can use against human beings: death. The State can persecute you, prosecute you, imprison you, exile you, execute you. All of these mean the same thing. The State can consign you to death. The grace of Jesus Christ in this life is that death fails. There is nothing the State can do to you, or to me, which we need fear.[31]

This was no idle or superfluous dispensation. The anti-war and freedom movements were on the brink of coming together when Martin King was killed. Malcolm X and a number of Black Panthers had been assassinated. Official guns would shortly be turned on college students at both Kent State and Jackson State universities. The power of death would make itself chillingly felt. The freedom to die, really the freedom of the resurrection, the freedom that baptism signals, the freedom to which Stringfellow testified, was the very freedom on which continuing resistance to the powers needed to be grounded.

One month after King's assassination at the hands of the powers, the Catonsville Nine acted. They were convicted in the dramatic public trial, but several of them declined to submit readily to sentence. Daniel Berrigan went underground, speaking, writing, and playfully eluding the federal authorities for several months. He was a walking festival of hope. When Dan was finally captured by the FBI, it was at the Block Island home of William Stringfellow and Anthony Towne. In consequence, the two were indicted for harboring a fugitive.

Though the indictment, clearly a political charge, was eventually quashed, this was a momentous event in Stringfellow's life. It was the first time he had personally suffered so bluntly the aggressions of the principalities. Given his state of health, it was indeed a bodily assault threatening death. But it was also his first experience of being vic-

---

30. *An Ethic for Christians*, 150.
31. For a longer version of his remarks, see his own account in *Second Birthday*, 33.

timized by the legal principalities that he had fought so vigorously on behalf of others, as a street lawyer in East Harlem during the fifties and early sixties. In many respects, the event seeded the energy of *An Ethic for Christians and Other Aliens in a Strange Land*. As it happened, Bill and Dan had sat at the dining-room table discussing the biblical bases of that book (the Babylon texts of Revelation) while, in all likelihood, the FBI listened in by high-powered directional microphone. Then came the indictment, a provocation further illuminating the texts, clarifying the mind. If the principalities and powers had known what they were doing, they would have let it slide. That book effected their complete exposure (becoming something of a theological handbook for the American resistance movement). Stringfellow claimed yet again the grace and freedom he commended. He was unintimidated, standing instead by his friendship with Berrigan.

Martin Luther King and the Giant Triplets

Perhaps no one, certainly no public theologian, more fully lived that freedom than Martin Luther King Jr. Before the night he spoke of being to the mountaintop, he had suffered many assaults: death threats and assignation attempts. And it would not be far-fetched to say that ultimately, he was killed for naming aloud the principalities in the moment of racial crisis and war-making. On April 4, 1967, he made his strongest anti-war statement at Riverside Church in a momentous speech known as "Breaking the Silence: Beyond Vietnam."

> I am convinced that if we are to get on the right side of the world revolution, we as a nation must undergo a radical revolution of values. We must rapidly begin the shift from a thing-oriented society to a person-oriented society. When machines and computers, profit motives and property rights are considered more important than people, the giant triplets of racism, materialism, and militarism are incapable of being conquered.[32]

Hereby Martin King names the principalities, singling out the three reigning powers in American life. It is somewhat rare among black preachers and theologians to hear the language of the principalities. The writings of Paul are not prominent in the African American canon. One, because of the household codes introduced into Colossians and Ephesians: "Slaves, be subject to your masters." And two, because of

---

32. Martin Luther King Jr., "A Time to Break Silence," in *A Testament of Hope*, ed. James M. Washington (San Francisco: HarperSanFrancisco, 1991), 240.

the cultural preference for narrative in the African American church for its preaching, Bible study, and music. In story, the focus is on Jesus, the Exodus account, and the prophetic narratives. The powers are certainly present as characters in the narrative forms—Go tell Pharaoh, whose army gets drownded—but not the specific language of powers and principalities. Yet in this address Dr. King essentially deploys that language. He puts his finger on what we would call the ruling ideological powers and virtually suggests what Walter Wink will come to call the *domination system*, where the powers coalesce into a systemic configuration. Just as Stringfellow's neighbors saw the powers arrayed against their Harlem community, so in Dr. King's speech we recognize the powers that are arrayed against human community in American life: racism, militarism, and materialism.

Between the Conference on Religion and Race in 1963 and his death in 1968, Martin King was growing ever-more deeply radical. In this period, he was trying to bring together movements already at work against each of these forces in American life. The Riverside Church speech attempts to connect the anti-war movement and the freedom struggle. The Poor People's Campaign, then in the works, would pull these strands together with movements for economic justice. It was, in effect, his success in making these connections that got him killed. Little wonder that when he links these dominating powers and their countervailing movements, it is actually over the objection of his friends and political companions. Many urged him not to make those connections: other civil rights leaders, the Urban League folks. His own board at SCLC (except for James Bevel) said don't do it. Don't jeopardize foundation funding, don't diffuse the focus. Never mind the complaints of his erstwhile political ally, Lyndon Johnson, or the darker threats of J. Edgar Hoover. Now there's a list of powers. Don't look deeper, they all say. And above all, don't go deeper.

Hence, Martin King speaks of the "vocation of agony" his decision provoked. He acknowledges that "silence is betrayal" and identifies seven reasons for which he is compelled to speak.[33] His first three reasons are these: 1) that the war is an attack on the poor, dismantling programs of support in order to fund it; 2) that it is a racist war, sending young men in brutal solidarity to burn huts in Vietnamese villages who wouldn't be able to live next door in Detroit; and 3) that he couldn't preach nonviolence to young people on the street without

---

33. Ibid., 232–34.

opposing the "greatest purveyor of violence in the world today—my own government." Notice that these are precisely materialism, racism, and militarism. Dr. King is viewing the war as an expression of the giant triplets, the ruling powers of domination!

His fourth reason is literally pivotal, dynamically cutting two ways: backward to the list of powers and forward to his vocational identity. On the latter, the voices of constraint would hold him back with a narrowing definition of his calling: "Aren't you a civil rights leader?" But even that compels him, since from the beginning the motto of SCLC had been "To save the soul of America." He understood the nation as a spiritual power, albeit a fallen one, but with a Constitution and a vocation that could be called upon. He cites Langston Hughes in his "concern for the integrity of life in America":

> "O, yes,
> I say it plain,
> America never was America to me,
> And yet I swear this oath—
> America will be!"[34]

Dr. King could lead a march walking the nonviolent way of the cross, and carry the flag along in train—summoning the best of the American tradition and so its hope. Later in this address, however, after naming the giant triplets, he comes to a very strong point: "Any nation that continues year after year to spend more money on military defense than on programs of social uplift is approaching spiritual death."[35]

It's interesting to set Stringfellow alongside King here. He too could point to the Constitution, to invoke its remedies against tyranny—the power of impeachment, for example—or to size up the public assault on its rights and protections. But his biblical radicalism led him increasingly to identify America with Babylon, to see it as the greatest purveyor of death in present history. Stringfellow wasn't at the Riverside speech (he was actually in L.A. that day), but he had himself by then visited Saigon, and saw the war as exemplifying in America "death as social purpose."[36] Spiritual death indeed.

Dr. King's reasons are also related to his "vocation," however agonized. The broadening and deepening of the sequence is noteworthy.

---

34. "Let America Be America Again," *The Collected Poems of Langston Hughes* (New York: Alfred A. Knopf, 1994).
35. "Let America Be America Again," 241.
36. *Ethic*, 68f.

Starting again with number four—he does base the opposition on his work as a civil rights leader and the task of healing the nation's soul. But further, he feels it incumbent upon him because of the Nobel Peace Prize, which he accepted as an internationalizing commission. It laid upon him a task of global nonviolence. And thirdly, reason six, he is compelled as a minister and disciple of Jesus. That is no small thing. For some, most religious, that would be the pinnacle of vocational cause, but Dr. King goes another step deeper: It is finally his connection with all humanity as a child of God. He speaks out of his vocation to be truly and fully human. In this, he couldn't agree more with Stringfellow on the meaning of vocation in baptism: It is the sacrament of the unity of all humanity in God.

With Jacques Ellul: In Creation or Fall?

Another influence on *An Ethic for Christians* was Jacques Ellul. *The Meaning of the City*, Ellul's sweeping biblical reading of urban civilization, had only just been published in English. Bill wrote to Ellul concerning the indictment against himself and Towne:

> It is difficult to put succinctly in a letter all that has happened and its background, growing out of the past several years in which this society has so much constricted and in which opposition to the regime has provoked a repression more serious and extensive than most people realize.... There is not the slightest doubt in my mind that charges were brought against us because we have openly expressed our opposition to the barbarism in Indochina and the threatening totalitarianism in America. One might even say that we are attacked by the government because we are Christians, although I would not want to put it that way without a more complete designation of what that means.[37]

These two lawyer theologians pursued for some thirty years a personal correspondence, though Stringfellow attributed to the Holy Spirit the coincidence that they would find themselves writing on similar biblical texts or with common reference to particular powers, since their letters never discussed what each would be working on next.

Consider these excerpts from an earlier letter of Ellul to Stringfellow:

---

37. WS to JE 2/23/71, Box 15 Stringfellow archives #4438, Cornell University.

Bien Cher: I have just finished your book . . . with great emotion—the description you give of the current development of the USA is almost unbelievable. In Europe, no one pays attention at all to this reality. . . . I often ask myself which is easier—on the one hand, to live, like me, in a country radically non-Christian, where the invocation of the Gospel means nothing to "the person on the street"—or, on the other hand, like you to speak in an officially Christian country, to have the facility that the message of the Gospel is normally well received, but where it's a matter of breaking through the misunderstandings, the hypocrisies, and giving the Gospel its revolutionary power. I was terribly pleased with your last chapter. You and I are trying to transmit an insupportable truth—and I sense in your pages the same urgency, the same passion that I feel in myself. I don't know how to tell you how near I am to you, how much it consoles me to know that there is, over there, a person chosen by God to carry on this combat which sometimes seems desperate to me.[38]

Stringfellow's first brush with Jacques Ellul was actually a near miss. Ellul, just then emerging from participation in the French resistance movement, addressed a conference of the World Student Christian Federation that followed immediately the Oslo gathering Stringfellow had attended in 1947. Unfortunately, the young Stringfellow attended instead a meeting of Anglican youth at Canterbury. Ellul's talk, nevertheless, essentially chapter two from his book *The Presence of the Kingdom*, was published in an issue of *The Student World*, "On Politics,"[39] which would catch and hold Stringfellow's interest.

Their first direct contact came about in connection with a major conference on theology and law that Stringfellow organized in 1958. Though Ellul ended up not attending (never coming to the U.S. for that matter), the gathering, hugely successful, was built, prepublication, around the English translation of Ellul's *The Theological Foundation of Law*. That volume, a radical Christian critique of natural law that happened to comport with Stringfellow's own position, is pertinent to the topic of principalities in a number of ways. Most importantly, Ellul there identifies institutions theologically with the principalities, powers, thrones, and dominions of the creation hymn found in Col 1:15.[40] That view is actually something of an anomaly in Ellul's writing, since he more generally rejects the view that the powers are creatures willed

---

38. JE to WS 11/16/66 Box 9, Stringfellow archives #4438, Cornell University; trans. Robert Rodes, Notre Dame University.
39. Jacques Ellul, "The Christian as Revolutionary," *Student World* 41, no. 3 (Third Quarter 1948): 221–26.
40. Jacques Ellul, *The Theological Foundation of Law* (New York: Doubleday, 1960). For more on the Colossians creation hymn, see chapter 2.

by the God of Jesus Christ that have been somehow deflected from their true and valid purpose. This, however, is precisely Stringfellow's view (and Wink's, who followed him) and it was most likely nourished by the book.

For Stringfellow, the principalities are indeed creatures, which is to say they have a life and integrity of their own.[41] He references them to the Genesis account as well as the creation hymn of Colossians. From his perspective, the creatureliness of the powers underscores that they are not actually under human control, whatever naïve misapprehension people may hold in this regard. He emphasizes the question of their vocation in the created and social order, which also signifies their standing before the judgment of God. In all of this, Stringfellow acknowledges that the exact origin of this creatureliness in the powers is a mystery. Human beings are obviously privy to the genesis of any number of institutions, but something more than human initiative comes into play.

In practical theological fact, though Ellul denies their creaturehood, his view is not all that different. Concerning the nature of the powers, he situates himself somewhere between two positions, sometimes emphasizing one aspect, sometimes the other: 1) that they are less precise powers than traditional demons, but still possessing "an existence, reality, and as one might say, objectivity of their own," and 2) that they are simple human dispositions, human factors that are constituted as powers by virtue of being exalted as such.[42] For example, he treats the city as a purely human creation, virtually an act of rebellion first by Cain against God. And yet, on the basis of an etymological argument, he observes that the word for city means also the Watching Angel, the Vengeance and Terror. "We must admit that the city is not just a collection of houses with ramparts, but also a spiritual power. I am not saying it is a being. But like an angel, it is a power on a spiritual plane."[43] Okay, not a creature with a vocation, but a mystery to which humanity has some privity and initiative.

In 1967, when the English translation of *The Presence of the Kingdom* (Ellul's postwar theological manifesto clearly charting the future course of his whole life's work) was republished, he asked Stringfellow to provide an American introduction. Bill Stringfellow wrote:

---

41. See *Free in Obedience*, 52–53; *Ethic for Christians*, 78–80; *Conscience and Obedience*, 27–32.
42. Jacques Ellul, *The Ethics of Freedom* (Grand Rapids, MI: Eerdmans, 1976), 151–52.
43. Jacques Ellul, *The Meaning of the City* (Grand Rapids, MI: Eerdmans, 1970), 9.

Few books by American authors purporting to deal with theological ethics discern the presence and power of death in this world, in this day, even in America, as an essential clue, to nations and institutions as well as individuals, of their radical alienation from one another and from themselves, that is to say, of their fallenness.[44]

On this matter of fallenness, Stringfellow and Ellul couldn't have agreed more. As far as the former was concerned, North American Christians were hopelessly (the word is used advisedly) naïve concerning the depth and ubiquity of the fall. Fallen creation included for him the distortion, confusion, and inversion of vocation in the principalities. This means they place their own survival above service to human life and creation. It means they blaspheme instead of praise; enslave instead of serve. It means, among other things, they usurp the place of God. It means they are become, every one, demonic powers—dehumanizing and dominating human life. In this, they share an array of stratagems and tactics, by his account: denial of truth, doublespeak, overtalk, secrecy, boasts of expertise, surveillance, harassment, exaggeration, deceptions, cursing, conjuring, diversion, demoralization. Because he gathers them all up as the tactics of "babel," they are heavily verbal in character.[45]

The structure of the fall in Ellul's work bears prominently on the common observation that he wrote in two parallel tracks. He would do sociological or historical analyses of political authority, say, or propaganda, or technology, and would match them with works of biblical theology, taking on 2 Kings, or Revelation, or a sweeping thematic study of the city in scripture. For example, take the volume that arrived at Stringfellow's door, just as he had completed a first draft of *An Ethic for Christians*. Ellul's book, *The Meaning of the City* (so radically pessimistic about human works and radically hopeful about God's grace in history), is in fact the theological counterpoint to *The Technological Society*, which is equally pessimistic about the tyranny of technique aggressively penetrating every aspect of human society. In this parallel process, Ellul made a rigorous methodological commitment to keeping his sociological analysis free of religious reference. He clearly desired the scathing sociological works to stand on their own as analysis, but he also wanted Christian readers to live with the dialectical tension of the two tracks. For many secular academics, his biblical

---

44. William Stringfellow, "Introduction," Jacques Ellul, *The Presence of the Kingdom* (New York: Seabury, 1967), 3.
45. *An Ethic*, 98.

theology was utterly unknown or dismissed as little more than some quirky hobby. In Detroit, a circle of lucid anarchists are Ellul devotees, yet they were nonplussed, dumbfounded would be more precise, to discover that he was a Christian, let alone that faith was the beginning and end of his work.

Let me insert that Stringfellow takes the opposite methodological tact. In writing on the principalities he moves seamlessly between social analysis and scripture or theology. It is all one for him. I believe that method is rooted, from his perspective, in a radically incarnational theology that refuses any otherworldliness. He considered the genius of the biblical witness to be that "the Bible deals with the very sanctification of the actual history of nations and of human being in this world as it is while that history is being lived."[46] I'm inclined to think that if you took *Technological Society* and *The Meaning of the City* and compressed them together under the weight of racial crisis and war-making in America, the dialectical sparks would fly upwards and you would get a book very like *An Ethic for Christians and Other Aliens in a Strange Land*.

Marva Dawn has shown very clearly that the concept of the powers is a point of departure for Jacques Ellul's social analysis and, in fact, the very tie between the two tracks.[47] What Ellul demonstrates empirically is that particular powers prove to have a life of their own, operating with an independence actually beyond human decision-making and control. The virtual autonomy of technology in shaping the course of its own development is a prime example. When he slips into appearing to grant it a mythic kind of will, he steps back with a sociological qualification:

> It is obvious—and this comment holds for all the rest of this discussion—that when I say technology "does not admit," "wants," etc., I am not personifying in any way. I am simply using an accepted rhetorical shortcut. In reality, it is the technicians on all levels who make these judgments and have this attitude; but they are so imbued, so impregnated with the technological ideology, so integrated into the system, that their vital judgments and attitudes are its direct expression. One can refer them to the system itself.[48]

---

46. *An Ethic*, 47.
47. Dawn, *The Concept of "the Principalities and Powers" in the Works of Jacques Ellul*, op. cit.; Sources and Trajectories (Grand Rapids, MI: Eerdmans, 1997); "Powers and Principalities: Yoder Point to Ellul," in *Faith and Freedom* 5, no. 1-2 (June 1996): 54-59. Just a further point, in her *Power, Weakness, and the Tabernacling of God* (Grand Rapids, MI: Eerdmans, 2001) she marshals Ellul in a significant critique of Wink.

Ellul's sociological synonym for the fall is "the logic of necessity," a kind of analytical equivalent for "the law of sin and death." It is the web in which all, all are caught. He employs it to gather up, as Dawn has put it, everything that "is unavoidable, the compulsion or constraint caused by circumstances or social conditions which make certain actions obligatory or inevitable."[49] His genius is in uncovering what I would call, to use a term of choice in Paul's epistles, the *stoicheia*, the elemental building blocks or rudiments of that necessity. With respect to technique, these are the means choosing the means. With respect to political power or violence, the same. Having identified the laws or mechanisms by which violence operates, he concludes, "The order of violence is like the order of digestion or falling bodies or gravitation." Then who can fight against it? For Ellul and Stringfellow both, we are caught in a horrifying bondage—which they describe with such unflinching honesty that we might be led to the brink of despair.

And yet.

Nevertheless. Paradoxically, shall we say? Beyond all imagining, they both proclaim a freedom from that bondage. Freedom from the logic of necessity is a kind of ethical Christian charism for Ellul. Stringfellow names it plainly: freedom from the power of death.

Actually, it is that freedom which enabled Stringfellow to look the Beast in the face without flinching, turning aside, or going weak in the knees. He lived and wrote in the freedom of the resurrection, the freedom to die. He wrote as it were in the estate of justification—free to stand at any given moment before the judgment of God. And he commended thereby an ethic, without principle or program, that was sacramental, improvisational, incarnational, and eschatological. An ethic of resurrection. He was simply convinced "that neither death, nor life, nor angels, nor principalities, nor things present, nor things to come, nor powers, nor height, nor depth, nor anything else in all creation will be able to separate us from the love of God in Christ Jesus our Lord" (Rom 8:38).

Engaging Walter Wink: The Conversation Goes Forward

Before his death, William Stringfellow had occasion to read *Naming the Powers*, the first volume of what has become Walter Wink's stunning trilogy (with the several supplemental works) on the principalities and

---

48. Jacques Ellul, *The Technological System* (New York: Continuum, 1980), 335n2.
49. Dawn, *The Concept of the Powers*, 173.

powers. In fact, with page proofs in hand, he and Wink jointly taught a two-weekend course on the Powers for Auburn Seminary. Between the first session and the second, two months later, he crossed over to communion of saints. But at that first weekend, he confided succinctly that it was "very good" and added with prescient emphasis, "It's going to be an important book." Little wonder he would think so. With careful and exhaustive New Testament research, Wink confirmed in the main what Stringfellow intuited over the years through his own Bible study and writing. Wink tips his hat to Bill Stringfellow periodically in those volumes, and specifically acknowledges having first conceived the entire undertaking in 1964 under the impetus of reviewing *Free in Obedience*.[50] He subsequently identified the extent of his debt:

> As I look back over that completed project and having now read through most of his opus (a few books for the first time), I am able to see how very deeply I owe the strengths of my series on the powers to him and how its weaknesses reveal my failure to take him more seriously. (I also realize how much of his thought I had internalized without giving him sufficient credit.)[51]

Naming the Powers lays the exegetical foundation for the project, tackling the word studies and closely reading the disputed or neglected passages in their first-century context. The second volume, *Unmasking the Powers*,[52] is a set of interlocking cultural essays on aspects of power addressed as the phenomenal categories developed in the first book. They are thoughtful reflections on topics long banished from our own rationalist and materialist vocabularies: namely, Satan, the demons, the gods, the angels of the nations, the angels of the churches, and the like. The essays are polemical insofar as they made frontal attacks on the ideology of materialism, but they are Christian apologetic insofar as they use sociological analysis and Jungian depth psychology to make these biblical persona more readily comprehensible. Between the two could be seen the attempt to define a "postmaterialist cosmology," as he termed it, by drawing on the biblical resources.

The culmination of the thirty-year project is *Engaging the Powers*, Wink's biblical "Ethic," his own book of "Praxis." It proves to be nothing less than a new and renewed theology of gospel nonviolence. The

---

50. "Stringfellow on the Powers," 25. Wink there identifies the review as written at the behest of *Christian Century*, but it was in fact the *Christian Advocate* (November 5, 1964). The same cannot be said with respect to Ellul. Wink found him "unreadable."
51. Ibid., 25–26.
52. Walter Wink, *Unmasking the Powers* (Philadelphia: Fortress Press, 1987).

fallen moral reality that Barth freely termed "Satan's" rule and Stringfellow called "the power of death," the estate of bondage that Ellul named "the order of necessity," Wink has dubbed "the Domination System." It is the versatile, aggressive, and self-replicating system of violence that enjoys a mythic, indeed theological, justification as creative and redemptive. Part one of *Engaging* unpacks the history, myth, and methods of that ubiquitous system we may recognize as our own. Part two sets beside it the domination-free social order that Jesus called "the kingdom of God," and details the means of subversion and the provocative tactics of transformation that it imagines.

Wink admits to launching the entire study under the naïve preconception that the powers of domination could be facilely "demythologized," that is, reduced without remainder into modern categories. Under the sway of materialist assumptions, he expected to find nothing more than institutions, social systems, and political structures, but he was in for an exegetical surprise: Their "mythic" spiritual dimension wouldn't go away. In the end, he was forced to argue that the principalities and powers are *simultaneously* the inner and outer aspects of any given manifestation of power. They are, in effect, at once visible and invisible.[53]

So, to take as example the central case of Jesus's trial and execution, the powers may be in one rendition, "the rulers and elders" or Pontius Pilate and, in another, "the rulers of this age" who crucified the Lord of Glory (see 1 Cor 2:7–8). The latter is no abstract theologizing or political misdirection;[54] both speak of the realities of political power in different aspects.

Or, to draw a striking instance from a different class of powers, the "prince of the power of the air" (Eph 2:2) is not to be cast off as some spooky and ephemeral first-century superstition. The power of the air may be recognized as identifying a kind of world-atmosphere, the general spiritual climate that influences human interaction, what Paul in another reference calls "the spirit of the cosmos" (1 Cor 2:12). It is, says Wink, the "invisible dominion or realm created by the sum total of choices for evil. It is the spiritual matrix of inauthentic living."[55] This pseudo-environment is the constellation of forces that he sees touched on by such contemporary terms as *zeitgeist* or ideology, cul-

---

53. See the further discussion of this in the next chapter. Also see the concluding personal appreciation, chapter 28, for more on his own spiritual history.
54. S. G. F. Brandon was among the early makers of this argument. See *The Trial of Jesus* (London: Paladin, 1971), 19.
55. Wink, *Naming*, 84.

tural expectations, climate of public opinion, mob psychology, even negative vibes. Essential to its functioning is that we are not even aware that it exists. To seem not to appear is part and parcel of its power. I have heard it said that at the Pentagon, the in-house term for its own military propaganda is "atmospherics."

While Stringfellow might not have shared Wink's "post-materialist cosmology" or "integral worldview," his own theology comported just fine with Wink's spiritual/material take on the principalities. Where the two were more in tension was around the possibility of the powers' redemption and transformation. Though radically hopeful, Stringfellow was less than optimistic about the possibility of such real institutional change. He emphasized that we live in the era of the fall and that all institutions and structures suffer it.[56] The powers could be rebuked and constrained. There would be events in which the renewal of life in the end might be glimpsed, but it was the height of naïveté to imagine that human beings could readily bring institutions in line with the realm of God. The work of ethics was to nurture human beings and human communities that could live in radical freedom from the bondage to death and so in living witness to the renewal of all creation in the *eschaton*.

Walter Wink works much more in the transformational mode. For him, creation, fall, and redemption are simultaneous processes constantly at work. Naming and unmasking and engaging the powers means summoning them back to their created vocations to serve human life.

As for myself, I hope not to be naïve about the fall, but as you will see, I embrace the radical freedom of Stringfellow's theology as crucial to the work of transformation. One transformation seeding the other. I compare it to Gandhi's "nonattachment to results" being crucial to the "effectiveness" of the truth warrior. At various places in these essays—perhaps because they are written over time or perhaps

---

56. Reflecting on his own approach compared to Stringfellow's, Walter Wink wrote: "My own natural tendency (against which I have striven mightily but with limited success) has always been to seek the *via media*. Principalities and powers are usually bad, but they also do good; therefore, they are a mix of good and evil, and need a bit of reform here and a bit of rebuking there, but they must not be demonized or rendered irremediably evil. Stringfellow found such thinking reprehensible. His own approach was paradoxical in the extreme. The powers are fallen, unequivocally. While some are less lethal, corrupting and venal than others, all are equally fallen, all seek their own survival as the highest good, all are complicit therefore in idolatry, all have thus become demonic. There is no room here for amelioration, for a continuum between good and bad. The Powers—all of them, without exception—participate in the kingdom of death." Walter Wink, "Stringfellow on the Powers," in *Radical Christian and Exemplary Lawyer*, ed. Andrew W. McThenia Jr. (Grand Rapids, MI: Eerdmans, 1995), 18.

because a moment may require either particular emphasis, one may be more in play than the other. Let the reader take note. It is certainly with this question that we are come right to the heart of practical theological ethics in engagement.

2

A Personal and Activist Appreciation: The Life and Legacy of Walter Wink (2016)

The times are the realm of hope.
The times are under the sway of death and despair.
The times require us to act on the fully human, and so perhaps redeem them.

I speak not so much as a scholar but more personally, as a friend and mentee, as pastor and nonviolent community activist. Also, as a white hetero male professional with a place-based vocation in and to Detroit.

I want to begin with a word about library as legacy. I'm so grateful that Walter Wink's collection has been joined here.[1] In Detroit, as elsewhere, libraries as an accessible commons are under assault and not just by digitalization, scanning, and stashing books in private clouds. In Detroit, where public education is being dismantled and privatized under emergency management, school libraries are literally left to collapse and mold on the floor. In Highland Park residents went through a dumpster salvaging, book by book, a collection of African American history and literature that had been trashed by the EM. You don't have

---

1. Remarks given at the Center and Library for the Bible and Social Justice, Stony Point, NY, October 21, 2016, on the occasion of Walter Wink's personal library being donated to the Center.

to appeal to *Fahrenheit 451* to understand libraries as resistance, especially in minority communities. Or what a gift it is to have access to a library, a community of thought, on the Bible and social justice.

A little backstory.... Two or three years ago June called and invited me to come visit, pick over Walter's shelves, and fill my trunk with whatever of his books I wanted. I knew this was a collection that needed to be kept together. I said, have you ever heard of the Center and Library for Bible and Social Justice? She had not. I sent some info and, by June's generosity, here we are. Walter's legacy is joined with a growing host of biblical witnesses. Thanks be to God.

I met Walter in 1971 when I began an MDiv at Union. That was a formatively important time for me; but looking back, it was also a pivotal period for Walter, filled with emblematic moments. Earlier that year, he spent time and study at the Guild for Psychological Studies, which shook his hermeneutics to the root. Then he was arrested at the White House, opposing the war, as pictured on the cover of his capstone book, *Just Jesus.* I believe it's fair to say that both these events figured into the writing of *The Bible in Human Transformation*, a little book, but a major event that in turn eventually drove him out of the seminary and onto the road. And then to cap it off, he and June married.

We were busted together twice in DC, two different wars. The cover of *Just Jesus: My Struggle to Become Human* shows his arrest at the Daily Death Toll project. Escorted off, he holds a Vietnamese peasant hat and wears a banner identifying himself with a monk. At the time, 300 people were dying each day in the air war. So cities up and down the east coast each took a day to send 300 people to a daily die-in at the White House gates. Other professors at Union sent us off with $100 in bail forfeiture money, but Walter went himself, body and soul. The only Union faculty member, as far as I know. I search for myself on the ground behind him in the photo, but I must be off the page or already in the wagon.

Earlier, as a pastor in Texas, he'd responded to Martin King's call to Selma and took that deeply to heart, telling the story and its lessons in more than one place. The entire time of his tenure at Union (1967–75) he was on the steering committee of Clergy and Laity Concerned about the War. Sixty-seven brought Dr. King's infamous speech "Breaking the Silence," which named the reigning American principalities, the giant triplets of extreme materialism, racism, and militarism. I don't know if Walter's CALC leadership preceded or followed the speech, but it's surely connected. I wonder if he wasn't present. Those years did include another event at Riverside Church, James Foreman seizing the pulpit and declaring the Black Manifesto in a call for reparations. Also the student takeover of Columbia University buildings. Walter was drawn variously into both. So: anti-war, student movement, racial justice struggle.

This activism was lifelong and inseparable from scholarship for him. I mentioned the later disobedience against the War in Iraq. While we were both in handcuffs he tutored me in the spiritual disciplines of writing. I was angsting about a book I was attempting to write, but stuck, about the principalities and liturgical direct action. He said firmly, "The Powers hate exposure. They are trying to suppress this book and you can't allow them to." I was fully encouraged. It got me moving and off the dime. I wrote. Only much later did it dawn on me how this wisdom was hard won from his own experience of struggling mightily to unmask the powers.

When he took a sabbatical, he used it with June to experience life under dictatorship—in Chile and South Africa. Both altered his life work.

There was the subsequent trip to South Africa, evangelizing the provocative nonviolence of Jesus amidst the anti-apartheid church struggle there. That saga includes the famous story, a mystery of providence, concerning his entrance illegally into the country from Lesotho. His book, *Jesus: The Third Way*, which had been widely distributed there in a plain brown cover, to pastors black and white, by the Fellowship of Reconciliation, was a focused biblical and theological participation in that struggle. That material was the script for his workshops and was eventually integrated into *Engaging the Powers*—a *magnum opus* that set forth a new and renewed biblical theology of nonviolence for North Americans and for global struggle. This is simply to say that Walter's legacy essentially includes the embodiment of engaged and transformational scholarship.

It was in 1971 that he studied with Elizabeth Boyden Howes at the Guild for Psychological Studies in San Francisco. The precursor to this was a powerful charismatic and Pentecostal experience of baptism in the spirit during college, which not only set up a long yearning to integrate reason and experience, but opened him to the possibility of healing and miracle. (I love his definition in *Engaging*: "Miracle is just a word we use for the things the Powers have deluded us into thinking God is unable to do."[2] Simply something the system has convinced us is impossible.)

The yearning for integration took him to the Guild, where the Jesus story was read employing depth psychology. For Walter, this meant bringing one's whole person, body, mind, and spirit to the reading of scripture, and it deeply implicated his own woundedness with that engagement. (Think of passages in the major theological works where he vulnerably brings his dreams to bear or shares his family history of abuse.)

You mustn't imagine that depth psychology meant individualization in Bible study. Quite the contrary. Carl Jung was the pioneer and vocalist of the collective unconscious who, under Nazism, could discern the Germanic god Wotan, once suppressed, rising with a vengeance in the Third Reich. Along with *The Human Being*, Walter's fullest use of depth psychology is in the second volume of the Powers trilogy, *Unmasking*. There he exposes not only the angels of the churches, but the angels of the nations, the angels of nature, the gods, Satan. Without making metaphysical claims—he was able to get at the inner dimension, the palpable spirituality of the principalities, partly by way of depth psychology.

Howes and the Guild altered forever his pedagogy. Within that same year he was my instructor for Introduction to New Testament. In the small-group session one day we were looking at the pearl of great price parable in Matthew. Part way into the discussion he said, "Okay, let's go round the circle and each say what it is we'd be willing to die for." Not your typical discussion starter in critical Bible study. He let the text question us. I venture to say it's a question no one should pass through seminary without being asked. Never mind baptismal preparation.

Next thing you knew, clay and paint were on the table with the text. With him I have considered Revelation 2 and discerned the angel of a congregation with clay in my hand. These in turn opened the way for the gifts that June brought to their marriage, their biblical partnership and collaboration—gifts his insights were crying out for but did not come naturally to him. In the love of their marriage were embraced left brain and right brain, inner and outer, conscious and unconscious, soul and body. He dedicates the Powers series to her with lines from Eliot's *Four Quartets*. "To June where the tongues of flame are enfolded." So, not only clay and pottery, but so much more: dance, drama, and body movement . . . all.

Perhaps his most notorious and oft-repeated bodily enactment was

---

2. Walter Wink, *Unmasking the Powers* (Philadelphia: Fortress Press, 1987), 303.

of the Sermon on the Mount texts, which he first workshopped in South Africa. Turn the other cheek, give your coat as well, and go the extra mile. Almost single-handedly he altered the way these have been read for near two millennia. Not milquetoast passivity, but uppity anti-imperial examples of exposure and ridicule. I was among those he would call on to appear at his local presentation with my swimming trunks on beneath my pants. Picked randomly like a magician's assistant from the audience, I would role-play the poor person who was being sued for my outer garment. Then in animated exasperation, "Okay, take it all, take my shirt, my pants . . ." suddenly "naked" (but with my bathing suit to cover). The last time, I hadn't foreseen that I'd be acting this out in the chancel of an African American church.

But it may be most important to press this back to its origin. I believe it was in acting these out bodily that it first became abruptly clear that striking someone on the right cheek was in fact necessarily a backhand, an insult, an act not just of violence but of power and status. Putting the whole person inside the text revealed its political context.

Phil Berrigan, also of blessed memory, used to say, "Conscience is about where you put your ass." The gospels are about body politics. They narrate where Jesus put his body, in what spaces, at what risk, in order to teach and act. This is my body. . . .

Anyway, it was this new approach to reading that prompted in 1973 (in the midst of my own time at Union) publication of *The Bible in Human Transformation*. It began, "The historical critical method is bankrupt" and went on to assail the reigning myth of scientific objectivity, the disembodied approach that kept the text at arm's length and preempted real engagement. He compared the writing of it to performing a "hermeneutical exorcism" on himself. It may have been a healing act and vocationally adept in the long run, but near term it was, as they say, a "bad career move." He was subsequently denied tenure and effectively "blacklisted" in the academy. He would later call this a providence. It pushed him from the seminary into the sanctuary and the street. He (and June with him) would go on the road, congregation to congregation, with their Bible study method. Church (and movement) had now become what he called his "community of accountability."

I think it's fair to say that this little book was and is a contribution to the conversation on liberative, popular, and contextual hermeneutics. His own activism meant praxis was in the hermeneutical circle. And the whole person, body and soul, meant not just bringing one's social location, but one's physical and psychic location to reading as well.

Walter's role in bringing the principalities and powers back onto the map of Christian social ethics is a substantial part of his legacy. It was a project seeded in 1964 when he was asked to review William Stringfellow's *Free in Obedience* and he began quietly gathering, through the Union period, materials that came to fruition in the trilogy. (Though by my count he actually wrote twice again that many books on the powers.) Once again, he is part of illuminating an aspect of the scriptures hermeneutically buried for 1700 years.

I put him in a line with Karl Barth and Jacques Ellul, for whom the crisis of Nazism first brought the principalities into high relief, and with William Stringfellow, who discerned them in connection with U.S. racial crisis and militarism. Walter and Bill read the powers biblically as creatures, in the analogy of the nations, standing before the judgment of God, accountable for their vocations to praise God and serve human life.

To ask the vocation of a given power proves to be a very radical question. What is the vocation of a bank? How is it called to serve God and human community? What is the vocation of a newspaper or the media? And how is that vocation turned upside down in the fall—to imagine itself as god and so to assault or enslave human life? One of his gifts to us is to make the principalities not only comprehensible, but functionally useful in movement struggle.

I first read *Naming the Powers* in jail for anti-nuclear resistance, actually subsequent volumes as well. I've written about how his theology helped shaped our participation in the Detroit newspaper strike, and now with respect to resisting Emergency Management and the water shut-offs.

I'm always struck how his language has entered into common parlance in theological, church, and movement circles: "The Powers are good; the powers are fallen; the powers must be redeemed," a structure of movement he found in Colossians 2, but also discerned overall in the second testament.[3] Its simplicity suggests a kind of spiritual polit-

---

3. Within recent memory of this reflection I can tabulate an impressive short list of instances experienced or overheard: 1) A Christian Peacemaker Team participant returns from work in Gaza and the West Bank reflecting on her experience through the lens of the "Myth of Redemptive Violence" and Wink's uppity reading of the Sermon on the Mount; 2) An Alinsky organizer with Gamaliel cites Wink in connection with understanding power biblically, commending prayer and contemplation to organizers; 3) A homiletics professor takes his class to Atlanta for prophetic street preaching and ends up writing a preaching text based on the powers; 4) A panel member at an advance retreat laying the foundations for the Greensboro Truth and Reconciliation Com-

ical agenda. Or take "the myth of redemptive violence" or "the domination system." He never came up with a similar synonym for the "kingdom": "God's domination-free order" never quite rolled off the tongue or took so readily. I like "the Beloved Community" myself.

His refusal to turn away biblically from the spiritual, interior aspect, of structural powers, has potent implication for movement struggle. We are not just up against material realities to be resisted or transformed. If we don't engage them in their spiritual dimension, we are fighting one-handed and blind-eyed. Liturgy, ceremony, lamentation, sacramental memory, muraling art, libation, storytelling and joke, chanting and song, fasting and prayer must all be movement tactics and resources. He underscored that for us. And we are taking it to heart in Detroit.

Certainly the most remarkable and practical legacy of the principalities work was that he pursued the powers straight through into a full-blown theology of nonviolence that articulated the love of enemies, the call to reconciliation, purifying our projections and inner violence, and the way of the cross. For evidence and example he collected stories of nonviolent transformation, large and small, which he compiled in a monthly column for *Fellowship*, not to mention culling the magazine archives for the essential collection, *Peace Is the Way*.[4]

I want to return to the language question and a legacy to ponder. At a certain point, early on, Walter determined to write in plain, commonly accessible language. His magisterial works could be painstakingly researched and massively footnoted, but still written in the common tongue, free of esoteric parlance and academic idiom. I think of it as a political commitment, a spiritual discipline all its own. Moreover, he would take an 800-page trilogy, strip it of 100 pages of footnotes, and boil it down to a popular paperback that could fit in a church pew rack, not a whit less scholarly.

His final book, posthumously published and as yet underappreciated, *Just Jesus: My Struggle to Become Human*, does something similar for his major volume, *The Human Being*. The latter is a theological treatment of the so-called "Son of Man" texts, which he offered in conver-

---

mission draws on the visible/invisible vocational structure of the powers as an aspect of their need in the reconciling process; 5) A restorative justice activist freely considers the "angels of the nations" in the work of forgiveness; 6) A nationally known anti-racism trainer wants to explore the practical implications of naming racism a demonic power; 7) A founder of the Jonah House resistance community addresses a group of Methodist activists in L.A. using the terminology of the "domination system," as though this were simply common parlance in movement circles.

4. Walter Wink, ed., *Peace Is the Way* (Maryknoll, NY: Orbis, 2000).

sation with colleagues in the Jesus Seminar. Both of these brought him back to Jesus, his first love in biblical work.

When he began *Just Jesus*, already diagnosed with Lewy Body Dementia, he was calling it "the autobiography of an exegete." In the end, with June's judicious help, it gathered up personal narratives from previous work and verily personified and practiced the methodology he had pitched when I was a seminarian. *Just Jesus* (along with *The Human Being*) is a last testament that fulfills and enacts *The Bible in Human Transformation*. Bookends of a collection. Frames of a great work.

What they point to is his life as a legacy. His beloved humanity, struggled for and worked at and become. Even in the end pared painfully and painstakingly down to its simplicity. Calling us to live into the humanity of God's very self. Thanks be.

3

Death Shall Have No Dominion: Daniel Berrigan of the Resurrection (2017)

> At this writing . . . Dan is the only remaining brother of the six; I believe that he is in close communication with his own dying and the life that awaits him and all of us. Like Phil, like Jerry, it looks to me as if Dan is in touch with the life that lies beyond this one.
> —Elizabeth McAlister, Preface, *The Berrigan Letters*[1]

I once had a conversation with Dan Berrigan (April 30, 2016) about his death.[2]

We were talking late into the night at the Block Island hermitage that William Stringfellow and Anthony Towne had built for him while he was two years in Danbury Federal Prison, in consequence of the 1968 Catonsville draft board action. He had by then foresworn Scotch, on doctor's orders, so I was being introduced to Manhattans, dry, which were somehow allowed. The place was fitting for the topic. On the wall above us was an exorcism poem that he had hand-lettered in a style familiar to Catholic Worker and resistance houses across the country.

---

1. Elizabeth McAlister, "Preface" to *The Berrigan Letters: Personal Correspondence Between Daniel and Philip Berrigan*, ed. Daniel Cosacchi and Eric Martin (Maryknoll, NY: Orbis, 2016), xvi.
2. Bill Wylie-Kellermann, "Death Shall Have No Dominion: Daniel Berrigan of the Resurrection," *CrossCurrents* (September 2016): 312–20.

> At landsend
> where this house dares stand
> and the sea turns in sleep
> ponderous, menacing
> and our spirits fail and run
> landward, seaward, askelter,
>
> we pray you protect
> from the law's clawed reach
> from the second death
> from envy's tooth
> from doom's great knell
> all who dwell here.

I'm certain I was the one to broach the topic of death. When we met in my seminary days in the early seventies, it was in the wake of notorious assassinations; Medgar Evers and Viola Liuzzo, Fred Hampton of the Panthers, Malcolm, King, the Kennedys. There was a certain youthful grandiosity in imagining that he or Phil or others who were such troublesome peacemakers would be similarly targeted. I braced my heart. I told him so. (Then he turned around and lived, thanks be to God, to ninety-four!) I probably mentioned Bonhoeffer or King and the way the blood of the martyrs is seed of movement or church, even yearning secretly myself for some sort of "meaningful death." He gently countered with Albert Camus's good life and the absurdly random car crash of his death. So, I was as much chastened as honored when he turned the conversation into a Block Island poem:

> Drinking one night, Kellermann and I
> talked the moon down, "Think of mad racers
> we're at the mercy of
> And stuttering engines of air craft
> so high the guardian angels peel away –
> Then street knifings. And bloody so on.
> It's certain we exist
> courtesy of bellicose junkers, by merest
> sufferance."
> Significant death?
> Gold leaf of history, cosmetic
> on a split skull.[3]

---

3. Daniel Berrigan, *Block Island* (Greensboro, NC: Unicorn, 1985), 67.

In point of fact, Dan had himself once wondered over the sort of death I imagined for him. In 1970, instead of submitting voluntarily to the Catonsville prison sentence, he had gone underground, slipping away from a very public event, under the noses of federal agents, in the oversized Bread and Puppet effigy of one of the apostles, Peter or John. During that notoriously public four months, he wrote a letter to the Weathermen, a cohort of war resisters whose tactics many found violent. There he said, "And this is why we accept trouble, ostracism, and fear of jail and death as the normal condition under which decent men and women are called upon to function today. Undoubtedly the FBI comes with guns in pursuit of people like me because beyond their personal chagrin and corporate machismo (a kind of debased esprit de corps; they always get their man), there was the threat that the Panthers and the Vietnamese have so valiantly offered."[4]

Our last conversation, less than a year ago, was again partly about Dietrich Bonhoeffer (April 9, 1945). The new Charles Marsh biography, so honest and revealing, was out. He'd not heard tell. His underground sojourn coincided with the appearance of the earlier definitive and elephantine biography by Bonhoeffer's beloved companion and student, Eberhard Bethge. It was actually on the twenty-fifth anniversary of Bonhoeffer's death by hanging in the Nazi prison of Flossenberg, that Berrigan went openly missing in 1970. That day he began a long poetic review of the new bio, publishing it in *Saturday Review*. Such publication was maddening to FBI Director J. Edgar Hoover. Like other initiatives, popping up to preach in a prominent pulpit or appearing on network television and then skipping out the back door, it improvised a nation of safe houses and kept Berrigan on the Most Wanted List.

In the review, acknowledging the footnoted churchy stuff, he honed on the distillate.

> Bonhoeffer: "I am working with all my might for church resistance. But it is perfectly clear to me that this resistance is only a temporary and transitional phase that will lead on to opposition of a quite different kind. . . . [P]ray with us that it will be a 'resistance unto death,' and that people will be found to suffer it."

> Berrigan: "To the question of whether the church should connive with the state in the suppression, deportation, and murder of Jews, he proposed a concrete answer: the formation at Finkenwalde, in 1936, of a [community]

---

4. Daniel Berrigan, "Letter to the Weathermen," in *America Is Hard to Find* (Garden City, NY: Doubleday, 1972), 92.

of young seminarians, to engage in study, discipline, and prayer, and (in the event, only known afterward) to prepare of resistance and death."⁵

When the FBI, disguised as the infamous birdwatchers, caught up with Berrigan on Block Island four months later, it was this very topic that he and William Stringfellow were discussing. Could such a seminary take form on U.S. soil in a different moment? Though they took this up again in earnest after Berrigan's release from prison, it would be wrong to think imprisonment was an interruption of some sort. It was, in fact, the immediate tryout behind bars. Pulling together a circle of draft resisters and conventional felons, Dan convened a group for study, discipline, and prayer, which eventually busted out upon the world. And only then would a group of us at Union Seminary be drawn into its next iteration.

While at Danbury prison, Berrigan wrote *A Letter to the Vietnamese*. Long and little known, it was published by the Thomas Merton Center in NYC, as a series of connected posters with art by Tom Lewis. I've no doubt it was hand delivered to its intended by way of his friend Thich Nhat Hahn, the Vietnamese Zen monk, then exiled in Paris. During the Tiger Cage Fast and Vigil in the summer of 1974 I committed the entire poem to memory while sitting inside a mock tiger cage cell, used for political prisoners in Vietnam, on the steps of the U.S. Capitol. By design they were too small to stand or stretch out, and accessed through bars above. With a little refreshment or prompting I can recite the letter still. It begins:

> Dear friends, your faces are a constriction of grief in the throat
> your words weigh us like chains, your tears and blood
> fall on our faces. Prison; Vietnam, prison; U.S.
> prison is our fate, mothers bear us in prison,
> our tongues taste its gall, bars spring up
> from dragons' teeth, a paling, impaling us.
> A universal malevolent will, crouched like a demon
> blows winter upon us, stiffens our limbs in death, the limbs of
> women and children.
> Here, they hawk death in the streets, death in the hamburger joint
> death in the hardware, death in the cobbler's hammer
> death in the jeweler's glass, the classy showrooms of death.
> Death, shouts the newsboy; death, oranges and lemons,

---

5. Daniel Berrigan, "The Passion of Dietrich Bonhoeffer," *Saturday Review* (May 30, 1970), 17–22.

death in a candy wrapper.
Death, the cinema blares it; death!

Further on in section IV he writes,

If the birth of a child is sufficient reason
To grace seasons in wedding garments,
To wreathe in smiles our stiff-jointed discontent,
Then it must be held with equally vigorous logic
That the death of a child is sufficient reason
To burn like trash or offal those hunting licenses
Which go by the civilized euphemism, draft files,
To endure imprisonment, the loss of repute,
The mark of cain burned by the perfumed hands
Of judges churchmen and politicos on the forehead of Abel.[6]

He does write in winter, even Christmastide as above, and one can feel the toll on his lifelong ailments of bone and back and limb. But each ache is a reminder, a connection, an intercession. He concludes with a line that still haunts my conscience, "It is snowing tonight as I vigil, the first white fall of winter, bitterly cold. I think on the fevers and horrors of Con Son. No to their No. Yes to all else."

Death, the great No with a capital N, is everywhere in the culture, riddling it all. How does one say No and at the same time Yes?

One way, of course, is the invention of liturgical direct action, with all its risks and consequences. Ritually damaging nuclear warheads in such as the Plowshares action (1980), or before that, the draft board raids like Catonsville (1968), burning the files with homemade napalm. Dorothy Day, in an address to the Liturgical Conference, called the latter an "act of prayer," and Stringfellow termed it "a politically informed exorcism." Here was a No in the form of a Yes.

Yet side by side with these, Dan was tending the dying. Like Camus's doctor in *The Plague*, he tended victims, all while saying No to the executioners. In the '80s he sat to the end with AIDS patients, the untouchables ravaged by both disease and culture. I have notes from him on cards depicting Christ crucified by AIDS. In *Sorrow Built a Bridge*, he recounted, eyes wide open with love, their crossings over.[7]

---

6. For an accessible version see Daniel Berrigan, "A Letter to Vietnamese Prisoners," *Radical Discipleship*, May 18, 2015, https://radicaldiscipleship.net/2015/05/18/a-letter-to-vietnamese-prisoners/ (accessed May 14, 2016).
7. Daniel Berrigan, *Sorrow Built a Bridge* (Baltimore: Fortkamp, 1989).

Earlier, he had done the same at a hospice for the dying in Manhattan—specifically, the dying poor with cancer. Needless to say, he made the connections—they were woven whole cloth into his life. He recognized Hiroshima as the emblem of unleashed fallout in culture, history, planet. Genes corrupted by the radioactive poisoning of water and air were simply to be seen as the ailment of this world. Cancer? They declare war on that, too. The targeting of civilians in the atomic bombing flowed from the long-time casting off and casting out of the poor. All one before Mars, god of war.

Berrigan also told their stories. *We Die Before We Live*[8] (he thought the order important) reads partly like a journal, feeling his way forward in the hospice halls, learning the clumsy arts of touch or silence or a word, even prayer. But largely the book collects vignettes, accounts of the dying, their ways and faces. Dan had been led to the hospice by a young Catholic Worker serving there as an orderly. I suggest the influence of the Worker here in a further way. Going back to the days of Dorothy, the New York paper had a practice, picked up by others around the country, of eulogizing guests who would ordinarily cross over in the silence of blank and nameless obscurity. Often as not, sizing up characters fit for a Dickens novel, these descriptions could be funny and heroic and quirky, but above all honest and loving. I always read them. And I know the style crept into my own approach to doing funeral liturgies.

If you find the gospel in someone's story only by smoothing the facts, then it's really less than the gospel and actually less than truly human as well. Consider how much of conventional burial liturgy is taken up with smoothing and fluffing as denial. Or saying carefully in effect nothing at all. Face-painting a corpse. Anyway, thanks be for the humor, poignancy, and refusal to look away, evinced by those tales.

In 1985, Berrigan preached Stringfellow's eulogy on Block Island. Beside a culture of betrayal—political, economic, spiritual—in the nation and on the Island, he set Bill as a nonbetrayer, a keeper of his word, indeed a keeper and guardian of the Word of God. He declared:

> My encounter with this spirit of Stringfellow and his non-betraying friendship dates notoriously from 1970 and events that occurred up the road from this chapel. I was lifted from the home of Stringfellow and trundled off the island into prison. From that vantage, I learned of the subsequent indictment of William and Anthony for the crime of harboring a

---

8. Daniel Berrigan, *We Die Before We Live* (New York: Seabury, 1980).

fugitive (a strange foretaste of the present sanctuary movement within the church). But for those few days, Stringfellow's home was the only church I knew. It was the only safe place in the universe.[9]

That arrest was a kind of watershed for Stringfellow too. As to the non-betrayal, he and Towne penned a classic statement in response to their indictment:

> Daniel Berrigan is our friend. We rejoice in that fact and strive to be worthy of it. Our hospitality to Daniel Berrigan is no crime.... We did "offer and give sustenance and lodging" to him. We did not "harbor" or "conceal" him . . . Father Berrigan has and had no need to be concealed. By his own extraordinary vocation, and by the grace of God, he has become one of the conspicuous Christians of these wretched times. We have done what we could do to affirm him in this regard. We categorically deny that we have done anything to conceal him. We are not disposed to hide what light there is under a bushel.[10]

They seemed to delight in being charged with a Christian virtue, hospitality.

Long before, at a festival of hope during the 1968 Catonsville trial, Stringfellow, weak and frail with extreme illness, had climbed the pulpit to utter, by Dan's account, a single terse testimony: "Death shall have no dominion!"[11] The congregation rose in a standing ovation.

Now in the wake of the arrest, Stringfellow found himself taking recourse to the book of Acts, specifically the account of the arrest of the apostles for healing the disabled beggar and for preaching the resurrection. It was the latter that so caught his attention. He read it and read it. What can "resurrection from the dead" mean if it is cause for arrest and imprisonment? He employed this text in preaching to his hometown congregation in Northampton a sermon called "An Authority over Death." Again:

> The preaching of the resurrection, far from being politically innocuous, and the healing incidents, instead of being merely private, are profound, even cosmic, political acts ... I do not imply that Berrigan is engaged in some self-conscious imitation of Peter or John or any other of the earlier

---

9. Daniel Berrigan, "A Homiletic Afterword," in *William Stringfellow: Essential Writings*, ed. Bill Wylie-Kellermann (Maryknoll, NY: Orbis, 2013), 231–34.
10. William Stringfellow and Anthony Towne, "Statement of the Accused," in *Suspect Tenderness* (New York: Holt, Rinehart & Winston, 1971), 120–22.
11. Stringfellow's self-accounting is somewhat longer. See Stringfellow, *A Second Birthday* (Garden City, NY: Doubleday, 1970), 133.

Christians; I simply mean that to proclaim the resurrection in word and act is an affront which the State cannot tolerate because the resurrection exposes the subservience of the State to death as the moral purpose of the society which the State purports to rule.[12]

Indeed. Daniel Berrigan enjoyed and exercised that freedom. Stringfellow once reflected on a visit to the prisoners at Danbury and how he there beheld a witness of the resurrection, specifically in Berrigan's demeanor. He told of arranging the visit and how the warden and the other authorities, even the chaplain, had seemed constrained, anxious, dehumanized, unfree in the fulfillment of their functions, unable to undertake the most ordinary decisions without consulting the Attorney General. Whereas the prisoners, on the other hand, though certainly inconvenienced by their confinement, seemed truly free and fully human, unconstrained and unencumbered by their location—exemplifying, he thought, the radical freedom of the resurrection.[13]

The night of our conversation about death, there was not yet a plaque of Dan's design on the wall behind us, but there soon would be. In the spring of 1986 we moved Anthony's ashes and joined them with Bill's beside the stone wall of the cottage. The plaque was a testimony terse: "Near this house the remains of William Stringfellow and Anthony Towne await the resurrection, Alleluia."

Now Dan's remains in earth, like his remains in us, anticipate that same freedom.

---

12. Stringfellow and Towne, *Suspect Tenderness*, 73, 74.
13. William Stringfellow, Programmed Leadership Tape #3 of *Study Guide for an Ethic for Christians & Other Aliens in a Strange Land* (Waco, TX: Word, 1977).

4

From the Beginning: Two Creation Liturgies

A recurrent stumbling block to comprehending the principalities exists, for many people, at just this point. Human beings are reluctant to acknowledge institutions—or any of the other principalities—as creatures having their own existence, personality, and mode of life. Yet the Bible consistently speaks of the principalities as creatures. . . . The typical version of human reluctance to accord the principalities their due integrity as creatures is the illusion of human beings that they make or create and, hence, control institutions and that institutions are no more than groups of human beings duly organized. How do these creatures called principalities come into existence? How does an institution originate? Where does tradition come from? When is a nation born? How is an ideology created? I am frank to admit no full answers to such queries and further to confess that I am more or less content to leave these questions unanswered. The exact origins of the creatureliness of principalities is a mystery in quite the same sense that the creaturehood of human beings remains mysterious.[1]

Thus the heavens and the earth were finished, and all the host of them. And on the seventh day God finished the work which God had done,

---

1. William Stringfellow, in Bill Wylie-Kellermann, ed., *A Keeper of the Word* (Grand Rapids, MI: Eerdmans, 1994), 206.

and God rested on the seventh day . . . So God blessed the seventh day and hallowed it . . . (Gen 2:1–3).

Conceived in Conflict: The Imperial Myth of Origins

We are accustomed to reading the first chapter of Genesis in the context of social conflict. It is a passage wrestled over and struggled for. One thinks immediately of its place in the Scopes Trial and the continuing, no less, debate between "creationism" and progressive evolution as ideologies. Moreover, this account is being read now in the light of the global environmental crisis. There is the famous essay by Lynn White that first laid the burden of Western domination at the feet of a text that urges a "subduing" of the earth.[2] No matter if this be a misreading of the text, that misreading has functioned historically with power. Likewise, there is no doubt that this narrative has been employed to justify a human-centered hierarchical vision. What an irony that the cornerstone of conservative creationism should also work as the sanction for scientific progress and technological domination. Against the latter, advocates of creation spirituality cite this same passage as the source for God's "original blessing," and the anarcho-primitivists, rightly as I will argue, would read this as a credo against the centralizing forces of civilization. Add to all this the various issues of gender and sexual politics implied by the male and female image of God in the "orders of creation" (1:27), and we have a truly embattled text.

What I want to suggest is that this story was conceived in conflict. We might productively read it as a text of liturgical combat. In its earliest version, this creation narrative from the "Priestly source"[3] has its roots in the midst of struggle, virtually as an act of cultural resistance. The roots of Genesis 1 go back to the Babylonian exile of the sixth century bce. The two kingdoms, Israel and Judah, had been crushed, the temple destroyed. The social world of Israel was literally unmade. The best and the brightest, namely the literary elite, had been dragged off to Babylon and, often as not, offered good government jobs. It

---

2. Lynn Townsend White Jr., "The Historical Roots of Our Ecological Crisis," *Science* 155 (1967): 1203–7.
3. It is standard in biblical scholarship to identify several strands or sources that have been woven together to form the Hebrew Bible in its present form. P or the "Priestly source" originated subsequent to the exile of 587 bce. The more ancient account from the J source follows in chapters 2 and 3. For a popular introduction to the Priestly source see Robert B. Coote and David Robert Ord, *In the Beginning: Creation and the Priestly History* (Minneapolis: Fortress Press, 1991). I will cite this in the pages to come, though its argument and view differ from the one set forth here.

was a time of confusion and cultural seduction. Who now to worship? Marduk and his kin of the Babylonian pantheon? They were literally overpowering. Hadn't they defeated Yahweh? That certainly was the Babylonian view made explicit in their own public celebrations. Specifically, the great imperial liturgy was the New Year's festival, which remembered the creation of the world as the founding anniversary of the empire. There the *Enuma elish*, the Babylonian story of creation, was dramatically reenacted.

Readers will recognize that I'm following Walter Wink who begins *Engaging the Powers* with his own reading of the Babylonian creation myth, though not, as here, with reference to the first chapter of Genesis.

At the crux of the Babylonian story is a great battle. Younger gods who have stirred the wrath of Tiamat, mother goddess of sea and chaos, turn in terror to Marduk the up-and-coming young male god. He offers a bargain: that he will fight the great dragon in exchange for undisputed sovereignty in the assembly of the gods. He does indeed engage her in fierce cosmic combat and prevails.

> Over the captive gods he strengthened his durance,
> And unto Tiamat, whom he had conquered, he returned.
> And the lord stood upon Tiamat's hinder parts,
> And with his merciless club he smashed her skull.
> He cut through the channels of her blood,
> And he made the North wind bear it away into secret places ...
> Then the lord rested, gazing upon her dead body,
> ... and devised a cunning plan.
> He split her up like a flat fish into two halves;
> One half of her he stablished as a covering for heaven.
> He fixed a bolt, he stationed a watchman,
> And bade them not to let her waters come forth.[4]

Victorious, Marduk has divided Tiamat's monstrous fishlike body, spreading it out upon the heavens, thereby imposing foundational order upon the world and paving the way for his enthronement among the gods as the very god of Order. In this act is the creation of the world. Thereafter, from the dripping blood of her consort, also felled, he fashions human beings to be slaves of the gods, go-fers doing the bidding of their imperial leisure.

---

4. *Enuma Elish: The Epic of Creation*, trans. L. W. King. From Tablet Four of the Seven Tablets of Creation (London: Luzac & Co., 1902).

Several things ought to be mentioned in connection with this creation myth.

As foundational myth, this is the story that legitimates and virtually creates the social world of Babylon. *It sanctions the Babylonian state as the real world of order.* (Indeed, the cosmos itself may be conceived as synonymous with the State.) The king as divine representative embodies the sovereignty of imperial order, a role authorized and ritualized in public festival. Paul Ricoeur describes this process in The Symbolism of Evil:

> The magnitude of the New Year's festival at Babylon is well known. A whole people, in the presence of the gods assembled in effigy, relives the fundamental emotions of the poem—the cosmic anguish, the exaltation of battle, the jubilation in triumph. By the celebration of the festival, the people place their whole existence under the sign of the drama of creation.[5]

Moreover, by this story, *human beings are assigned a place in the created social order: they are servants and slaves.* The story not only grants meaning to the empire, it clarifies the significance of each person's life in relation to the world, social and political.

Evil, in Babylonian theology, precedes creation. That, above all, was Ricoeur's brilliant point. Chaos and evil predate the world. They have a kind of metaphysical primacy. As he put it: "[T]he origin of evil is coextensive with the origin of things; it is the *'chaos' with which the creative act of the god struggles.*"[6] And this, quite naturally, has enormous consequences for how one views life and this world.

Several things are being conquered here. Not the least of these is the feminine. It is no small point that this origin narrative recounts the defeat of feminine evil, by masculine good. *Maleness is glorified* and this historical period does indeed mark the rise not only of state and empire, but patriarchy.[7]

It issues equally in *the preeminent theology of war.* This is classic military imperial mythology. Might makes order makes right. And it is practically the primeval Orwellian equation: destruction is creation.

---

5. Paul Ricoeur, *The Symbolism of Evil* (Boston: Beacon, 1967), 192. I have previously written about the myth, drawing on Ricoeur, with reference to the mythic structures of nuclearism. *Seasons of Faith and Conscience: Kairos, Confession, Liturgy* (Maryknoll, NY: Orbis, 1991).
6. Ibid., 172.
7. See Riane Eisler, *The Chalice and the Blade* (San Francisco: Harper & Row, 1987), for a detailed study of this view. Walter Wink, *Engaging the Powers* (Philadelphia: Fortress Press, 1992), 36–39.

This mythic ideology identifies every enemy with the original enemy, Chaos—and every victory creates anew the world of Pax Babylonia.

Pretty primitive people, no? If it seems so foreign and ancient, perhaps it is because this comes so close to home. I first took interest in Babylonian mythology in connection with the mythic meaning of the Hiroshima bombing. Here was a historical act perceived as primordial, primeval, mythic event. In nuclear mythology, and Hiroshima as creation drama, Babylon finds a typological kin. The war fought to make the world safe for democracy, to preserve Western civilization, was won by the purveyor of unimaginable destruction. By that bombing the postwar world was virtually created. Salvation and creation were one and the same.[8]

As noted, Walter Wink begins *Engaging the Powers* with an analysis of this same myth.[9] Following Riane Eisler, he considers identifying its emergence with a concrete historical moment of "the fall," virtually one with the rise of imperial and patriarchal civilization. Wink demonstrates how this "myth of redemptive violence," as he calls it (though it might equally well be termed the myth of *creative* violence), permeates American culture. For example, he undertakes, among other things, a devastating survey of cartoon plotlines to show how our children are being fed "Babylonian mythology" with their breakfast cereal. In this cartoon catechism Marduk and Tiamat fight it out in an infinite variety of costumes but with the same mythic plot, the same redundant meaning.

As this is written, the U.S. wars against Iraq are currently ongoing. Especially in the first Gulf War, much was made in certain circles of Iraq as ancient Babylon. Yet in terms of actual Babylonian mythology, recall that it was the Presidents Bush, at least as much Saddam Hussein, who evinced and employed the myth. Hussein may have once invoked the "Mother of All Battles," but it was George Bush, the father, who declared that this war would create the "New World Order," and it was George W. Bush, the son, who proclaimed from the pulpit of the National Cathedral, "Our responsibility to history is already clear: to answer these attacks and rid the world of evil."[10]

It is in light of our own imperial mythology that the liturgical resistance of Israel in Babylon may be most edifying. To reiterate their situation: the Israelite exiles were inundated in the empire's myth; their

---

8. See Bill Wylie-Kellermann, *Seasons of Faith and Conscience* (Maryknoll, NY: Orbis, 1991), 58f.
9. Wink, *Engaging*, 13–17. I am generally following his theological analysis here.
10. Cited in Jim Wallis, "Dangerous Religion," *Sojourners*, September–October 2003, 24.

children were being taught it; and they suffered the massive spectacle of the annual New Year's festival.

Against Marduk: Creation as Resistance Liturgy

Believe it or not, since the discovery of the Babylonian creation myth over a hundred years ago in the library of Ashurbanipal, biblical scholars have been touting it as the source for Genesis 1. The echoes are treated as an act of mimicry, a replication. A plagiarized creation story as the highest form of cultural flattery.

The Marduk/Tiamat image does get taken up in Hebrew scripture, notably in the royal psalms:

> You divided the sea by your might;
> you broke the heads of the dragons in the waters.
> You crushed the head of Leviathan;
> you gave him as food for the creatures of the wilderness. (Ps 74:13–14)

> For who in the skies can be compared to the Lord?
> Who among the gods[11] is like the Lord . . .
> You rule the raging of the sea;
> when its waves rise you still them.
> You crushed Rahab like a carcass;
> you scattered your enemies with your mighty arm. (Ps 89:6, 9–10)

When it does appear in the exilic poetry of Second Isaiah, it is in direct association with the memory of the Exodus Red Sea crossing:

> Was it not you who cut Rahab in pieces
> who pierced the dragon?
> Was it not you who dried up the sea,
> the waters of the great deep;
> who made the depths of the sea a way
> for the redeemed to pass over? (Isa 51:9–10)

In Genesis, however, the borrowed elements are better heard as a cunning act of subversion.[12] Read in the exilic context, the Genesis 1 account, with its stunning rhythm and its drama of voices and refrains, may be understood nearly as a refutation of the Marduk tale. It would be an alternative creation liturgy for exiled Israel. As it stands we have

---

11. *bene elohim*—often translated "sons of God" or "heavenly beings."
12. Portions of this section were first published as "Genesis as Resistance," *The Witness*, October 1992.

it in cultic Temple form, orchestrated for full choirs,[13] but imagine it more as a leaflet transcribed and passed hand to hand for recitation in home use around the kitchen table. This literally is a case of singing the Lord's song in a strange land.

Whereupon several counterpoints may be noticed:

This story also creates Israel's social world. The world that has been destroyed by Babylonian might is reconstructed in household liturgy around the family table. An identity and community are actually sustained without the benefit of either Temple or State. Oh, chaos is here, the formless void over which the Spirit hovers, but it is the chaos of imperial culture, which imagines itself to be right order. In new creation is the yearning for return, back to origins, seeded now in memory and imagination.

The recitation establishes a spiritual and social rhythm in the life of the exiled community. The sabbath as a seventh day of rest largely originated among the exiles.[14] Insofar as this was a public act of rest, it declared a different worldview, an alternative allegiance. Resting with Yahweh. This is not to suggest that the Sabbath was a periodic strike day, but one has to wonder how such a coordinated work stoppage would play in Babylonian society. The Israelites were certainly marching to a different cultural drummer. It recalls a more current nonviolent tactic of the Intifada, where for a period of time the Palestinians set their watches forward an hour. At one point, Israeli soldiers of the IDF were stopping people and smashing their watches if they showed the "wrong" time. What time you kept would signal an allegiance of resistance.

It is fundamental to this story that *creation is not by the sword, but by the Word.* In this sense, the biblical roots of nonviolent transformation go back to day one, page one. True creation, say the exiles and their God, is not by violence, but by love and delight. By Word. This is also, notice, the prophetic tradition of social transformation in Israel. The prophets act as though the truth (or better, the Word of God) uttered in the streets has history-making power. They speak, trusting quite simply that a change is thereby set in motion.

---

13. When read from the standpoint of the second temple, this text may be understood to have legitimating functions in that context. See Coote and Ord, *In the Beginning*.
14. Coote and Ord identify the seven-day sabbath with the Priestly source, but locate its origin in the post-exilic Temple cult. Coote and Ord, *In the Beginning*, 78, 84. In Babylon, which employed a lunar calendar, the 7th, 14th, 21st, and 28th days were regarded as "unlucky" (see Roland se Vaux, *Ancient Israel* [New York: McGraw-Hill, 1961], 187). Though on a lunar cycle of twenty-nine or thirty days, this counting would begin anew each month, it is striking to think of unlucky or "evil" days in the culture being marked as sacred days of rest by a counter-community of faith.

Above all, *the gods are creatures.* This is the sly sleeper of the story, and seminal for a theology of the principalities, all of which "imagine themselves" to be gods. The gods of empire are all included. Here dualistic (Persian) gods of light and dark are discovered to be no gods at all. They are uttered and named by the Word. The great sea monsters (like Tiamat and her progeny) are reduced to being simply ennumerated in a list of sea-animals, not evil but good. Fertility, rather than vested in Baal and his cults, inheres in creation itself. Egyptian sun gods and moon gods with their "rule," along with the astral deities—all are likewise creatures.

In the Hebrew Bible, "host of heaven" most often refers to the stars, the sun, the moon, but it may also, by a *studied ambiguity* (such a useful literary device), portray the court of Yahweh, the heavenly council. The two are rendered in parallel by God's creation song, the answer to Job:

> Where were you when I laid the foundation of the earth?
> . . . On what were its bases sunk,
> or who laid its cornerstone,
> when the morning stars sang together,
> and all the gods[15] shouted for joy? (Job 38:4, 6–7)

Not to be missed here is the element of wry political humor, seeing them grouped in obeisance round about the throne as advisors, messengers, choir members, subordinate go-fers and lackeys. Sing, ye gods, ye angels of the nations.

The same debunking element of withering Jewish humor is operative here in Genesis. The *Enuma* is a "theogony"—it details the origin of the gods. It includes a standard refrain, "These are the generations of the gods. . . ." The liturgists of Israel say, "You want a theogony? I'll give you a theogony!" And so the homespun creation liturgy concludes with a punchline. "These are the generations of the heavens and the earth when they were created" (Gen 2:4). It's been called in this regard a "theogonic satire."[16]

All told, the narrative functions to withdraw the mythic projection that in Israel is called idolatry. As God warns elsewhere: "Beware lest you lift up your eyes to heaven, when you see the sun and the moon and the stars, the whole host of heaven, you are drawn away to worship

---

15. Again, *bene elohim*—often translated "sons of God."
16. James Sanders, "God Is God," *Foundations* 6 (October 1963): 349f.

and serve them, which Yahweh your God has allotted to all the nations under the whole heaven" (Deut 4:19). This remains a perennial problem, against which the creation account inveighs.

More: *Creation is good.* In fact very good. The Hebrew word *tov* connotes such intense delight, that it has been suggested a better translation might be "fantastic!" Richard Lowery calls it "God's cosmic WOW."[17] This seems perhaps a small point, but it is every bit as momentous for how one views the world as the Babylonian conviction that evil precedes creation. This story flatly counters and reverses that view. Sin is here subsequent (see Genesis 2 and thereafter). Evil is derivative and secondary. It has no claim to metaphysical preeminence. Practically on this point alone, the Creation spirituality folks stake a worldview they claim is decisive for planetary survival.

Human beings, the liturgy asserts, are created in the image of God. Here is an idea that's incredibly subversive and may be the most politically loaded claim of all. Who in Babylon, not to mention virtually the whole of the ancient civilized world, was the image of god? The King, of course, who stands in for Marduk, and whose authority is annually legitimated. Who is it, however, in the liturgy of Israel? Humanity as a whole. Women and men. Human beings in community. This is a subversion and affront to every imperial authority. It's practically anarchism. In this counter-story, human beings are not fashioned from the blood of a murdered god, created as slaves of the state. They are made for freedom and responsibility.[18]

Especially since the Marduk story is so permeated with patriarchy, showcasing the masculine overcoming the feminine, *it is a momentous theological counter-assertion to cast humanity in the image of God as both male and female.* One could hardly suggest that patriarchy is not inscribed into texts upon text of the biblical witness. However, at the outset, in knowing conflict with the Babylonian worldview, a certain equality is declared.

Human beings are made for filling and pre-serving creation. The charge to humanity in Genesis 1 is, "Be fruitful and multiply; fill the earth and subdue it; have dominion over the fish of the sea and over the birds of the air and over every living thing that moves upon the earth" (1:28). This, of course, is the very text seized upon by the mythmakers of

---

17. Richard Lowery in *Sabbath and Jubilee* as cited in Ched Myers, "To Serve and Preserve," *Sojourners,* March 2004, 31. The suggested translation of *tov* is from Myers.
18. Walter Wink confessed that it never occurred to him to set the Babylonian creation myth side by side with the Genesis 1 account. In *The Human Being* (Minneapolis: Fortress Press, 2002), he quotes an earlier version of this very pargraph (p. 28).

modernity to justify the subjugation of nature, so we readily hear in it the very theology of domination. Yet to the contrary, to fill and to multiply is an aspect of human vocation shared with all creatures of earth and air and sea. As Ched Myers writes:

> But the exact invitation has been made to the other creatures as well (Genesis 8:22), a sharp reminder that *homo sapiens* is not the sole tenant on the Earth. This refrain emphasizes that the creation in not static but dynamic, ever regenerating, spreading fecundity. Even after the Fall, life may continue through this sustaining reproductive grace: The invitation is reiterated in the Noahic covenant, again to both animals (Genesis 8:17) and humans (9:1, 7). Faithful caretaking must value these life forces *above all else*... [In] Genesis 1:28, human rule over the rest of creation does not connote this kind of subjection. It doesn't even include *eating* the fauna (which isn't allowed until the Noahic "concession" of 9:2-5). Indeed, the very next verse reminds us that humans must share with "every other thing that has the breath of life" the earth's flora.[19]

There is in the charge an undeniable element of authority implied, suggesting both freedom and responsibility. That may be considered over against the enslavement implied in the Babylonian theological construction. Moreover, as we shall see, Stringfellow fastens on this suggestion of human dominion, and so to it we shall return.

A Creation Hymn: Shaking the Prison Walls

> [Christ] is the image of the invisible God, the firstborn of all creation; for in [Christ] all things in heaven and on earth were created, things visible and invisible, whether thrones or dominions or rulers or powers—all things have been created through [Christ] and for [Christ]. [Christ] is before all things, and in [Christ] all things hold together. [Christ] is the head of the body, the church; the beginning, the firstborn from the dead, so that [Christ] might come to have first place in everything. For in [Christ] all the fullness of God was pleased to dwell, and through [Christ] God was pleased to reconcile to himself all things, whether on earth or in heaven, by making peace through the blood of the cross. (Col 1:15-20)

This is an early Christian hymn, which we receive as set within a prison letter. The voice of Paul, as a prisoner of imperial Rome, cries out at the letter's conclusion: "Remember my chains!"[20] In such a context

---

19. Myers, "To Serve and Preserve," 32-33.
20. For the importance of this plea in interpreting the letter see Rick Cassidy, *Paul in Chains: Roman Imprisonment and the Letters of Paul* (New York: Crossroad, 2001), 85-94.

the hymn's joy is by no means mitigated, but an edge is put upon it. One thinks immediately of Paul and Silas singing hymns in jail as narrated in the Acts whereupon the foundations of another Roman jail are shaken, the prisoners set free, dramatic conversions effected, and the authorities confounded. We ought to take care when and where we sing such hymns—and this one is indeed a foundation-shaking hymn, which rightly sung and rightly heard has the capacity to free us from our captivity. It too is subversive liturgy.

All the commentators agree that this is an early Christian hymn and line it out poetically. What they can't agree upon is its precise structure, whether it had a pre-Christian source from which it was lifted and adapted, what that source might have been, whether there are additions and insertions made to the hymn, and whether those were added prior or by the author of Colossians (who might or might not be Paul). All those queries, though not a matter of indifference, we more or less set aside here. In the main, we shall read it in the light of the Genesis 1 creation liturgy, which it clearly echoes and reflects, reading it specifically for what it says about the principalities and powers.

This Christological hymn makes an explicit and fundamental claim that the principalities and *powers are creatures.* Perhaps this echoes forthwith. The very thing that Genesis 1 says about the gods of the nations, this hymn says of the powers. Insofar as they imagine themselves God, the hymn is a humiliating corrective. This is not to suggest we are reading any sort of satire, but it certainly makes an inherent rebuke to idolatry. Here as well is a counter-creation liturgy in the context of imperial pretension. The hymn likewise follows, if you will, the method of Genesis in withdrawing the mythic projection the powers enjoy. To be concrete within the Colossians letter, these tend to reference the law, philosophical systems (elemental spirits), the empire itself.

Sadly, patriarchy has become embedded uncritically in the epistle, especially by the household codes of chapter 3, but also in the hymn itself—though I have minimized its presence above by replacing the obsessively redundant male pronouns with their antecedent, Christ. This is actually more in keeping with the biblical sources for the construction of the hymn, which comes from partly from the Book of Wisdom, where Sophia is the preexistent one holding all things together.[21] So ironically the hymn might originally be sung to a subject of "she."

---

21. See the numerous parallels: Wisdom 1:7, 14; 5:23; 6:21–22; 7:8, 24, 26, 29; 8:1; 9:12.

Nevertheless, we take note of the possessive claims of the principalities upon scripture and grant a wide birth for hermeneutics of suspicion.

In *Naming the Powers*,[22] Walter Wink makes several points about this text on which we want to build, even using them as a framework for developing further the theologies of Stringfellow and himself. He observes the hymn's implication that *the principalities are both visible and invisible, heavenly and earthly; they are material and spiritual.* This, in fact, is one of the key insights of that work. His admission has been noted to beginning the overall study with the naïve preconception that the powers could be facilely "demythologized," and readily reduced to modern categories. In the end, he has come to argue that they are *simultaneously,*

> ... the inner and outer aspects of any given manifestation of power. As the inner aspect, they are the spirituality of institutions, the "within" of corporate structures and system. As the outer aspect they are political systems, appointed officials, the "chair" of an organization, laws—in short, all the tangible manifestations that power takes. Every Power tends to have a visible, an outer form—be it a church, a nation, or an economy—and an invisible pole, an inner spirit or driving force that animates, legitimates, and regulates its physical manifestation in the world. Neither pole is the cause of the other. Both come into existence together and cease to exist together. When a particular power becomes demonic, placing itself above God's purposes for the good of the whole, then that Power becomes demonic. The church's task is to unmask this idolatry and recall the Powers to their created purposes in the world—"so that the Sovereignties and Powers should learn only now, through the Church, how comprehensive God's wisdom really is" (Eph 3:10, JB).[23]

A Theological Tool for Social Analysis

In the hymn there appears a series of these: thrones, dominions, rulers, and authorities. This is hardly intended to exhaust the powers. It is, however, a suggestive way of invoking them all. One of the general observations that Wink stumbled upon in his early survey of the New Testament terrain was that terms for power tend to be paired (as in principalities and powers, or scribes and Pharisees) or rendered into series or strings, "as if power were so diffuse and impalpable a phenomenon that words must be heaped up in clusters in order to catch a sense of it's complexity."[24]

---

22. Walter Wink, *Naming the Powers* (Philadelphia: Fortress Press, 1984), 64–67.
23. Wink, *Naming*, 5.

Stringfellow also has picked up on this New Testament style, though rather than articulate it expressly, he has mimicked the form in an exaggerated fashion. Notice his stress on "all."

> The very array of names and titles in biblical usage for the principalities and powers is some indication of the scope and significance of the subject for human beings. And if some of these seem quaint, transposed into contemporary language they lose quaintness and the principalities become recognizable and all too familiar: they include all institutions, all ideologies, all images, all movements, all causes, all corporations, all bureaucracies, all traditions, all methods and routines, all conglomerates, all races, all nations, all idols. Thus, the Pentagon or the Ford Motor Company or Harvard University or the Hudson Institute or Consolidated Edison or the Diners Club or the Olympics or the Methodist Church or the Teamsters Union are all principalities. So are capitalism, Maoism, humanism, Mormonism, astrology, the Puritan work ethic, science and scientism, white supremacy, patriotism plus many, many more—sports, sex, any profession or discipline, technology, money, the family—beyond any prospect of full enumeration. The principalities and powers *are* legion.[25]

Talk about heaping up terms. The structure of Stringfellow's list holds some interest for the development of his thought. The first three he names, "institutions, images, and ideologies," reflect his earliest understanding of their primary categories as developed in *Free in Obedience*, but go on to include additional categories such as movements, traditions, and methods. The next sentence series tends to exemplify institutions and corporations. The one thereafter ideologies. And the last series comes round to echoing the answer of Karl Barth to Stringfellow's question in Chicago in 1962.[26]

Without straying from the assertion that the Colossians list is meant to evoke the totality of the powers, it is also interesting to look closely at this list as well. Wink provides detailed and nuanced definitions of each term[27] to which we may add some concrete examples.

Throne (Greek *thronos*) is the seat or symbol of institutional power. This is a term that carries over into our own usage, such that the head

---

24. Ibid., 8.
25. William Stringfellow, *An Ethic for Christians and Other Aliens in a Strange Land* (Waco, TX: Word, 1973), 78; see also Bill Wylie-Kellermann, ed., *A Keeper of the Word* (Grand Rapids, MI: Eerdmans, 1994), 205. Stringfellow employs "legion" in its common biblical usage as "many," oddly, given his political understanding of empire, without observing that in the context of Mark 8, this is a Roman imperial military term.
26. Wylie-Kellermann, *Keeper*, 190.
27. Wink, *Naming*, 65–66.

of board has a "chair," the judge a "bench," and the bishop a "cathedra." If we were to apply this term, say, to the presidency of the United States, the analogy would be fairly simple: the throne would be the White House, or better, the Oval Office. Perhaps Air Force One is a portable throne. With the current President we need to ask if Trump Tower is not yet another seat, though extra-governmental and more secret.

Dominion (Greek *kyriotēs*) is the realm, territory, or sphere of influence. With respect to the presidency this might seem to be fairly straightforward. One thinks most readily of the territorial boundaries of the United States, and the new President in his campaign made much of this, speaking repeatedly of building a border "wall" and expelling people from the country. However, as Commander-in-Chief the President projects American power around the world pretty much at will. Not only has Latin America been for more than a century our "backyard," but the dominion of the presidency has taken on a global scope. Merely consider all the forward American bases in other client states, or the penetration of sovereign states by surveillance and killer drones. From a constitutional perspective, the dominion of the Presidency is limited and circumscribed by the legislative and judicial branches, though it still includes not only armed forces, but the huge bureaucratic territory of agencies like Homeland Security or Housing and Urban Development, the Education and the EPA. Even there expansions are rife. Think of extra-constitutional authorities like the CIA or the National Security Administration, whose budgets escape democratic oversight. Think further of the contractual privatization of bureaucracies, even military services. More. To think in yet another dimension, ask how far into the lives of citizens does the presidency penetrate? Does it get even into our dreams and our psyches? Dominion may be understood to have many dimensions.

Ruler (Greek *archē*) is the "prince," not as person, but as agent-in-role, as ruler-in-office. Hence the ruler in the White House as I write would not be Donald Trump, but President Trump.[28] It is the fusion of person and power of position. A big question hovering here is whether the person takes possession of the presidency or whether the presidency takes possession of the person. One recalls in this regard someone like Jimmy Carter, who campaigned on a platform of nuclear reduction and disarmament, but seemed utterly incapable, practically

---

28. See Chapter 28 for further reflection on this matter and moment.

powerless, to pull it off. It was Carter who signed Presidential Directive 59, authorizing a formal policy of first strike, and who brought in the first-strike technology: the neutron bomb, the cruise missile, and the deadly Trident submarine. It is almost as though to be President is to stand at the vortex of such forces that one is a pathetic victim. How this will play out in the present administration remains to be seen. In many instances, it may even become a matter of pastoral concern. Hear Stringfellow in this regard:

> The American problem is not so simple that it can be attributed to a few—or even many—evil men in high places, any more that it can be blamed on long-haired youth or on a handful of black revolutionaries. Besides, our men in high places are not exceptionally immoral; they are, on the contrary, quite ordinarily moral. In truth, the conspicuous moral fact about our generals, our industrialists, our scientists, our commercial and political leaders is that they are the most obvious and pathetic prisoners in American society. There is unleashed among the principalities in this society a ruthless, self-proliferating, all-consuming institutional process which assaults, dispirits, defeats, and destroys human life even among, and *primarily* among, those persons in positions of institutional leadership. They are left with titles but without effectual authority; with the trappings of power, but without control over the institutions they head; in nominal command, but bereft of dominion. These same principalities, as has been mentioned, threaten and defy and enslave human beings of other status in diverse ways, but the most poignant victim of the demonic in America today is the so-called leader.[29]

Authorities (Greek *exousiai*) are the sanctions and legitimations by which power is maintained, in particular its rituals, symbols, and images.

To make presidential examples of each of these three, consider first the heavily ritualized legitimations that do attend the office. The campaign and election must be considered as rituals of legitimation. Some might even regard the campaign process as a variety of spiritual formation for the presidency—little wonder one so brutally softened up might be ripe for moral victimization by the office. Ritually, the inauguration is a key legitimation, though so are press conferences, Rose Garden bill signings, and photo ops. The playing of "Hail to the Chief" is certainly a ritual and one than needs to be enacted—whenever it is used, it must be played by live musicians.

---

29. Stringfellow, *An Ethic*, 89.

We might recall a presidency that virtually lacked this form of legitimization at the outset. Perhaps half the nation regarded him as "selected, not elected," and George W. Bush limped through the first year in office as a premature lame duck. Hobbled and hampered. It was not until September 11, or better, until he decisively exercised the powers of commander-in-chief, that he was legitimated in his presidency. This, actually, marked a very dangerous situation—to have a leader legitimated by war-making. Not only because that's pretty much the definition of fascism, but because war becomes urgently necessary for a yet another "reason": it sanctions and legitimates ongoing political authority. War-making itself becomes a ritual of legitimation.

The Obama administration was beset with false accusations seeking to question its legitimacy, to the extent that the president had to produce his birth certificate to public view.

As to symbols, the most obvious is the presidential seal set affixed to his podium, the bully pulpit, and imprinted on letterhead. But there is a sense in which the constitution itself is a symbol of legitimation. It stands for the history and tradition and legal apparatus by which power is maintained.

With respect to images, one readily thinks of the Roman emperors placing their images in the public square of cities within the empire, or setting their image before the Christians and requiring them to burn incense as a measure of allegiance. The equivalent with the presidency is not so much the official photo in government offices or even the pictures of the "dead presidents" on coins and bills (though monetary images do come up in the gospels—Matt 22:20; Mark 12:16; Luke 20:24). The image most pertinent is the one put in living rooms, kitchens, family rooms, and bedrooms of virtually every good American family—by way of television, or virtually anywhere and everywhere by tablet or smartphone. In terms of legitimacy, it is not even so much the sound bite, the content, the line of the day, but the redundancy of the image itself that sanctions the ruler-in-office.

At this writing, the impending inauguration of Donald Trump raises an entirely different question of reverse legitimation, whether his election will sanction and authorize, virtually unleash, a national and street-level *zeitgeist* openly authorizing white supremacy, harassment, misogyny, homophobia, Islamophobia, xenophobia, and the like. And not just attitudes but a multitude of overt acts. Some of what carried him into office is rendered in turn normative and acceptable. The underside of that is the atmosphere of terror and dread in certain communities. Evidence in the weeks immediately following suggests so.[30]

All of this is hardly to suggest that this early Christian hymn is doing sociological analysis, but it is striking that these political terms heaped up practically comprise an analytical tool that could be employed to survey most any institution, government body, or corporation.[31]

A Theological Movement: Vocation Lost (and Found?)

If read closely, a theological movement may be detected in the hymn. In this creation vignette, the powers are understood to be "good," fashioned by Christ and for Christ. However, by the concluding line, they are understood as being in need of reconciliation to God by the blood of the cross. This punchline is the sly sleeper of the hymn. It changes everything. The one who holds things all together is the crucified. Here the scholars squabble. Was this the method by which a gnostic hymn was Christianized? Was it the author of Colossians (perhaps even Paul himself) who cunningly modified the hymn? Whichever it may be, note that to Christianize it means that a hymn that otherwise might ritually sanction the powers and encourage unquestioned obedience to the authorities becomes one in which the powers are understood to be separated from and at odds with the creator. They are regarded as needing to be reconciled by the cross. In the final version of this early Christian creation hymn, the movement is from Creation to the blood of the cross.

What is implied, unspoken? The theological move is from the powers being good to the powers being redeemed. What is assumed by the Christians is that the powers are fallen. They are alienated from God in Christ. They are separated even from what they were created to be. Wink identifies this sequence (actually he argues that all of these are happening simultaneously) with a basic theological framework: The Powers are good. The Powers are fallen. The Powers must be redeemed.[32]

It is here that another implication, perhaps only hinted by the hymn, comes into play: that of vocation. As creatures, the powers each have a

---

30. https://www.forbes.com/sites/niallmccarthy/2016/11/30/report-trums-election-led-to-a-surge-in-hate-crime-infographic/#61dd5c972cf5 (accessed March 3, 2017).
31. "That all these terms were in fact used of social structures in the New Testament is beyond question, as our earlier survey shows. Whether the author intended such an analysis of social structures here is an open question." Wink, *Naming*, 66.
32. Wink, *Engaging*, 65f.

vocation, a calling, an authentic identity—who they are uttered in the Word of God to be. Stringfellow says that the vocation of the powers is to praise God and serve human life, though each has a more specific vocation. So, of any given principality one might ask after its identity and calling: How exactly is it to praise God by serving human life?

Strikingly for our comparison here, Stringfellow himself rooted the vocational question less in Colossians than in the first chapter of Genesis. As creatures the principalities are made for worship and subject to the authority of human life.

> In the biblical understanding of creation, the principalities or angelic powers, together with all other forms of life, are given by God into human dominion and are means through which human beings rejoice in the gift of life by acknowledging and honoring God, who gives life to all and to the whole of creation. The dominion of humanity over the rest of creation, including the angelic powers, means the engagement of human beings in the worship of God as the true, realized, and fulfilled human life and, at the same time and as part of the same event, the commitment by them of all things within their dominion to the very same worship of God, to the very same actualization of true life for all things. All persons, all angels, and all things in creation have origination, integrity, and wholeness of life in the worship of God.[33]

Notice that he vests the accountability of the powers to human life in the dominion passage of the creation story. While "dominion" has been made problematic in the context of its appropriation by Western domination theology, and especially in relation to environmental assault, here in the context of fallen powers, its use makes for some very interesting assertions. For Stringfellow, the fall signifies both the loss of authentic vocation for the powers and the loss of human authority over them. In fact, he witnesses an "inversion of dominion," such that *those powers called to praise God and serve human life, now imagine that they are God and enslave human life.*

> Pretending autonomy from God, these creatures are autonomous from human control. In reality they dominate human beings. Relying upon the biblical description, I have come to think of the relationship of the principalities and persons as if the Fall means that there has been not only a loss of dominion by human beings over the rest of Creation but, more precisely than that, an inversion or a reversal of dominion. So, now, those very realities of Creation—traditions, institutions, nations—over which

---

33. Stringfellow, *Free in Obedience*, 1964, 52–53.

humans are said in the Genesis creation story to receive dominion, and the very creatures that are called thus into the service and enhancement of human life in society, exercise, in the era of the Fall, dominion over human beings (Gen 1:26). The work of the demonic powers in the Fall is the undoing of Creation (Gen 6:11–13). The gravest effort of the principalities is the capture of humans in their service, which is to say, in idolatry of death, whatever external appearance or particular form that may assume.[34]

Jesus testifies to this inversion when he sets it right, "The sabbath was made for humanity, not humanity for the Sabbath" (Mark 2:27). I've heard it said of Florence Nightingale that she once quipped, "I may not know what a hospital is for, but I'm pretty sure it's not the spread of disease." Much as Jesus once quipped, "I may not know what a Temple is for but I'm pretty sure it's not to be a den of thieves." We may rejoin with any number of present-day powers: "I may not know what the media is for, but I'm pretty sure it isn't to repeat high-frequency lies."

To put the vocational question in any given situation becomes a radical act. Ask, for example, What's the vocation of a bank? Though the first uncritical reply might be, "to make money," things can be pressed a little further. For what might a bank be held accountable to human life? How might a bank praise God, by serving human life? By supporting neighborhood investment? Redistributing the resources of a neighborhood to others by credit? The question summons to thought a long-forgotten purpose.

Once, at a street rally of the Detroit newspaper strike in the nineties, I asked the picketers and protesters if they had ever read the Detroit News Building, and pointed to the balustrade ledge above us. High above the stage and the street, nearly out of sight and entirely out of mind, were to be seen etched in stone a series of epithets, among them: Friend of Every Righteous Cause, Reflector of Every Human Interest, Mirror of the Public Mind, Dispeller of Ignorance and Prejudice, Bond of Civic Unity, Protector of Civic Rights, Troubler of Public Conscience, Scourge of Evil Doers, Exposer of Secret Iniquities, Unrelenting Foe of Privilege and Corruption, A Light Shining in All Dark Places. At each recitation of a name, I would get a great laugh, as the strikers knew the bitter truth in each instance.

Were these posted intentions a laughable pretense from the begin-

---

34. Stringfellow, *An Ethic*, 82.

ning, a mere "façade" covering the machinery of power and profit, or did they publicly remember the true vocation, the calling, of a community newspaper? I want to believe it is the latter. These phrases written in stone, romantic and pretentious though they be, actually suggest the very bases on which Detroit Newspapers Incorporated is accountable to human life and so also stands before the judgment of God. For some, the former may be easier to swallow theologically than the latter. Yet, just as the prophets brought the nations before the bar of God's judgment—the nations and not just the kings or the individuals comprising them—so all the powers may be thought likewise subject to the judgment of God.

How comes the vocation of the powers to be lost, forgotten, distorted, inverted? Human idolatry is perhaps primary. Recall Wink: "When a particular power becomes demonic, placing itself above God's purposes for the good of the whole, then that Power becomes demonic [and] the church's task is to unmask this idolatry and recall the Powers to their created purposes in the world." Stringfellow would state the idolatry question in yet another way. He suggests that the powers forget their calling when they substitute for it a preoccupation with their own survival. Ironically, the flipside of imagining that you are gods is anxiety about your mortality. For Stringfellow this means that all the powers operate with a logic of survival. Theologically, this fear of death names their bondage to death, names their homage to death, such that Death is ordained the Power behind the powers.

The Image of God, the New Humanity, and the Lordship of Christ

Where, one may ask, at least in the hymn, does the accountability to human life appear? To that let another question be joined: Do you read the image of God in the hymn as a human title or a divine one? (Here another echo of the Genesis account, no?) Even should you say both, there is implied in the Lordship of Christ as emblem of the new humanity, a renewal of human dominion over the powers. That is in part what the Lordship of Christ means—much like the title, "son of man" (the human one), with which it is directly associated.[35] Both are effectively human titles. Just a note for those who follow "dominion theology" and its theocratic approach to authority—all too popular in certain circles—this is not to suggest that the Lordship of Christ signals the renewal of Christian authority over the powers, but human authority.

---

35. See Wink's discussion of Daniel 7 in *The Human Being*, 51–54.

The difference may seem slight, but in practice it is momentous. And it is raised with emphasis here.

To Disarm and Reconcile: The Power of the Cross

Return to the punchline and the blood of the cross. We've no end, within scripture and without, of theological explanations as to how God reconciles individual persons through the blood of the cross, but what and how would it mean to reconcile the powers? Perhaps the first and most important thing to note is that it was the rulers and authorities, the principalities and powers who killed Jesus (1 Cor 2:7–8). Not only did the Constantinian reading of scripture write the powers off the map into outer space, it wrote them largely out of the creeds and out of responsibility for Jesus's death. As players in the biblical drama, they are rendered invisible. The basic formula says that Jesus died, not that he was killed. The former may rightly emphasize both his agency of freedom and his human mortality, but it simultaneously lets the powers off the hook. They are veiled in a passive voice.

It is edifying in this regard to read a tad further in Colossians. Here the personal reconciliation is inseparable from the political as it were: "God made you alive together with [Christ], forgiving us all our trespasses, erasing the record that stood against us with its legal demands. He set this aside, nailing it to the cross. He disarmed the rulers and authorities [principalities and powers] and made a public example of them, triumphing over them in it" (Col 2:13–15). What clues here? One concerns the meaning of triumph.

It names perhaps the single most edifying point to be made, that Jesus was killed in a Roman liturgy of political execution. Ched Myers is one who has recognized this most clearly in his commentary on the Gospel of Mark:

> When the Roman security forces have completed the deeds of the torture-room, Jesus is marched out of the city to the place of crucifixion (15:20). The drama of the via dolorosa, like so many other aspects of the gospel narrative, has become in churchly tradition a pious exercise in personal anguish, replete with self-flagellation. Gone is its true signification: the political theater of imperial triumph.[36]

---

36. Myers, *Binding the Strong Man*, 384.

He points to Rome's well-documented practice of parading its defeated military foes through the streets. We know this best from Josephus, who describes the imperial liturgy, the great Roman victory parade concluding with the ceremonial execution of Simon bar Giora, self-proclaimed king of the Zealot Temple occupation. After the siege and destruction of Jerusalem by Roman legions, Simon was transported to the capital for a formal political humiliation.

> The triumphal procession concluded at the temple of Jupiter Capitolinus, where . . . Simon bar Giora, who had just taken part in the procession among the prisoners, and, with a noose put over him, was dragged by force to the proper spot at the forum, all the while being tortured by those who led him. It was at that spot where Roman law required that those sentenced to death for villainy be slain. When his death was announced, it was greeted with universal acclamation, and the sacrifices were begun. (*Wars*, VII, v, 6)[37]

In Rome the standard procession of a full triumph rolled by with a particular order, granting ceremonial places to various parties: captured arms and spoils of war, including in this case Temple vessels and a portable tableau depicting the siege of Jerusalem, gifts presented by conquered (so-called liberated) peoples, oxen to be sacrificed to Jupiter (as in Josephus's reference), captive prisoners in chains—including the conquered king, magistrates, and senators, of course; the *triumphator* himself in a chariot; and finally the soldiers wearing laurel-wreaths on their heads and singing.[38]

Out in the occupied provinces, with lesser, upstart kings, a return to Rome and full triumph could be dispensed with. However, a less grand onsite version served to make the same point for the locals. The public march in which the "king" was made to carry the implement of his own torture and death to the site of execution served precisely the same ceremonial function, and sufficed to convey the same message of imperial omnipotence. The cross, of course, was the standard Roman instrument of this public "ritual." And Golgotha was the local ceremonial site.

This understanding is reflected in the famous passage from Colossians: "He has cancelled the bond which was outstanding against us

---

37. Ibid., 384–85. In *Wars*, VII, v, 4–7, Josephus describes to considerable effect the magnificence of this procession in full: its pomp and prayers, images of the gods and an excessive show of wealth, detailed battle portraits of the war, its trophies (especially those taken from the Temple), and the feasting that followed.
38. As cited by Wink, *Naming*, 56n46.

with its legal demands; he has set it aside nailing it to the cross. There he disarmed the powers and authorities and made a public spectacle of them, leading them as captives in his triumphal procession" (2:14–15). In a wonderful twist of gospel irony, the liturgical procession is alluded to, but its meaning is exactly opposite of what the powers intend. In the crucifixion, it is the authorities that are paraded, humiliated, exposed, and even rendered powerless.[39] This of course, is the hidden political meaning of the Way of the Cross which, over against interpretation, always needs be rediscovered. Not pious and private anguish, but public exposure and, in truth, victory.

The claim is bold to say the least. For some it is utter foolishness. Perhaps it can be understood that pushed to the limit, the powers have been driven into the public arena and their reliance on death as sanction, as their sole moral authority, is exposed. Remember, there is only one thing the powers can do to you, and that is to kill you. The violence of Death and its substitutes is all they have in their arsenal. And that is hung out there for the whole world to see.

Martin King wrote in a similar vein on Easter morning from the Birmingham jail in response to the public assault of the local moderate pastors who accused him of bringing violence to Birmingham. But the violence was already there day in and day out. He wrote them to this effect in his public reply:

> Actually, we who engage in nonviolent direct action are not the creators of tension. We merely bring to the surface the hidden tension that is already alive. We bring it out in the open, where it can be seen and dealt with. Like a boil that can never be cured so long as it is covered up but must be opened with all its ugliness to the natural medicines of air and light, injustice must be exposed, with all the tension its exposure creates, to the light of human conscience and the air of national opinion, before it can be cured.[40]

Exposure, the subtle debaters of this present age might argue in turn, is one thing. Disarming and dethroning is quite another. Where do you see this in present history? We reply, trembling to be tested: in the life and freedom of the community that lives by the cross. Jesus exhibits an astonishing freedom in the cross. He is free from the grip of the powers, free both from their seductions (as summed up in the temptations)

---

39. I can only commend again Walter Wink's important discussion of the Colossians passage. See *Naming*, 55–60.
40. Martin Luther King Jr., "Letter from a Birmingham Jail," April 16, 1963.

and from their intimidations (as encountered in the garden just prior to his arrest, their hour and the power of darkness). He virtually seems free to die, free to stand in this moment's notice before the judgment and mercy of God. Elsewhere Paul calls this justification by faith. In Jerusalem, on trial and before the execution, it might better be called Jesus's freedom of the resurrection.

The cross for Jesus, as for his disciples, is neither desperation nor suicidal despair. He is not throwing himself, a last absurd gesture, like a wooden shoe into the cogs of history's machinery. He goes up in the conviction that God is entering, cracking, turning, and breaking open history. It is an irrepressible act of hope.

As to myths of origins and creation stories, the question is this—Who is the true creator, the one who kills or the one who dies? Ernst Käsemann reads in Colossians a baptismal liturgy.[41] In the moment when the catechumens are being transferred from the power of darkness into the realm of Christ (Col 1:13), the creation hymn is sung. Foundations shake. A new world is announced. As though when anyone is in Christ, there is a new creation. A new person. A new humanity. A new community. Indeed, a new world.

All this from beginning to end will be denounced and repudiated as naïve and foolish by think tank scholars, worldly-wise politicians, the negotiators and experts, the purveyors of hardware and software wisdom, the subtle debaters of this passing age—indeed, need it be said, the rulers and authorities. But to those who are called, who are prepared to walk its way, it is the power of God and the wisdom of God, the very means of the end which is the beginning.

---

41. Ernst Käsemann, "A Primitive Baptismal Liturgy," in *Essays on New Testament Themes*.

PART II

Particular Powers

5

Barbed Wire and Beyond: The Freedom to Unmake Nuclear Weapons (1983)

Author's Note: Nuclear weapons may be thought the preeminent principality. They are the final word in escalation dominance—and so the current emblem of the domination system, the very power of death targeting the planet as creation. My own practical understanding of the principalities and powers was worked out, book-length, precisely in their guise.[1] Given that account, they are actually under-represented in this volume, yet they are the place to begin. When I wrote the following about them in 1983,[2] I was preparing with friends for an Easter morning liturgical action at a Strategic Air Command Base in Michigan. Because in that action we would cut the barbed wire as a symbol of breaking and entering with the gospel, I focused this reflection on the barbed wire itself. It is only long since that I have come to understand that barbed wire is a principality. As a weapon itself, cutting into flesh, it figures into the ideology of property, the practicalities of Manifest Destiny in taking the West, in the walled demarcation of nations, and the power of prisons and concentration camps. It circumscribes the ecology of modernity.[3] And so it is also thereby a

---

1. Bill Wylie-Kellermann, *Seasons of Faith and Conscience: Kairos, Confession, Liturgy* (Maryknoll, NY: Orbis, 1991).
2. Bill Wylie-Kellermann, "Barbed Wire and Beyond," *Sojourners*, May 1983, 20–22.
3. See Reviel Netz, *Barbed Wire: An Ecology of Modernity* (Middletown, CT: Wesleyan University Press, 2004).

fitting place to begin. At the conclusion of the essay, I have appended a short account of the Easter-morning action, written separately.

> Warning! On May 30, two persons were observed trying to look over the wall surrounding the concentration camp in Dachau. They were of course immediately arrested. They explained that they had been curious to see what the camp looked like inside. In order to give the opportunity to satisfy their curiosity they were detained overnight. It is hoped that their curiosity has now been satisfied in spite of this unforeseen measure.
>
> We wish to still the curiosity of all those who might ignore the warning by informing them that in the future they will be given the opportunity of studying the camp from inside for longer than just one night.
>
> All inquisitive persons are hereby warned once more.
>
> In charge of the Supreme S. A. Command
> Special Commissioner Friedriche
> Published in Dachau
> June 2, 1933[4]

Who, in heaven's name, were these two people? It's tempting to wonder aloud. Were they just dear friends out for a walk and a talk, only to happen upon some new construction along their old familiar road? Were they conscious political voyeurs, looking to be titillated by the suffering of others? Or were they conscientious citizens, refusing "from the git-go" to be good Germans? Were they perpetrators or bystanders, innocent or guilty?

Such questions one might contrive to answer with a short story, imagining the dialogue between the two and their angry captors. In my version of the story, these friends are local Christians. They took note in the newspaper last month about the opening of this curious facility in the suburbs. Already the thing has begun to haunt them, intruding on their conscience, their dreams, and now their conversation. They muster each other's courage, maybe even praying first. "Let's at least go look." And the visit, as the published report attests, is a real eye-opener.

When they are sent home, chastised and duly intimidated, perhaps they pray some more. I suppose it's possible, in fact, that they went back again and suffered a solitary fate, which the papers neglect to

---

4. Barbara Distel and Ruth Jakusch, eds., *Concentration Camp Dachau 1933-1945* (Dachau: Comite International de Dachau, 1978).

report. In my fanciful version of events, they return (against all common logic) with a whole confessing congregation of sisters and brothers. I picture this crowd standing early one morning with candles along the stretch of fence, praying once more and looking deep into the barbed wire.

I knew a man once, as it happens, a Russian. His own memories were of Soviet fences and walls. He said, "If you want to deal with the nuclear arms race, the first thing you're going to have to come to grips with is barbed wire." That is a true saying. And I've often thought of it since.

Another friend of mine, Peter Weber, who years ago cut the fence at the Rocky Flats nuclear weapons plant and went in to pray, talks about barbed wire as an idol. If so, the cutting of the fence is a true act of iconoclasm.

Am I saying that barbed wire is more than barbed wire? Or fence more than fence? Well, sort of. When the powers string it up, it gets charged with authority and fear. A circle of space is laid claim to.

The power of barbed wire is not so much in the physical barrier, but in the authority it defines and projects. The wire is revered as sacrosanct. It is a petty idol set up to mark and guard the threshold of profanely "sacred" space. Rituals of security and clearance attend it. We bow to its power by turning our heads. No looking or thinking or questioning beyond this point. The barrier is really to consciousness itself.

Among the political and theological issues here is the question of sovereignty. That barbed wire, and the law that runs through it like an electrical charge, are simply the front for bigger idols behind. The claim of the nuclear-armed powers is to more than just a circle of turf or even a realm of technology; the claim is to history itself. They pretend to direct it, manipulating events with the perpetual threat of death. They fiddle with the fate of the earth. Any challenge to those big claims will sooner (most likely) or later meet up with the lesser pretensions of barbed wire.

Some years ago, a Methodist church in Detroit publicly declared its sanctuary a political refuge for resisters to draft registration. This declaration is simply an acknowledgment of what every act of Christian worship proclaims: that God is sovereign in our lives and in history. The claim of the church has been that when push comes to shove, the long arm of the law, or better, the reach of political authority, stops at the sanctuary door. A limit is affirmed.

All this comes back around to barbed wire because in recent decades, Christians have been taking their prayer and worship to the boundaries of nuclear weapons facilities. By this means, the way of the cross is lifted up as a real alternative to the way of massive violence. Our stand on the question of security is clear: We celebrate the sovereignty of God in history over against the arrogant and truly blasphemous claims of the powers. Divine sovereignty is enacted in a liturgy of trespass. No legal right is being asserted as such; a holy truth is simply demonstrated.

A very good film came out some years past, called *Day After Trinity*. It is a movie about physicist Robert Oppenheimer, the scientific city of Los Alamos, and the making of the first atomic bomb. The film tells the story of Oppenheimer, who was driven and single-minded in his preoccupation with the breakthroughs and necessities of building the bomb. The biographical account begins with his poetry and politics, passes through the scientific enthusiasm of the Los Alamos days, and ends showing him tragically broken (even his security clearance withdrawn) on the trash heap of the McCarthy attacks. It is, the filmmakers imply, a tragedy of classic proportions.

But we might be more precise. At one point, a young scientist reflects that Oppenheimer had made a "Faustian bargain" with the Pentagon's General Groves, who was able to offer him all the resources in half the world to do history-making physics on a grand scale, in simple exchange for certain successful products. Oppenheimer delivers, it seems, heart and soul. With both political fervor and scientific fascination, he is captivated and captured. His personality changes. The metaphysical poet becomes the great administrator. His ego inflates. I hope I'm neither unkind nor unfair to say, at least on the evidence of the film, that this is a classic instance of possession in a very concrete and demystified sense.

This possession, be it moral, spiritual, or political, can happen to entire cities as well. The top secrecy of Los Alamos was a great barrier to the release of any news and information about what happened there, but that same security and secrecy was an even bigger barrier to the penetration of certain concerns into the premises. The New Mexico desert and another strand of barbed wire are the perfect elements for moral isolation. Here again, I can't help picturing a handful of foolish American Christians trekking across the desert in their tennis shoes with a banner that says, "Stop!" and bearing leaflets that invite people to consider what they are doing and who will feel the fire of grand physics. Such a Christian walk and prayer, regardless of liturgy or rite, may freely be called an exorcism. The intrusion of the simplest light is nothing less than the casting back or casting out of the power of dark.

Letting in the Light

It has been noted that with an amazing and unwitting consistency, people who have entered high-security nuclear weapons facilities for prayer and disarmament actions have commonly been instructed by the fifth chapter of Ephesians. They have attended there by way of preparation and meditation. The passage itself has become a source of light and a beacon to discernment. "Take no part in the unfruitful works of darkness, but instead expose them. For it is a shame even to speak of the things that they do in secret; but when anything is exposed by light it becomes visible, for anything that becomes visible is light" (Eph 5:11–13).

Darkness: string up a circle of barbed wire and the most hideous crimes and horrifying weapons can be prepared and hidden within. Light: walk in, eyes and heart open. Look around. Pray, and maybe weep. Do the time.

Such deeds of worship and faithfulness are more often akin to holding a candle over the abyss than to lightning over the moral landscape (as we always wish). Still, if they are undertaken and offered in the gospel spirit, there is an element of exposure and true light, whether that can be readily calculated or not.

One element of exposure may come because trespass actions and their like yield some attention by the press. If the things they do in secret are mentioned in the headlines, all to the good. The papers might, thereby, fulfill some vocation to illuminate the truth, instead of aiding secrecy with silence. However, a caution is in order against measuring light by the column inch or confusing true illumination with news airtime. In the end this exposure runs quickly thin.

The public prayers of Christians are forever to God and not to the cameras. An action faithfully discerned and offered as a prayer, whether noticed by the media or not, may shed light that is unplanned, unexpected, and even unnoticed. More often than not, the light born to dark places comes back to the community of faith. It is among ourselves and the church that so much light is wanted.

Bishop Leroy Matthiesen of Texas, who in the early 1980s urged members of his diocese to leave their work at the Pantex nuclear weapons plant, testified about this kind of unexpected light that brought his own awakening to the dark truth of the arms race. He explains that he used to drive regularly by the Pantex plant near Amarillo, where the components of all U.S. nuclear weapons were assembled. The facility is a mere four miles from Saint Francis parish, where he was pastor before becoming bishop.

He confesses to never thinking seriously about what went on inside. It just blended, for him, into the landscape of business-as-usual. It was just another fence on the treeless, wind-swept pasture and crop land of his parish. Then a handful of Christians early one morning transgressed that fence to pray inside, setting off an alarm and landing in jail for a year. It was as though a light went on for Bishop Matthiesen.

No one is talking here about credit or causality or even political effectiveness; there is simply a rejoicing in the work of the Spirit in and through events.

In speaking of the faith community, there is the suspicion that trespass turns quickly back on ourselves. One very tough question to be met here is the matter of secrecy in the movement. There are certain actions worthy of consideration, prayer, and embodied deed that do require an element of discretion simply to pull off. Surprise is a needful part of the entrance and the drama. The doves may need to operate with the craftiness of serpents. But (said with some trepidation) there is also a subtle temptation to draw our own circles of darkness. By justifiable degrees it's easy to mimic the masters of security, even to parody their rituals, drawing lines through the faith community.

The remedy for this temptation is not some absolute principle, Gandhian or otherwise. It has more to do with accountability to friends and community and, needless to say, the Lord of Light. It means a readiness to take the consequences—sticking around to take the heat with the light. There is a need, finally, to stand with our lives exposed.

We are not, ourselves, let it be remembered, the light. The preface to John's Gospel identifies the light with Christ Jesus. He is the one shining in the darkness and not overcome. It is abundantly clear that the light is not at all welcome in the world. He is not recognized or received, but hated and rejected. From the standpoint of the world and its claims, the incarnation is an intrusion, a divine incursion. It is, I suppose, a kind of cosmic trespass.

I am led to think of the way the New Testament speaks of the Lord's coming as a "thief in the night." The metaphor has always been troublesome to me. It evokes a little cringe. Our Lord the cat burglar. The point, of course, is the unexpected timing of things, but I suspect a further implication. Perhaps this glorified "breaking and entering" implies the breaking of our false securities. Our lives are penetrated and vulnerable. We are broken into. Here again, we find the truth sneaking in our back door.

The implication of every trespass action is the confession of our own vulnerability. People often cite (and often unfairly) the qualms that Dorothy Day reputedly had about the draft board break-in by the Catonsville Nine in 1968. Her sense of golden-rule nonviolence caused her to picture the same moral incursion into the front parlor of the Catholic Worker. I don't have the same qualms, but do regard the practical application as a spiritual insight. The Worker, of course, endured such intrusions (they poured in the front door) as part of its daily life.

Dan Berrigan, who was part of the Catonsville action, once told of being at the Pentagon with a symbolic action. A military officer stormed angrily up to him and said, "How would you like it if we did this at your house?" The implication that the Pentagon was his home is interesting in itself, but there is something provoking in the question. Berrigan, responding instinctively, promptly offered his address and said, "Why don't you come over for dinner and we'll talk?"

The practical flip side of trespass is hospitality. It is no coincidence that so many of those who cross lines open their front doors to the homeless and the stranger. And the spiritual flip side of climbing and cutting barbed wire is our own openness and vulnerability to truth.

In a liturgy of trespass we need to leave our arrogance behind. We are not the children of light facing off with the children of darkness. The sovereignty of God is not to be proclaimed as if it were really our own, as if it were a moral front, as if it were a theological extension of our certainties and claims.

God's sovereignty dictates our humility. It is practically another name for it. Before the barbed wire we need to pause, take a deep breath, and imagine that we may truly need to be forgiven for our trespass.

And then, with that freedom, in the end before God, we go ahead and act boldly. My prayer is that we do precisely that.

(Author's note: Here follows the account of our action at the SAC base.)[5]

---

5. From the Introduction to *Seasons of Faith and Conscience*, xix–xxvii.

It was Holy Saturday 1983.

We had gathered, a group of friends, in the woods of northern Michigan. Darkness settled in about our cabin and with it the cold of night.

Less than a mile up the blacktop road was Wurtsmith Air Force Base, home of the 379th Bombardment Wing of the Strategic Air Command. Sixteen B-52s with nuclear mission targets in the Soviet Union sat on the runway. They were just in those days being further armed with cruise missiles, a nuclear weapon of pinpoint accuracy which extended the bombers' range and capacity to fight in a first-strike nuclear attack.

The arrival of the missiles and the arrival of Easter occasioned our presence there. Together they defined a moment of historic and personal import.

For months, we had been gathering periodically in retreat for Bible study, prayer, and discernment. Each of us (a Methodist pastor, several members of the Catholic Worker movement, a handful of Catholic priests with experience in third-world or inner-city ministry) had come with some urgency to this point of considering a direct action with more risk than we had undertaken before. Given the times, where were we called? Hence the topic of our prayer.

Because the cruise was raising opposition in Europe that we wished to support, and because of its role in first-strike scenarios, we had settled on Wurtsmith as the focus of our action. All of us had come long ago to conclude that such weapons were not only illegal by international standards and immoral by ethical ones, but also theologically blasphemous, the power of death writ large. In the course of discussion, one of my friends said, "You know what I'd like to do? Celebrate the Easter Vigil Liturgy walking onto the base." In that moment I recall a nearly audible thump in my own heart, an immediate confirmation of personal certainty. Quickly, almost effortlessly, after months of uncertainty, we all agreed. Not to say there wasn't more to be agonized over details and risks, but the direction of things was set.

So here it was, the eve of resurrection. And we were gathered to act.

At two a.m., we began the liturgy of the Word. Those who know the Easter Vigil will recall that there is in Christian liturgy no finer collection of readings from the Hebrew scriptures: the story of creation, the flood, Abraham's sacrifice of Isaac, the Red Sea crossing, Ezekiel's new heart and spirit, the valley of dry bones called to live, and the like. A feast of faithfulness, passage, and hope.

There in the cabin we also made intercession, marking names and peoples upon a sheet subsequently to be used as an altar cloth: children (by name), the poor, friends in prison, soup kitchen guests, the dead and disappeared of Central America, peacecampers at Greenham Common, members of parishes back home, families. A communion of the living. A solidarity of the spirit, this prayer for passage, this claim upon the future.

After singing a hymn, we exited into the night. Against our expectations, it had begun to snow, heavy and wet. Single file from the road through the woods to the extreme end of the runway, the snow fell about us like a dense silence. It felt for all the world like setting out for an action from Thomas Merton's monastic hermitage in the Kentucky hills.

At the barbed-wire fence we paused and circled as a group, here for two symbolic deeds. The first was to light the Paschal candle. Into these, our dark times, enter the light of Christ. So we prayed, flame in hand. The second, indeed one with the other, was to cut the fence. From our Bible study we were mindful how the seal on the stone of the tomb is against tampering, a legal barrier backed up, by one account, with force of armed guard. Twang! The security of death guarding death was broken in liturgy. The wall was breached.

Thereupon seven of us began our three-and-a-half-mile trek toward the high-security area, the loaded B-52s. It had been our intention to paint at the foot of the runway, in six-foot-high letters legible from a landing plane: CHRIST IS RISEN! DISARM! We toted along supplies sufficient: buckets of yellow paint, brushes, rollers, all. The wet and freezing snow, however, foreclosed that plan.

We walked on mostly in silence, lying down periodically in a fumbling comedy, to avoid the view of patrolling security cars. As the nuclear storage bunkers came into sight, we arrived at a small building, the enclosure for some sort of electronic equipment. Here on the walls we inscribed our message, paint congealing in the freezing drizzle. And here we carried the vigil liturgy another step forward: we renewed our baptismal vows.

I had not foreseen the personal power of that moment: to look down the runway toward the machines and their cargo, and there to "renounce Satan and all his works." There I promised in a way not fully understood before, to "persevere in resisting evil, and, whenever I fall into sin, repent and return to the Lord." A life may be called back to such moments, indeed may turn on them.

The sky had begun to lighten. Birds were rousing. Shivering, we conferred: enough of the dodging and weaving. Let us proceed upright with dignity, in the manner of right worship. Here an astonishing phenomenon occurred, one reportedly not uncommon in such undertakings: We passed unseen. On one side were the bunkers, encircled with barbed wire, lit like perpetual noonday, driven round about by a constant patrol of vehicles, and observed from above by watchtowers, beneath which we processed. On the other side, parked for maintenance or refueling, huge bombers stood in a line equally well lit. It was as though the waters had parted. We walked unhindered to the open entrance of the high-security area where planes on alert stood ready to fly given the command.

There, measured by a sudden flurry of activity within, we were finally noticed. Armored vehicles and pickup trucks rushed to surround us. We spread our altar cloth of intercessions on the runway. About it we scattered blood, brought in small bottles, to signify the blood of the innocents, the blood of the Lamb. Producing the elements of the Eucharist, we completed the service at gunpoint, surrounded by young airmen armed with automatic weapons.

We were a disheveled band. Bedraggled, dressed in plastic garbage bags in makeshift protection against the unexpected weather, we were soaked nonetheless and cold to the bone. In weakness and exhaustion, we fought and suffered a sense of our own foolishness.

The airmen held us in their sights, but did not approach. Extending the service, we sang plaintive gospel songs and hymns of resurrection. At long last, an officer approached us tentatively. "Are you," he asked, "base personnel?" No. "Do you work on the base?" No. Then surveying the scene yet again, "Well, would you pick up your trash and leave?"

It was clear almost immediately that our breach of security was so severe an embarrassment that should we simply depart quietly, no record or mention need come to the attention of community public or even military higher-ups within the system itself. We consulted among ourselves, and declined. The liturgy was complete in its own right, but it had momentum and direction that we did not intend to flee. Herded into a bus, strip-searched, interrogated by various agencies military and civil, we were in the end dumped unceremoniously at the front gate without charges.

Our friends awaited us with leaflets in hand. At the gate to the base and the doors to the churches in town, we distributed the news. The leaflets described the cruise and its meaning for policy. They described our pilgrimage. And they offered this simple confession of faith:

We believe that God has already intervened in this dark history of ours.

We believe there is hope. Many people have yielded to despair. They can already hear the terrible sound of the door slamming shut on human history. But we are here to say otherwise. Someone is hidden at the heart of things, breaking in to break out, on behalf of human life.

We believe that God rules our common history. Not the Soviet Union. Not the United States. Not the NATO or Warsaw Pact forces. Despite their big and competing claims.

We believe that human beings (so says Easter) are free from the power of death in all its forms and delivery systems. We are not stuck with the balance-of-terror arrangements. We're not in bondage to these weapons. We are truly and fully free to unmake them. Now. Not tomorrow or next week or next year. But this very morning.

We believe that God who raised Christ from the dead will also quicken our imaginations, and thereby our bodies and lives.

We believe this is the meaning of the resurrection. And we've come to say so.

***

Was anything actually accomplished? Many will ask. In a certain sense, that is the central question of this book. Oh, that Easter Vigil was the first in a now long series of actions and leafletings, trespasses and arrests, an ongoing campaign of presence and resistance at that Air Base. As I write this, a friend sits in jail, a six-month sentence, for a subsequent entrance to leaflet at Wurtsmith.

But the fact of the ensuing campaign does not fully answer the question. Is such action a proper and effective form in the struggle against these weapons and the system of which they are emblems?

I have told the story in detail because through it, my growing sense of what I will make bold to call "liturgical direct action" was further formed.

I tell it not because it is so remarkable and rare, but contrariwise, because such actions in this last decade have become commonplace in the faith-based nonviolent movement of resistance to the arms race, to third-world intervention, and even to ecological destruction. Examples abound. I name these almost arbitrarily.

Advent 1986. An Episcopal bishop celebrates the Eucharist outside Williams International, a Michigan cruise missile engine manufacturer that is the focus for a series of Christian civil disobedience actions. Several hundred people participate. The service is right out of the *Book of Common Prayer,* but the context magnifies certain meanings, certain hopes, certain calls to repentance. Its significance is not lost on the diocese.

Epiphany 1987. Four people enter the Willow Grove Naval Air Station, outside Philadelphia. With hammers, they damage a P-3 Orion anti-submarine nuclear-capable aircraft (with a role in Pentagon first-strike scenarios), and two military helicopters of the sort employed in Third World intervention. They celebrate the feast day of Christ's appearance by enacting Isaiah's prophecy that "swords will be beaten into plowshares." Since the first one in 1980, over 100 people have participated in such "plowshares" actions, disarmament at once prayerful, symbolic, and concrete.

Lent 1990. Beginning on Ash Wednesday and continuing through Holy Week, a series of groups gather in Las Vegas to enter the desert. They are going to the Nevada Test Site, where nuclear weapons tests (for upgraded warheads, stockpile maintenance, and new systems such as Star Wars) are carried out approximately once every three weeks. The groups pray together, consider the meaning of temptation and repentance, and conclude by entering the property, there to be arrested. The continuing witness, called the Nevada Desert Experience, was begun by a group of Franciscans a decade earlier and is now facilitated by a team of organizers year-round in Las Vegas. Just inside the main gate to the site, two permanent large barbed-wire holding pens have been constructed for the processing of "demonstrators."

Good Friday 1989, in Detroit. As every year for the last decade, and in a manner similar to many other communities, the Stations of the Cross are walked in a public and political way. Seeing the crucifixion of Christ in the suffering of victims, three hundred people process through the streets of Detroit pausing to pray at places where suffering is manifest (neighborhoods neglected and destroyed, the county jail, the site of a handgun shooting), where needs are ministered to (a soup kitchen, a free health clinic, a shelter for runaways), or decisions made (a city-county building, the federal building.) The meditation booklet from which they read specifies the connection of this suffering to the arms race. In addition, this year the day coincides with the anniversary of Oscar Romero's assassination. His memory and the suffering of the Salvadoran people are prominent in the litany.

Pentecost 1989. It is a "Faith and Resistance Retreat." These have become common, especially throughout the Midwest. As with others, this one is ecumenically called by Episcopal, Roman Catholic, and United Methodist bishops, and by the Presbyterian Church. In the course of the weekend there is Bible study given to the lections of the season, political analysis, nonviolence training, and some guided instruction in personal discernment. The Spirit is invoked and wrestled. On Pentecost proper, there is a brief service outside the gate of a missile engine factory, whereupon a smaller group of people climb over the fence to plant a tree, nurturing hope. They are arrested and sentenced to thirty days in jail.

These instances are exemplary and typical. The sites vary from the Pentagon to its missile silos, from nuclear labs and think tanks to Trident submarine bases, from corporate headquarters to SAC Headquarters, from manufacturing facilities to the arms bazaars where the weapons are marketed. The list goes on, covering the continental map.

In 1989, there were some 5,500 arrests at seventy-four different sites in the United States and Canada for actions of resistance to nuclearism.[6] In a year that properly touted the nonviolent resistance of movements in China and Central Europe, it was a record number, gone nearly unnoticed in the American media. Add arrests for resistance to homelessness, third-world intervention, and environmental degradation, and the figures would nearly double. I hazard to suggest that the vast majority of these were Christians, and that many of the actions were of the sort I have described.

This is an attempt, from within that movement, to make biblical, theological, political, and even liturgical sense of these actions. It is on the one hand addressed to that same wide community in hopes of clarifying what we have been instinctively about for the last decade or more. (The instincts have been right and good.) It reflects on our common experience and is written in hopes of nourishing our movement further.

It is also addressed to the church. I am convinced that these actions constitute a virtual "liturgical renewal movement" in the streets. They are a gift to the life and faith of the church. They illuminate the simple fact that every act of worship, every occasion where the sovereignty of the Word of God is celebrated, every instance where the realm of God is acknowledged, is always and everywhere expressly political.

It is inevitable, I suppose, that some will complain this reduces worship to an instrument or a tactic of social struggle. I can only testify to the faith of those who undertake these actions, and my own. I fear and delight to place my life in the hands of the living God. Prayers and

---

6. Jack and Felice Cohen-Joppa, "Nuclear Resistance, 1989," *The Nuclear Resister* 67 & 68, January 25, 1990, 1. During the 1980s they counted upwards of 37,000 anti-nuclear arrests.

praise arise from the deeps of my heart. I understand, however, that this is also a choice, call it Christian discipleship, if you will. That choice implies much, including many things still hidden from me, but I comprehend at least that it is a choice to stand under the sovereignty of God, in actuality to declare that sovereignty in history. It is a choice for that community, for that social world commonly called the "kingdom of God." It is a reality upon which I bet my life. Liturgically put: Yahweh reigns! and Christ is risen!

6

Discerning the Angel of Detroit: The Spirits and Powers at Work in One City (1989)

THE CITY [in Hebrew] is *'iyr* or *'iyr re'em*. Now this word has several meanings. It is not only the city, but also the Watching Angel, the Vengeance and the Terror.... We must admit that the city is not just a collection of houses with ramparts, but also a spiritual power. I am not saying it is a being. But like an angel it is a power, and what seems prodigious is that its power is on a spiritual plane.

—Jacques Ellul, *The Meaning of the City*

This essay was originally published in Sojourners *(October 1989) and also appears in my recent book,* Where the Water Goes 'Round: Beloved Detroit *(Eugene OR: Cascade, 2017). Also included there are successive reprises of the article in different historical moments: "Resurrection City: Detroit," from* Sojourners *(May 2009), and "Detroit: Is Your City Next?" The Catholic Worker, New York, Jan/Feb 2014.*

In the hot summer of 1988, something happened in Detroit. A well-financed campaign to legalize and develop casino gambling as the panacea for the city's desperate, ongoing economic crisis was rejected overwhelmingly at the polls. Oh, yes, there was a hard-working, no-budget counter-campaign by neighborhood organizations, and a stiffening in certain city pulpits. But perhaps something more was at work....

One neighborhood activist who served a token appointment on the mayor's blue-ribbon committee studying the issue offered a minority report of solid arguments and reasons, then groped further, to the brink of something more: "I don't know, I'm not sure how to say this. Detroit is a blue-collar town. Its essential character is just a bad fit for casinos, with their big money and glitz. From an image perspective, it just doesn't work." What if the city of Detroit, its spirit and identity, was an ally, most unacknowledged, in the fight against the casino invasion? That would be a political (and theological) insight worth pursuing.

Recent exegetical work and theological reflection on the principalities and powers suggests a versatile but coherent New Testament cosmology that recognizes the spiritual dimension of institutions and social structures. One that may be verified in our experience.

As the letter to the church in the city of Colossae implies, these structures are simultaneously material and spiritual, seen and unseen, interior and exterior, earthly and heavenly. They are expressed in two poles of reality as it were. "For in [Christ] all things were created, in heaven and on earth, visible and invisible, whether thrones or dominions or principalities or authorities—all things were created through Christ and for Christ" (Col 1:16).

It is an interesting exercise in first-century "social analysis" to apply these political categories to the city of Detroit:[1]

The *throne* is the seat of power; that is, the mayor's office, the council chamber, the Monoogian Mansion where the mayor lives.

Dominion is the realm or territory, even the sphere of influence. Here one thinks first of municipal boundaries, such as Eight Mile Road. But its social and political influence (much diminished these days) in the Tri-County area or the State Capitol should be counted as well. Dominion consists of those places and ways the city's authority penetrates the lives of its people.

The *principality*, the prince, is the agent-in-role, the ruler-in-office: with respect to the executive, not Coleman Alexander Young, but Mayor Young.

Authorities are the range of sanctions and legitimations by which authority is maintained. A longer list comes to mind, from the cops and

---

1. I am fleshing out once again, the clue from Walter Wink's word study, *Naming the Powers* (Philadelphia: Fortress Press, 1984), 64–67.

courts to rituals like election campaigning, press conferences, groundbreakings, and photo opportunities; or symbols like the city charter, the seal, those billboards proclaiming city sponsorship at this or that development site, and the mayor's image hung in front offices everywhere, from city clerk to neighborhood police ministration. You can think of more.

The elements are not exhaustive. Among other things they omit economic seats of power such as the auto companies or bank boardrooms or the multinational powers of illegal commerce like the drug cartels that open street-level "branch offices," each of which has its own spirituality.

Moreover, the political administration and the city as an entity name two very distinct powers. The City of Detroit (which one may look up in the telephone book) is not the same in this sense as Detroit the city. It may presume to speak for the city, but the two voices are not one and the same. It may try to claim the rich history or the spirit of the city, but these are not its own to manipulate or dispose of.

The City as a Spiritual Power

After the biblical manner of the angels of the nations (portrayed most dramatically in Daniel 10) or the angels of the churches (addressed in the opening chapters of Revelation), I have begun to speak of the "angel of Detroit." The term piques and intrigues. By it I mean what has been called the "actual inner spirituality" of the city. I mean to get at its identity and vocation, its character and personality, its potentiality as well as its fallenness before God.

One of the first to write about the city in this fashion was Jacques Ellul. Because his book *The Meaning of the City* was something of a theological companion to his devastating sociological work *The Technological Society*, but also because Ellul's theology simply goes this way, it is relentlessly pessimistic about the character of the city as a human work and its predatory fallenness as a spiritual power. (One hastens to add that in keeping with his theology, he is also radically hopeful about God's grace, judging the city but adopting it nevertheless as an instrument of grace.)

The idea that the city is at once a human work and a spiritual power is a mystery key to any understanding of the principalities (of which the city may be said, in Ellul's view, to be the very prototype). It is in this regard that Ellul mines the mythic primeval history of Genesis with astonishing results.

Who, do you happen to recall, was the first builder of a city? It was Cain. As a resident of Detroit, whose media monikers notoriously include "Murder City," I find my ears perk up.

Banished to a life of wandering and insecurity, "He built a city and called the name of the city after the name of his son Enoch" (Gen 4:17). By murder Cain has broken his relationship to humanity, to God, and even to the earth (which received Abel's blood and cried out to the Lord). He has destroyed his home and so sets out to build his own security, the city named Enoch, meaning "initiation" or "dedication." Cain's bold pretension is to construct and dedicate his own new world. Violence is the kernel of alienation by which the brave new city is seeded.

And idolatry. Here we think most readily of the tower of Babel. "And they said to one another, 'Come, let us build ourselves a city, and a tower with its top in the heavens, and let us make a name for ourselves'" (Gen 11:4). The tower, says Ellul, is not the center of the narrative; the city and the name are. The one is the means to the other. But name here means not so much reputation and notoriety as becoming independent, making their own name.

It is now widely understood that naming in Israelite culture has a supreme importance. It signifies dominion. It is a token of spiritual power. The city, then, is not a Promethean act reaching up to God. It is the act of making an identity by making a world, an urban environment, a great city. It is the act of excluding God from creation. It is incipient and express idolatry. So Ellul's radical pessimism.

Here we are at the mystery of works become fallen, of demonic powers. Here is the truth of Enoch and Babel and Babylon and Rome and New York and, alas, even Detroit. Insofar as human beings find meaning and justification and identity in the city, they make its angel a fallen angel.

William Stringfellow used to say that the vocation of the principalities was to praise God and serve human life. I like the image of Detroit singing in the courts of God, not to mention serving its own inhabitants. I know, however, that it suffers blindness, confusion, inflation, and distortion in the Fall.

As Jesus approached Jerusalem, he paused to address it. "Would that even today you knew the things that make for peace." (Jerusalem's name means "city of peace," though it suffered a deep confusion and blindness.) "But now they are hid from your eyes. For the days shall come upon you, when your enemies will cast up a bank about you and surround you, and hem you in on every side, and dash you to the ground, you and your children within you, and they will not leave one stone upon another in you; because you did not know the *kairos* of your visitation" (Luke 19:42–44).

Walter Wink points out that each of the Greek pronouns in this passage is second-person *singular*. Jesus addresses the city as an entity: *You*. Dare we say he has discerned the angel of Jerusalem and spoken to it? First he names and addresses it, claiming the dominion of the Word of God, then he enters its symbolic center with the strong action at the temple.

Several things strike as noteworthy clues within. One, if we accept the synoptic portrayal of events where this is his first physical glimpse, Jesus discerns the angel of Jerusalem (Luke 13:34–35) in Galilee! Perhaps this should not be so surprising. The city's dominion, its sphere of influence spiritual and political and economic, dominated the region. To abide with the poor of Galilee was to feel the weight of the Temple City, to know its true character, because they were beholden to its aristocracy, its obligations, its interests.

In Galilee, Jesus felt its influence, as evidenced first by his temptations and again later through its intimidations. "O Jerusalem, Jerusalem, killing the prophets and stoning those who are sent to you! How often would I have gathered your children together as a hen gathers her brood under her wings, and you would not! Behold, your house is forsaken" (Luke 13:34–35). (The pronouns are once again singular in Greek.)

There is love here. It is the agonized love that causes Jesus to break down in tears, even as he approaches the city to confront and rebuke its power. By such accounts, Jesus loves Jerusalem, longs for it to praise God and serve human life. I don't know if that is prerequisite to discernment, but he does yearn that it should recognize this *kairos*, this opportunity wherein it might repent and recover its calling before God.

All right, emboldened by the Lord, I admit it: I love Detroit. In so many ways. I love that it's a movement town. The home of the sit-down strike. Rich in a history of struggle. Martin King tried out his "I Have a Dream Speech" first in Detroit. It flew and triggered the March on Washington.

I love the black majority and revel in the scandal that it is to the American norm. The '67 rebellion burns in my high school consciousness like a revelatory moment, a personal and political turning point.

Not that de facto segregation doesn't carve up neighborhoods (and churches), but I delight in the wealth of street culture.

There's so much of the South in Detroit's black, and white, community—family and extended kinship and hospitality and old-fashioned morality. Waves were drawn north by the auto companies, much like the Europeans before who still cluster by culture in neighborhoods. I love the Latino barrio on the southwest side where we live, and the fact that Detroit has the largest Arab population this side of the Middle East.

I love the legacy of Motown soul, the gospel music, and the Detroit jazz within it. I love Tiger Stadium and confess my loyalty to certain of the city's athletic teams.

I love the river. The straits, from which the French name derives, *des troits*, is our link with the Great Lakes ecosystem. I love Belle Isle, the huge island park that is the chief recreational resource of the city's poor. There mix the smells of river water and barbecue.

I love the city. And I dread it, too. And sometimes I weep. So, is that prerequisite to discerning the angel of Detroit? Maybe.

In spring 1989, a handful of activists and church people who are engaged in ministry or social struggle in Detroit met for six weeks with this precise project in mind. They committed themselves to bringing the city as an entity into their established spiritual disciplines. To intercede for the city in prayer. To hold it in heart during scripture study. To attend to its spirit in journal keeping.

The immediate concrete project was to write something in the voice of the city or to address the Word to Detroit in this historical moment, much like the Revelation 2 letters, "To the angel of Detroit write this...." (The latter may seem at first blush pretentious, but no more bold, really, than a preacher taking the pulpit week after week to speak the Word to a congregation.)

A first question we asked one another concerned geography. Implicitly a question about social location (as Jesus with the Galilean peasantry), it is also a matter of physical place and a stimulus to imagination. John had his Patmos for divining the angel of Rome. Where would we stand to listen for the voice of the city?

By the river at Belle Isle? Above one of the freeway canyons that riddle the city? At Solidarity House, union headquarters? At an empty lot in a devastated neighborhood such as the Cass Corridor? Surrounded by the famous Diego Rivera mural depicting with care and irony industrial Detroit? In Elmwood Cemetery, which retains one of the few plots of original pre-urban terrain?

A few years earlier, by virtue of my part in a neighborhood organization, I had represented the community on a development coalition composed elsewise of institutional and corporate types. Their vision and agenda were different from ours. Still, if we met in the neighborhood, the reality of food lines and housing needs, the lives of people, were never completely out of sight and mind. But when they took to meeting in a conference room in the heady heights of the Renaissance Center, a downtown megastructure, our community faded literally into the distance and a different spirit presided.

Outside the City-County Building is a large sculpture called *The Spirit of Detroit*. Its image is reproduced on city letterheads, documents, and building project signs. More than the city seal, it is the official symbol of Detroit. For that reason the spirit has some currency in political discourse. It is claimed and abused and struggled over.

Sometimes dubbed the "green giant," the sculpture was completed in the '50s by an artist known for war memorials and works on a grand scale, such as the world's largest crucifix in the woods of northern Michigan. Inspired by 2 Corinthians 3:17, that "where the Spirit of the Lord is there is liberty," he set to work. A large figure of humanity, quite male and European, holds a golden sphere of the deity in his left hand; and in his right hand, toward which he looks, a nuclear family lifts its arms to heaven.

A museum curator whom I asked about the sculpture thought the divine sphere signified "science and the industrial genius of the auto companies." (There is an annual car show called the Spirit of Detroit.) A city government publication avers, "For many it symbolizes the city's new spirit of renaissance and rebuilding." The City Council confers Spirit of Detroit awards on prominent and worthy citizens. But a group of community organizations fighting for neighborhood priorities over downtown development in the city budget calls itself the Save Our Spirit Coalition.

The sculpture itself marks out a kind of public political space. It is the common site of demonstrations against city administration policies. I once saw a coven of witches gather there to invoke Hecate and curse the world's largest trash incinerator being built within city limits.

Most intriguing is a weekly vigil of the Anti-Handgun Association. At the foot of the sculpture they read aloud a small booklet of facts and the stories of victims. It is a kind of meditation, a liturgy really. Included is a modified verse of the black spiritual, "Were you there when each day a child was shot?" But the refrain at the close of each small section is "Spirit of Detroit, save our youth!" I believe the angel of Detroit is being named and addressed in this little event.

On the other hand, as part of a 1988 ad campaign, a gigantic fez cap (you know, with tassels like the Shriners wear) was set upon the statue's head to coincide with the appearance of billboards bearing a similar image and announcing that "Conventions are the Spirit of Detroit." Which is to say again that the spirit of the city is a matter of dispute. It is subject to diverse claims, humiliations, and manipulations.

That dispute and the "conventions-as-the-spirit" claim call to mind that Detroit, like so many other cities (or like the nation for that matter or even the global economy), is a tale of two cities. One is the living city composed of neighborhoods where poor and working people reside, almost entirely in single-family homes. (Until the late '60s, Detroit was the largest homeowning city north of the Mason-Dixon Line.) The other is the new downtown of government-subsidized megastructures: arenas, the convention center, hotels, commercial space, luxury high-rises, and office buildings, all connected by an elevated railway going in circles. Conventioneers and executives never need set foot on the streets of the city.

It is on those megastructures that the administration is banking and betting. Mortgaging the Block Grant budget, funneling grants to large-scale private development, and hustling tax abatements is the official order of the day.

A five-tower skyscraper, this weird urban stalagmite is the emblem, anchor, and centerpiece of the scheme. Spearheaded by auto money, it was built in the wake of the '67 insurrection. Intended to signify a rising from the ashes, a mock resurrection, it was called the Renaissance Center and intended to make a name for Detroit: Renaissance City.

The influence of the riots is in its bones. It has an imposing and inaccessible structure, literally defensible. Ringed with a concrete embankment, one readily imagines the location of gun turrets.

I used to think of drafting a theological leaflet summarizing Ellul's Babel reflections and distributing it within. But the only time I ever attempted to leaflet there, we were swarmed by plainclothes private security bearing walkie-talkies and summoning the city cops, who arrived in a flash. (The marketplace at the Renaissance Center as elsewhere is no longer public. It is privately owned. The streets may belong to the people, but the streets are disappearing.)

The RenCen marketplace is a failure by and large. Its three-story shopping mall, with an endless series of circular passages, is a nightmare to navigate,[2] the reputed "easiest place to get lost in Detroit." It signifies the failed attempt to move the suburbs downtown, to reverse the drain that has been going on since the first shopping mall in the world, Northland, was built in Detroit—or, more precisely, just outside of it.

Detroit photographers with an eye for the human or the ironic never tire of juxtaposing a glass-strewn lot or the burned shell of a building with the shining towers of the RenCen. The view of one city from the other. In the decaying neighborhoods, there is a phenomenon that is also a metaphor: brick thievery. An unlicensed dump truck jostles and pulls at the walls of abandoned apartment buildings until the façade collapses. The driver, a maverick subcontractor himself, pays street people day-labor wages to clean and load the bricks into his truck. Neighbors, slow on the uptake, imagine the city has sponsored the demolition. (Indeed, 150,000 Detroit homes—nearly half the total—have been burned or bulldozed in recent years. And by current count there are more than 15,000 abandoned buildings in the city.) Come evening the truck is gone and the frame shell of the building, more exposed and unsafe than ever, remains standing in a pile of rubble. The bricks go for top dollar in the suburbs where patios, I suppose, get that aged urban character.

Like the suburban boom still going on, downtown development by and large sucks the life, including city-budget priorities, out of the neighborhoods. The new office towers drain the business from the older addresses, leaving empty aging tombs on the marginal skyline.

The most notorious and blatant example of such megadevelopment was the 1980 condemnation and destruction of an entire integrated, ethnic neighborhood of 1,200 homes to build a highly automated Cadillac plant. (Two older General Motors plants, including one just blocks from my house, closed simultaneously for a substantial net loss in jobs.) In the Poletown neighborhood, arson aided and abetted the project by driving out the resisting residents and making demolition easier.

The Poletown project marked a turning point in recent Detroit history. A friend of mine calls it "the official sanction to devastation."

And it is also the emblem of Detroit's bondage to the auto industry, to principalities and powers that have fed on the city, its human pop-

---

2. See Gloria House, *Tower and Dungeon: A Study of Place and Power in American Culture* (Detroit: Casa De Unidad Press, 1991).

ulation, and now have grown larger in scale and scope than the city itself. They move capital, exporting jobs south, or south of the border. By that freedom and threat, they blackmail the city for tax abatements and land. No longer, Do you want General Motors, one of the world's largest corporations, in Detroit? But, Do you want Detroit in General Motors?[3]

Growing up here I shared the fascination with the motorcar. My wife still marvels at my unsuppressed enthusiasm for the useless skill of distinguishing a '55 Chevrolet from a '56. The automobile is deeply entangled not merely with the economy, but with the collective psyche of Motor City. Detroit is a ruined shrine to that version of American consumer idolatry.

At one session of our "Discerning the Angel" group, we tried to bring our own unconscious resources, our right brains, as it is said, into the process by forming an image of Detroit's angel in clay. I found myself shaping up a figure crying out in the grip of a gigantic hand. Was that hand the power of the multinational auto companies? I think perhaps it was. Though it might in equal portion have been the grip of the cocaine powers.

Not many years ago, one citywide drug-dealing organization, Young Boys, Inc., did $400 million of business annually. Today, crack cocaine sales top a billion dollars a year. The market includes a broad range of users, from the auto worker pulling down $35,000 and spending half of it on crack, to members of the permanent underclass being paid, in effect, in crack "rocks" for the goods they've stolen from their neighbors' homes. The average user has a $250-a-week habit.

Crack houses vary, too. On one end is the social crack house, like the "blind pig" of Prohibition days with its "tavern culture," diverse and illicit services, ersatz community, and personal interaction. On the other end is the fortified abandoned building where sales are made through a slot in the door. Some set-ups, as suggested, are fencing operations that exchange cocaine for stolen merchandise.

All of them are arsenals full of weapons. And not just handguns. (In Detroit there are already two of these for every man, woman, and child.) Semi-automatics and Uzis are rife. Enforcers patrol the streets in four-wheel-drive jeeps with tinted glass. Same vehicles and weapons and methods as the Salvadoran death squads, say.

Earlier this year, in a neighborhood on the Northwest side, a wave of

---

3. I'm referencing a telling mis-speak by James McDonald, GM President, from the film *Poletown Lives!* See Appendix IV.

crack houses invaded. Now with such invasions comes a simultaneous arrival: a palpable spirit of fear and intimidation. You can almost taste the acrid smell, a shadow of death settling in. Against the houses and their spirit, residents made repeated police calls but without response. Finally one day the cops made a bust, a buyer coming out. Across the street, an older black woman who had made the call raised her arms and rejoiced, "Thank you, Jesus! Thank you!" Some would say she was unduly and indiscreetly bold. The next morning an ambulance arrived at her home, summoned by a 911 call. A shooting had been reported. She was dumbfounded; they had been misinformed. She didn't know who had called. On the following day arrived the "dead wagon," as she calls it, from the nearby funeral home. They had been called to pick up the body.

Now these are death threats in the concrete, and sophisticated ones at that, but the older woman was having none of it. She consulted her friend, another senior citizen veteran of the civil rights movement (with which the city is filled), and together they convened a meeting at her church on Rosa Parks Boulevard. "My dreams," one of them later reported, "overtook my fears."

On Friday night next, they met in a storefront, were led in prayer by their Baptist pastor, and there began a slow procession through the community, pausing in front of the known crack houses and singing, "We Shall Overcome." Every third Friday they do it again. And it's catching on in other neighborhoods.

This is an exorcism, dear friends. It is a discernment of the spirit of death and a public rebuke. A refusal of its claim. This is a public liturgy of freedom, for person and community. On a scale at once modest and bold, it is an attempt to set at liberty the neighborhood, indeed the city of Detroit, its angel. Most of us in the angel discernment group have joined them on one occasion or another.

Discernment of spirits. Among the so-called charismatic gifts, it is the political sleeper. But how to go about it, this odd and intuitive grace? In our little group, we did Bible study of Luke, Colossians, Daniel, Cain, and Babel. We heard a poet read glimpses of his loving urban realism. We watched a film and played with clay. We talked and talked about what we love and hate about Detroit and how it is at a historical turning point. But in the end we listened. We found the time, chose geography (I did go to Belle Isle), and sat to listen and write. The most wonderful things came forth.

At our last group session, we read our work to one another. It was nothing less than a liturgical event. More than once we came to tears. One of these "prophecies" (let's call them that) was a plaintive plea in the city's voice, "Here I am, listen to me now." Weak but not beaten, tired but not driven out. A voice cries and whispers from the river, the alleys, the boarded homes and closed shops, and the places of power. A voice driven underground, but yearning to be called out and heeded. Another was confessional and repentant, naming its pulsing heart in neighborhood life, but confessing the temptations of big-ticket development.

One, in the loving voice of the Lord God, chastised the angel for succumbing to the seductions and illusions of material affluence, the appetites that willingly tolerate injustice for the continuing paycheck. And for failing to take on the struggle against the multinational corporations that left Detroit, a losing struggle but one which, if articulated, could have helped save the soul of the city's people. Yet another was a meditation focused on the sculpture, "A Message to the Spirit of Detroit from the One who was dead but now lives." It called the spirit to attend to its family, especially the children and youth, by turning its eyes to the divine energy that alone can renew.

There were more. I do none of them justice. Were they definitive? No. Were they subjective? Admittedly and necessarily so. But they got at something easily neglected; they pointed to something real. Something in need of healing within and without. Ourselves and our city. Someone suggested they might well be used as readings to begin a neighborhood meeting. Just so. In such a paraliturgy, could they revive in others what had come alive again in us? Our love for Detroit, its people, its spirit. A realism and a vision. A sense of the times.

In that spirit, I put down here the concluding portions of my own attempt, written and rewritten. May it be a true word to the angel of Detroit:

Die and arise. In your weakness is your hope. You are at an end and a beginning. Recollect your best history and come alive.

You will do this if you set the lives of your people above your own. Attend to the least, the poorest, the homeless. Defend them from the ravages of corporation and economy. In their empowerment is your life.

Cast off your bondages. (This too may feel like dying.) Begin with drugs and guns. Your people pray for this; join them in action.

Instead of Murder Capital, become the city of nonviolence. It can be so.

Your industrial heyday has gone to rust. You will not see its like again. Now think small. Encourage the modest, an economy of creativity and self-reliance. Nourish the projects of human scale, the works of community and struggle.

Let your empty lots bloom green; you will find there a hidden economy all its own.

Sit light upon the river, but not as real estate frontage for the rich. Be in right relationship to its life, and through it to the region, to earth itself.

For your sins, enough. Now you have my blessing. Sing to glory and come to life.

Let it be so. Amen.

7

Fallen: The Law and the State (1991)

> There is no other honest way to describe the relation between the law in America and American blacks, between this principality and these human beings, than in terms of the aggressions of the legal system against human life. For blacks in the U.S.A. (to cite no other nonwhites of which the same must be said) the law, in a quite overwhelming sense, in the legislatures, in the courts, in law enforcement and administration is now, as it always has been, an enemy: a harasser, an invader, an oppressor. And this is the law's reality not only in notorious circumstances, like chattel slavery or the era of the lynch mobs or the generations of voter intimidation and disenfranchisement or in the assassinations of black leaders or in the vindictiveness of welfare policy or in the official persecution of black politics or in the ingenious and tireless evasions of school desegregation (contrived as much in the White House as in any school board) or in the sometimes fatal abuse of black prisoners, but also, and perhaps more significantly, in the apparently petty, routine, daily assaults and importunities which blacks suffer under the guise of legality.
> —William Stringfellow, *An Ethic for Christians*

It is the powers, the rulers of this age, who crucified Christ.[1] That is perhaps the single most edifying point in comprehending them. They

---

1. One of my earliest attempts to work with powers theology as a practical political tool, particularly with respect to liturgical direct action, was *Seasons of Faith and Conscience: Kairos, Confession, and Liturgy* (Maryknoll, NY: Orbis, 1991; 2nd ed. Eugene, OR: Wipf & Stock, 2008). This is a portion of chapter 4, "Principalities and Powers That Be."

are at best confused and blind to their vocations. And if all the New Testament references are amassed, from the lowliest human agent to the powers in high places, from the Sadducean party to the Beast rising out of the sea, the preponderance of them report demonic agencies, a host in rebellion against God. They are among the forces that separate human beings from the love of God (Rom 8:39); they blind the minds of unbelievers (2 Cor 4:4); they enslave human beings (Gal 4:1–11); they are in league with death (1 Cor 15:24–27); and they are the true forces against which believers, in faith, contend in mortal combat (Eph 6:10–20).

How comes this state of affairs?

The powers are fallen by virtue of idolatry. In the biblical saga, human beings neglect the stern warning, lifting up their eyes and worshiping that which is not God. In consequence they come into bondage, and the powers are twisted and inflated, mushrooming out of control.

We might easily take the nations as the ready example of this. Israel's history is surely a litany of suffering one imperial occupation after another. The social order of creation was experienced as corrupted and in disarray. From one prophet to the next the cause of this is laid to idolatry.

Let us, however, try an example closer to home, at least firstly to Paul's home: the law. The law is no mean principality. It must be so counted and numbered. Moreover, it is the one with which he is most intimately acquainted. He knows it as agent and insider. With legal credentials he's been jealous on its behalf even to the point of official violence. No wonder, this side of his conversion, the question that exercises his mind so much in correspondence is how could the law, a good gift of God, become an instrument of blindness, a vehicle of ignorance, a tempter to sin, an ally and accomplice of death itself?

The law is a good creation of God (Rom 7:13). It has a given vocation in the social order. It probably is imprecise to speak of an angel of the law, though there is a tradition mentioned in Acts (8:53) and cited by Paul in Galatians (3:19) that it was delivered by angels. As we have come to expect of the powers, there is certainly a visible aspect to the law (the written code, the public symbols and rituals of interpretation) and there is most assuredly an invisible, interior aspect. (Even today a lawyer will argue a case on the "spirit of the law.") But how does it come to be in a trio of powers, in alliance with sin and death?

To draw on G. B. Caird, he recounts a brief literary history of Satan.[2] The survey doubles as something of a parable that illuminates the mystery with which Paul struggled. "Satan" means adversary, and early on that came to have a legal meaning in relation to divine judgments. In the prologue to Job, the Satan is one of the angels with rightful access to the heavenly court of Yahweh, there to serve as public prosecutor, defender of the law. In that pursuit, Satan goes to and fro upon the earth garnering evidence. (Notice that even in the New Testament period certain juridical duties remain. Satan is the legal adversary in 1 Pet 5:8, and in 1 Tim 3:6 those who are conceited come under his legal condemnation.)

Later, in Rabbinic literature, Satan has a tendency to be executioner as well, dishing out punishments in accord with the sentence. Paul himself reflects this when he mentions a person being handed over to Satan "for the destruction of the flesh, that his spirit may be saved in the day of the Lord Jesus" (1 Cor 4:5). In the extreme Satan becomes Destroyer, holder of the power of death.

Meanwhile, he expands his responsibilities with the zealousness of an agent provocateur, canvassing business for the law-courts, inciting people to disobedience. By degrees the servant of God has become the enemy of God, with whom Jesus contends in the gospels. Concludes Caird:

> We cannot say that in the process he loses anything of his original character. Throughout his tragic history his zeal for justice remains unimpaired. He is a martinet, who demands that men shall be dealt with according to the rigor of the law, and will go to any length to secure a verdict.[3]

Satan has made an idol of the law and so becomes himself the raging power of death. The "fall" of Satan appears here to be one with the idolatry of law. Not that we should let the "parable" confuse us on this point: *idolatry is a human act*. Think on the zeal of Paul himself. All of the principalities become inflated in their power; they are all implicated in the fall; they are confused in their vocations; they usurp the very place of God—*because* human beings grant them worship.

In the case of law, that comes of mistaking something derivative, secondary, and conditional, with the absolute will of God. It comes of seeking self-justification, meaning, and identity in law. (To seek justification by the law is the form of idolatry that most concerns Paul.) In consequence the law itself becomes accuser, tempter, and executioner.

---

2. G. B. Caird, *Principalities and Powers* (Oxford: Clarendon, 1956), 31–39.
3. Ibid., 37.

Human beings are then "in bondage to beings that by nature are no gods" (Gal 4:8). To put it another way, the law was made for humanity, not humanity for the law. Paul never quite speaks of it so, but I believe he experienced his relation to the law as a kind of possession. The sudden violence of his conversion, as portrayed in Acts, may suggest its powerful grip upon him.

While there is little difference in the ancient world between nation and state, they do name distinct principalities in our own. Much is written on the state in New Testament literature, a preponderance focused upon Romans 13, because it has been so abused as an isolated text sanctioning an unqualified obedience of Christians to any established regime. I forbear to dwell on it, but the passage does speak of the vocation of political authority to order society. The word Paul uses for "authorities" is the same one he employs in other places referring to the angelic powers, which is to say their heavenly, interior aspect, and most often with respect to their demonic rebellion against God. In the thirteenth chapter of Romans the reference is clearly to the most mundane human agents (who wield the sword, and issue taxes). Their authority, says Paul, comes from God. They are servants of God. All in all, not that different in conception from the subordination of the nations to Yahweh's divine sovereignty. (And not that different from what Jesus is reported in John 19 to have pluckily said to Pilate on the occasion of his sentencing to death.)

This admonition of Paul to obey the state authorities is often rightly juxtaposed with the version of the Roman state portrayed in Revelation 13: the Beast rising from the chaos of the sea. There the angelic being "behind" the Beast is the Dragon, an "interiority" from hell itself. In this vision the state has lost any vestige of legitimate vocation in a frenzy of idolatry and blasphemous pretention. It is experienced as virtually out of human control, transfixing and enslaving human beings, demanding their worship. This is an image that has provided grist for thoughtful meditation in our own time.

Second Thessalonians, a Pauline letter, seems to combine the views:

> Let no one deceive you in any way; for that day will not come, unless the rebellion comes first, and the man of lawlessness is revealed, the son of perdition, who opposes and exalts himself against every so-called god or object of worship, so that he takes his seat in the temple of God, proclaiming himself to be God. Do you not remember that when I was still with you I told you this? And you know what is restraining him now so that he may be revealed in his time. For the mystery of lawlessness is already at work;

only he who now restrains it will do so until he is out of the way. (2 Thess 2:3–7)

To say the least, this is a more ambiguous view of the state. In a narrow historical sense it may reflect the impact of Caligula's decree (never accomplished) that his image be erected in the temple of Jerusalem, but more broadly it evinces an understanding of the general idolatrous tendencies of political authority. That a restraint is seen (perhaps in Caligula's removal) implies the continuing vocation of the state, not as yet altogether lost. However, the fact of deep corruption remains, a fallenness that seen full-blown could be adequately described only with recourse to the beastly images of apocalypse.

8

The Machinery of War: Technology and the Powers That Indwell (1991)

> No one has ever yet been able to find the basis of political power or the reason why people always irresistibly and irremediably obey it. . . . Political power has many dimensions, e.g., social, economic, psychological, ethical, psycho-analytical, and legal. But when we have scrutinized them all, we have still not apprehended its reality. We cannot say with Marx that power is an ideological superstructure, for it is always there. The disproportion noted above leads me to the unavoidable conclusion that another power intervenes and indwells and uses political power, thus giving it a range and force that it does not have in itself. . . . One might ask whether technology is not also one of these powers. The answer seems simple enough.
>
> —Jacques Ellul, *The Ethics of Freedom*

This essay first appeared in Sojourners, *April 1991. For a fuller summary of Ellul's analysis of technology, its logic and mechanisms, as a power, see my* Seasons of Faith and Conscience: Kairos, Confession, and Liturgy *(Maryknoll, NY: Orbis, 1991; 2nd ed. Eugene, OR: Wipf & Stock, 2008), chapter 4.*

The most prominent public feature of this deathly Gulf War has been the celebrated vindication of the American technological myth. This technological superiority is evinced in the heaviest (and ostensibly most accurate) bombing in the history of the world. People of faith and conscience have felt the spectacle of this "triumph" as a dark weight on their souls, indeed as a heartsickness.

The American people and the nations of the world sit transfixed before images of technical prowess. The machinery of warfare has been named and paraded, analyzed and glorified to death. On television, people watch laser-guided missiles float in the front door of buildings, as if this were the finals of some video-game championship. The papers are full of diagrams and technical descriptions. Popular knowledge of the planes, the weapons systems, and the esoteric acronyms becomes a mark of the well informed.

What goes unnoticed is the extent to which technology itself has been a driving force in the creation of this war. The technological system has a mind and a logic, an independence and momentum all its own. It is indeed one of the preeminent principalities of the present age.

By way of analysis, this is not to minimize the pursuit of resources to oil the imperial machine, the geopolitical realignments, certain economic considerations, the politics of the home front, or any other factor—but merely to say the weapons have been ravenous for new targets. They have in and of themselves been hungry to be used. I do not personify them unduly. It is plain biblical literacy to comprehend these technological systems as having an inner driving spirit to them. As much as anything, that predatory technological hunger has been pressing toward war.

Technology is a realm of the "sacred" in secularized American culture. High technology saves, mystifies, and accomplishes miracles. It is esteemed as the source and basis of our way of life. Moreover, it has its own priesthood ranked in hierarchies of expertise (and security clearance). Certain things are held beyond the comprehension of an ordinary human being, the "layperson." We have witnessed an astonishing array of military technicians conversing knowledgeably with the nightly news anchor people. The former are matter-of-fact, the latter filled with reverence and awe.

This idolization inflates the power of technology, rendering it at once "necessary" and demonic. Biblically, of course, this is the experience with all the principalities and powers. They are, every one of them, understood as fallen. Claiming to serve life, they are in fact become minions of death. It is, for example, the powers who coalesce and conspire to crucify the Lord (1 Cor 2:6-8). In history they are unleashed and out of control.

Plainly put, we are in the possession of our technology, not (as we suppose) the other way around. Jacques Ellul, the French theologian and social historian, is the most lucid commentator on technology as a power. He has spent his life documenting and analyzing the logic and method by which technocratic systems and societies grow and move. I here suggest an urgent rereading of Ellul in light of this war. Four decades ago he observed the separation of means from ends that was rendering life in Western society absurd.

> All that science can do will be used to save one life, and then millions of men will be massacred by bombs, or in concentration camps: both are products of the enormity of means. . . . In this terrible dance of means which have been unleashed, no one knows where we are going, the aim of life has been forgotten, the end has been left behind. Humanity has set out at tremendous speed—to go *nowhere*.[1]

The Gulf War is illustrative on the face of it: the official ends and objectives have been repeatedly shifted, but ever since the first placement of offensive troops and equipment, the means have been constant and clear. They predominate utterly over the elusive ends (no matter how fervently and redundantly the President stresses that we all *know* why we are there).

Those who have struggled with the powers of nuclearism have come to understand in some measure how technology determines policy, not vice versa. First-strike counterforce targeting has been less a military and strategic doctrine in search of a means, as it has been an emerging capability: "modernization" and improvements in accuracy issuing de facto in a policy of first strike.

The cruise missile, which was the first line of attack in the Gulf War, is something of a technological parable in this regard. Cruise missiles are small pilotless jet planes. (Saddam Hussein's "grossly inflated figures" of planes shot down apparently include these. American figures exclude them because they are flown, in effect, by "robots"). They combine evasive, radar-ducking, treetop altitude with pinpoint accuracy.

---

1. Jacques Ellul, *The Presence of the Kingdom* (New York: The Seabury Press, 1967), 69.

The Pentagon claims they could launch one from San Francisco and put it through the goalposts at Soldier's Field in Chicago.

Their history originates with Hitler's World War II buzz bombs: part rocket, part airplane. Early Pentagon attempts to develop the weapon further were essentially abandoned with the successful deployment of ICBMs. However, in the early 1970s several simultaneous technological breakthroughs—miniaturization of jet engines (accomplished a few miles from my own hometown), miniaturization of nuclear warheads, electronic mapping and computer guidance elements, and the concentration of jet fuel, combined in ensemble to represent the possibility of an accurate and effective cruise. Henry Kissinger took the possibility, and threatened its development as a "bargaining chip" in arms control talks. Once developed, however, all branches of the military fell in love with it. The cruise was promptly deployed in a variety of land-, air-, and sea-based systems. Moreover, its deployment in the early 80s coincided with the development of the nuclear war-fighting doctrine called "protracted nuclear war," wherein a limited nuclear exchange in a particular theater of war, Europe say, is envisioned to result not in a full-blown nuclear war, but in a long, slow, "protracted" series of nuclear shots escalating horizontally, as they put it, into other theaters. This global test of wills was featured to last for a period of weeks or even months. The policy was formalized in the Single Integrated Operational Plan, specifically SIOP-6, the master targeting plan set in place under the Reagan administration.

To reiterate more simply: an ensemble of technologies makes a weapon possible. It is developed as a bargaining chip, but once developed is withdrawn from the table and deployed. Its deployment issues in a new rung on the ladder of escalation dominance; a new element of policy is formalized. Furthermore, it is a policy not of deterrence but implying first-use and nuclear war-fighting scenarios.

Now comes the Gulf War. No surprise really. With the thaw in the Cold War and the demise of Soviet power, it took little imagination to predict that new targets (which is to say new enemies) needed to be located. And so we have (thus far) a "conventional" war in which the cruise has functioned as the first-strike weapon.

Listen again: The enthusiasm for success of the Patriot missile is quickly marshaled to fund the SDI/Star Wars technology. Another first-strike system finds a new mission and new targets (yes, third-world ones) in the "new" world order.

The fact is barely mentioned in public: this war (like Panama) has made first strike ever more palatable and morally justifiable to the American people. They are simply "preemptive" of a greater evil on the horizon. Then again, first-strike weapons, like cruise and stealth, get hungry to try their bite.

I keep thinking of the bombing of Hiroshima. Toward the end of World War II, the Japanese were suing for peace through various channels. An end to the war might have been negotiated. But there was this atom bomb secretly in the technological pipeline. It needed to be used. The will to use it against human beings had to be demonstrated. So "unconditional surrender" was the only offer. It sufficed to continue the war long enough to "test" two bombs against human populations. That is the only way I can understand the abiding refusal to negotiate an Iraqi settlement. The infamous deadline was no international diplomatic lever. It merely bought time required to set in place the machines, their mechanics and massive infrastructure. Finally, the weapons were in place, arched and ready to devour.

I have also been thinking, even as we are urged not to, of Vietnam. In that instance the incremental commitment to war was also led by technology. The "technologization" of the war went hand in hand with Nixon's later policy of "Vietnamization." Too many American body bags were piling up on the planes home. Just as U.S. soldiers were being replaced by South Vietnamese troops, they were also being supplanted by the technology of the "electronic battlefield." The precursors of today's smart bombs were directed by on-ground sensors monitored from computer stations in Hawaii and elsewhere. In Vietnam, automated air war technology sought to reduce political costs at home. In this Gulf War, it is clear that one lesson of Vietnam has been learned: no more body counts. Pentagon briefings only confirm in a general way, if emphatically, that we are "killing them."

One suspects (two and a half weeks into the war) that the land assault predicted to take a toll in the lives of U.S. soldiers would be foregone entirely in favor of the unrelenting air war, apart from the fact that other varieties of technology, other "tools in the box" like M1 tanks and infrared night vision equipment, also need to strut their stuff.

The war in Vietnam entailed not only a systematic attack on truth, but on language itself. We are seeing that carried forward from the outset in the Gulf. At press conferences, military technicians speak in a language that is esoteric, arcane, and euphemistic, a jargon of coded phrases and acronyms. They do not expose the truth of reality, but mask it. That is how we are hearing about this war, in the hermetic language of technique. Cluster bombs (developed for Vietnam) and now in use are not described as weapons of terror, spraying metal fragments suddenly and indiscriminately into human flesh (military or civilian), at unpredictable times long after the bombing raid. (By any honest reading, these things are as illegal under international law as gas, or germs—or nuclear weapons, for that matter.) With Orwellian aplomb, they are simply termed "area denial devices." Let's leave it at that.

Vietnam was the war that television technology brought into our living rooms. That is so with the Gulf War, though in a vastly different and more sinister way. Think again of those images from the early days of this war: the missiles floating through the front door, or guided down the air duct of the building. Many have noticed the video-game quality of those images, but the observation stops there. This is the first war to be sold to a generation captivated by Nintendo, raised with their hand on the joystick and finger on the button. (We had heard how military recruiters hung out at video arcades ready to entice the quick of eye and hand with offers of "the real thing.") So, who are the good guys? Simply, the ones on this side of the screen. And Who are the bad guys? The ones in the target sight. Point the camera, settle the question, and push the button. The consummation of technology utterly replacing ideology is at hand.

Moral solidarity, whether you experience it as patriotism or heartsickness, euphoria or dread, has been fully exposed. The difference in moral culpability between the F1 pilot seeing the target blow on his screen and us seeing it blow on ours, is negligible. And who imagines the people inside?

What we are witnessing is the fusion of the television camera with the weapons themselves. One and the same device. And, in a weird inversion, who is the real target? And why do we feel so deadened and powerless? And why has the media never seemed so fully claimed as an organ of the empire? One and the same device.

9

Confronting the Drug Powers; Freeing the Captives (1992)

> For we are not contending against flesh and blood, but against the principalities, against the powers, against the world rulers of this present darkness ... (Eph 6:11)

William Stringfellow, the theologian who may be justly credited with reviving in this country a theology of the principalities and powers, claimed to be first put onto them by his friends and legal clients in Harlem who experienced, among many other things, the mafia and its network of runners and dealers as a predatory force invading their families and neighborhoods. His years of lucid reflection began in a concrete sense with their intuitive theological street wisdom.

It is thereby all the more remarkable that in the churches' struggle against drugs there has been such meager theological reflection. Indeed the notorious frustration and substantial failure of the church in confronting the drug problem, so-called, may be partially rooted in this fundamental shortcoming: the failure to comprehend drugs biblically, that is, as numbered among the principalities and powers. The officially sponsored "Just say No" approach and its churchly equivalents effectively mask the character of the drug powers. While intimating resistance ("say No"), it first reduces the struggle to ("just") an individual exchange, an illegal street-level deal. The principality in its economic, political, cultural, and above all spiritual aspect remains hidden and is given a free hand to go about its deadly business.

Because the church's approach is firstly (and rightly) pastoral, the individualist temptation predominates. It is, however, especially pastoral care that requires the fullest comprehension of the powers.

To comprehend drugs as a power means, on the one hand, to see it whole, as an entity, the drug system: a configuration of competing underground corporations, economic arrangements, illegitimate operations, and cultural forms. It means seeing the system of transnational-national enterprises, akin, say, to the military-technological complex. What has been written about the political economy of drugs begins to get at this.

As an economic entity, the system reaches across the planet. Between the poppy or coca fields and the hustling street vendor lies this huge enterprise. In certain respects it is a network marketing operation (of the variety mastered legally by Amway) with a 700- to 2,000-percent markup from one end to the other. Moreover, it conforms to the patterns of and crosses the boundaries of the two-tiered global economy. Above, elites dominate production, manufacture, and global export, with a middle-management operation overseeing regional distribution, paramilitary security, money laundering, and the like. Below are the peasant farms (third-world raw materials) and the crack houses or their equivalent feeding on cheap labor.

Legally it's an elaborate conspiracy, but as with any structural power the whole is greater than the sum of its parts. In the name of Adam Smith's invisible hand it takes on a life of its own, claiming those who claim to control it. Moreover, since it operates illegally (the free market truly unleashed) it has a phenomenal vitality, an inordinate versatility. For example at street level the crack houses on my block can rapidly shift their mode of operation from infrastructure support with runners for the open drug bazaar in the park, to drive-up operations going night and day, to some setup involving the prostitutes who make the trek back and forth continuously to the main drag. The social traffic pattern and even the personnel can change, but it is the same operation. For this same reason jailing a "kingpin" changes nothing. It's not a conspiracy, but a structural power. Change the faces top to bottom, yet the principality abides.

> The "principalities and powers" are the inner and outer aspect of any given manifestation of power. As the inner aspect they are the spirituality of institutions, the "within" of corporate structures and systems, the inner essence of outer organizations of power.... Every Power tends to have ... an invisible pole, an inner spirit or driving force that animates, legitimates, and regulates its physical manifestation in the world.[1]

When the drug powers invade a city neighborhood, they are attended by a palpable spirit. You can almost taste it, though it's tougher to name: fear and seduction breeding on despair. It is truly predatory and invasive, bearing along the real presence of death. Admittedly, in the era of the fall, as the New Testament attests, all the principalities are minions and servants of death. However, in the case of the drug powers, much like military ones (with which they have more than a little traffic) death wears no silk glove here. It is blatant and forward, idolized and invoked, named as an omnipresent threat. In popular discourse this is often recognized as the "violence of the drug culture." It is indeed endemic. But this is more than the rituals and codes, the pervasive trappings of a subculture; the spirit of death is exposed and raw. This is not to suggest that the drug powers are any more fallen or demonic than the Pentagon and its surrogates. On the contrary. It is merely to observe that on the domestic scene, it is the one accounted, even in popular culture, as most enthralled with death.

This spiritual dimension has everything to do with the stronghold grip that drugs exercise on lives and communities. Yes, there is a biochemical dependency that may be clinically observed. But chemistry is not social determinism. Chemical dependency is the emblem, the coin of exchange, of a larger and deeper spiritual claim. Even those in the system (be it corporate gang members, or money-laundering wizards) who by discipline "stay clean," are nevertheless subject to this same bondage.

> The scene of turmoil and confusion associated with the demonic powers becomes acute when it is recognized that these are rival, competitive powers despite the fact that, at times, they seem to confront human life as compatible or collaborating powers. All alliances among the principalities (the reciprocal arrangements of the Pentagon, some self-styled think tanks, and the weapons industries furnish an example) are transient and expedient. Such liaisons are aptly described in Revelation by terms like "fornication," "sorcery," or "playing the wanton" (Rev 18:7–15, 23).[2]

---

1. Walter Wink, *Naming the Powers* (Philadelphia: Fortress Press, 1984), 5.

In the pantheon of current powers, drugs evince this pattern of rivalry and collusion, often simultaneously. The following are offered as examples.

In my own town, the *city administration* and its police force are geared up in a fight against drugs. At the same time they are in convenient collusion with them. I do not refer to the corruption of the police force or the current scandal concerning embezzlement of unaccounted drug seizure funds, but the way in which incursions of crack houses decimate a neighborhood that has been identified for clearing and redevelopment. A community that stands in the way of a ballpark, an airport expansion, or a new auto plant will suddenly find itself deep in struggle with an influx of drugs. What housing market there is drops; renters depart; homes are abandoned and eventually burned; neighborhood organizing is deflected and dissipated; the logic of redevelopment is reinforced in the public mind. In the main the mechanism is simple: cops are less likely to risk their necks for a neighborhood already designated as having no future. There doesn't even have to be a conspiracy in some fourteenth-floor meeting room. And yet I once heard the City's director of economic development describe a police strategy of "corralling all the dope houses into one neighborhood" (in this case one slated for development), "so we can drop the net on them." Nonsense apart from incipient collusion.

Another more obvious example of collusion is the symbiotic connection between the drug powers and the *financial industry*. This is true at every level—from the International Monetary Fund to auto dealers selling cars for cash in small denominations. When the IMF puts the squeeze on third-world nations, they force peasant farmers further to the brink of survival and push them toward the lucrative drug system. Juan Valdez and friends are compelled to alter their cash crop of choice. The permanent third-world debt crisis has addicted whole national economies to the underground drug trade, and the international bankers blithely take their interest in drug dollars. The financial powers are also deeply entrenched through various money-laundering operations. The going rate for turning hot cash into electronic balances is estimated at 7–10 percent.[3] Since converting to a dollar economy, Panama has been and remains to this day (the "Just Cause" Noriega war notwithstanding) an international laundering center. In the States, one

---

2. William Stringfellow, *An Ethic for Christians and Other Aliens in a Strange Land* (Waco, TX: Word, 1973), 210.
3. Eva Bertram, "It's Worth the Risk," *Christian Social Action* 6/90, 12.

only has to call to mind the number of failed Savings and Loans that were gutted, under deregulation, by certain international dealers and brokers with access to drug dollars.

Perhaps the most notorious example of conflict and collaboration is the involvement of the CIA in international drug traffic. The U.S. is only the most prominent in a list of nations whose clandestine agencies have linked up with traffickers: Nationalist China, Pre-War Japan, Gaullist France, French Indochina, Thailand, and Pakistan.[4] CIA involvement goes back nearly to its inception, though its best documented complicity was with the heroin trade of Southeast Asia, forming an alliance with the opium-growing Hmong tribe. The agency helped eliminate competitors and provided transport via its front airline services, in exchange for the tribe's part in the American war. (This activity, incidentally, coincided directly with the period of heroin epidemic that swept U.S. inner cities.) Familiar more recent alliances include the Mujahedeen in the Afghan war and the Contras in the undeclared war against Nicaragua. In general, the theme of rivalry and collusion is signified by the relationship of the Drug Enforcement Agency and the covert operations of the CIA. The international investigative and enforcement efforts of the former bump heads with the hands-off "national security" claims of the latter. In effect the CIA grants cover and de facto immunity to the drug powers, often at critical periods that allow them to expand, forging connections to new markets.[5]

There is a further irony with a bitter edge: the "War on Drugs" is itself a form of collusion. By way of analogy, before the end of the Cold War certain East European Greens were referring to the arms race as a "single two-headed monster." Their idea was that by mirroring and justifying one another the superpower military establishments were held in an elaborate interlocking structure. (Third-world peoples long ago experienced and named this as the common struggle of North vs. South.) Arms-control agreements were nothing more than the institutionalization of their co-dependency. The Pentagon was crippled and panicked by the demise of the Soviet Union. By partially filling the Cold War vacuum, the Drug War has demonstrated elements of a similar collusion, though perhaps the relationship is less mutual. The Pentagon at the moment needs the drug powers more than vice versa.

---

4. Alfred McCoy, "Drugs and Covert Ops: A Brief History" (excerpted from *The Politics of Heroin*), *Convergence* (Fall 1991): 3.
5. Ibid., 4.

An immediate need was to find new "enemies" to replace "communists" in the ongoing manufacture of public consensus. "Narco-terrorists" and "narco-guerrillas" remain viable candidates. The media enlisted in the drug war (nearly to the extent and degree they marketed the Gulf War), scripting a sensational crisis right from administration press releases. Needless to say, Pentagon technology has been drafted into the effort—AWAC airplanes and over-the-horizon Backscatter radar systems have new surveillance missions in the interdiction effort. Military aid to countries with atrocious human rights records may be masked and enmeshed in the drug war effort. Interventions, as the war against Panama demonstrates, may be successfully sanctioned and justified under its rubric. Among those who lay odds on "the next war" (Bush's "October Surprise 1992"?), many name Peru a top pick. Guerrillas and coca fields abound. The U.S. already has military advisors on the ground.

Domestically, the war has furthered the assault on civil liberties. Search without warrant, property seizures, surveillance and ID systems for public housing, youth curfews, extended pre-trial jail time, large-scale police incursions—these unconstitutional legal practices are merely the necessary "war powers" the authorities expect to employ. The "enemy" at home is also a political necessity that justifies and inflates state power. In the process, African American males are made a criminalized and endangered species.

Racism is an ideological power that insinuates itself in a variety of institutional structures. It is at work in the drug war—and it collaborates simultaneously with the drug powers. Combat and collusion. There is a TV ad currently running on the east coast in which a voice over urban images intones indignantly: "Forty-six percent of the drug use in the New York area is in New York City!" The implication is clear and commonplace. Then following a pregnant pause the voice asks further, "Where do you suppose the other fifty-four percent is?" The point comes home. Surveys indicate that the typical crack addict is a white middle-class male, though you'd never know it from either media portrayals or arrest records. Only 12 percent of those using illegal drugs are African American, but they constitute 44 percent of those arrested for simple possession.[6] Add in the pervasive racial bias in prosecution and sentencing and you have a formula for a booming prison industry feeding on African Americans.

---

6. Pat Coy, "Conscientious Objection to the Drug War," *Christianity and Crisis*, August 6, 1990, 245.

The same bias is in league with the assaults of the drug powers themselves. One thinks of the cinematic representation in *The Godfather*: the Dons sit at table debating the wisdom and morality of a mafia entrance into the drug business. It is a dispute already threatening war among the families. Marlon Brando steps forward to deliver the acceptable compromise: We will sell, but only to Negroes. The scene, needless to say, has its corollaries.

Because periods of intense activism in the African American community are often followed (and dulled or dissipated) by an influx of narcotics, activists have often suspected, in such case, a *political* conspiracy. In general, though, it is a structural collusion of the powers that is at work in targeting the black community. The simple logic of profit makes them a target market for the trafficking principalities. The economic devastation of the inner cities (is any documentation needed for the history of racism there?) affords a hospitable environment for the underground economics of the drug powers. It's the domestic equivalent of the IMF. And the atmosphere of despair is part of the spiritual matrix that opens the door. There is a surrogate economy, though it is largely delusional. Drug marketing offers black youth the same long-shot, hit-big options as professional athletics or the lotto. Drugs are one of the few things that bring suburban money into my neighborhood; however, in keeping with conventional patterns, the lion's share goes up and out to the middle management and their bosses. Still, it fires the mind to imagine what the Detroit-area billion-dollar-a-year business of the drug powers might mean converted to a genuine local alternative.

> In order to perceive the Addictive System for what it is, one must be *in* it but not *of* it. In other words, one must be in recovery from its effects.[7]

There is a question, at once sociological and theological, a debate of more than passing interest, that bears fundamentally on one's view of recovery, of freedom from the drug powers. It's this: Are we talking about one society or two? It is patently clear that we live in a two-tiered economy—one with a widening gap and ever-more rigid barricades. But are the drug powers a creature that flourishes in the "culture of poverty"? Are they the de facto and extra-legal rulers of those under chemical apartheid? Does freedom mean being liberated from

---

7. Anne Wilson Shaef, *When Society Becomes an Addict* (New York: Harper & Row, 1987), 5.

the darkness of the street and baptized into the mainstream productivity of the dominant American culture?

Perhaps I've begged the question, but let me suggest that the drug powers are as American as Apple computers. The percentages ought to ring a bell if we acknowledge that while Americans are 6 percent of the world's population they consume 60 percent of the world's illegal drugs. Narcotics are the ideal consumer product in a culture of consumption. Every manufacturer would love to have the consumer loyalty that crack cocaine engenders. A product to die for. Moreover, it is consumer products that are the conspicuous emblem of the urban hustlers: from shoes and coats, to gold chains (ironically from South Africa), to car phones and luxury rides. The drug powers are not consumerism gone awry but carried to its deadly conclusion. They are its shadow, mirror, and mime. We have only to recall the multinational corporate character of the powers, one that is born out at street level as well. Gangs in my own city, as elsewhere, mimic well-organized business formations. A recent study of corporate gangs in Detroit found that members had never heard of Thurgood Marshall, but every last one of them knew of Lee Iacocca.

Moreover, addiction itself is deeply entrenched in, some say intrinsic to, the dominant culture. More and more there is talk of the "Addictive Society." This is a social analysis discovered in the therapeutic work of recovery. Counselors have come to understand that addicts of various stripe are regularly participants in a dysfunctional family, or a *system* of relationships that are all cooperating and co-dependent with the addict. It has been a short leap to recognize that the same mechanisms and patterns operate on the larger scale of culture. Anne Wilson Schaef is one popular author who has now named as the Addictive System what she formerly called the White Male System.[8]

Within an array of common mechanisms people may be addicted to more than agents of chemical dependence: food or any consumable, of course, but also "process" addictions like sexual patterns, or work or making money, even religious fixations. It doesn't take long to perceive that an entire culture may be organized around these mechanisms. There is a shock of recognition in seeing writ large in culture, the patterns of the individual addict and family system: Power and control are the ultimate goal. The lie is the norm and everyone cooperates in its perpetuation. Memory is conveniently short so no lessons may be

---

8. Ibid., 14.

learned. Scarcity is the model, with everyone competing for a limited amount of attention or "love." Confusion is manufactured. Projection becomes a standard form of denial. Fear, though unacknowledged, permeates the system. These are but glimpses, though they couldn't ring truer.

These comprise the social and spiritual matrix in which the drug powers flourish. The mechanisms of addiction are endemic to the culture and synonymous with its spirit.

> They came to the other side of the sea, to the country of the Gerasenes. And when he had come out of the boat, there met him out of the tombs a man with an unclean spirit, who lived among the tombs; and no one could bind him anymore, even with a chain; for often he had been bound with fetters and chains, but the chains he wrenched apart, and the fetters he broke to pieces; and no one had the strength to subdue him. Night and day among the tombs and on the mountains he was always crying out and bruising himself with stones. (Mark 5:1–5)

Recent interpretation of this most political exorcism is intriguing within the context of our current discussion. Literary critic René Girard has commented on the relationship of the townspeople to the demoniac. How does he survive and grow strong among the tombs? Are they feeding him? Is it really impossible to fashion unbreakable chains? Is there collusion in some ritualized drama of violence and restraint repeated over and over? The suggestion is that the Gerasenes and their demoniac have settled into a pattern of "cyclical pathology,"[9] an elaborate co-dependency of sorts. They enable his madness.

Beyond that, he is their "scapegoat" for the violence they are unable to face in themselves. On the one hand he acts out their rage to be free. (The entire region was under the chains of Roman domination.) On the other hand he "stones" himself—internalizing the violence of both the occupation and their unexpressed revolt. In third-world situations of oppression this phenomenon of the self-destructive urges is sometimes called the "colonization of the mind." The empire has fractured him. He lives openly with death and the dead. As the representative of all Gerasa, his theatrics dull and deaden their pain and violence. For our purposes here it is ironic, to say the least, that the Greek name for scapegoat (as Girard points out) is at root the word for drugs, *pharmakos*.

---

9. René Girard, *The Scapegoat* (Baltimore: Johns Hopkins University Press, 1986), 168.

It need hardly be argued that drug addicts are scapegoated in this country: a New York City councilman once suggested chaining them to trees, so that passersby could spit on them!¹⁰ There is of course the redundant call, uttered even from the White House, for the enactment of the death penalty in connection with drug cases—and one recalls the notorious public statements of drug czar William Bennett that he had no problem morally with *beheading* drug dealers!

Addicts in turn evince the pattern of illicit freedom that is really bondage and self-destruction. Or consider the parallel of the street gangs who demonstrate all the dramatic flash and color of rebellion or revolt, but without political effect; they are beating themselves to death. They affect the consumer trappings of the dominant culture and shoot themselves with its weapons.

With respect to the Gerasene demoniac, it is the most striking gospel instance of a demon being named as a systematic structure of violence and power, in this case the "Legion." (During the period when all the synoptic gospels were written, an entire Roman legion was indeed quartered at Gerasa.¹¹) This is a suitable name for the very power that conspires with others, to kill Christ.

We should not underestimate the risk Jesus assumes in the encounter with the demoniac. One who cannot be bound rushes out to meet him as from the grave. He is a storm incarnate. The demoniac is a fragmented confusion of conflicting impulse and emotion. Jesus is perceived clearly as a threat, someone with no business here. But he stands his ground and responds in the single-minded authority of love. They hold a conversation, the Lord asking his name. The spiritual power of domination, the pathology, inner and outer, the mechanisms of scapegoating, the specter of violence are all gathered and present, but it does not obscure the love of Jesus for the demoniac. The power present is overcome, in history and heart, not by will or violence, but by grace. Jesus, in the encounter, exposes the power of death and with a word dismantles the scapegoat mechanism. In that is the beginning of freedom and release.

At the conclusion of the episode the townspeople come out to find the two thousand drowned pigs and the demoniac "clothed and in his right mind." They are upset and afraid, pressing Jesus to depart the region. It is possible the economic loss of the herd is at issue. (In Acts

---

10. Walter Wink, "Biting the Bullet: The Case for Legalizing Drugs," *Christian Century*, August 8–15, 1990, 738.
11. Walter Wink, *Unmasking the Powers* (Philadelphia: Fortress Press, 1987), 45.

16 Paul and Silas are beaten and jailed for an exorcism that costs some slaveowners their hope of financial gain.) But more likely it's the revolt of a dysfunctional arrangement against newfound wholeness. Such a healing is often less welcome than one might imagine. When the man begs to join the disciples as they depart, Jesus sends him back into Gerasa, to friends and family. "We know from family systems therapy," writes Wink, "what a threat this can mean to a sick system, which must repossess its former victim or find a new victim if it is not to explode."[12]

> Therefore take the whole armor of God, that you may be able to withstand in the evil day, and having done all, to stand. Stand therefore, having girded your loins with truth, and having put on the breastplate of righteousness, and having shod your feet with the equipment of the gospel of peace; above all take the shield of faith, with which you can quench all the flaming darts of the evil one. And take the helmet of salvation, and the sword of the Spirit, which is the word of God. Pray at all times in the Spirit, with all prayer and supplication. (Eph 6:13–18)

Viewing drugs biblically as a principality would seem certain to alter the church's ministry in the whole area. It cannot be said to dictate any particular course of ministry, but does suggest a change in orientation.

Confession, for example, rather than condescension or self-righteousness, would need be more a point of departure. If the drug powers are the shadow children of American culture, then any church bound to the materialist interests of the addictive society will be hard pressed to offer anything more than spiritual cover-ups to the addict community. Insofar as the church itself is an addictive organization, as some contend, it will afford little in the way of alternatives or freedom. A church that needs enemies and scapegoats will likely be unable to truly love and serve those who have been treated as either.

In the manner of biblical realism, to recognize the drug powers is to be disabused of our naïveté. Girded with the truth, we get a fuller sense of what we're up against—more than a chemical agent, truly a system and a spirit. The depth and dimension of the struggle is revealed. The accompanying danger is to become, thereby, disempowered and overwhelmed by despair: Who is like the drug powers and who can fight against them? Wherever the church has struggled with the powers, Nazism, say, or nuclearism, or the demons of racism and sexism or any similar principality, we have experienced the same temptation to turn

---

12. Ibid., 48.

away in despair. That, more than anything else, is their power. This is also to say, we are from the git-go thrown upon grace (which is their downfall).

The alternative, long practiced, is biblical illiteracy and theological ignorance. The powers, unseen in their economic, political, and above all spiritual dimension are given free reign. Not to know is bondage. In this sense biblical realism, publicly practiced, is itself a *tactic*—by naming and exposing the drug powers their cloak is torn away. Part of God's work in the cross of Christ is this very work of unmasking—the powers are actually prodded into the arena and publicly exposed.

A certain work of exposure is going on in the relentless, if not obsessive, campaigns of the Christic Institute folks. They have sought, in particular, to expose the collusion of the drug powers and the covert operations. Because of the need for and the inherent difficulty of documentation it is a variety of exposure that takes on a conspiratorial cast. Their work, which would benefit from conscious theological reflection, needs to be supported but broadened and expanded by the church. Where can we see institutional and structural collusion? How would the church's gift of discernment bear on understanding the spiritual reality of this collaboration? Can this systemic comprehension make a difference to addicts? to street-level communities? Do gang members know their place in the political economy? Would it make a difference if they did?

An interesting version of street-level exposure has been simply for the community simply to be a very public presence on the drug corners (sometimes even with video cameras) shining the light of day on the traffic. Buyers move on and out.

The church probably needs to expose the drug war, which is to say renounce and resist it—at least as officially cast—a militarized assault abroad and a paramilitary one at home. At the height of war's political profile, some people were indeed calling themselves "conscientious objectors."[13] The war on drugs has only been a success in the manipulation of consensus. Apart from that it is a measurable failure. No surprise to those attentive to the spirituality of the power. When you fight violence with violence, violence is what increases and prevails. Violence against the drug powers only inflames and spreads and fuels them.

Drawing upon other struggles and other contexts of war, the church

---

13. Coy, "Conscientious Objection to the Drug War."

needs to claim the charisms of nonviolent battle mentioned in Ephesians. In Philadelphia a congregation near a notorious drug-marketing corner spent time together in prayer and active nonviolence training before undertaking a bi-weekly prayer vigil on the street.[14] I have written before (see chapter 6 in this volume) about the movement of crack marches in Detroit that process throughout the neighborhoods chanting and singing to reclaim them from the pervasive spirit of despair. Such refrains as, "Up with hope! Down with dope!" or "Pack up your crack and don't come back!" resound through the streets. There is something akin to an exorcism in this, casting out of the neighborhood a pervasive spirit of fear and despair. But exorcisms can be dangerous ventures. Casting out the demons may be readily confused with demonizing people. (Jesus himself suffered such innuendos and accusations.) I have come to appreciate the approach of the Glide Memorial congregation in San Francisco's Tenderloin district. They too have marched chanting and singing on public housing projects, but instead of a pack-up-and-go approach, the challenge has been, "Come on down, It's recovery time." The invitation, which takes the community treatment resources and congregational commitment to back it up, is: come home, get free.[15]

In Detroit, one of the most successful and intriguing ministries has been undertaken by Joy of Jesus, a charismatic neighborhood ministry with a phenomenal sense of "parish," a neighborhood territory or turf for which they take responsibility. A network of block clubs based on the "principles of Christ" undertake everything from pastoral referral to housing rehab and economic development. They are building a neighborhood that refuses the cocaine economy. One can only imagine a city in which all the churches took their "parishes" seriously as turf to care for against the incursions of all sorts of powers, from drugs to gentrification. Joy of Jesus combines this parish mentality with an understanding of drugs as a spiritual power (though admittedly less as a structural or global system), which means they practice a variety of prayer counseling with addicts and their families in which "prayer warriors" are a silent but present part of the counseling process. In doing so they uncover patterns of abuse that go deep, and often back to several generations of dysfunction. They contend that "anything short of dealing with the spiritual roots is simply conformity, to law or will

---

14. Betsy Schwarzentraub, "Neighborhood Defense: 'It's Recovery Time!'" *The Witness*, November 1991, 8–9.
15. Ibid., 8.

power—trading one addiction for another." They get secular and community funding for the program, because it's one of the few with a history of success.

Prayer has generally been trivialized or ignored in the struggle with the drug powers. Exercising the common power of collectively praying at all times, in all prayer and supplication, is decisive in the struggle with the powers. In worship, it publicly redefines the possible, changes the atmosphere of nonviolent combat, and creates openings for God's activity.

In that new atmosphere of parish and with an inkling of the powers in their various dimension, the kid on the street, say, can "just say no" as an individual exchange that understands the scope of the powers in their various dimension and is surrounded by the spiritual and material support of a community. It's the difference between a Negro woman refusing to give up her seat and move to the back of the bus because she's tired, and Rosa Parks refusing in the understanding that she is confronting a whole system top to bottom in that act, and doing so with spiritual, and eventually political and economic, support of her community. It's a genuine freedom.

The freedom is deeper even than that. What we require is the freedom that comes from the knowledge that in Christ, the drug powers have already be dethroned and defeated. If we know it, the struggle is wholly different.

10

Family: Icon and Principality (1994)

> [Such] are all principalities. So are . . . white supremacy, patriotism plus many, many more—sports, sex, any profession or discipline, technology, money, the family—beyond any prospect of full enumeration. The principalities and powers *are* legion.[1]
> —William Stringfellow, *An Ethic for Christians and Other Aliens*

This essay first appeared in The Witness, *December 1994.*

The holy family is an icon of Christmastide. It is an image of humanity, speaking of God's love for and presence with us all. It stands virtually as the seasonal emblem of love. We must not forget, however, that this is love under pressure. Here the family is beset, a family in crisis. They must overcome the public shame of unwed motherhood. They are moved about by government order. They are foreigners without resource or shelter. They become the target of violence and flee as political refugees. In these and other ways the family of Jesus represents the experience of family today. It is beset by the principalities and powers.

---

1. William Stringfellow, *An Ethic for Christians and Other Aliens in a Strange Land* (Waco, TX: Word, 1973), 78.

However, if we are to defend the family as such and speak on its behalf, family itself must also be numbered among the principalities and powers of this world.

Bill Stringfellow certainly counted it so—including it in one of those interminable and exhaustive listings of the powers that be: with all institutions, ideologies, and traditions, with the likes of the Pentagon, the Ford Motor Company, and Consolidated Edison, with sports, sex, technology, money, and a host of others. More than once he pronounced that he must write something on the topic: family as principality.

To name it so means to recognize in the family a social reality with a life of its own, a structure with a vocation to praise God and serve human life, indeed a creature accountable to judgment—to the sovereignty of the Word of God. It also means that we acknowledge the family as subject to the fall, as suffering a confusion and utter distortion of vocation, as enslaving (instead of serving) human beings, capturing them in the bondage of death.

Amidst the call for attending to the family and its values—and I am one prepared to join that call—we'd best be thoroughly realistic about the fallenness of this "most basic social unit of human society."

A Fallen System

One gentle way into this is via the therapeutic community's understanding of "family systems," let's say with respect to alcohol addiction. Years ago the alcoholic was treated in isolation as a solitary individual afflicted with a disease, a genetic or personality or behavior disorder. Subsequently, members of the family were brought into the treatment process for the sake of supportive relationships. But lo and behold, as theory and experience developed, these very family members were discovered to be "enabling" the addiction. The family member called upon for support turned out, often as not, to be a co-dependent. Finally, as the history of family counseling has gone forward, it's been recognized that the family is a configuration, a system of relationships. Even in its most dysfunctional state it operates to bind its members in a status quo, to hold and conform them to a "homeostasis"—"the tendency of any set of relationships to strive perpetually, in self-corrective ways to preserve the organizing principles of its existence" (Friedman[2]). Healing, apart from addressing this entire system, is often misdirected if not futile. The one who is sick or addicted may be merely the place where the pathology of the whole system has surfaced. The people are in the pattern and the pattern is in the people. It operates with a kind of spiritual force. While "dysfunction" is hardly an adequate synonym for the distortion of the fall, it is not unrelated. One may be literally in bondage to a position in the dysfunctional pattern. Naming and seeing (and then breaking) that pattern are key to healing and freedom.

Family and Violence

Going a step further, such patterns are regularly replicated generationally in what therapists call the "family field." So it is that violence, particularly against women and children, and sexual abuse are not only handed down but carefully and systematically maintained. The family, in this regard if no other, presents itself as a fallen principality.

In *For Your Own Good*,[3] psychoanalyst Alice Miller recounts the internal and systemic mechanisms by which the "silent drama" of humiliation and abuse is played out from one generation to the next often in the guise of discipline, which is to say, corporal punishment. Because of their utter dependence upon adult family members, because their love and tolerance for their parents knows no bounds, children are completely vulnerable. Their sense of betrayal, their anger, even (as we now know) their painful memories can only be repressed to be discharged later in adulthood against others—most often their own family members—or themselves.

The statistics of family violence horrify. Some 1,200 children die each year from abuse or neglect.[4] One in six Americans claims to have been physically abused as a child; one in seven report being sexually abused.[5] Of the 11,000 handgun deaths each year in the U.S., the great majority of these occur within the family.[6] Each day, four women die at the hands of their male partner. As the Surgeon General recently put things, "The home is actually a more dangerous place for women than city streets."[7]

---

2. Edwin H. Friedman, *Generation to Generation: Family Process in Church and Synagogue* (New York: Guilford Press, 1985).
3. Alice Miller, *For Your Own Good: Hidden Cruelty in Child-Rearing and the Roots of Violence* (New York: Farrar, Straus & Giroux, 1983). I am indebted to Ched Myer, *Binding the Strong Man* (Maryknoll, NY: Orbis, 1988), for his useful and pointed summary of her work.
4. Stephanie Coontz, *The Way We Never Were* (New York: Basic Books, 1992), 229.
5. 1989 national poll cited in Coontz, p. 3.
6. Benjamin Spock, *A Better World for Our Children* (Bethesda, MD: National Press Books, 1994), 80.
7. *Christian Science Monitor*, October 28, 1991, 20 as cited in Coontz, p. 3.

The family, called to love, to nurture, and protect human beings, turns out to be often as not the very site of violence, raising up members of society readily conformed to the larger—even global—systems of domination. We are in the pattern and the pattern is in us.

A Biblical View

The Bible is not unfamiliar with such patterns. It betrays and exposes them. When Phyllis Trible exegetes her biblical "texts of terror"[8] for women, all but one of them arise from the violence of power in family relations. Moreover, in scripture the first murder, that seminal act whose consequences mushroom in myth and history, takes place among siblings of the first family of creation (Gen 4:1-16).

Biblically, the legacy of family is plainly synonymous with patriarchy, though this is not (as much of the Christian family movement would suggest) grounded in the natural orders of creation but explicitly in the fall. The creation story clearly identifies the domination of men over women as a curse (Gen 3:16), the consequence of disorder and confusion, a very emblem of brokenness. And for a book that has been used to propagate patriarchy, it is striking how often the narratives of the Hebrew Bible, from Jacob to Joseph to David and Solomon, subvert the conventions of primogeniture—the inheritance of the eldest son is repeatedly preempted in the twists and turns of God's working.

The ancient Hebrew family bore little resemblance to the American nuclear family so often romanticized. It was an extended family and then some. The common Hebrew term is literally "house," as in "Abraham's house" (no small entourage moving to Canaan let alone trailing through history) or that most famous royal family field, the "house of David." As a social unit the Hebrew family embraced more than just those united by blood. It included servants and slaves, widows and orphans, resident aliens—all those who lived under the authority and protection of its head.[9] Where there were several wives, a practice also related to the fall (Gen 4:19) though common in Semitic culture and in Israel prior to the monarchy, the family clan would be clustered into distinct mother-centered circles.

In the gospels, the fallen character of the family is practically a theme. Walter Wink points out how often it is cast as a barrier to discipleship.[10] Whoever comes without hating father and mother, wife and

---

8. Phyllis Trible, *Texts of Terror* (Philadelphia: Fortress Press, 1984).
9. Roland de Vaux, *Ancient Israel* (New York: McGraw-Hill, 1965), vol. 1, 20.

children, brothers and sisters, cannot be a disciple (Luke 24:26). Is this a hard word or what? I came not to bring peace but father against son, mother against daughter, whole families divided by crisis (Luke 12:51–53). The call to discipleship supersedes family obligations: leave your dying father's bedside, never mind the funeral, come follow me (Luke 9:59–60). Family comes off largely as an impediment to the kingdom movement, an arena of temptation and betrayal (Mark 13:12).

Jesus's experience of his own family, where mentioned in the gospels, is most often recorded as a hindrance to his ministry (Mark 3:21, 31, even Luke 2:48 and John 2:4). At one point his family becomes convinced he's gone off the deep end and they come to fetch him home. He won't even go out to them, turning their intrusion to a teachable moment: Who are my mother and my brothers? . . . Whoever does the will of God (Mark 3:33, 35). Is Jesus not making a clean break with the bloodlines of patriarchy? Remember he may well have been of the "house and lineage of David." If so, the remarkable thing is that he never claims the authority of such birthright, almost always preferring Son of Man/Human One to Son of David, and even rejecting the latter as a messianic title (so Mark 12:35f.).

Neither was Saint Paul big on family. Among his notorious opinions in 1 Corinthians 7 one might extract some one-liners to render as principles of a Christian family movement. He does offer certain words of encouragement and advice. But read the chapter whole cloth and it's hardly an admonition to marriage and family. On the contrary, in preaching the radical urgencies of Christian expectation, Paul counsels a freedom from family's binding obligations and thereby from the driving anxieties of the whole world system. He may be, Wink suggests, closer to Jesus on this score than commonly acknowledged.[11]

Family as Image and Idol

Idolatry is an issue here. Isn't it always whenever a principality blocks the call of God or becomes confused in its own vocation? When the family places itself, or is placed, above the good of its members, it has become an idol supplanting God.

An example from the therapeutic realm again illustrates. In a dysfunctional family—be the issue alcohol addiction, spouse abuse, or incest—there is a tremendous pressure to keep up appearances, to pre-

---

10. Walter Wink, *Engaging the Powers* (Philadelphia: Fortress Press, 1992), 118–19.
11. Ibid., 120.

serve the family by projecting the image of normalcy. All members conspire to this conformity of appearance. Care of the image is made more important than the health and well-being of individuals, more important than truth. Denial and idolatry go hand in hand. The image is a lie.

The culture also sponsors images of family normalcy. Television images come to mind right off. In this respect we're still "playing old tapes" of Father Knows Best. In *The Way We Never Were: American Families and the Nostalgia Trap*,[12] Stephanie Coontz identifies the TV image around which a new configuration of family values coalesced in the 1950s. The happy homogeneous white suburban nuclear family that we all remember was uniformly portrayed in an array of programs. That image belied the diversity of experience and social reality of large segments of the population. It was a cultural exercise in denial. At the turn of that decade a third of the children in American families remained poor. African American families suffered the systematic brutalities of Jim Crow in the south and ghettoization in the north. Here in Detroit, when all normal TV families had moved to the suburbs, 10,000 black men crossed the city line to work in the Ford plants of Dearborn, and not one of their families could live in that near suburban municipality.[13] And in an era in which gay-baiting was nearly as common as red-baiting, many people were forced into the family closet.

Say it again: the image functioned as an idol.

This is pertinent in reflecting critically on the Christian family movement. There are some good things to say about that movement—and I will try to say a few further on. For the moment it is significant to note that much of what this movement yearns for is actually nostalgic worship of that cultural image. It would return in many respects to denial and conformity. It would urge family members to find their meaning and worth, their justification (the theological term is used here advisedly), in the family itself. St. Paul would be more than wary of any such source of justification save in God's grace alone. Apart from that, the term for him was nearly a synonym for idolatry.

Consumption and Political Economy

In the postwar period it was women above all who were urged to locate personal worth and justification in the family. At least for the

---

12. Ibid.
13. *Life*, April 11, 1957, 161, cited in Coontz, p. 31.

moment as the boys came home, Rosie the Riveter was being demoted and forced out of the plant, her services no longer required. The family image was sold in government films. Babyboomers were getting born.

And for all the "durable goods," the stoves and automobiles of postwar industrial conversion, the family became the basic unit of consumption. The American Dream had a new emblem: the single-family home with a car in the driveway. In the mid-fifties nearly the entire increase in the gross national product has been attributed to spending on durable goods and residential construction[14]—all marketed to that newly reconfigured social and economic power: the nuclear family.

Think of Ozzie and Harriet holding conversation in the kitchen. That Hotpoint refrigerator (proud sponsor of the program[15]) was nearly another character in the scene—the defining prop of any heartwarming American family. Or recall Richard Nixon's shrewd political instincts for taking on Nikita Khrushchev in the famous impromptu "kitchen debate." Here, he proclaimed, was capitalism's reply to communism. Never mind the nuclear bomb. We would bury the Russians beneath the superior conveniences of the nuclear family's buying power.

Here is the period in which the American doctrine of justification shifted from the "work ethic" to the "ethics of consumption." Though it initially fostered the nuclear family and claimed it as a locus, in the long run the consumption ethic is proving disastrous to family values. It "constitutes the major source of materialistic individualism in American life, creating powerful pressures against long-term commitments and social solidarities" (Coontz).[16] Throwaway culture comes home to roost.

This is only one way of saying that, overall, the commercial principalities of capitalism have not been particularly kind to the family. They have broken it down, inside and out. Early American families were held together with a measure of self-sufficiency: the family farm, the cottage industry and family business. Industrial capitalism removed its members one by one from the home, turning them into wage-earners. The Victorian family, sometimes touted as another traditional image, was made possible and sustained by African American families torn asunder in the cotton fields, the child-labor of the industrial mills, and the cheap domestic "help" drawn from immigrant fam-

---

14. Ibid., 25.
15. Ibid., 175.
16. Ibid.

ilies. The economic exigencies of the nuclear family have made the truly "traditional" extended and multigenerational family a thing of the past. The ethics of consumerism (now less and less focused on the home) have rendered small two-earner families the most common American variety. They lament having little time left for their children, or even for having children: all those "empty-nesters" and DINK households (dual income no kids).

The families most ravaged by the economic powers are the very ones most often scapegoated for the family crisis, those in the black community. In the economic interests of chattel slavery this breakup was a conscious and systematic strategy of repression—to fracture kinship solidarity and render the lot more manageable. Capture and the middle passage did its work, the block in the slave market divided further, then masters would regularly dissolve and scatter families. African filial names and traditions were suppressed, forbidden, and replaced.

Nevertheless, family became virtually a form of resistance and social survival. New forms of extended kinship and childrearing were improvised from African traditions. The "grandmothers" stepped forward as primary anchors. And "roots" were carefully tended to in oral memory and record. Even now here in Detroit an August weekend is special for black family reunions. Our municipal island park overflows with wall-to-wall picnics often with common commemorative T-shirts and always with honored elders.

Given the relentless assault of poverty linked with racism, given the mechanisms in which the regulations of the welfare apparatus often enforce family breakup, what is most astonishing is the utter resilience of the African American family. It has fulfilled its vocation serving human life. For this very reason grave worry arises as families seem to unravel.

In *Race Matters*,[17] Cornel West includes these same "sustained familial and communal networks of support" among the ingenious legacy of black foremothers and forefathers that have served as a buffer against despair. They "equip black folk with cultural armor to beat back the demons of hopelessness, meaninglessness, and lovelessness."[18] West is concerned that these cultural shields are now failing. A deep and active despair he calls nihilism, driven by market forces and market morality (touched upon above), has penetrated even black families. This he regards as a spiritual crisis. He writes critically of conservative behav-

---

17. Cornel West, *Race Matters* (Boston: Beacon, 1993).
18. Ibid., 15.

iorists who speak of values and attitudes in a vacuum, as if political and economic structures barely existed. Their calls for personal responsibility end in contributing to despair by blaming the victims. However, he is equally critical of liberals who see things only in terms of economics and politics, remaining blind to cultural issues of meaning, spirit, personal responsibility. Beyond both he calls for a "politics of conversion," which remains alert to the structural conditions that shape people's lives (one might say—remains radically realistic about the fallen powers and authorities), but which meets the threat of nihilism head-on as a matter of the heart, meets it locally and at home with nothing less than love.[19]

A Rightness of the Right?

It may be that something similar is also the best impulse of the Christian family movement. To suggest this does not mitigate in the slightest the idolatry of nostalgia, the naïveté concerning the family's place in an array of fallen structural powers, the homophobic ideal type that conforms and excludes, the principles of male headship that seek patently to reestablish patriarchy, or the narrowing of social obligation to a kind of self-interested privacy—all of these are deeply and perhaps essentially entangled. Still, goodhearted Christians (even at the mercy of cynical political powers) have become convinced that the family is in a cultural and spiritual crisis, that it needs renewing in its vocation, that time and long-haul commitment and personal responsibility will be required, that open and honest communication—even prayer and worship together—are key to this renewal. I dare say they are to that degree right. And that Christians of the left have been wrong in the degree to which they have utterly ceded the concern or simply re-upped in the culture war against "family values." Radical Christians ought truly to be family advocates, structurally alert to the assault it suffers, and nurturing its vocation in new and renewed forms through the politics of conversion.

I look around my own community committed to nonviolence and simplicity, committed to life in the city of Detroit, committed to the work of social transformation—and I am struck how much of our energies are devoted to life in families of one sort or another. Occasionally I worry that we are being domesticated by a familial principality (and need I say it's worth being realistically wary on that score). But in my

---

19. I am selectively summarizing his argument from "Nihilism in Black America," 11–20.

heart I know this concrete work of love is not a substitution but one and the same with the other commitments. We see the future (and seed it) through our children. (I have heard Rosemary Ruether say that one of the most revolutionary efforts around is the time and involvement a new generation of feminist fathers give to raising their children.) We resist the cultural breakdown of the century, by holding together. We honor the promises of partnership and marriage.

Resistance and Transformation

Amidst imperial culture in the exile of Babylon, the Hebrew family became a focal point of cultural resistance. It rose to the crisis of history. In the absence of temple and state the family-based festival of Passover was a vehicle of memory, grace, and survival. One thinks again of kinship networks bearing the humanity and hope of American slaves through a long dark time. How might the family in this our own imperial culture praise God and serve human life—even serve all creation—as a circle of resistance? How can the unconditional love of long-term commitments resist the market morality of consumption, resist the plague of materialistic individualism? How might new forms and ways of ordering family life and childrearing seed a nonviolent future free of patriarchy and domination?

Jesus once uttered a strange promise: "Truly I tell you, there is no one who has left house or brothers or sisters or mother or father for the sake of the good news, who will not receive a hundredfold now in this age—houses, brothers and sisters, mothers and children, and fields with persecutions—and in the age to come eternal life" (Mark 10:29f.). Houses and lands? It sounds like he had some new economy in mind. And this, inseparable from new patterns and definitions of family, must surely have been a scandalous pronouncement. It appears he described the "kindom" movement (to use a feminist term now current) as precisely that, a new family—simply one not constituted exclusively on bloodlines. "Looking at those who sat around him, he said, 'Here are my mother and my brothers! Whoever does the will of God is my brother and sister and mother'" (Mark 3:31f.).

Imagine families a very form of the gospel.

11

Spiritual Warfare and Economic Justice (1994)

> Christ is the image of the invisible God, the firstborn of all creation; for in Christ all things in heaven and on earth were created, things visible and invisible, whether thrones or dominions or principalities or powers—all things have been created through Christ and for Christ.
> —Colossians 1:15–16

This essay first appeared in The Witness, *May 1994. Also published as "Before Courts Human and Divine," in* Who Is My Neighbor? Economics as If Values Mattered *(Sojourners, 1994).*

Among the most important (and most neglected) biblical resources for Christian economic thinking is the theology of principalities and powers. William Stringfellow, who must be credited with the theological and political discernment that awakened much of the recent practical interest in the powers, first began to speak on the topic in the early '60s. Slated to give two identical presentations in Boston—one at the Harvard Business School and another at a nearby seminary—he had a strange encounter.

Stringfellow debated with himself about excising any explicit biblical reference or language from the business school version, but decided in the end to let it stand intact. As it turned out, the business school students engaged him thoroughly, bending his ear long past the hour appointed with numerous examples from their own experience of corporate dominance, of distortion and possession by the commercial powers. Their experiences verified his own observation.

Irony upon irony, at the seminary the identical speech was ridiculed and written off: ruling authorities, principalities, world rulers of the present darkness? Come now! These were but the incidental vestiges of a quaint and archaic language, an esoteric parlance now obsolete, with no real meaning in history or human life. Such was the debasement and neglect of the biblical understanding then current.

Stringfellow's insight from scripture—the one that rang true with the business students—was that economic institutions were creatures with a life and integrity, even a vocation, of their own. He recognized them, however, as creatures utterly fallen and in bondage to death. Comprehending this alone will alter substantially the character of our economic practice.

A certain public acknowledgment of this is present in the legal convention that considers corporations as "persons" before the court. More is here than anthropomorphic fiction: corporations are treated whole, as living entities. And, as is often the case, that whole is something more than the sum of its parts. The whole has a life and a momentum, almost a will of its own, transcending or overshadowing, even directing the wills of those who presume to direct the corporate body (so the business students confirmed). Here is an experience not far from Adam Smith's notion of the "invisible hand" moving in a pattern that no individuals completely control.

Insights into the "invisible" aspect of economic life provide Christians with the greatest opportunity to contribute. As the Colossian hymn attests, the powers are both heavenly and earthly, visible and invisible. Theologian Walter Wink has developed most thoroughly this understanding of the "spirituality of institutions"—recognizing their invisible, interior dimension. Beginning with the biblical record, he has inferred that "every Power tends to have a visible pole, an outer form—be it a church, a nation, or an economy—and an invisible pole, and inner spirit or driving force that animates, legitimates, and regulates its physical manifestation in the world."

General Motors, let us say, has a particular spirit to it (as does the food co-op down the block). Anthropologists brink on understanding this when they speak of "corporate culture." To join the corporation fully is to enter into that spirit and identity. And because of this common spirit, one could replace the executives, shuffle personnel, even modify the product line, but little of substance would actually change overall. Each institution's interior gyroscope maintains the direction and fundamental character of its values.

We are only just beginning to surmise the implications of this for the work of economic transformation on scales both large and small. Conventional economic analysis, whether of the Left or the Right, is notoriously materialistic, which is to say blind to fully half of social reality. We must be alert that real, substantial, systemic change entails a spiritual transformation as well.

The creatureliness of the powers also means that they stand as "persons" not only before the courts, but also before the judgment of God. As with human creatures, they are accountable for fulfilling their God-given vocations, for being who they are uttered in the Word of God to be. As Colossians puts it, they were created in and through and for Christ—which is to say for humanity in its fullness. Stringfellow used to say that the primary vocation of the principalities was to praise God and serve human life. Imagine General Motors or General Dynamics (or even the local co-op) held to such an account.

Of course each power has a more particular and concrete calling. The vocation of the commercial media, for example, might be to serve human beings by getting the truth out; the vocation of the healthcare system is to nurture and heal; the vocation of an auto company, I suppose, is to serve creation by facilitating transportation.

As a tool of analysis and discernment, "vocation" is at once a simple and radical idea. It means Christians begin by asking about root purposes. What is a bank for? What is a healthcare system for? What is even an economy for?

To some, these queries will seem naïve or simple-minded, because certain purposes are assumed beyond question, or threatening, because certain vocations have been forgotten or even inverted. For example, contrary to popular assumption, the purpose of an economy is not "to grow" or to centralize or to globalize.

Florence Nightingale: "I may not be sure what a hospital is for, but I'm pretty certain it's not for the spread of disease." Personally, I'm not sure what a defense industry is for, but I'm pretty sure it's not domination and annihilation. And I'm pretty sure the vocation of the media has nothing to do with turning a profit by the repetition of lies or official disinformation. As Jesus once put it (in loose translation), "I may not be sure what a House of Prayer is for, but I'm pretty certain it's not to be a den of thieves."

The assorted economic principalities suffer a radical confusion of vocation. It is part of their fallen character. They forget who they are called to be. Instead of praising God and serving human life, they imagine they are gods and dominate human life. They become literally demonic. Were economic institutions made for humanity, or humanity for the institutions? The bumper sticker logion "people before profits" is a theological affirmation.

Some years ago in Detroit, a bank ran an ad campaign averring itself to be the bank "where the bottom line is you." This of course is a bald-faced lie, as could be demonstrated in court, human or divine. At that financial institution, the bottom line is the bottom line. Though in the ad, it must be granted, some vague notion remains—a haunting commercial memory—of what the vocation of a bank ought to be.

The simplest confusion, the initial act of forgetting a creaturely vocation, stems from a power making its own structural survival the first and final priority. In the institutional realm of economic powers, this leads to a deadly "ethic of survival"—and becomes virtually the *only* morality that governs among them.

We witnessed this during the Cold War era in the clash of competing economies which, arming themselves to the nuclear max, were prepared to incinerate half the planet for the sake of "survival." It was plain in the deadly and death-dealing bureaucracy of Eastern bloc command economies (where Marxist eschatology had envisioned the benevolent withering away of such powers).

We see it in the predatory combat of corporate takeover with its contempt for human consequences in the devoured corporation. It is attested where companies move their operations (south of the border, for example), blithely abandoning communities to which they are truly indebted. It is plain in the famous "war" of capital against labor—the exploitation of human beings as workers.

It is apparent in the production and aggressive marketing of commodities known to be harmful to human beings—from cigarettes to handguns, from Pintos to Dalkon Shields. It is exposed in the contempt for the ecosystem, pouring toxic by-products into rivers and airstreams. In these and endless examples that might be named, the willingness to spoil creation and to dominate human beings, for the sake of corporate survival, is manifest.

The principalities' radical anxiety about survival is in fact their homage to death. It signifies, in Stringfellow's view, at once a worship of and a bondage to the power of death. Wink's term for the ethic of death, its spirit and logic, is the "domination system." Both are apt and accurate.

A few years ago in Detroit, one teenager was killed by another over a pair of fancy new tennis shoes—an incident replicated too many times in too many places. The event could be analyzed in terms of their family and social histories, but it is edifying just to identify a few of the economic principalities hovering about, at work in the deadly moment.

There is, of course, the international shoe-manufacturing conglomerate, paying women (likely in Korea) the barest wages to make the shoe. There is the ad agency, virtually indifferent to the actual product, whose work is to make the "name" of the shoe a household desire. (They certainly had a billboard just up the street.) "Name," incidentally, in the biblical scheme may itself be considered a principality—as in "above every power and name."

Then there are the principalities of commercial sports and in particular the "image" of the sports personality that has been associated with the shoe to inflate its value and meaning. The "image" also is a distant principality—often incorporated itself (and thereby having the standing of a person before the courts!). It would, I presume, be theoretically possible for Michael Jordan, the human being, to sue "Michael Jordan," the incorporated image!

There is the handgun manufacturer, probably based in Connecticut, muscling for a share of the $16 billion annual market. Here again there is a chain of marketing and distribution principalities—including some 4,000 licensed dealers in the Detroit area, and of course one of the most powerful political lobbies in Washington, the NRA, to keep the product flowing.

Finally, there is the general spirit of consumption, in which false needs are rendered virtually an addiction. All of these, and more, are at work in the shooting. This is not to say the boy who pulled the trigger and ran is not personally responsible; it is merely to acknowledge and name the powers, visible and invisible, who play an aggressive and predatory part in the death.

Jesus spoke of the spirituality of "Mammon." His ministry included a number of instances of naming and rebuking the principalities in a concrete and demystified sense. The action at the temple currency exchange was surely one of them. None, however, was more explicit and forthright than tagging money or wealth as Mammon. He literally named it for us. This is more than a quaint or archaic synonym: Jesus identifies Mammon's aggression in competing with God for human allegiance. You cannot serve both, he says.

Jesus points to money's invisible power. We are deluded to imagine that it is a mere passive medium of exchange, an abstract reference or token of balance. Mammon itself is a spiritual power that acts with a kind of autonomy, directing and controlling and, finally, possessing human life. We must not be naïve in this regard if we are to imagine and create new economic forms.

Actually, Karl Marx had a related idea about money as a spiritual power. He, of course, described it as alienation. Specifically, he recognized the projection of human labor and human life onto money in such a way that it takes on "life" of its own.[1] It takes on a religious aura and is made sacred. This is his theory of "fetishism" in which money (or commodities or capital) is "personified" and human beings are "commoditized." (A familiar inversion or reversal, no?) He even identified it with the anti-Christ, with the mark of the beast in Revelation 13! Money becomes an autonomous power determined not by the will of human beings, but instead by the logic of exchange itself.

How do we break the grip of this idolatrous power onto which we project our lives? Jacques Ellul writes in *Money and Power* of a certain freedom as the very thing that profanes the sacred power of money:

> Now this profanation is first of all the result of a spiritual battle, but this must be translated into behavior. There is one act par excellence which profanes money by going directly against the law of money, an act for which money is not made. This act is *giving*. Individuals as well as authorities know very well that giving attacks something sacred. They know full well that it is an act of profanation, of destruction of a value they worship.[2]

Where this happens liturgically, albeit unbeknownst and unrecognized, is in the Sunday-morning offering. We are accustomed to imagining (often as a thin guise for money-grubbing utilitarianism) that money brought to the altar is thereby set apart as "sanctified." Let the profane be made sacred—so go our prayers. To the contrary, says Ellul, exactly the opposite transpires: It is desacralized. I suppose money's vocation to praise God and serve human life may also be restored in the

---

1. See Franz Hinkelammert, *The Ideological Weapons of Death* (Maryknoll, NY: Orbis, 1981).
2. Jacques Ellul, *Money and Power* (Downers Grove, IL: InterVarsity, 1984), p. 110.

context of worship. There is something wondrous in imagining a new economy beginning at the altar, beginning literally in Eucharist.

Stringfellow thought the church had a unique vocation to be the "exemplary principality," the one that was not to be caught up in the survival ethic because it was not to be anxious about its own death. The church was to be the institution that knew the freedom to die—and thereby was the institution free to risk everything, all its resources, even itself.

One smiles at bitter ironies . . . but also at wondrous possibilities. Churches may indeed prove to be the very place that a new and renewed economy can begin. If we are willing to risk.

How does a biblical understanding of the powers affect our new economic practice? It is theological framework that invites us to discern the invisible dimension of economic power. It encourages radical questioning about the vocation of economic institutions and their confused inversions. It authorizes action that confronts and rebukes commercial principalities, calling them to repentance—to the restoration of their creaturely vocations. It nurtures in us a freedom from the spirit of consumption, and the grace to break the law of money by creating a culture and economy of gift. It thereby frees our collective imagination for completely new forms.

Perhaps last and more important, it may grant us the wisdom to recognize that our new efforts will not escape the Fall. Our land trusts and co-ops and neighborhood entrepreneurial projects will become petty principalities, will forget where they began, will be tempted by a survival mentality. It is, alas, even so with exemplary powers. They too, we pray, will be summoned now and again and always to praise God and serve human life.

12

The Powers in Healing and Hospital Ministry (1996)

> Who shall separate us from the love of Christ? Shall tribulation, or distress, or persecution, or famine or nakedness, or sword? As it is written: "For thy sake we are being killed all the day long; we are led as sheep to be slaughtered." No, in all these things we are more than conquerors through the one who loved us. For I am sure that neither death, nor life, nor angels, nor principalities, nor things present, nor things to come, nor powers, nor height, nor depth, nor anything else in all creation can separate us from the love of God in Christ Jesus our Lord.
> —Romans 8:35–39

This chapter was first published in The Witness, *June 1996.*

How many times have pastors read this passage at a hospital bedside where the extremities of pain and fear and death hover? Here is compressed a seminal confession of faith that often serves in those moments as the preeminent word of pastoral care. Yet one may be struck how it actually names the principalities and powers (not to mention their main methods of operation) in a personal and presumably private word of comfort. What gives? Is this a mere quaint circumlocution or do the scriptures offer the serum of truth, making us utter what we knew not, preparing us to expose the powers in a hospital room? I suggest the latter.

But be warned: the implications are great. If the latter, then the entire formula of pastoral care is altered. Instead of a schema in which the relationship of the pastor (or the pastoral community) to the person is featured as nurturing an uninterrupted relationship with God, we get a picture rather in which additional forces, visible and invisible, are at work. Systems and structures and spirits intervene designing to separate us from the love of God. Any pastoral work that is oblivious to these forces is at best hampered in the work of nurturing whole personhood, and at worst may in fact end up serving these very powers, aiding and abetting them, conforming and adapting human beings to their wiles.

For example, in the hospital room, it is astonishing how many illnesses are actually attributable to the powers. Cancers and birth defects, allergies and immune deficiencies, which are the assault of toxins loosed upon our bodies and earth. Addictions fostered in cold calculation by the powers of commercial greed. Corporate stress rupturing hearts. The hurry-up indifference to hazards of the workplace. All the grinding and chronic ailments of poverty. The epidemic of gunshot wounds pouring in the emergency room door, which can be traced back to the shipping docks of the domestic armaments industry. Hell, the economics of the insurance industry and government policy turning certain people away, gradually or finally, at those hospital doors. And this is just to name a few. Tribulation, distress, persecution, famine and sword—we are led like lambs to be slaughtered.

The pastoral effort is modified if an illness may be understood not merely as the tragedy of happenstance, but the assault of the principalities. Hospitals are probably the buildings in which more prayer is uttered per square foot than anywhere. But is it healing prayer that accounts for the work of the powers, creating a space for freedom and seeking to break their binding grip? Intercessions in this pastoral theology take on a new focus and fuse necessarily with advocacy or resistance. This is to say we are not mere passive victims in relation to the principalities. In so many of the above, be it violence, stress, or addiction, we are complicit in our own bondage. We cooperate in our own crippling ailments. Pastoral ministry, witness the healing work of Jesus in the gospels, involves nurturing or affirming this renewed freedom in the victims: Take up your bed and walk.

A bridging analogy from the therapeutic community to this kind of pastoral theology may be found in the emergence of family systems theory. An addict, say, once treated in isolation as having an individual physical or psychological problem, has, by virtue of understanding co-dependency, come to be seen often holding a place in a dysfunctional family system. In a sense the addict is simply the position in which the systemic ailment erupts, or is acted out with the cooperation and support of others in the system. All parties are in a kind of self-chosen bondage. The people are in the pattern and the pattern is in the people. In such cases treatment apart from naming the pattern and addressing the whole family system is all but futile. In fact, as Anne Wilson Schaef has pointed out, the system is much larger than the family. The patterns and mechanisms of addiction are endemic to our culture—they are replicated and writ large in what she terms the Addictive System, a synonym for the cultural bondage in which so many of our illnesses occur.

All this means that pastoral work, in the hospital as elsewhere, relies heavily on discernment. As William Stringfellow aptly put it:

> This gift enables the people of God to distinguish and recognize, identify and expose, report and rebuke the power of death incarnate in nations and institutions or other creatures.... Similar to the discernment of signs, the discernment of spirits is inherently political while in practice it has specifically to do with pastoral care, with healing, with the nurture of human life and with the fulfillment of all life.[1]

It is no coincidence that Stringfellow, who may be credited with reviving the current interest in the principalities, hammered out his theology of the powers partly from a hospital bed. He had been prompted to explore this biblical understanding first by the people of the ghetto with whom he lived and worked. The way they spoke of the police, the mafia, the social work bureaucracy, or absentee landlords as predatory beasts eating them alive pushed him toward the biblical texts. "In the wisdom of the people of the East Harlem neighborhood, such principalities are identified as demonic powers because of the relentless and ruthless dehumanization which they cause." But subsequently in the grip of dire illness, in his own experience of pain and even of commercialized medicine, he recognized the same forces at work. He described his experience of the sixties in this way:

---

1. William Stringfellow, *An Ethic for Christians & Other Aliens in a Strange Land* (Waco, TX: Word, 1973), 139.

The decade locates me, at its outset, deeply in the midst of work as a white lawyer in Harlem, but it closes in fragile survival of prolonged, obstinate, desperate illness. It begins in social crisis, it ends in personal crisis. For me, these are equally profound *because* the aggression of death is the moral reality pervasive in both and, moreover, the grace to confront and transcend death is the same in each crisis. Indeed, I do not think the two episodes, which roughly mark personally the boundaries of the last decade, are essentially distinguishable.[2]

The story of that illness is recounted in the second, and least-known, volume of Stringfellow's "autobiographical trilogy," called *A Second Birthday*. Here is a book, if only for the theology of pain it articulates, that ought to be a standard text in courses on pastoral ministry. It ought to be stashed, in paperback version, in bedside tables of hospital rooms. It ought to be prominent, next to flowers and greeting cards, in the lobby gift shop. That it is not, however, may be attributable to its being too hot to handle. When it names the powers, it includes the principalities of commercialized medicine. It names and exposes the hospital itself.

This is a key point for pastors, but even more for chaplains and for that matter any Christian working the hospital system. In Stringfellow's thought the hospital must be regarded as a creature standing before the judgment of God with a life and integrity of its own, a living creature called to praise God and serve human life, but one whose vocation is distorted and confused in the fall. This question of vocation is no small matter. And, as with any institution that wants its purpose and calling presumed beyond question, it is quite a radical and provocative query to put. It goes to the roots of creaturely identity. A hospital is called specifically to praise God and serve human life by . . . what? Offering hospitality in an environment, spiritual and physical, of healing? Serving patients by nurturing their health and wholeness? No training for hospital chaplaincy should conclude without putting and probing *and discerning* this question.

Equally radical is to comprehend the degree to which that vocation has been confused and forgotten in the fall. To the point is Florence Nightingale's barb, "I may not know what a hospital is for, but I'm pretty sure it isn't the spread of disease." The vocation of a hospital is distorted, often to demonic proportion, in a variety of ways. Certainly by the market mentality that puts profits before patients, seeing them

---

2. "Harlem, Rebellion and Resurrection," in *Christian Century*, vol. 87, December 11, 1970, 1345–48.

virtually as servants of the hospital rather than vice versa. By the idolatrous inflation to which medicine, as a purveyor of life and death, is inherently subject. By turning the person from the subject to the object of care. By the rapid multiplication of technology and technique in the practice of medicine. By the competitive anxiety concerning institutional survival, which supplants any and every other purpose.

Anyone working in a hospital setting will be effectively asked to serve these distorted purposes, which Stringfellow saw in league with death itself. Who, for example, does the chaplain serve? Is his purpose to be alert to ethical issues, intervening mainly so as to prevent the hospital from being sued? Or does she intercede and advocate on behalf of the patient? Does she smooth things pastorally in large part for the efficient running of the operation? Or does she risk rebuking and challenging the hospital in the name of health? In short, does the chaplain look for ways to renew the hospital's true vocation, calling it back to itself, to its identity in the Word of God? (This latter is the best service a Christian can render the hospital itself.)

It is when I have raised these questions in Clinical Pastoral Education seminars, that I've gotten the biggest rise. On the briefest of experience, students already understand the ways in which they are actively constrained in their ministry by the spirit of the hospital, which hovers over their work, requiring their allegiance and hemming them in. They perceive it as a moral dilemma in their role and identity.

A factor in how such questions are answered is often predicated on who pays the chaplain. To whom is she accountable? To the church or to a medical bureaucracy? It's the difference between the jail chaplain who has the keys locking the prisoners in behind as he departs, or one who waits the wait of prisoners in order to see those whom she serves. It's the seductive confusion of the military chaplain whose career is measured by the stripes on his sleeve.

Frankly, anyone exercising "the grace to confront and transcend death," as Stringfellow put it, may find themselves in trouble. In fact, the gospels are adamant to the point of redundancy that real healing may get one into political straights. Think of those Sabbath healings that so gall the scribes and pharisees. Recall how perturbed and provoked the authorities become should Jesus, God forbid, forgive sin to effect a healing. There is that long story of the man born blind, dragged before a grand jury of sorts and interrogated about the details of his recovery—eventually to be cast headlong out of the synagogue. And in John's Gospel it is the raising of Lazarus—a healing in the nth degree—which is the last straw in the arrest and execution of Jesus. Nor do the disciples escape this fate. In Acts they are repeatedly arrested in a chain of events set in motion by the healing at the Beautiful Gate.

I believe that is so because one power or another is invisibly involved in each of these situations, be it the law (purity code and debt code) or the turf and dominion of certain rulers, not to mention the power of death itself. I believe the love of Christ is at work in each of those healings, subverting the domination of principalities that manufacture, profit by, or sustain illness. In our ministries, we simply witness that nothing in all of creation can separate us from that love.

13

Death Has Its Day: The BP Oil Spill (2010)

The heart aches with another apocalyptic wound opened in creation, deep and gushing. Instead of the real healing for which it cries, poisons are poured upon it, dispersing and hiding the mushrooming bleed of underwater clouds. Death will have its day. To one degree or another, all flesh of earth and sea will know it. Suffer the sting.[1]

In the lust for oil, drones sail the deserts and robots sink to the deeps. Thus far the reach of the military corporate maw. And the doxology their choristers chant: Drill, baby, kill! Make no mistake: The powers, and behind them death, are at work. In their own deregulated design, they slip the grip of accountability to human life. They pretend to sovereignty in heights and depths. They set limits to their own culpability. They make themselves, in the imagination of their hearts, too big for political containments. They place their survival, nay their eternal increase, above the common life of all creation. It is time to name their blasphemies and prosecute their crimes. The Mother of us all will not be mocked.

You and me? With our southern Gulf shore? Our freeways and our ignition keys? Our transcontinental vegetables? We are complicit in our own captivity. We are guilty bystanders to planetary domination.

---

1. *Sojourners*, August 2010.

We are the users in a culture of addiction. Such is the bondage of sin and death.

Which is also to say: The healing of the planet and the healing of ourselves, inside and out, are one. Apocalyptic events reveal the truth, pull back a veil, break the seal, set us free. Such is grace. We best get with the transformation, dear friends. Be accountable to the Spirit and community of creation. Another world, one oil-free and domination-free, is actually possible. With earth itself, let us fight for it. Heal into it. Let it be.

14

Readers before Profits: The Detroit Newspaper Strike (1996)

> These corporations have no loyalty to the city of Detroit, no respect for our culture as a union town, no concern for the Detroit strikers and their families who are in danger of losing their homes as the strike drags on.
> —Grace Lee Boggs, community activist

First published as "Readers before Profits," Sojourners, January/February 1996.

It has struck me more than once how thoroughly our response to the newspaper strike ongoing in Detroit has been shaped by a theological comprehension of the principalities and powers. It proves both illuminating and practical.

The situation is this: Last July, six unions representing 2,600 workers were forced to strike when the company demanded another round of deep job cuts and refused to operate under the old contracts while bargaining new. Almost immediately it announced the hiring of "permanent replacement workers."

"The company" in this case comprises the two largest newspaper conglomerates in the country. Gannett, owner of the *Detroit News* (not to mention *USA Today*), holds eighty-one other papers, by which it made profits last year of $636 million. Just a week after the strike began, Gannett initiated purchase of Multimedia Inc. for $1.6 billion. The *Detroit Free Press*, meanwhile, is owned by Knight-Ridder, which has twenty-seven other newspapers and took $170 million in profit for 1994.

Together their business operations are fused in a "Joint Operating Agreement," which preempts competition, reduces the workforce, presents a single bargaining front, and last year earned profits of a million dollars a week.

It's clear the conglomerates are prepared to expend (pre-tax) losses of more than $100 million to bust the unions. That expense is already paying off in Philadelphia and Miami, where they are exacting substantial concessions.

In a long front-page article on November 11, the *New York Times* essentially declared victory for the company. The announcement was premature. This is an important strike. And the wider union movement knows it. The election of activists John Sweeney and Richard Trumka to AFL-CIO leadership has already yielded commitments of funds, staff, and vision. It may be a truly long haul.

The theological question that we have been asking publicly is both simple and quite radical: What is the vocation of a newspaper? All principalities are called to praise God and serve human life. In this case, specifically, that service is to the larger Detroit community by shedding the light of truth, by facilitating communication and public conversation. This, indeed, is discernibly the calling to which the paper is held accountable in the judgment of God. In the distortion of sin and the Fall, however, that vocation of service becomes confused, preempted, or inverted. The newspapers serve first and foremost the corporate chains, absentee owners with no stake in or commitment to the community, conglomerates who imagine the vocation of a newspaper is little more than to clear 15 percent profit. In that demonic confusion, truth or discourse becomes a matter of indifference; contempt for their workers is one with a contempt for their readers. Frankly, this is a pattern that may be recognized all across the country.

To frame the question as Jesus once did: Were the newspapers made for human beings (the community, readers, workers), or were human beings made for the newspapers? The slogan "Readers before profits" becomes a theological aphorism in this light, no?

Readers United (RU), a group that's been formed virtually out of meetings in our living room, has taken that phrase as its organizational maxim in attempting to be an independent voice of the community within this labor struggle. It was amazing how eager people have been to identify with the project or lend us their names. In a series of public demonstrations—one where we dramatically burned the scab papers, section by section—we have tried to broaden and reframe the issues at the front door of the company, particularly the matter of their role as members and servants of this community. In that light we've rebuked their bad-faith bargaining, violence, and contempt for the workers.

While the company daily runs slick commercials attacking the striking workers and their unions, we are organizing toward a citywide forum for early in the year to keep reiterating the fundamental point: What is a newspaper, and how does the community hold it accountable to that calling?

One tactic and handle of accountability we've just begun to reflect upon is the corporation charter. There is, of course, no mention of corporations in the Constitution. They assume the status of "persons" and a legal right to protection of life, liberty, and property under an 1886 court ruling initiated by the railroads. Ironically (to say the least) that ruling was predicated on the 14th Amendment, just then ratified to protect the rights of freed slaves!

Historically, corporation charters were granted by states for limited and fixed terms to be renewed only if the corporation could demonstrate that it was fulfilling its purposes (its vocation). Previously, corporations were prohibited from owning other corporations. Nor could they participate in the electoral process, financially or otherwise. Today every state (except Alaska) retains a charter revocation clause.

We are asking: Is it possible that this could be an avenue for reclaiming community accountability over the conglomerates? As Grace Lee Boggs of the RU steering group puts it, "We need a landmark decision in the mounting conflict between the interests of local communities and absentee corporations which will do for today's movement what Brown vs. Kansas Board of Education did for the civil rights movement."

Readers United has also pushed the vocational question with the unions themselves. Since a newspaper, being part of the community's life, is a substantially different product than steel or cars, the strike itself must be fought in a distinctive way. Asking readers, for example, to boycott the scab papers (even the company acknowledges circulation is down 25 percent) is to leave them in the dark concerning crucial local news—some with urgent political implications. It's not only strategically smart, but part of the unions' responsibility to the community to provide a genuine newspaper, at least for the duration of the strike.

This we have said in letters and leaflets, face-to-face conversations, and news interviews—recirculating a practical proposal made in midsummer. Finally, just before Thanksgiving, *The Sunday Journal* became a reality. So now? Now we urge broader community editorial participation. We urge the paper to be more than just a strike tactic, but likewise to honor fully the vocation of a newspaper.

This is to say, we are not unmindful that unions are principalities as well, called under the sovereignty of God to serve human life by serving their members' interests, by honoring the worth and dignity of all human labor, and by risking themselves in engagement with the commercial powers. And they too have a responsibility to the community.

However, in the Fall that vocation also gets corrupted. Unions may become more preoccupied with institutional survival and self-preservation than with the human needs of their members. Leadership may serve other interests in pursuit of reelection or be more concerned with guarding the coffer than with justice. Readers United stands with the striking workers, but all the while voicing a call that the unions too be servants of the community.

Violence remains the toughest issue. I speak of that initiated by the company, first the structural violence assaulting people's lives and jobs, but more directly violence on the picket line, especially where workers have tried to block vehicles from delivering company papers. Repeatedly, trucks have driven into crowds of strikers, resulting in a number of injuries.

Often as not those trucks are driven by Vance Security, the Pinkerton-like, paramilitary force hired by the company. Vance, which came into its own during the 1989 mine workers strike, advertises itself as specially skilled in documenting (by photo and video evidence) the violence of strikers in order to secure injunctions (the company managed to get one forthwith) and to portray violence as the tactic of protesters.

I have been present when riot-equipped forces charge or posture to provoke a reaction, filming from the roof. Driving a truck into an angry crowd does draw sticks and rocks, equally photogenic. The company's ubiquitous commercials "deplore striker violence" (in order to mask its own). Some of them show burning vehicles that I believe were actually set afire by their own security.

Yet the unions have been slow to embrace disciplined nonviolent action (after the pattern of the United Mine Workers, for example). An ambitious plan of escalating nonviolent action, prepared last August, was cast aside when the injunction came down and the trucks ran the crowds. Moreover, the most creative and militant caucus among the strikers adheres to the slogan "By any means necessary."

One witness of nonviolence has been Bishop Tom Gumbleton, of the Catholic Archdiocese of Detroit, who has been active from the beginning, heading up statements by religious leaders, speaking publicly and in the media, testifying against company violence on the line, confronting and mediating with the police. In his connection with Readers United, he has met with union leadership to urge the production of a strike paper and to exhort a disciplined nonviolent approach that could include religious-based direct action.

To my mind the question hanging fire remains: Will the unions embrace a thoroughgoing strategy of this sort or will the nonviolent initiative need be seized entirely by groups in the community like Readers United?

***

Postscript: That spring, beginning Easter week 1996, Readers United organized a series of ten nonviolent direct actions blocking the entrances to the Detroit News Building. I myself was arrested in four of those. Readers United was eventually summoned to appear before a hearing of the National Labor Relations Board on a "fishing expedition," though without any charges ever brought against the Council of Newspaper Unions. The boycott of the papers (RU declared them "morally unreadable"), though compromised in the city proper by the unions' own history of racism, took a toll on the papers from which they have never recovered, downsizing circulation, print days, operations, and profits. Nonetheless, the New York Times, *even if premature, proved right. The corporations prevailed at great cost to themselves, their workers, and the city of Detroit.*

15

Labor Unions and the Principalities (1998)

Thus, the Pentagon or the Ford Motor Company or Harvard University or the Hudson Institute or Consolidated Edison or the Diners Club or the Olympics or the Methodist Church or the Teamsters Union are all principalities. So are capitalism, Maoism, humanism . . . and the Puritan work ethic . . .

—William Stringfellow

First published as "The Power of Alliance: Why the Church and the Labor Movement Belong Together," Sojourners, September/October 1998.

Biblically, theologically, ethically, even pastorally, it is incumbent upon the church to stand with workers, to be with them in the struggle for justice, to join them in holding corporations accountable to human community.

The day before his death, in a prescient sermon immediately famous, Rev. Martin Luther King Jr. urged pastors and laypeople to support the striking sanitation workers of Memphis, Tennessee, by turning to Luke's parable of the Good Samaritan. In summoning the congregation to break the court injunction by marching the day following, he detailed the risks of that biblical "bloody pass," the winding road from Jerusalem down to Jericho. He allowed that the priest and the Levite may have been simply afraid, warily wondering if the robbers still hovered about, or if the victim was himself a thief lying in wait in wounded disguise.

> And so the first question the Levite asked was, "If I stop to help this man, what will happen to me?" But then the Good Samaritan came by. And he reversed the question: "If I do not stop to help this man, what will happen to him?" That's the question before you tonight. Not, "If I stop to help the sanitation workers, what will happen to all of the hours that I usually spend in my office every day and every week as a pastor?" . . . "If I do not stop to help the sanitation workers, what will happen to them?" That's the question.[1]

The Brickmakers Local

Not long ago I heard Rev. Joe Lowery of the Southern Christian Leadership Conference preach at a striking workers' prayer service, "The first labor negotiations in history took place between Pharaoh and Moses." Actually, Exodus portrays a pretty remarkable piece of negotiating (seven chapters' worth), with offers and counteroffers, nudges and reversals aplenty.

God, of course, had heard the cry of the brickmakers, on whose lives and sweat the very foundations of empire were being laid. Moses is sent. But after the initial meeting, Pharaoh responds in hardball fashion, in effect demanding the same productivity on fewer resources ("Let them gather their own straw," Exod 5:7). It is a demoralizing tactic: At the first sign of protest, make working conditions even worse. Needless to say, Moses comes to the table with no small leverage, those plagues, but Pharaoh's heart is hardened in a manner all too familiar to poor and working people today. In the end the people of Israel walk out for good, learning to make, by God's grace, a whole new economy.

When the prophets took measure of the nation's health, they always looked to the least—the widows and orphans and sojourners in the land, but also (the law spells this out—Lev 19:13; Deut 24:15) to the fate of workers. King Josiah got it in challenge from Jeremiah: "Woe to him who builds his house by unrighteousness, and his upper rooms by injustice; who makes his neighbors serve him for nothing, and does not give them their wages" (22:13). The book of James echoes that spirit: "Behold, the wages of the laborers who mowed your fields, which

---

1. Martin Luther King Jr., "I See the Promised Land," in James Washington, ed.. *A Testament of Hope* (San Francisco: Harper Collins, 1991), 285.

you kept back by fraud, cry out; and the cries of the harvesters have reached the ears of the Lord of hosts" (5:4). Notice a number of echoes here, in fact.

The Carpenter and the Fishermen

It hardly needs saying that Jesus heard such cries and pronounced similar woes upon the rich. He gathered a movement of spiritual and social transformation among the poor and unclean, among dispossessed peasants and common laborers. Notorious in this last group of working stiffs were certain fishermen of Galilee on whose callings recent archeology and scholarship have cast new light.

Richard Horsley and Neil Silberman have recently written on changes in this political economy.[2] For millennia, fishing on the Galilee had been a very local, self-reliant, and seasonal affair in the lakeside villages. Rapid spoilage fixed a limit on the market, localizing a self-sustaining economy. However, under the tetrarchy of Herod Antipas, who was anxious to make his backward region productive for Rome (by both taxes and exports), and with the development of preservative techniques in which hauls of sardine and carp could be pickled or salted, the pressures of a wider market seem just then to have been altering the Galilean economy. Romans developed a taste for salt-fish. Spicy sauces and fish stews were highly valued as both condiment and medicine. Magdala, lakeside hometown of the disciple Mary, became a kind of factory town nicknamed Taricheae, or the "Town of Salt-Fish." The Galilee, little more than a large freshwater lake, was becoming virtually "industrialized" and perhaps even overfished.

Against such a background the gospel stories of disciples fishing all night and coming up empty, not to mention those miraculous net-busting catches, take on a different cast. Nobody was organizing a maritime union, but when Peter and friends dropped their nets to follow Jesus they were certainly signing on to a movement that offered a sweeping alternative community—economic, political, and spiritual—to the dominating imperial system of Rome.

---

2. Richard A. Horsley and Neil Asher Silberman, *The Message and the Kingdom* (New York: Grosset/Putnam, 1997), 22–26.

Corporate Powers That Be

In thinking through the church's role to support workers in the face of forces that abuse or exploit them, there is no resource in the scriptures more pertinent than a theology of the "principalities and powers," evinced especially in the New Testament. Rediscovered and reclaimed in recent years by the likes of William Stringfellow and now Walter Wink, this biblical theology identifies the whole range of institutions, ideologies, and other structures of power as aspects of the created order, creatures, in fact, that have a life and integrity of their own and are accountable to the judgment of God.

Stringfellow averred that the vocation, the calling, of every power was to praise God and serve human life (see Col 1:15–20). Imagine General Motors or United Parcel Service or Caterpillar held to such an account.

Of course each power has a more particular and concrete calling. The vocation of the commercial media, for example, might be to serve human beings by getting the truth out and providing a forum for public discussion; the vocation of the healthcare system is to nurture and heal; and so on. As a tool of analysis and discernment, "vocation" is at once a simple and radical idea. It means Christians begin by asking about root purposes. What is an auto company for? What, even, is an economy for? In every case the answer must identify its servanthood to humanity, to the community in which it functions, even (and here we arrive at a crux) its own employees.

The problem, deep and ubiquitous, is that in the Fall these vocations are necessarily distorted, confused, even inverted. The corporate powers forget who they are called in the Word of God to be. In the fallenness of life, the powers cease to praise God and serve human life. Instead they imagine they are god and they enslave human life. The assaultive contempt that so many corporations demonstrate for their own employees is virtually one with the contempt they show for the wider society, and for the Earth itself.

Frankly, though it is a task largely unclaimed, the church proclaims the redeeming work of Christ in large part by exposing this dehumanizing distortion and calling the powers, including the corporations, back to their created vocations (Eph 3:9–10). A friend of mine, a Catholic sister active in all sorts of social movements, says that the only time people ever walked out on her in church was when she explained that papal encyclicals and Catholic teaching placed labor above capital.

With respect to corporations, the mechanisms and forums for accountability are becoming fewer and farther between. Shareholder meetings have sometimes been an arena for church suasion and action. Now they are more and more obviated by mutual fund managers who hold controlling interests from above in the name of indifferent market players. Corporate charters issued by states were once for limited periods and required the scrutiny of annual renewal and review. Now they are a legal formality, a pretense without teeth.

Corporations have been subject to the law and constrained by government regulation. Now, as corporations become larger than many nation-states and as capitalism moves into global hyperspace without the restraints of local or democratic regulation (as per NAFTA, GATT, or MAI), there may cease to be any effective point at which they can be held accountable to human life. Theologically, this hastening arrogation of global sovereignty portends not merely idolatry, but a kind of blasphemy.

It is also, as corporations shake off the remnants of political and economic restraint, behind much of the union-busting assault now at work on so many fronts. Hence, when churches stand with workers in the struggle for justice, it is (as in the past) a solidarity, a preferential option expressly urged upon us by scripture. However, (at present) it is also potentially an alliance on behalf of human life, a forum where the corporate powers may be reminded of their vocations and for that matter their creatureliness, a locus where the sovereignty of God may be in effect proclaimed, and a place where the interests of local communities, or even the Earth itself, may be defended. If this sounds as much like a call to the unions as it is to the church, then so be it.

Powers Closer to Home

Last year I had occasion to address a conference of United Auto Worker chaplains—a wonderful collection, it seemed to me, largely of Baptists and Pentecostals on the shop floor. I offered a principalities view of corporations, predatory and expansive. The chaplains and their union leaders loved it. I explained how the church too is a principality, confused in its vocation. In the death of Christ it is freed from bondage to the powers yet it is divided and ruled by mammon, racism, and the like. In the resurrection of Christ it is freed to risk it all, to die, and yet it remains obsessively anxious about its own survival. They nodded in knowing agreement.

I drew a breath and told how movements and unions are likewise powers subject to the Fall, whose vocations can be forgotten and corrupted, and need to be called back again and again to the roots of their identity, a task chaplains were perhaps well placed to undertake. The congregation voiced scattered "Amens." The leadership at the table behind me went cold. Applied close to home, a theology of the powers often meets a mixed reception.

Ask: The vocation of a union is what? Well, I suppose, to praise God and serve human life, human communities, by honoring the integrity of labor everywhere; connecting workers in the struggle of justice for one another; giving them public voice (or voices); resisting the assaults of capital and wealth; furthering the development of democracy and nonviolent action, acting on behalf of justice in communities and society . . . and more I'm sure.

Be biblically realistic about the Fall: Organizations born in battle and risk become consumed with shoring up, above all else, their own institutional survival; lawyers and coffers dictate strategy; movement becomes bureaucracy; solidarity becomes turf war or "interest group" politics; alliances become power for sale; workplace democracy gives way to overpowering incumbency (and its mechanisms) . . . and more I'm sure. However much the oxymoron "union bosses" may be caricatured and exploited in the media, it can signify in a nutshell the inversion of fallen life.

The vocational question, in both its root and fallen aspect, must be put again and again firstly by workers in their own movements. However, it also must be asked by the church in a way that gives encouragement to those within the labor movement working tirelessly for reform and renewal. As with the larger picture, the church's natural bias from within the union is also from below, beginning with rank and file, from the bottom up. Here, putting the vocational question, no matter how sometimes troublesome, is in fact an open gift of churches to labor.

Roles and Charisms of the Church

This is to say that when clergy and churches at their best enter into alliances with labor unions they do so while maintaining, nonetheless, a certain freedom and independence. They come without laying down critical biblical faculties. They come bearing whatever moral weight they publicly retain, but do not simply throw the cloak of morality over any given struggle. They must come as partners, clear about their own vocation and identity. They ought, I believe, to come with an active bias toward creative and redemptive gospel nonviolence. And because the churches intercede for the whole world, they would bring a broadening perspective to the table. They ask not only how the community can support this fight, but how this fight can serve the wider community.

One gift a church may bring, to any social struggle, is discernment. If the powers-that-be are realities both material and spiritual, as the scriptures suggest (being "visible and invisible, heavenly and earthly"—see Col 1:16), then comprehending their workings would take an eye and a heart for the spirit. All too often churchfolk enter coalitions relying on the otherwise excellent social analyses of their partners, without remembering that this is only half the picture, and that they have (however atrophied) gifts of spiritual listening to offer at the strategy table.

In like manner, half of any struggle is a spiritual battle. (Sometimes the corporate types understand this better than the children of light and engage a sort of "spiritual warfare" of their own, setting about systematically to break the spirit of hope and solidarity with despair.) Prayer and fasting and public worship and singing and signs of imagination are among the tactics of any movement that knows it wrestles not merely with flesh and blood (see Eph 6:10–18).

If the church is to step up to this alliance, it better be doing good theology. That might seem to go without saying—especially in light of the powers discussion foregoing, but I'm thinking particularly of the theology of work itself. Given the rhythm of work and rest identified with the blessings of creation in the first chapter of the first book of the Hebrew Bible, we are on a foundational theme. Given the entanglement of work in the curse of the Fall, in the broken relationship between human beings and the creation, in the inversion of dominion suggested above, it is hardly to be ignored. Moreover, all of this is reiterated and reworked in the Sabbath/Jubilee approach to economics (Leviticus 25; Exod 21:2–6; 23:7–11; Deut 15:1–18; Isa 61:1–4; Luke 4:17–21), which runs throughout the biblical witness.[3]

We ought, however, to be chastened to recall the historical import of such previous theologizing. The Protestant work ethic may be today so thoroughly supplanted by the "ethics" of consumption that it's all but forgotten, yet it played a supporting role in the rise of capitalism

---

3. Ched Myers, "God Speed the Year of Jubilee!" *Sojourners,* May–June 1998 and "Jesus' New Economy of Grace," *Sojourners,* July–August 1998.

itself. The exalted individualism and moral virtue, justification really, that it imputed to work, lubricated (if not drove) the social machinery of industrial capitalism.

With the apparent triumph of consumer capitalism so touted in the global economy, we are at a moment of crucial and perhaps radical rethinking about work. Questions abound. What is work? What does a biblical theology say about the basis of and right to meaningful work? Can labor now be decommodified? Can it be separated from the corporate provision of "jobs"? What is the relationship of labor and land? Of work and community? Can new forms of work be generated by communities, for communities, from the bottom up? Certain of these questions will be welcomed by the labor unions. Others will stretch their limits.

In all of this, the church will be stretched as well. Such are the gifts of the alliance table. What if at the turn of the millennium, labor were renewed as movement? What if the church were too?

16

Exorcising an American Demon: Racism Is a Principality (1998)

> But now in Christ Jesus you who once were far off have been brought near by the blood of Christ. For he is our peace; in his flesh he has made both groups into one and has broken down the dividing wall, that is, the hostility between us. (Eph 2:13–14)

It is commonly understood that racism is more than individual attitude. It is prejudice with power behind it. Yet looked upon with a biblical and theological eye, white racism may be recognized to be even more than that: it is itself an active and aggressive principality, a "power" that appears to move, adapt, and grow with a life of its own.[1]

In 1963 William Stringfellow made precisely this point in a brief speech at the first National Conference on Religion and Race in Chicago. Addressed by Martin King, Sargent Shriver, and Abraham Heschel, the conference, ecumenical and interfaith, was the first major foray of the mainline denominations into the freedom struggle. Stringfellow's remarks were controversial for a variety of reasons, among them that he excoriated the gathering as "too little, too late, and too lily white" (a phrase he would come regularly to employ in

---

1. *Sojourners*, March/April 1998.

prodding and provoking the church). However, his most provocative and remarkable observation was this:

> From the point of view of either biblical religion, the monstrous American heresy is in thinking that the whole drama of history takes place between God and humanity. But the truth, biblically and theologically and empirically is quite otherwise: the drama of this history takes place amongst God and humanity and the principalities and powers, the great institutions and ideologies active in the world. It is the corruption and shallowness of humanism that beguiles Jew or Christian into believing that human beings are masters of institution or ideology. Or to put it differently, racism is not an evil in human hearts or minds, racism is a principality, a demonic power, a representative image, an embodiment of death, over which human beings have little or no control, but which works its awful influence in their lives.[2]

Many at the conference were scandalized because they heard in Stringfellow's statement an invocation of despair. And yet it is just such scandalous biblical realism as this, which is prerequisite to hope for America.

What would be the implications of comprehending racism as a principality? What insights, spiritual and practical, into the nature of our struggle does the biblical view begin to afford?

In such a light, racism must still be regarded as sin, but in a much broader and deeper sense—as individual and collective collusion with established evil. It is willing complicity in our own enslavement to privilege (or limitation). It is giving ourselves over to an animate system of domination. It is thereby distorting our humanity and, as we shall see, submitting ourselves to an idol.

Viewed biblically, a power (and racism is virtually emblematic in this regard) may be identified as both structural and spiritual—having these two aspects in one reality. This is underscored in the creation hymn of Colossians 1:15–20 where the assorted powers and authorities are described as both heavenly and earthly, visible and invisible. Walter Wink (whose analytical work on the powers over the last several decades was seeded by Stringfellow's scriptural intuition) has concluded that "every Power tends to have a visible pole, an outer form—be it a church, a nation, or an economy—and an invisible pole, an inner spirit or driving force that animates, legitimates, and regu-

---

2. William Stringfellow, "Care Enough to Weep," *The Witness*, February 21, 1963.

lates its physical manifestation in the world." These are simultaneous aspects of a single reality.

In the struggle for racial justice the recognition of "institutional racism," that insidious structural element far beyond personal prejudice, was a huge step toward seeing racism as a principality. Ironically, however, the liberal preoccupation with its institutional character would prove progressively blind to its overpowering spiritual dimension. The African American freedom struggle, founded under SCLC's early banner, "To Heal the Soul of the Nation," tended to become more and more a civil rights movement with a largely legislative agenda. In the several decades since Stringfellow's address, the legal apparatus of our American apartheid has been all but dismantled. End of racism, right? No. We ignore its spiritual reality at the peril of our national soul. And there is no force in our history that has proven more relentless or devastatingly resilient than white racism. It is empirically a demon which again and again rises up transmogrified in ever-more predatory and beguiling forms, truly tempting our despair. The frustration we suffer is not unlike that of the disciples who were gently upbraided by Jesus, "This kind can only be cast out by prayer and fasting."

Generally, with respect to powers theology, the effort is often to convince theological liberals that institutional structures have a spiritual dimension that must be taken with equal seriousness, and then to convince theological conservatives that principalities are not airy beings waiting to swoop down on unprepared individuals, but that they invariably have their feet on the ground, being embodied and incarnated in social forms and cultural structures.

With respect to racism and social transformation, the struggle before us remains necessarily two-handed or two-edged, fusing social analysis and institutional reconstruction with discernment, prayer, and worship-based action. These may be held together conscientiously in parallel tracks or welded in a single spiritual-political act. It's no tactical coincidence that in the best of the freedom movement, the church was "the place to go out from." Prayer and preaching and knock-down singing were introit to action. And one with it. Under the charge of benediction, people would pour down the aisle and out the doors to march or sit-in or boycott. The powers of racial injustice to be confronted in the street had already been named and met and brought down before the sovereignty of God in worship. Their spiritual claim already shaken.

Prayer and worship are crucial to anti-racism work in large part because racism is fundamentally an idolatry. George Kelsey, one of Martin King's professors at Morehouse, wrote decades ago:

> Although racism did have its beginnings in a particular constellation of political and economic events in the early modern world, it has developed into an independent phenomenon, possessing meaning and value in itself and giving character to all the institutions of some societies. . . . When men elevate any human or historical factor to so great a height that it has the power to give substance and direction to all cultural institutions, no matter what the *raison d'être*, that human or historical factor has become a god.[3]

Idolatry is perhaps the primary spiritual mechanism by which a glorious human diversity, created by God for praise and delight, becomes in the fall a power of division, a device of injustice, a demonic servant of death. This reversal and inversion of God's good gift is synonymous with the fall. And it is predicated on the distortion of misplaced worship.

Another way of putting the idolatry question is to say that racism is an issue of justification. "Moral worth" and meaning are imputed to certain people or communities on the basis of their "whiteness," say. We are actually here on firm New Testament turf. Paul, by way of wrestling with the law, concluded that claims of justification, meaning, and self-worth, located in any ideology or institution (indeed anything but God's grace alone) ultimately prove bondage to sin and death. Consider the frightful energy of pure "righteousness," which fuels racial violence and hate crimes. Moreover, "whiteness" is itself an ersatz cultural reality, a social artifice without real substance, virtually a fabrication and a falsehood. That a lie should preempt and usurp the truth of God's grace is, well, the work of death's power in this world. Those of us who enjoy privilege on the basis of race, or who seek justification there, are truly pathetic victims, cut off from the rich gifts of our own humanity. (We are also cut off, not incidentally, from the richness of our own histories and cultures—all sold for a mess of whiteness.)

Of course, this false justification in race is elicited to begin with at cost to others, namely colored peoples, whose justification and moral worth, in exact proportion, are commonly seen as less. They are dehumanized—unjustified, if you, before the gods of this world. The assault

---

3. George Kelsey, *Racism and the Christian Understanding of Man* (New York: Scribner, 1965), 27.

on their humanity, which this both represents and sanctions, is practically definitive of the demonic.

When the power of racism reigns within the church, it is noticed in several ways—but primarily in the suppression of gifts. The Word of God in the Holy Spirit is forever busy stirring up and calling out boldness in people to exercise their gifts and faculties on behalf of the community and in service to humanity and all creation. Meanwhile, the power of death in the demon of racism is busy intimidating people, or suppressing, refusing, devaluing, and denying those very gifts and facilities, rendering them unknown or inaccessible to community and creation. (The same experience may be recognized with respect to the demons of sexism and homophobia.)

The more visible scandal to the gospel perpetrated by the rule of this principality in the church is division. The body called to witness Christ in and through its visible unity, instead replicates the de facto apartheid of our society. It is conformed. Be it by congregation or denomination, the segregation of the white church compromises, nay refutes, the gospel.

Read in dynamic analogy, the "wall of hostility" identified in Ephesians (2:14) bears upon us. The hostility referred to there is not racism as such, but the division between Jew and Gentile which the church had finally resolved to overcome in its life and community. The wall, in one sense, was quite literal. There was in the Temple a barrier defining and setting off the court of the Gentiles. On it was posted a notice, literally a death threat, a sign forbidding Gentiles entrance into the interior courts of the Jews. Paul, as a matter of fact, was accused of transgressing that very wall with a friend in the Book of Acts (21:27-36). He was arrested and imprisoned, a circumstance that drives the narrative of that book to its conclusion.

The wall, however, was more than a wall. It worked to represent all the boundaries of purity, the social architecture—often invisible, that separated the two communities. The law, in this case the purity code, which once praised God and served human life by preserving community boundaries and resisting the seductions of imperial accommodation in Babylon, had been made an idol now binding people to sin and death, and cutting them off from allies, brothers and sisters with whom they ought to be in community. The wall had become itself the very spirit of hostility incarnate.

We all know how boundaries are reflected in social geography, how patterns of power get laid out in space. I think about Detroit where

I live. Such geography has been enforced over the years in a variety of ways. Going back to 1827, the "Black Laws" attempted to exclude African Americans altogether from the territories by requiring them to register, showing a freeholders certificate and posting $500 to "insure good behavior." As recently as 1953 "restrictive covenants," real estate deed clauses forbidding sale to blacks, were still legally enforceable in the city. When housing discrimination was made illegal, the real estate industry took to "block busting" in the sixties, my high school days on the Northwest side, making bundles of cash on white flight (from whites who sold cheap and African Americans who bought dear) by concentrating the market on a narrow moving boundary line, one block at a time. In a further level of sophistication, "redlining" by banks systematically withheld housing loans from identified neighborhoods. Even now a more subtle and nearly imperceptible marketing device of real estate "steering" maintains such boundaries. And then there is the palpable spirit of hostility that lets you know that you are simply out of place, entering or traversing the wrong neighborhood. In Detroit, as elsewhere, there are certain thoroughfares (and not just expressways) that function as walls between racial communities. The streets themselves possess that palpable spirit which says, for example, "Don't cross Eight Mile."

Ephesians, which comes to us as a jail letter from Paul, argues that in Jesus's death and resurrection, the dividing wall of hostility has been broken down, and a new humanity thereby created in the one who is our peace. It continues:

> For this reason I, Paul, a prisoner for Christ Jesus on behalf of you Gentiles—assuming that you have heard of the stewardship of God's grace that was given to me for you, how the mystery was made known to me . . . that is, how the Gentiles are fellow heirs, members of the same body, and partakers of the promise in Christ Jesus through the gospel. Of this gospel I was made a minister . . . to preach to the Gentiles the unspeakable riches of Christ, and to make all see what is the plan of the mystery hidden for ages in God who created all things; that through the church the manifold wisdom of God might now be made known to the principalities and powers in high places. (3:1-10)

Observe how lucid the prisoner has become concerning the principalities. It's almost as though he sees in the wall a living reality. Something there is which does not like a wall to come down. It is as if taking the good news to the Gentiles requires addressing the powers themselves. Putting the wall itself on notice.

The Gospel of Mark, as scripture scholar Ched Myers has shown, knows the same experience in a different image. There Jesus is forever sending the disciples over to "the other side" of the "sea." Mark is the first person ever to call that turbulent Galilean lake a "sea," thereby invoking not only the power of chaos but the whole history of crossing to liberation. Among other things, this redundant phrase, "the other side," is tipoff to the fact that in Mark's story and geography, there is a Jewish side of the sea and a Gentile side. (Jesus feeds the people on one perimeter and then the other. He does parallel healings or exorcisms similarly on both sides.) And what should happen when he sends the disciples to cross over? Death threatens. The storm rages. Heavy weather would swamp or drown or blow them off course.

What could be truer to our own experience of trying to build alliances or friendships or communities with sisters and brothers on the other side? Something is there that says, "Stay home," which strikes fear in our hearts and prompts our despair. It may be a silent storm within, simply awkward and cool, or raging with hostility. Once again, that storm, that blustering barrier, must be named and rebuked with authority. It's nothing short of a baptism to set off in faith into those troubled waters.

William Stringfellow's source of authority and hope at the Chicago conference was tied to baptism:

> [Racism] is the power with which Jesus Christ was confronted and which, at great and sufficient cost, he overcame. In other words, the issue here is not equality among human beings, but unity among human beings. . . . The issue is baptism. The issue is the unity of all humanity wrought by God in the life and work of Christ. Baptism is the sacrament of that unity.[4]

As the Ephesians letter (which itself may be read as a baptismal meditation) puts it: the new humanity in Christ's body breaks down the wall of hostility (2:14–16). In this new humanity which baptism seals and affirms, our relationship to every other human being, every human community, indeed to every creature, is renewed. The wall has no claim upon us. The powers do not rule in our lives and community. We have died, with Christ, out from under their spirit and dominion (Eph 2:1–8).

---

4. William Stringfellow, "Care Enough to Weep."

The rite of baptism always has about it an element of exorcism. We vow to "renounce the spiritual forces of wickedness, reject the evil powers of this world, and repent of sin." In more ancient language, we "renounce the devil and all his works." That, I believe, is where the struggle against racism needs to be rooted, in the promise and grace of our baptism.

When the community that gathers around the Catholic Worker in Detroit renews their baptismal vows by candlelight in the Easter Vigil, they get scandalously concrete and specific about these promises. They pledge to "renounce racism, nationalism, sexism, and all other barriers to human unity...." They reject "the idols of money and property, race and class...." That, of course, is not the end of anti-racism work, but it is the proper place to begin. In worship. Under the sign and hope of resurrection. In freedom from the power of death. Where the principalities are already declared undone.

17

The Fall in Play: Sports as a Principality (1998)

> Human beings are veritably besieged, on all sides, at every moment simultaneously by these claims and strivings of the various powers, each seeking to dominate, usurp, or take a person's time, attention, abilities, effort; each grasping at life itself; each demanding idolatrous service and loyalty. In such a tumult it becomes very difficult for a person even to identify the idols which would possess one.
>
> Commercial athletics for example, represent a prominent and aggressive principality and—one might suppose—a more or less innocuous one. Yet the operation of this demonic power has significant *political* importance. By diverting citizens from politics and preoccupying their concern with sports instead of with politics, by distraction and also by substitution, it provides a vicarious involvement in the place of politics. American commercial sports have a political significance in this nation remarkably similar to that of circuses and athletic spectacles in Imperial Rome.[1]
>
> —William Stringfellow

When William Stringfellow queried Karl Barth face to face in 1962 concerning the nature and identity of the principalities and powers, Barth

---

1. William Stringfellow, *An Ethic for Christians and Other Aliens in a Strange Land* (Waco, TX: Word, 1973), 90.

named a handful of them: ideology, money, the state, religion, tradition, and fashion.² He also named sports.³ In Barth's view, sport, as a power, could be seen as a human capability that, in the alienation of the fall, becomes isolated and separated from human beings, experienced thereby as over against human life, virtually dominating it.

It is perhaps only a minor distinction to note that Stringfellow viewed the powers theologically as creatures in their own right, each with a particular vocation to praise God and serve human life. In the fall, that vocation is distorted and inverted, becoming an idol that usurps the place of God and enslaves human life. A theological analysis of sport within this simple framework is truly intriguing.

For one thing, at the core of sports there is a free realm of play, an activity, in itself as useless as praise, near to pure joy and delight. It is a bodily glory, an incarnational rejoicing before God that can indeed serve human life. For the Ojibwe, the Iroquois, the Creek, and Cherokee—virtually all the tribal nations of Eastern North America—the sport now called lacrosse was understood virtually as praise:

> The game of lacrosse was given to our people by the Creator to play for his amusement. Just as a parent will gain much amusement at the sight of watching a child playing joyfully with a new gift, so it was intended that the Creator be similarly amused by viewing his "children" playing lacrosse in a manner which was so defiant of fatigue. This is our belief, and when the Four Great Messengers came, the Creator reiterated to us that this game should be played.

Fifty years ago, Johan Huizinga wrote a study of the play element behind culture titled *Homo Ludens*. As captured in the name, he argued that play was essential, even definitive of human being. Next to the designations *Homo sapiens* (humanity as wise) and *Homo faber* (humanity as builder and maker) belongs *Homo ludens* (humanity the player). He summarized the formal characteristics of play in this way:

> We might call it a free activity standing quite consciously outside "ordinary" life as being "not serious," but at the same time absorbing the player intensely and utterly. It is an activity connected with no material interest, and no profit can be gained by it. It proceeds within its own proper boundaries of time and space according to fixed rules and in an orderly manner. It promotes the formation of social groupings which tend to surround

---

2. *The Witness*, January/February 1998.
3. "Introduction to Theology: Conversation with Karl Barth," *A Keeper of the Word*, 190.

themselves with secrecy and to stress their difference from the common world by disguise or other means[4].

As play, sport draws a boundary in time and space, defining and consecrating a field, setting aside a sacred interval, be it marked by a game clock or a cyclic rhythm of innings, say. The Kevin Costner film *Field of Dreams* (which has been the subject of innumerable topical sermons and enjoys an astonishing continued popularity) conveys this virtually sacred sense of time and space. There, a farmer's absurd and obsessive impulse to lay down a baseball diamond in his cornfield becomes a mystical pilgrimage of imagination into history and his own psyche. In fact, there is a key instant in the film that vividly demarks the sense of transcendent time and space. In a moment of crisis a rookie player from the past, getting a second chance to play, must choose to step across the enchanted boundary line back into ordinary time and space for the sake of saving a child's life.

Sports as Religion

It is a frequent observation, nearly a commonplace these days, to note that sports function as religion in America. This, of course, is a broad jump from "play as praise" to something more akin to "sport as idolatry." It is pertinent to a theology of the sporting powers.

The big three in America, baseball, football, and basketball, comprise a complete liturgical cycle for the year, each culminating in a massive festival, be it a World Series, a Super Bowl, or a playoff tournament. The arenas and stadia, with names like Palace or Coliseum or Kingdome, take on a temple-like character, overlaid with an accumulation of legendary history, collectively remembered. Bright liturgical vestments distinguish the teams (and even more so their followers).

There is a palpable spiritual element to sports—on the one hand regulating the enterprise, a kind of gyroscopic spirit of the game—and on the other the spiritual struggle of the competition. This latter is not underestimated by either player or fan. The combat on the field or the court is predicated on skill and strategic preparation, but above that (and within team and player) there is a battle of spirit at work. A better team can collapse mentally and go down to defeat under this shifting wind. For that reason fans chant and sing hymns (often to organ accompaniment). The home court advantage has less to do with know-

---

4. Johan Huzinga, *Homo Ludens* (Boston: Beacon Press, 1950), 13.

ing the particulars of the physical space, than with its meaning, with controlling the atmospherics of the contest. Fate and providence, "the breaks of the game," figure into this and may be influenced by the intercessory noise of the crowd. In homage to the fates, elaborate rituals of private superstition also arise.

Players prepare for the game under a rigorous mental and physical discipline, what the Greek athletes called *askesis*. (The monks, by the way, borrowed the idea of "asceticism" from the athletes, not vice versa.) Spiritual values are much touted in sport. An interesting recent example, somewhat New Age, is represented in *Sacred Hoops: Spiritual Lessons of a Hardwood Warrior*, by Phil Jackson who coache the Chicago Bulls.[5] It proffers a kind of Zen mindfulness that takes compassion and oneness to the court within the frame of a Native American wisdom. Or there are the more conventional spiritualities. In the wake of a conversion Mike Ditka takes his coaches and football players on a Jesuit retreat. I suppose it is no coincidence that Promisekeepers, the family revival movement begun by a football coach, fills stadia to overflowing with men. Something overlaps.

The players themselves become a host of saints, vying for a place not only in the book, but in the national shrine. Their lives become the subject of hagiography in the bookstore sports isle (which here in Detroit I recently noticed was larger than Political Science and Sociology combined). If the players are an athletic priesthood, then the media commentators (electronic and print) become resident theologians.

Dispassionate sociologists looking at American culture and pulling out their Durkheim (or their Marx), observe all the above along with functions of massive human bonding, social control, integration or legitimation, and draw the logical conclusion. It sure looks and quacks and walks like a religion.

Not all of them are critical. In the sixties, the neoconservative Niebuhrian and well-heeled Catholic theologian Michael Novak wrote a book called *The Joy of Sports*, which he has since republished.[6] It is a swooning tome, full of good writing and some sharp insight precisely about the religious character of sport, but (apart from some snide remarks here or there—about Muhammad Ali, for example) astonishingly uncritical. Confessing that sports are part of his religion "like Christianity, or 'Western civilization,' or poetry or politics," he acknowledges that the book is also written for "unbelievers" (non-

---

5. Phil Jackson, *Sacred Hoops* (New York: Hyperion, 1995).
6. Michael Novak, *The Joy off Sport* (Lanham, MD: Rowan & Littlefield, 1993).

sportsbuffs), "that they may gain a larger, ecumenical understanding of religions not their own." And waxing hyperbolic he is capable of writing as a chapter punchline, "If you think football is a violent liturgy, reflect upon the Eucharist." A certain confusion is afoot.

In the Mouth of the Beast

The religious function of sport is not new, of course, with U.S. culture. In ancient Greece, spread of the gymnasium with philosophy and athletics exercised variously around the altar was part of its cultural expansion (resisted, in fact, as idolatry by the Jews in the Maccabean period). In Athens, athletic contests fusing beauty with truth and good in striving for perfection of the ideal were held under the patronage of gods and to their honor. Olympic games were always set within the context of sacred festivals.

In Rome the games took a darker, though still thoroughly religious, tone. Contests originally held in honor of the gods became more regularly dedicated to the emperor. They often celebrated military victories, and became themselves more bloody. Today, we would say they enacted liturgically and athletically the myth of domination. At the dedication of the Colosseum, 5,000 animals died fighting one another or being hunted down. In the amphitheaters and circuses, schooled gladiators re-presented battles to the death. Criminals condemned to die (including Christians during the persecutions) were sometimes dressed to reenact mythic tales in the arena: one might represent Medea's rival wearing a garment that would burst into flame, another play Heracles burned upon the pyre, or another might fall from on high like Icarus into a sea of beasts, and yet another as Pasiphae bear the embrace of a bull. And not in the imperial city alone. Bread and circuses were propagated programmatically in the provinces as part of Pax Romana—with all attendant worship.

If Christians warmed slowly to sport, it is because in the first centuries they experienced them from the sand of the arena, as victims. They knew the games as imperial liturgies, one with the power of death. They saw them exposed straightforwardly in the cross. Here we might rightly reprise: if you don't think being thrown to the beasts a violent liturgy, reflect again upon the Eucharist.

Theologically the movement from "play as praise" to "sport as imperial liturgy of death" is known as the fall. It is not so much a temporal trajectory as one inherent in history. It is a movement we may recognize in our own history and culture. Sports retain their vocation to delight and praise God and also to serve human community, and yet in the inversion that is the fall, in the distortion of "religious" idolatry, they usurp God and enslave human life.

Of Idols and Images

The extent to which vast numbers of people find their meaning, what the New Testament calls their "justification," in the realm of sports is remarkable. The burgeoning market in uniforms, jerseys, and paraphernalia is literally emblematic of this. This widespread projection of identity and self-worth is straight-up idolatry from the standpoint of the gospel. It is in this regard that the religious character of American sport is so disturbing.

The notion of "sports idol," of course, is popular parlance within the U.S. Globally for that matter. Within the pantheon of sports, they function as demigods. Images of the stars hang like shrines on the bedroom walls of aspiring talents. (For urban youth these are saving images, not only of pride, but of exodus from the ghetto.) Because of the deep hunger for justification, their names on consumer items inflate the market value. They share in the wider cult of celebrity common to the age.

Michael Jordan is arguably the best to ever play the game of basketball. His hangtime moves punctuated with a one-hand dunk (from which the nickname "Air") replayed in slow motion are truly stunning. Chicago jazz ballet. His uncanny consistency to deliver with seconds on the clock have brought the Bulls a string of back-to-back championships. He has, as they say, "changed the game."

For what he can do with a basketball Jordan is among the most recognized figures on the planet. It is, at present, possible to market a new cologne with nothing more than the silhouette of his shaved head. His quick smile hawks everything from Wheaties to Coke, McDonald's to Haines jockey underwear. People yearn to "be like Mike." His signature on a variety of Nike shoes is worth tens of millions of dollars. Indeed it was calculated several years ago that his contract with Nike was greater than the entire payroll of the Indonesian factories that make the shoes. Of course, the Indonesian women stitching them were making $.82 a day.

Within the dominion of global media, Jordan's image is itself a principality distinct from his person. Incorporated as a commercial entity,

I suppose theoretically it would be possible for Michael Jordan the human being to sue Michael Jordan the incorporated image. (As a corporation the latter has legal standing as a separate "person" before the law.)

I remember reading some years ago Jordan's complaint that his image had taken on a life of its own. "It's like it is controlling its own self now . . . My situation is totally outrageous. People ask me to explain it and I can't . . . I'm like this little machine that's got to direct it, so that it acts the way most people perceive it should act." This alienated way of speaking, which in fact raises enormous pastoral questions on his behalf, is actually typical of what the New Testament hints at concerning the spiritual and structural power of "images," "virtues," and "names."

When Jordan retired briefly from the sport in 1993, the entire city was bereft, as if its own image had suffered a blow. "His shocking eclipse leaves Chicago groping through a temporary identity blackout," wrote one columnist. "It was like waking up and finding a vacant lot where the Sears Tower used to be," wrote another.

Big League Cities

To touch on the connection of sports teams to their cities is to consider the relationship of one principality to another. (A similar phenomenon abides with respect to university teams and entire states in many instances.)

To hear a sports broadcaster's report, one would think that one city took on another. "New York laid waste L.A. today . . ." In fact the identification is substantial. This year when Detroit's hockey team won the Stanley Cup, a million people (more than the population of the city proper), flooded into downtown, largely from the suburbs. An enterprising and very committed fan sewed a gigantic Red Wings jersey to adorn the sculpture of the "Spirit of Detroit," which it dutifully wore for days sitting before the City-County building.

Names and emblems often do reflect the city's history or economic base or identity. Bulls in Chicago, Magic in Orlando, Pistons in Detroit. A few years back, when Detroit was reputed murder capital of the world, the basketball team indulged and cultivated their mix-it-up image as "the Bad Boys." More clashing anomalies like the "Utah Jazz" or the "Nashville Oilers" come about when teams up and move (in these cases, from New Orleans and Houston).

As team offices become thoroughly corporate, attendant only to market's bottom line, they often have indifference or contempt for issues of history and identity, and are prepared "as the market dictates" to jump town. Here the symbiotic relationship is exposed as competitive. Cities aspiring to "world class status" want to be on the map as big-league towns. They need the Goodyear blimp to pan back from the field in a god's-eye-view to show their skyline as if in a set-piece commercial. Governments will raid their block grant budgets to write down land costs and finance absurd new stadiums. They permit themselves to be held hostage to the sports industry.

The Green Bay Packers, last year's Cinderella Super Bowl champs, are a refreshing exception. Here is a team virtually owned by the community, which bought shares in it years ago. It may sound like Wisconsin socialism, but the fan loyalty of cheeseheads will not be squandered by a franchise jump to a larger market. The Packers may be the true "America's team" precisely because they honestly have a hometown.

The Economics of Addiction

Insofar as fans themselves are alert to the powers in sport, it is with respect to economics. Salaries and salary caps, ticket prices, owner profits, destruction of legendary stadiums, the disruption of the games by advertising, and the general wreckage of spirit and tradition by the corporate front office are all grist for call-in sports radio and bar talk. People rail against the distortion of the game by big money. They know it in their bones. After the last baseball strike, fans stayed away in doves, dispirited and fed up. "A plague on both your houses" was the popular sentiment toward millionaire players and owners alike.

Just to get a sense, Super Bowl tickets these days run upwards of $300 and advertising air time goes for a $1 million per minute, in the main to hawk beer, automobiles, shaving cream, and assorted sports paraphernalia (shoes whose price is almost entirely the cost of advertising). I recently heard someone describe TV marketing as a physical process wherein the show (usually by way of violence) hypes the viewer into a state of internal agitation followed by commercials offering an array of solutions soothing to the psyche. Athletic competition is ideally suited, pumping our own adrenalin into our veins in pulses and cycles.

Put that together with the ritualized addictive quality of sports and you have a corporate advertiser's dream. The ordinary mechanisms of addiction, so endemic to our culture, are linked to a mood-altering substance produced by our own bodies. Those with ESPN simply mainline the stuff. I'll bet Marx's take on America would have been that sports are the opium of the people.

Habituated By-Standers and Violence

William Stringfellow highlights the debilitating impact of sports as a power in the political realm. Americans are controlled by them, he avers, being preoccupied with the distraction and substitution. Above all viewers are habituated in a spectator posture, which preempts their participation in real events, real decisions. Just as those in the provinces of Rome were rendered spectators by spectacles in the circus, Americans are pitifully pacified in this regard. Pax Americana.

President Nixon epitomized and caricatured this function during the War in Indochina as hundreds of thousands crowded around his house during the November 1969 Moratorium March. He let it be known to the press that he was not much aware of the demonstrators because he was engaged, as most ordinary Americans would be, in watching a football game. In fact Stringfellow considered the spectator element of sports watching to lay the groundwork for public violence: "It is a short transition from such popularized arena events, diversion, and entertainments to the staging of persecutions, punishments, and executions as public spectacles. . . . The political inattention and default occasioned by preoccupation with conventional commercial sports is just one way in which people are morally softened to the point where they become ready to be spectators at official persecutions and to applaud the lions when they devour their prey."[7]

There is a recurring debate about violence in sport. Some argue that it sublimates and controls violence, others that it socializes us to it, making violence legitimate. Novak is more with the former. He argues not so much that football can purge the human heart liturgically of violence, as expose the delusion of trying, though he does stress that police officers around the country know that during Monday-night football, crime rates fall dramatically. He seems not to know what battered women around the country do, that Super Bowl Sunday is regularly the day highest in incidence for spouse abuse. All that testosterone saturated in adrenalin and alcohol. Then half the men in the world's largest viewing audience come up losers for the day. I suppose they either buy something or beat somebody.

---

7. Stringfellow, *An Ethic*, 90.

If football is indeed a religion, Mars is no doubt its god. Martial ritual predominates in marching and formation. Famous coaches have also been warfare strategists. Its military lexicon (bomb and blitz, flank and platoon) as well as its turf-taking rules are long noted.

Perhaps it's no odd coincidence that urban gangs looking for colors to identify their members settle on coats and shoes and team paraphernalia.

Community, Play, and Redemption

Can sport recover its vocation to praise God and serve human life? I believe so. The powers may repent, as it were. And though we can hardly escape the fall, but we may slip their grip. All the above suggest certain responses. I won't pretend these are solutions in any sense, just hints and clues.

For play to be praise and delight, sports must actually be played, and for the sake of joy. Spectatorism may be the first alienation, the initial distortion in sport. This implies a participatory remedy, one that de-commodifies the games, de-commercializes them, de-industrializes. Put sports back in the common space: streets and parks and playgrounds (and without the shadow of professional sports distorting even the play of elementary schoolkids.) What if these became again spaces for transcendence, realms of freedom and grace where, as Huizinga says, "no profit can be gained." The best sports may be those with minimum paraphernalia, least vulnerable to commercialization. (Though it is astonishing how even pursuits like surfing or jogging become "technologized industries.")

Refuse to be a habituated spectator, be it in play or politics or the work of social transformation.

Get wise to the powers. Recognize their wiles and ways. Trust God alone for justification. I'm not being ingenuous. So much of the powers' grip upon us and our culture stems from the search for meaning and identity they cultivate in themselves. Withdraw that projection and refuse that claim. If you spectate, delight in the play, honor the tradition, but don't be a religious fan.

Where corporate teams occupy your community, hold them accountable as any corporation to the community as its servants in every respect. For God's sake don't mortgage the block grant budget at the expense of the poor, for the sake of the rich.

Boycott corporations that ravage the third-world workers under the cloak of consumer economics. Better yet, don't buy empty consumer sports goods.

Resist violence. Practice freedom.

Play ball and (as in everything) praise the God of all creation.

18

Global Economy: False Gods and the Power of Love (2003)

When Walter Wink was writing *Engaging the Powers*, the practical magnum opus of his book series on the biblical concept of principalities and powers, he stumbled over economics.[1] One long chapter turned into two and then was withdrawn altogether over doubts that he'd sufficiently treated the mushrooming complexity of the commercial powers. Ironically, nowhere is the "domination system" that Wink identified in his series more prominent or pertinent than in corporate globalization.

Globalization, broadly, is a moving theological target: a historic configuration of economic, technological, political, corporate, ideological, cultural, even religious powers in processes of competition and collusion, whose outcome is far from certain. Still, we'd best look this thing biblically and theologically in the face.

To the bewilderment of our churches and communities, urban neighborhoods are being altered beneath our feet—by globalization, above all by its corporate form. Family farms, campos, and swaths of countryside are being seized and decimated. Local cultures and

---

1. "False Gods and the Power of Love: Principalities of the Global Economy," *Sojourners*, November/December 2003.

political economies are being strip-mined, preempted, or in some cases flat-out destroyed. Creation is being assaulted and despoiled. Even the terrorism that so exercises the American consciousness is a fact of globalization. Its emblem, the 9-11 tower collapse, was reputedly set in motion by an expansive religious and ideological network that turned the vehicles of global transport against the central symbols of worldwide economic and military power.

In Walter Wink's biblical analysis, as in William Stringfellow's theology, the powers are seen to be creatures, at once material and spiritual (Col 1:15f.), with a life and integrity of their own, fashioned to serve humanity (Genesis 1), and subject to the judgment of God. The issue of that judgment is each power's particular vocation to praise God in serving human life. But in the ubiquity of the Fall, confused by human idolatry, and subject to anxiety about their own survival, those vocations become distorted and inverted: The powers, instead, imagine they are gods and enslave human life. They slip the grip of human accountability and service to creation. Instead of "holding together in Christ," they coalesce into a system of domination. They serve Death.

History as Parable

In the 1700s, given three-continent slaving operations and royally chartered corporations like the East India and the Hudson Bay companies that were specifically designed for colonial extraction, the new Americans had good reason to be wary of these "creatures" (corporations) and set out to keep them on a short lease.[2] Initially, only state legislatures could charter corporations, with the charter specifying a narrow and discrete purpose that would contribute to the common good. Each charter had to be renewed annually, subject to public debate about its fulfillment of this purpose. (Notice the relation of this purpose to the theological matter of vocation.) Charters had a twenty- to fifty-year limit and could be revoked at any time (their finitude was named and underscored). Owners were held responsible for injuries. Corporations were forbidden from owning other corporations or from participating in political life in any way, including financial contributions (already then an obvious conflict of interest). The amount of capital they could amass was strictly limited, and shareholders were required to be local residents. We've come a long way, no?

---

2. David C. Korten, *When Corporations Rule the World* (West Hartford: Kumarian Press, Inc. and Berett-Koehler Publishers Inc., 1996), 55.

For a century these restrictions were the subject of legal battles. Then, during the Civil War, corporations proliferated in providing munitions, supplies, and food for the military. Following the war, the constraints against corporations were virtually unwritten at their own behest through court rulings and legislative action. Soon corporate charters were issued in perpetuity (now *there's* a theological shift); owners and managers were relieved of their accountability. A watershed 1886 Supreme Court ruling, truly incoherent and without argument, applied the 14th Amendment (written, so goes a bitter irony, to guarantee the rights of former slaves) to corporations, granting them status as "persons" before the law. In a single blow this struck down scores of local, state, and federal laws designed to hold them in their place or protect human communities from their abuse, vastly expanding the realm of corporate freedom.

Theological aside: The "personhood" of corporations would seem to comport strikingly with their creaturely status before God. But to grant them "equality" with human beings while simultaneously advancing their scope, scale, and freedom—not to mention supplying them in perpetuity the delusion of eternal life—is a theological confusion fraught with dire spiritual and political consequences we have only begun to reap. In this parable of the Fall, the corporate powers are well on their way to imagining they are gods and enslaving human life.

At times human communities have attempted to rein them back in. The rise of organized labor as a countervailing force on the side of workers furnishes one example, though even that the corporations sought to co-opt into a compromise arrangement that they abandoned once it became inconvenient. Another example, anti-trust legislation, attempted to break up monopolies and regulate capital consolidation, but enjoyed temporary success at best.

Slipping the Grip of Human Accountability

Fast-forward to the present moment. For a decade or more, half of the world's largest economies have been global corporations. The trend is not slowing. In that same period, the corporate powers have been less concerned with altering local and state legislation than with drafting a whole new body of international law. Under the rubric of NAFTA and GATT and finally with the 1995 creation of the World Trade Organization, a global superstructure is forming to serve their interests. Through closed-door panels that negotiate down "trade barriers" and so manage the global markets, the corporations have engineered a means to preempt, obviate, and abolish not only local legislation and regulation, but state and national law as well. They place themselves, or their "rights," above the law as it were, but mainly above accountability to human communities. (It's only a short theological hop, perhaps one and the same, to presuming as well their exemption from the judgment of God.)

For this reason among others, corporate globalization is a systematic assault on community, indeed on faith and politics. For their money and by their lights, the corporations see the market itself as the last vestige of accountability, be it the stock-invested "owners" or consumers themselves. So goes their vision and plan for democracy: one dollar, one vote.

The Preeminent Power?

Thirty years ago William Stringfellow wrote that the power-wielding apparatus of the state was the preeminent principality. He was right, certainly in that moment. Among the de facto hierarchy of powers, the state still holds an archetypal preeminence, in part because its authority—in taxing, policing, imprisoning, or war-making—is most explicitly the power of death.

Corporate security forces are not yet private armies (though that day may come—glimpse the oil companies' employ of paramilitary forces in Colombia or Nigeria). But given the overbalancing scale of corporate economies and the way they more and more direct state power, we may find ourselves at a historic, even theological, watershed. It is a shifting point where, for example, debtor nations—under the structural readjustment pressures of the World Bank and the IMF—are essentially being forced to abdicate not only their sovereignty but their vocational responsibility for the common good, privatizing services and resources, eliminating protective regulations, cutting government programs for education and the poor, opening markets to predatory global powers. Downsizing government in every way except militarily. Hell (I use the theological expletive advisedly), the so-called industrial powers are doing the same thing, sometimes willingly, often as not under the sway of indebtedness.

Most striking currently is the revised role of American empire. At the very moment that the global corporations are drafting a new body of international law to secure their virtual deification (or "apotheosis," in theological language), U.S. preemptive war (along with its systematic withdrawal from treaty after treaty) is shredding a previously longstanding body of international law regulating nation-states.

The "National Security Strategy" of the current U.S. regime is much discussed, particularly this policy of unilateral preemptive war called the Bush doctrine (to use a term hinting at theology). What seems less noticed is the fusion of that imperial policy with the agenda of the global corporations, specifically these very same articles of faith: privatization, deregulation, free markets, and political downsizing. Iraq is to be the proof of the pudding: If petrodollars render a national economy impervious to structural adjustment, and a decade of sanctions can't bring its dictator down, can the extraction be simply imposed by military power?

The Strategy document spends a full chapter on the administration's commitment to "ignite a new era of global economic growth through free markets and free trade": the power of death and the power of mammon made one. Wendell Berry argues in "A Citizen's Response to the National Security Strategy of the United States of America," an essay first published in *Orion* magazine, that this fusion is an absurd and unworkable contradiction. "How nations, let alone regions and communities, are to shape and protect themselves within this 'global economy' is far from clear," he writes. "Nor is it clear how the global economy can hope to survive the wars of nations."[3] Like nothing else it epitomizes the odd mix of collusion and competition that Stringfellow called the "realm of chaos" in which the fallen powers abide.

One key question of theological ethics and practice in the present moment concerns whether Christians should be siding with the nations as a countervailing force to constrain the global corporations or whether place-based local resistance and spiritually grounded community alternatives are actually more faithful and effective.

An Ethic of Un-Finite Growth

When Stringfellow pulled together his most lucid statement on the principalities thirty years ago, he also identified the powers as dominated by an "ethic of survival"—one rooted in anxiety about their own finitude and death. This ethic, essentially an idolatry that denies the mortal creatureliness of the principalities, is the mechanism by which

---

3. https://orionmagazine.org/article/a-citizens-response-to-the-national-security-strategy/ (accessed June 8, 2017).

their vocations to praise God and serve human life are supplanted and lost. It is emblematic of the Fall.

In the present configuration, however, one notices an ethic not merely of survival but of infinite growth. Insofar as the global corporations are predatory of one another, survival is an issue, but more often predation and merger are indistinguishable, and both are driven by growth. Growth also supplants vocation, only more so. Human beings, their jobs, and communities are swept aside and shed as so much surplus baggage in the process. Expansion of capital, expansion of markets, expansion of market share are endless and in principle eternal. In a living organism (which is precisely what these powers are!) uncontrolled growth would be called a cancer. It would be named as a form of death. Indeed.

If there is an idol behind the idols of corporate globalization, it is Mammon. Here is the spirituality that drives the logic of growth. Capital consolidates. Money begets money. The rich get richer. The bottom line is acquisitive. Name it as you like. As gift has given way to exchange, now exchange gives way to expansion. And because money has this numinosity—this almost sacred or spiritual nature—because it is the realm of the "holy" in this global culture, growth is somehow mysteriously beyond question. It goes without saying. It possesses an ontological birthright. It simply is.

The Spirituality of Resistance

Love hopes all things (and casts out fear). This is to say that the tactical question already mentioned is inseparable from the spiritual resources of faith community. Mammon's grip will not be broken merely by dismantling and restructuring. Corporate powers in their fallenness have an invisible spiritual dimension that can only be met with the weapons of the spirit. David Korten, an economist and global analyst not widely known for his mysticism, writes:

> It is well demonstrated that people who experience an abundance of love in their lives rarely seek solace in compulsive, exclusionary personal acquisition. In contrast, no extreme of material indulgence can ever be "enough" for the emotionally deprived as all the riches of the material world become insufficient to support the demands placed on them. Thus, a world starved of love becomes a world of material scarcity. In contrast, a world with abundant love is also a world of material abundance.[4]

If theological ethics in the present moment is required to be richly diverse and, as Stringfellow put it, improvisational, it will nonetheless consistently entail the renewal of our humanity and building up of community in love. In everything we do. Whether we are recovering spiritually from the most recent war, or resisting the manipulated fears of terrorist attack, or suffering the temptations of consumer culture, or summoning the resources to confront the corporate powers, we need to attend together constantly to our hearts and our humanity. We need to make prayers and music and poetry. And in so doing, remember that we are beloved.

Love can neither be individualized nor commodified (though Lord knows the powers and the market mightily try). It is always embodied in a beloved community. All that we do in response to corporate globalization should be one with building community, be it protest and organizing or local development.

In Greensboro, North Carolina, a recent struggle at a corporate warehouse threatened to divide workers on racial lines. But local pastors understood that this was not just a labor dispute but a community struggle, and they named it so. Their direct action and local boycotting was more than just labor solidarity, it was the opportunity to nurture the beloved community. Their successful campaign (which in fact yielded a union contract) is being commended as an important model to the labor movement, whose traditional shop-floor, place-based organizing has been so undercut by globalization.

If the corporate powers are to be confronted and rebuked, if they are to be summoned to accountability and called to the renewal of their own vocations to serve human life, it will only be by those on the way to beloved community.

The churches, at least ones rooted in scripture, know a thing or two about this. For us, love is a gift of the one who has entered history and our hearts, changing everything. The incarnation is itself the renewal of our humanity, and the ground of our hope as well.

Specifically, the incarnation means that God has entered into human history and community. Invisible as a back-alley birth or a backwater resurrection, love is at work, hidden in the depths of history, breaking

---

4. Korten, *When Corporations Rule the World*, 267.

in to break out. Things are way more dynamic and alive than the powers calculate. Their self-constructed claim to be in control is actually self-deceived. Their new configuration, this apotheosis of domination, is already crumbling at the base. The sand shifts beneath its foundation. Love will out.

19

Unholy Alliance: John Wesley and Global Powers of Slavery (2003)

> And what is their gain? Is it not the blood of these men? Who then would envy their large estates and sumptuous palaces? A curse is in the midst of them: The curse of God cleaves to the stones, the timber, the furniture of them. The curse of God is in their gardens, their walks, their groves; a fire that burns to the nethermost hell! Blood, blood is there: The foundation, the floor, the walls, the roof are stained with blood![1]
>
> —John Wesley, *Thoughts on Slavery*

Now, it is your money that pays the merchant, and through him the captain and the African butchers. You therefore are guilty, yea, principally guilty, of all these frauds, robberies, and murders. You are the spring that puts all the rest in motion; they would not stir a step without you; therefore, the blood of all these wretches who die before their time, whether in their country or elsewhere, lies upon your head. "The blood of thy brother" (for, whether thou wilt believe it or no, such he is in the sight of Him that made him) "crieth against thee from the earth," from the ship, and from the waters. O, whatever it costs, put a stop to its cry before it be

---

1. "Thoughts Upon Slavery," *Works of John Wesley*, ed. Thomas Jackson, 1872, vol. XI, 59–79.

too late: Instantly, at any price, were it the half of your goods, deliver thyself from blood-guiltiness! Thy hands, thy bed, thy furniture, thy house, thy lands, are at present stained with blood.[2]

—John Wesley, *The Uses of Money*

These two texts which, apart from certain archaisms, ring like copy for a passionate leaflet at a Pentagon or a WTO direct action, are actually remarkable utterances of prophetic ire by John Wesley, founder of Methodism in the eighteenth century.[3] What may indeed be most striking is that both concern economic violence, though in their similarity the first is directed to the distillers and the second to slavers.

This same ethical coincidence is reiterated in Wesley's general rules, the lifestyle discipline of the Methodist movement. Under the rule of nonviolence ("do no harm") are found these same two injunctions side by side: against "buying or selling slaves" and "buying or selling spiritous liquors."

What is so remarkable about this conjunction is that without benefit of the modern tools of social analysis as such, John Wesley has put his fingers instinctively on the two pivots of the transatlantic triangle with its infamous "middle passage." He had thereby set the Methodist movement not merely against a set of immoral practices, but effectively against a deadly structure, an imperial system with a global reach.

In its most straightforward version, the notorious triangle worked like this: sugar cane, which had been brought to the Americas by Columbus, was grown with slave labor in the West Indies, first Barbados and then Jamaica among other islands. Molasses, a by-product of sugar refinement, was taken by ships to their homeports in New England (Boston and Newport primarily) where it was distilled into rum. Much of this spiritous liquor was in turn loaded back onto the ships sailing for the Gold Coast of Africa at which point it was used to purchase slaves who were packed as human commodities into coffin-like holds and taken to the West Indies to work the sugar plantations. From whence, says Wesley, from sea and earth, their blood cries out to the God.

Two bitter ironies of this system occur. One is that the slaves were forced to produce the very thing that procured their enslavement. (To think of it, this is actually the case with most all forms of domina-

---

2. "The Use of Money," in *Sermons on Several Occasions* (Naperville, IL: Alec R. Allenson, Inc., 1944), 581.
3. *Christian Social Action*, July/August 2003.

tion and exploitation, though perhaps not with such immediate clarity.) Another is that in the historical scheme of things, New Englanders were the slavers, and with respect to capital development New England was benefiting more than the southern colonies from slavery.

A similar, earlier, and more original triangle—at first by a monopoly corporation chartered by the Crown—had its homeports in London, Liverpool, and Bristol, England (evangelical homeports of the Methodist movement as well). This preceding, overlapping, and competing triangle, which arose in the seventeenth century and matured in the eighteenth, figured into the political collision course set between the mother county and the colonies.[4] But it was momentous in a variety of other ways as well.

The connection of the slave trade to the Industrial Revolution itself is much debated. The enormously profitable traffic in human beings and the fruits of their labor taken by force is said to have virtually financed industrial development in Europe.[5] A ship making a cycle of the triangle could be counted upon to make anywhere from 100 to 1000 percent profit (not a bad return even by today's accounting standards). Allowing for the risks and losses (think nightmarish deaths in the dark holds of the middle passage), slaves that cost $50 in Africa would be sold for up to $400 in the West Indies. Though the Liverpool slave-trade oligopoly was tied up by a mere ten firms, many slavers were financed by a more "democratic" pooling of resources by "attorneys, drapers, grocers, barbers, and tailors" who were shareholders in these capital ventures.[6] Such pooling was precursor to publicly held corporations. And then there were the jobs: it is calculated that by 1800, over 18,000 British seamen were directly or indirectly employed in the slave trade. Plus the spinoff employment of shipbuilding itself: clerks and bookkeepers, sailmakers, riggers and ropeworks, ironmongers and, of course carpenters to build those coffin-sized compartments below decks. It all added quickly up.

Moreover, sugar and rum comported well with the quickened tempos of urbanized working-class life. So it was that their increased consumption also coincided with the Industrial Revolution. Initially a luxury confection of the aristocracy, sugar became the first mass-produced exotic "necessity" of working people. England's sugar imports

---

4. Sydney Mintz, *Sweetness and Power: The Place of Sugar in Modern History* (New York: Viking Penguin, 1985), 43.
5. See the classic initiation of this argument in Eric Williams, *Capitalism and Slavery* (Chapel Hill: University of North Carolina Press, 1944).
6. Williams quoted in Mintz, *Sweetness and Power*, 168.

came consistently to exceed its combined imports of all other colonial produce, though a goodly portion was slated for refinement and export. By 1771 England was also importing 2 million gallons of rum a year—over and above its own distillery production and not mentioning that which was smuggled in. In Bristol, dock workers were paid partly in rum (talk about being bound in addiction to your job) and the industry was further institutionalized in national policy when the English Navy rum ration for adult sailors was set at half a pint in 1731 and increased to a full pint a few decades later.[7] The social mechanisms of consumer addiction were in the making.

This is to say that Wesley's opposition and marshaling of the Methodist movement was equally momentous. Note that in his prophetic rant the economic dimension is stressed. It is the "buying and selling" which is at issue, the money that "puts all the rest in motion." John Wesley certainly denounced drunkenness, but he was not opposed to beer and wine as such, both of which he enjoyed and even recommended within limits. His prophetic rage against the distillers, as with the slavers, was rooted in concern for the amassing of wealth by exploiting people and holding the poor in bondage.[8]

Biblically and theologically, his critique was predicated on the humanity of the victims and the justice of their cause. "O earth, O sea," he would say, "cover not their blood." Their lives in bondage and death cried out, like Abel's blood, to God. The humanity of the kidnapped Africans effectively summoned the slavers, the distillers, indeed their very system, before the judgment of God.

Wesley employed a striking range of tactics in the struggle against slavery, the first being what we'd call "media work," exposing it to the light of day. Telling the truth. He published a little book both in England and in the States, titled *Thoughts Upon Slavery*.[9] With such resources as he had, Wesley described the culture and politics of the African nations from which the slaves were abducted. It comes to a striking conclusion: "Where shall we find at this day, among the fair-faced natives of Europe, a nation generally practicing the justice, mercy, and truth which are found among these poor Africans?" It was a justice and mercy, as he observed, not introduced but disrupted by the arrival of the Christians upon their shores! Moreover Wesley graph-

---

7. Ibid., 44, 138, 174, 171.
8. Ted W. Jennings Jr., *Good News for the Poor: John Wesley's Evangelical Economics* (Nashville: Abingdon, 1990), 73.
9. *Works of John Wesley*, ed. Thomas Jackson, 1872, vol. XI, 59–79.

ically details their capture, branding, sale—and above all the conditions of the middle passage—such that of a hundred thousand human beings taken every year, "thirty thousand die, that is, properly, are murdered." He calls things what they are.

Tactically, he brought the movement of evangelical renewal into alliance with the broader abolitionist movement, throwing their weight behind it. He made coalition as it were. The last letter of his life was written to William Wilberforce, the Anglican layman who led the legislative struggle for abolitionism in the House of Commons. Wesley wrote:

> Unless the divine power has raised you up to be as "Athanasius against the world," I see not how you can go through your glorious enterprise in opposing that execrable villainy, which is the scandal of religion, of England, and of human nature. Unless God has raised you up for this very thing, you will be worn out by the opposition of God and devils. But if God be for you, who can be against you? . . . O be not weary of well doing! Go on, in the name of God in the power of His might, till even American slavery (the vilest that ever saw the sun) shall vanish away before it. Reading this morning a tract wrote by a poor African, I was particularly struck by the circumstance, that a man who has black skin, being wronged or outraged by a white man, can have no redress; it being a "law" in our Colonies that the oath of a black man against a white goes for nothing. What villainy is this! That He who has guided you from youth up may continue to strengthen you in this and all things is the prayer of, dear sir,
> Your affectionate servant, John Wesley.[10]

Here, the distinction between coalition and intercession is negligible. Which is to say, John Wesley treated engagement with these powers and institutions to be substantially, or at least in part, a matter of the spirit. In accord with this, he organized the movement to fast each Friday, "that God would remember those poor outcasts of men; and (what seems impossible with men, considering the wealth and power of their oppressors) make a way for them to escape, and break their chains in sunder."[11] Indeed, that God would make a way out of no way.

In England, God did. Within a month of Wilberforce's own death, his legislative abolition passed Parliament, but in the newly independent States the institutional possession and entrenchment was deep. Wesley's intention at first made its way into the American movement cum

---

10. *Letters*, VIII, 265 (Balam, February 24, 1791) as found in Albert Outler, *John Wesley* (New York: Oxford University Press, 1964), 85–86.
11. John Wesley, *Journal*, March 3, 1788, IV: 408, cited in Jennings, *Good News for the Poor*, 88.

church. At the founding Christmas Conference the anti-slavery plank of the discipline was written into the rules. And early on it became a badge of virtue among converted Methodist slaveholders to free one's slaves.[12] But as the bulk of membership, little by little shifted south, the commitment fell to the tempting compromise of mainline convenience. A committee was formed. By 1816, it was compelled to report to General Conference:

> The committee to whom was referred the business of slavery beg leave to report, that they have taken the subject into serious consideration, and, after mature deliberation, they are of the opinion that under the present existing circumstances in relation to slavery, little can be done to abolish a practice so contrary to the principles of moral justice. They are sorry to say that the evil appears past remedy; and they are led to deplore the destructive consequences which have already accrued, and are likely to result therefrom.[13]

It was surely a failure of faith: as though even God could not make a way. If the evangelical flame burned pretty low, it was not entirely out. From Methodist ranks rightly arose not a few of the young abolitionist preachers of the nineteenth century. Wesley, no doubt, smiled down. His engagement with a global system of injustice was not done, nor is it yet. We can only hope his intuitions and intercessions for a movement on the edge of a church might yet bear fruit.

---

12. Outler, *John Wesley*, 85n1.
13. James H. Cone, *The Spirituals and the Blues* (New York: Seabury, 1972), 147.

20

Be Not Awed: The War in Iraq (2003)

> The reign of death and, within that, the pretensions to sovereignty over history of the principalities, is brought to an end in Christ's resurrection. He bears the fullness of their hostility toward him; he submits to their condemnation; he accepts their committal of himself to death, and in his resurrection he ends their power and the power they represent. Yet the end of the claims of the principalities to sovereignty is also the way in which these very claims are fulfilled in Christ himself. The claim of a nation, ideology, or other principality to rule history, though phony and futile, is at the same time an aspiration for salvation, a longing for the reality that does, indeed, rule history.
> —William Stringfellow, *Free in Obedience*

A Preemptive Judgment and the Judgment of God

There is a sense in which violence always involves idolatry.[1] Follow the blood of the innocents to the foot of the idols. For what and for whom are human beings willing to kill? Even against the "guilty," violence involves an idolatrous and preemptive exploit of the divine prerogative. This is more than merely "God on our side." Whether it is in the death penalty or war, the exercise of official violence generally pre-

---

1. *Catholic Agitator* (LA Catholic Worker) April 2003 and *On the Edge* (Detroit Catholic Worker) April 2003.

sumes to know or to execute (which is to say, usurp) the judgment of God who alone holds the power of life and death.

In this respect, Gandhi, who more generally rooted his nonviolence in a metaphysical anthropology, who counted it the essential nature of the divine and the truly human, once said something to this effect: In humility I'm willing to die for the truth, but I am not so certain of it as to kill in its name. It was a backdoor commitment, a way of having no idols. He was faithful to the first of the ten commandments.

Awe: Who Is Like the Beast?

And yet something more explicit, actually more blasphemous, is going on in the present moment. I've been led to think about it from the Pentagon media catchwords of "shock and awe." The Bush regime and their military minions really do expect a kind of fear and worship, precisely reminiscent of the thirteenth chapter of Revelation: "Who is like the Beast and who can fight against it?" Here despair and idolatry are meticulously fused as one.

This program of shock and awe targets more than Iraqi civilians and soldiers. These military theatrics are intended as a political liturgy for the entire world. In that sense, if not so much its effects in terms of casualties, this is a deed remarkably similar to the bombing of Hiroshima. As we've long come to understand, Hiroshima was not so much the last act of World War II as the first act of the Cold War. We used the bomb against the Japanese in order to use it against the Russians. We wanted them to know that we had the bomb and that we were willing to use it massively against human beings—twice just to underscore the point. That act of destruction marked the formation of the postwar world. Just so, the Bush regime has expected this show of military technological force not merely to turn the quick tide of the war in Iraq, but to shape the post-9/11 world. Beyond the war on terrorism, beyond regime change, beyond remaking the Middle East map or establishing new forward bases, beyond even the oil, the U.S. has gone to war against the Iraqis firstly to let the rest of the world know that it is willing and overwhelmingly able.

Legitimated Domestically by Violence

It is best to recall that this is an administration that prior to September 11 was of questionable legitimacy in the eyes of many. Elected by a minority. Selected by Supreme Court intervention. Half the nation questioned the political legitimacy of this regime. It was hobbled and hampered. However, it was in actuality legitimated after September 11 by exercise of the authority of commander-in-chief. It was legitimated by war-making. You can look up for yourself the political terminology for a government legitimated by military power. Nor should this be underestimated or ignored in the current crisis. The U.S. has invaded for a variety of reasons. One further is to seal the continuing legitimacy of this Presidency.

Above the Law

There are those who argue that the date for the start of this war was essentially set last summer and that the diplomatic effort was little more than a matter of killing time while the forces of scale were arranged. In large part due to street-level movements around the planet, that diplomatic ruse proved a disastrous theological self-exposure. In the unilateral move to war, the U.S. has not only shredded the fabric of international law, it has virtually declared itself above the law. This should be no surprise. Over the course of the past year, since "unsigning" the agreement on the International Criminal Court, the administration has been trying to negotiate, country by country, an imperial exemption to prosecution in the court. This is not merely to protect Kissinger from his crimes in Chile and Indochina, or the Reagan administration's in Central America; they have been carefully consulting lawyers over war crimes they have been planning to undertake. They DO know what they do. And they are doing it anyway.

Here's their claim theologically implicit: they are not accountable to human life; they are above the law. All the talk about prosecuting Saddam Hussein or his own minions in the international court of law, howsoever truly legitimate, is freighted with supreme irony and projection. Let's prosecute them in a court to whose authority we ourselves refuse to submit. Virtually everything we say about them, true as it may indeed be, can be said about ourselves. Start with inventing, developing, and using weapons of mass destruction, truly illegal under international law, and threatening or using them against human beings or making them the foundation of foreign policy for half a century. Or start with a definition of state terrorism. Whether we are talking about the UN Charter, or the 1928 or 1949 Geneva Accords (never mind the War Powers clause of our own Constitution), this administration as much or more than previous administrations, counts itself above the law. That entire legal structure has been waved off as "irrelevant" to national security and imperial design. This is a theological pretense of divine sovereignty.

The Presumption of Omniscience

According to the President this war is predicated in part upon U.S. knowledge of the future. A threat we will face five years hence is sufficient reason to invade now. Never mind if someone were to project the curve on SUV fossil fuel consumption, I suppose if they did the math on oil needs for the American military five years from now, it would bode ill to say the least. Still, the claim of historical omniscience ought to be theologically suspect. (Who knows? Five years from now the American military may have collapsed of its own weight.)

In like manner, it is sometimes presumed that the electronic mapping of Baghdad from the satellite heavens, or the latest report from a roving predator robot, is a god's-eye view. (Biblically, of course, a view from God's eye would actually be in the streets and hospital beds of the city under attack, not from the computerized and abstract distance on high.) Domestically, the parallel claim is the presumption to invade citizen email or phone conversation without restraint. To put citizens in the FBI dock. To see everywhere. To invade and know the thoughts of human beings.

The intention and the pretension are one and the same. Another usurpation.

Omnipotence: In Control of History

The Bush administration imagines itself calling shots in history. This level of imperial arrogance is what the Bible calls blasphemy. So prophesies Babylon: "I am. And there is none beside me" (Isaiah 47). It seizes, as the current National Security Strategy proclaims, the "vast, new opportunities" opened by September 11 for "cooperative action with the other main centers of global power." By preempting divine judgment, acting as the lawless one, and claiming to know or the right to know all, this regime asserts it is in control of history.

The Good News

Here is some good news: it's not.

The incarnation means that God has entered into human history. Invisible as a back-alley birth or a backwater resurrection, the Word is at work, hidden in the depths of history, breaking in to break out. Things are way more dynamic and alive than they calculate. Those who claim to be in control are self-deceived. They can choose their full-moon timeline, but people rise up unaccountably in the streets. They can shred the fabric of international law and find themselves not endorsed, but utterly exposed. They can plan a great and precise military victory celebrated live on primetime, and find perhaps that it marks the onset of their great unraveling and collapse. God, thanks be, is not mocked.

Dear friends, we enter this period of struggle with a movement spiritually deep and broadly connected. Keep connecting across barriers of faith and ideology. We have not collapsed or imploded with despair at the start of this war, but understand that now a deeper resistance is summoned of us. We are being strategic. We are being faithful. We are being human. We must keep at it. Conspire the next steps. Be in the streets. Be in conversation. Be in community. Refuse taxes. Refuse to fight. Disrupt business as usual. Prefer poetry to ideology. Pray for victims before nations. When you pray for nations, let it be for the best of their tradition, for their renewal and repentance. When you light a candle, let it mean intransigent resistance. When you pray, imagine a new world possible.

Death appears to reign. But it is undone. Live in the freedom of the resurrection. In short, dear friends: Be not awed by anything but the God who raised Christ Jesus from the dead.

21

Katrina and the Wrath to Come (2005)

The Wrath of God is a difficult, if not problematic theological notion.[1] It would seem to impute to God, some would say project onto God, the very violence we have ourselves embraced as human beings. And yet from another angle it is in effect the consequences of our violence, our folly, and our sin come back round. It names in essence the spiritual cycle of violence to which we have allowed ourselves to be bound as captives.

In May of 1964, brushfires of racial violence had erupted in American cities, but the major uprisings and rebellions were yet to come. Stringfellow addressed a Council of Churches gathering in Washington, warning that the Day of Wrath to Come was now at hand.

> As the day of wrath dawns—let it come as no surprise, especially to white people, either Senators or common citizens. After all, what is involved is not merely the frustrations of these past several years of peaceful protest, nor just the insensibility of the Senate, but the inheritance of the past three centuries of slavery and segregation.[2]

---

1. First given as a part of a talk at a Word and World gathering in Minneapolis, 2005, this material was incorporated into the "Introduction" to *William Stringfellow: Essential Writings* (Ossining, NY: Orbis, 2013).
2. "Through Dooms of Love," *Fellowship*, July 1965. Cited here from Martin Marty, ed., *New Theology No. 2* (New York: Macmillan, 1965).

Recognizing a structural cycle of violence, he foretold clearly that on the day of wrath the prospect was not reconciliation, but overwhelming counterviolence, driving the nation irrevocably into a police state that would abort the revolutionary aspirations of freedom.

> In the day of wrath, what could save the nation from such a calamity is the recognition by white people that every hostility or assault by [black folk] against whites and against white society originates in the long and terrible decades of exclusion and rejection for blacks by white men. [Black] violence now is the offspring of white supremacy. The sins of the fathers are indeed visited upon their sons.[3]

Personal note: I witnessed that day of wrath myself, at least from a distance. I graduated from Cooley High School in Detroit in 1967. I was living on the northwest side when the city erupted in flames. I have a vivid memory; I actually picture myself in the middle of Grand River Avenue—one of these radiating spoke streets of Detroit and looking downtown toward the city in flames. (It was for me a moment, perhaps, like the falling towers are for another generation.) The real estate blockbusters would turn those flames into cash, ramping up the process already apace: "white flight." But my senior year in high school, I'd been reading not only Dr. King, but William Stringfellow. Both marked for me a theological and political awakening. So in that vision of flame, I witnessed the structured cycle of violence and heard there the groan of creation and the cry of the poor. I stood in the middle of Grand River and wept. My heart was pierced and my vocation clarified.

When Jesus looked upon Jerusalem, he did indeed foresee the destruction of Temple and city. In the movement he brought to town he set before the city a real alternative to its destruction. If you want to know the things that make for peace, do the things that make for justice. He could read the signs of the times, he could read Jerusalem with the prophets in the other hand. He witnessed the oppression of imperial occupation, foresaw the revolt, the uprising against the structures of violence—and imagined clearly the inevitable counterviolence of imperial repression. The Roman boot coming down. He did so in tears—weeping for the women and children who would be caught in the crush of historical events. In the collapse not one stone would be left upon another.

---

3. Ibid.

Is it likewise possible to see in the falling Twin Towers, a day of wrath come down upon global empire and economy, even while praying for a break in the cycle of violence, and weeping for the human lives caught in that collapse?

Or think of Hurricane Katrina and the devastation of New Orleans. In an early lead, the *New York Times* described it as a catastrophe of biblical proportion. Theological innuendo penetrates the headlines. In point of fact, there are many ways in which Katrina offers us, literally, an apocalyptic glimpse into America as it were. "Apocalyptic," firstly, in its sense of unveiling, revealing, exposing the apparatus and machinations of history. Can it be a parable of living history where the veil of denial is swept away in wind and flood?

A short list of exposures would include the urban architecture of race and poverty. Look in the faces of those abandoned and left behind. (The phrase "left behind," is used quite intentionally—mindful of the popular apocalyptic theology that presumes to know the judgment of God and sanctions the divine abandonment of whole populations.) Consider the levees untended of late by the Corp of Engineers, the choppers requisitioned and the National Guard shipped out to Iraq. These lay bare the relationship of war-making to the life and health of American cities. The gutting of emergency services for the common good and their realignment in the war on terror exposes the human consequence of such suicidal priorities. Cities, let it be said, are always an assault on the natural environment, but there are ways to sit more lightly in a bioregion, to honor earth's integrity. Katrina makes plain the human and environmental cost of wetland destruction, coastal sprawl, and runaway development.

Stringfellow observed that the weather was the one arena in which the sovereignty of God is popularly acknowledged, and yet he regarded it as the realm of chaos and the fall. Spoken like an Island resident at the whim of the winds. So, compounding ironies, perhaps the most precise theological framing is that which has identified the Wrath of Katrina. Insofar as the frequency and intensity of such storms is related to global climate change, a few degrees of Gulfstream warmth ramping up the severity, is this simply one in a series of unnatural catastrophes? (At this writing New York City sits devastated by the winds and floodwaters of Hurricane Sandy.) If American cities, and even more the suburbs, are based foundationally and architecturally upon cheap oil, what does it mean to see earth and sea, ironically, rise up and tear loose oil rigs, shut down refineries, and drive SUVs from the road with flooding and spiked gas prices? Is that a wrath at which heaven may rejoice, even through tears for the victims of its flood? Apocalyptic is always a call to community—not merely how the church can begin to prepare for disasters to come, but: How does it summon us simply to reweave the spiritual fabric of community in our own place?

Stringfellow anticipated "the impending devastation of political authority" in the imminent judgment of the Word of God.

> Judgment—biblically—does mean the destruction of the ruling powers and principalities of this age. I am aware that this is, for professed Christians in America and in many other nations, an unthinkable thought even though it be biblical (1 Cor. 15:24-28; cf. Acts 2:34-36, Rev. 18-20). . . . Christians rejoice, on behalf of all humanity and, indeed, all creation, at the prospect of the judgment because in that Last Day the destruction of political authority at once signals its consummation in the kingdom of God.[4]

He thought this expectation to be the characteristic stance of biblical people. The loss of that attitude contributed to the "Constantinian confusion" where Christians and church had turned to empire and the powers for "security" and thereby lent themselves to bondage. But it is also to say, conversely, that in the lively expectation of powerly dethronement and destruction lies a certain freedom for human action in relation to them.

---

4. William Stringfellow, *Conscience and Obedience* (Waco, TX: Word, 1977), 80-81.

22

Surveillance and Impeachment (2007)

> Ancillary to secrecy in politics and commerce and in other realms is surveillance and the abolition of human privacy. The prevalence of industrial and commercial espionage; the monitoring of shoppers and elevator passengers and similar, now commonplace, so-called security precautions affecting ordinary business; the everyday atmosphere of apprehension in which people have come to live in America—all have worked to enlarge greatly the tolerance of citizens toward political surveillance and the loss of privacy. The kind of open society contemplated by the First Amendment seems impossible—and, what is more ominous, seems undesirable—to very many Americans. So there is little outrage when Senate hearings expose illegal military oversight of civilians or when the unprecedented political espionage at the Watergate is exposed or when education (if that is what it can then still be called) is conducted in so many schools in the presence of the police or other "security" forces.
> —William Stringfellow, *An Ethic*

What follows is a talk presented in a series calling for the Impeachment of the President and Vice-President, which was organized at Loyola University by my daughter Lydia Wylie-Kellermann.

I believe I was present when this series was conceived.[1] It seemed to arise full-blown in Lydia Wylie-Kellermann's mind. We'd attended the

Detroit Town Hall on Impeachment. It had some high-powered participants at the table like Bill Goodman, recently of the Center for Constitutional Law in NYC, and Ray McGovern, former CIA, and Col. Ann Wright, who resigned her commission the day before the invasion of Iraq, but also some irrepressible local voices. It was done here in Detroit substantially to hold Congressman John Conyer's feet to the fire as it were. As minority leader of the House Judiciary Committee, he had done all the groundwork for impeachment proceedings, but now that he is chair of the committee and in a position to move it, he has allowed political pressures and considerations effectively to slow him. As we walked out into the parking lot, following the passionate remarks of all on the panel, Lydia said, "You know this could be done as a series, building a document of impeachment, article by article, week by week." She invited many of the same folk to come lay out the constitutional basis and then week by week to build articles on *habeas corpus*, on torture as administrative policy, on invasion and occupation in the context of international law, even on Hurricane Katrina as signifying an article of high crime and misdemeanor. She secured me to do this piece on "surveillance."

I will pretend no expertise as such in these matters, but I have done some ordinary reflection on personal experience of political surveillance.

Twenty-five years ago I was part of a direct action campaign at a cruise missile engine plant outside of Detroit. At one point the company and the prosecutor upped the ante by presenting several of us with conspiracy charges. In the course of prosecution, state and county police infiltrators who had been with us in prayer and nonviolence training testified against us. They argued on the stand that nonviolent activists needed to be surveilled because active nonviolence could cross over into violence and terrorism. In the end a jury acquitted us of conspiracy, though we did the time for the actual trespass.

Then last spring I was traveling to a U.S.-Canadian conference on Peace in the Middle East to be held at the University of Windsor in Ontario. It was mostly to be academics, but there was an afternoon panel of activists to which Id been invited. At Canadian customs, the booth official asked several questions and then shunted my car to Immigration. There, nothing more than my driver's license turned up a long rap sheet of direct action arrests, including the cruise missile

---

1. *On the Edge*, 2007.

doings and several conscientious acts at the Pentagon. Whereupon I was denied entrance. If I want to eat any longer at my favorite Vietnamese restaurant in Windsor, I'm required to apply first at the consulate for a temporary residency permit. Elsewise I am subject to "enforcement." Now I hear that a couple of weeks ago the same thing happened to Col. Ann Wright, because she had been arrested for conscience sake. Her name was found on an FBI watchlist that apparently equates nonviolence with the threat of terrorism. Now I wonder if that's what I stumbled upon as well.

Biblical and Theological Reflection[2]

Because it is so often associated with the intrusions of technology, we tend to regard surveillance as a modern phenomenon, but it's generally been more labor intensive and is in fact quite ancient, as old as empire itself. For Israel, the Babylonian, but even more the Persian empire was a security state with an extensive surveillance apparatus.

In the New Testament, Caesar Augustus issues the decree that all the world should be enrolled—a measure intended not only for taxation, but for population control of an oppressed and occupied people. In Matthew's Gospel, Herod the Great attempts to draw the magi into his own web of information gathering, of search and destroy.

By the Gospel accounts, Jesus is subjected to a constant barrage. "So they watched him and sent spies who pretended to be honest, in order to trap him in what he said, so as to hand him over to the jurisdiction and authority of the governor" (Luke 20:20). By my count, I find in the synoptics and John, forty instances where Jesus or his followers are watched or sought, and twenty-five references to plottings against him. If you can read the gospels without getting paranoid, you're not paying attention.

In John there is the notorious case of the man born blind and the elaborate scrutiny of his healing. It goes on for a full chapter. His parents are interrogated. And though the intention is to silence and intimidate him, he only grows bolder as the story proceeds. Spies are sent to entrap Jesus, the tax-resistance question is chief among them, which generates testimony that comes forward at his trial.

However, the two most central events of the narrative involving political surveillance are related to denial and betrayal, to Peter and

---

2. For a description of surveillance in the gospels see Bill Wylie-Kellermann, "Wise as Serpents, Gentle as Doves," *Sojourners*, February 1986.

Judas. The latter is a paid informer within the most intimate community. At the last supper he is the eyes and ears of the authorities—and not only in that safe house where the supper is convened but leading the police (the temple cops by some versions, or a Roman cohort in another account) to the secret place of prayer in the night.

In Peter's case, he is recognized in the courtyard, fingered and identified by one of the high priest's staff. It becomes for him a crisis of discipleship. Will he deny himself, or deny his friend and teacher? When he breaks and denies Jesus it is a crushing spiritual blow. Say that again: surveillance is "intended" as a spiritual assault—personally, as in the case of Peter, communally, as in the case of Judas. It is designed to create fear, mistrust, division, and death.

At the height of the surveillance campaign against Martin Luther King Jr. by J. Edgar Hoover and the FBI, an internal memo put forward the following objectives: to discredit, expose, and neutralize him. The memo was concerned with the state of his mind and sought specifically to exacerbate the tensions and stress under which he lived. Employing bugs and taps, they sent him material that could be truly embarrassing if made public and threatened to do so. Sent anonymously with a tape, the letter called him a fraud, Satan (Jesus was called that too), "an evil, abnormal beast." The letter suggested that suicide was the way out. In a phone conversation, known because also tapped, he said, "They are out to break me."

As theologian William Stringfellow put it,

> Typically, each and every stratagem and resort of the principalities [including surveillance] seeks the death of the specific faculties of rational and moral comprehension which specially distinguish human beings from all other creatures. Whatever form or appearance it may take, demonic aggression always aims at the immobilization or surrender or destruction of the mind and at the neutralization or abandonment or demoralization of the conscience. In the Fall, the purpose and effort of every principality is the dehumanization of human life, categorically.[3]

Jesus spoke of being "troubled in spirit." The word in Greek, *tarachthēnai*, means to be stirred up, agitated, distressed and perplexed of mind, to be struck with fear and dread. It is used with regard to Jesus in the face of death itself, but also notably in connection with his awareness of Judas's betrayal, with Peter's denial, and the approach of the authorities. In each the ruler of this world is drawing near.

---

3. Stringfellow, *Ethic*, 97.

I will forbear to detail the freedom and versatility of Jesus and the discipleship community in response to surveillance, but I'll conclude this section with a succinct theological comment. Aggressive political surveillance signals on the face of it a pretension to divinity. It is the drive toward omniscience undergirding omnipotence—each a claim of false sovereignty in history.

The Normalization of Surveillance

In brief, surveillance has readily become banal and mundane. It is so commonplace as to be ubiquitous. There was a time when cameras in public places felt intrusive. They made people angry. As college students, you are part of a generation that has grown up with cameras and databases. You have no memory of the time before.

A primary acquiescence is to commercial surveillance. It is tied to our refined consumerism. It is the marketeers who drop cookies in people's computers compiling and recording and catering to Internet preferences. At the grocery store or big box, buyers trade cheap shampoo for access to individual buying habits. At checkout, computers spit forth personalized coupons suited to taste. AND this is neither frightening nor disconcerting to most people, especially in your generation.

If you google "surveillance" it doesn't turn up theological reflection or impeachable offenses, it directs you to listings of where to buy the technological equipment so you too can watch your enemies, competitors, intimates, or those otherwise targeted by your voyeurism.

The technology of surveillance is exponentially intrusive. The lookdown accuracy of spy satellites is already notorious. On the other end, the miniaturization of cameras and transmitters is bringing at hand the day when "bug" or "fly on the wall" will have entirely new levels of meaning.

In the so-called "post-9/11" world, the fear of terrorism is so politically enhanced and manipulated that it accentuates the normal and necessary. The rituals of airport security are part, for the traveling class, of what is allowable. It is now normal and acceptable that the authorities know what you carry in your toiletries bag. The most personal and intimate readily suffers violation. The line-waiting and the passage through the detector have a ritual meaning. They signify submission and compliance. The line, of course, can be lengthened to a heightened level of inconvenience should political exigencies require an enhanced dose of fear. Lydia recently noticed an occasion of ethnic profiling that pulled aside an Arabic man for extra scrutiny. What struck her was how angry people around her got, not at the screening and surveillance process, but at the man himself for slowing things down.

These are but hints offered to suggest that normalization and "necessity" have weakened outrage and blinded us to the constitutional crisis we now face.

Impeachable Offences and Political Legitimacies[4]

Specifically on December 17, 2005, it was revealed that four years prior the President had authorized and ordered National Security Administration to conduct warrantless electronic surveillance of U.S. citizens, primarily with respect to phone and email communications.

This is flatly illegal on the face of it. Such communication between citizens and those outside the U.S. is covered exclusively by the Foreign Intelligence Surveillance Act (of 1978). All of what NSA claims publicly to want is covered by FISA, but it requires the authorization of a special court set up to monitor. We are here precisely at the point called "separation of powers" in the constitution, where Congress enacts and legislates, and where the courts limit and adjudicate.

The President, however, signed an executive order circumventing overriding FISA. This is an actual claim to be above the law, arrogating to himself and his office extra-constitutional authority.

This is an offense (one of several impeachable) specifically aimed at the Bill of Rights. It is the fourth amendment that forbids unreasonable search and seizure—of persons, houses, and papers. Sometimes called the "right to privacy," the history of judicial interpretation has included phone and electronic communication in this right.

The actual breech under discussion involves "data-mining," using search-engine and voice-recognition technology to scan phone and email communications. The NSA has big listening ear discs in Sugar Grove, West Virginia and Yakima, Washington that can intercept and monitor such communication, but they have also received upon request massive data from telephone companies like AT&T and Verizon. Quest, who declined to provide similar information on the premise that it was protected, subsequently lost substantial government con-

---

4. In the following I draw upon Center for Constitutional Rights, *Articles of Impeachment Against George W. Bush* (Hoboken, NJ: Melville House, 2006); and Gail Presbey, "Scrutinizing Justifications of Increased Surveillance," *Human Rights Global Focus*, December 2006, vol. 2, no. 4.

tracts. As these remarks are offered, the President is seeking legislation that would retroactively exonerate the cooperating phone companies for their violations, presumably placing them, as with the President himself, above the law.

To some this will seem a minor transgression. The problem is that any breach establishes and precedents "lawless authority" in its wider intentions. I believe the impetus behind this and other violations is a systematic expansion of presidential power, virtually an assault on the constitutional constraints.

Among the justifications put forward by both Bush and Cheney for the legal circumvention is a congressional resolution, the "Authorization for the Use of Military Force" in Afghanistan. That in itself was a shadow, an attempt to preserve the barest semblance of Congress's sole right and responsibility to "declare war." The President argues that this authorization granted him broad powers to make war, which necessarily include surveillance. The claim, in effect, is that spying on U.S. citizens is inherent in the power to make war, in the powers granted the Commander-in-Chief.

Pay attention here. This is a presidency that at the beginning was not regarded by many Americans to be legitimate. George Bush did not receive the majority of votes nationwide, and a recount of questionable votes in Florida was preempted by Supreme Court action. There was widespread anxiety about the president's legitimacy, and his first year was hampered by that perception. It was not until September 11 and the exercise of his powers as Commander-in-Chief, that his "legitimacy" was realized. Say again: this is a Presidency that established its political legitimacy only by making war, even then a war illegal by all international standards. Think about this. That other high crimes and misdemeanors have been done in that same guise should be no surprise.

Impeachment is not a mechanism for getting someone out of office. It is not a glorified recall campaign. It is the remedy for addressing a constitutional crisis. We are in such a crisis, dear friends. For the sake of democracy's remnant. For the sake of Afghan and Iraqi victims beneath illegal war. For the sake of those beneath the torturer's hose. For the sake of conscience. Yes, even for the sake of the constitution itself, impeach Cheney and Bush.

23

Lest Death Prevail: Harry Potter and the Principalities (2011)

For a decade now, we have read as a family J. K. Rowling's magical Harry Potter books aloud to one another in beds and cars and cottages.[1] A bookstore friend mailed us the first, which caught and held with our two girls. Except for the last that she never saw or heard, the subsequent volumes served for us as a therapeutic backstory to my wife's struggle with cancer. Here was a lively gift of diversion and delight, which we increasingly read as rich in themes biblical and Christian. It was as if the Oxford Inklings (C. S. Lewis, J. R. R. Tolkien, Dorothy Sayers, and Charles Williams, among others) had hoisted a pint and admitted a new voice to the table.

That itself was an irony beside the early uproar in certain evangelical communities against what was taken to be its witchcraft-laden, dark and cultic assaults on the faith. Night-fears that the kids in backyard play would lay down their guns and take up wands.

Last summer's release of the final film *Harry Potter and the Deathly Hallows, Part 2* rings down the curtain on this ten-year pop-cultural love

---

1. "Harry and the Principalities—Review of *Deathly Hallows 2*," *Sojourners*, November 2011.

affair with Harry and Hogwarts. Now it seems the burgeoning industry of theological commentary upon it will only grow.

In times such as these, with crises rife and death on the planetary prowl, one pauses deep before spending comment on popular culture. Unless they all be connected.

By my lights, in the final film, J. K. Rowling gave away the gospel store. I say that presuming her role of holding its center through the twisted turns of assorted screenwriters and directors, not to mention commercial powers. (Who knows? I may be wrong there.) But here's what I mean. In the final volume, of both book and film, after a long wilderness testing (with a portable tent and a light no less), the more messianic themes come to a head.

As an infant, Harry survived Voldemort's Herodian attack to become "the chosen one." On Christmas Eve, Harry and Hermione visit the site of that attack and his parents' graves, which are marked with a passage (unidentified) from 1 Corinthians 15:26 (KJV): "The last enemy to be destroyed shall be death."

When the climax of series and story nears, when Harry moves inexorably to his face-off with the Dark Lord, he meets Voldemort with a gracious freedom to die. Spoiler alert: And die he does, for the sake of his friends, for the sake of the struggle, because he is called to. And yet. Passing through a conversation with his mentor in the shadowless white light of King's Cross station, Harry rises to another encounter.

Here to the main point. In the books, Harry never kills anyone. He scatters dementors with his patronis charm; he stuns opponents; he walks into danger with deceptive incognitos. Once he wounds his student nemesis, and once in anger he causes torturous pain. But Harry never kills. In fact he is so quick to use the disarming jinx, *Expelliarmus*, that it becomes his signature spell, the way he is verily recognized.

In the final moment, on which everything turns, Voldemort shrieks the death curse *Avada Kedavra*, and Harry "yells to high heaven" his disarming charm *Expelliarmus*, which brings the Dark Lord's wand tumbling through the air toward Harry. Or so it goes in the book.

In the film *Deathly Hallows, Part 2*, Voldemort does *not* die by his own rebounding curse. The final "battle" scene in the film is greatly extended. Voldemort's immortal power is lost when his last revivification talisman, the snake Nagini, is destroyed. Harry sees his adversary fall, vulnerable, and readies his next spell. Silently, Voldemort casts one more curse at Harry—the deadly green sparks flow—and without a word, Harry counters. The two spells collide, but this time Harry forces the Dark Lord's curse back until the death-telling green seeps through the wand and engulfs Voldemort. He shatters apart.

The sparks may differ, red and green; the wand may fly through the air; but deep difference has been silenced: Neither wizard utters aloud curse nor spell. We have no *Avada Kedavra vs. Expelliarmus*. It is not the curse of death versus the nonviolent disarming of the opponent (in the book, with a humanizing invitation to remorse, repentance, transformation). It is just plain Might and Right become one. Voldemort dies at the hand of a stronger wizard with a more powerful claim on the wand. Which is to say, finally Harry kills. The real victory of death.

I do understand what it takes to turn a gorgeously written 700-page novel into a screenplay, even two. I am not among those who lament long over treasured characters or dialogue lost to a tighter narrative path. Okay, grant that I didn't understand why the final scene wasn't in the Great Hall with the truth-unveiling conversation, but let the expository details go. Nor may I like it in the least, but I even get where they are building theme-park rides into the plot or multiplying the pyrotechnics for the 3D crowd.

But when it comes to the genuine crux, as it were, the heart, the center, I counted on Rowling to fight for the life of this thing. Live like Harry, I say. Stand the ground.

At the turn of the millennium, Walter Wink wrote about the myth of redemptive violence. "In short," writes Wink, "the Myth of Redemptive Violence is the story of the victory of order over chaos by means of violence. It is the ideology of conquest, the original religion of the status quo. The gods favor those who conquer. Conversely, whoever conquers must have the favor of the gods. The common people exist to perpetuate the advantage that the gods have conferred upon the king, the aristocracy, and the priesthood."[2]

This is the myth built into the narrative structure of popular imperial culture, the repetitive story that might makes right, that violence creates and redeems and justifies. It is the order of the day among the crises that prowl our planet. It is the main Hollywood script. The military press release. The corporate commercial. The story we are all impressed into serving and buying and living. It is the plotting that bought or bullied its way into final installment of the Harry Potter films. It is the gospel story hijacked and inverted.

This is a constant of the domination system, including its Hollywood

---

2. http://www.ekklesia.co.uk/content/cpt/article_060823wink.shtml (accessed March 26, 2017).

minions. I remember my similar dismay more than a decade ago when the first *Matrix* film brilliantly transposed the Jesus story, politics and all, only to have it turned on its head (with death and resurrection still to come), pivoting on one decisive line from Neo: "Guns. Lots of Guns." And the killing began.

In the *Deathly Hallows Part 2*, can so small an omission in the Harry-Voldemort face-off bear such pivotal weight? In some ways that's the very point. In a subsequent closing cinematic scene, Harry considers his rightful claim on that Elder Wand—the most powerful wand in his world. It is like one of the three great temptations—and he resists, breaking and throwing its parts into the abyss. Good that. But one can't help thinking the wand is destroyed, but the Myth of Redemptive Violence survives. Even prevails, aided and abetted.

So bring on the forward bases and targeted drones, the endless trillion-dollar wars, the spills and the fracking, the budget standoffs, the mass incarcerations, more. Popular culture will not merely divert, but back it all up.

Perhaps I'm unfair to Ms. Rowling. Perhaps her authorial role to stand against the powers and hold the story's heart was long since spent. But if she has any remorse, I hope she will declare it. We need a different ending than the one now playing out in the theaters of history. We need the one in The Book.

24

Coming to a City Near You: Emergency Management (2014)

> Christ drove the money lenders out of the Temple. But today nobody dares to drive the money lenders out of the Temple . . . because the money lenders have taken a mortgage on the Temple.
> —Peter Maurin

This chapter published first in The Catholic Worker, *January-February 2014.*

Let me tell you about a new form of urban fascism, one that is the template for direct corporate rule. Though it comports fully with what is happening in most of the global south, this despotism called emergency management is being deployed in Michigan, and Detroit is its major test ground. Since March of 2013 we have been living under a nonelected government thoroughly allied with the banks and corporations.

Start with the political structure: an Emergency Manager (EM) appointed by the governor over a municipality or school district holds in their person all the powers of government plus more. In a city, the EM immediately supplants the mayor and city council, eliminating even those checks and balances. So an Emergency Manager can write laws with the stroke of a pen, repeal ordinances, fire employees, set budgets, sell assets, privatize services and departments—and, two further extraordinary powers, unilaterally break contracts whether union or otherwise, and even rewrite the city charter. Though Detroit is much in the news, you are not likely to get this from broadcast media, from reading the Detroit dailies, or the *Times* for that matter.

In the fall of 2013 organizers got 250,000 signatures to put the repeal of the EM law on the ballot, but it had to go to the State Supreme Court to overrule the board of canvassers' decision that the typeface of the title was microns too small. It was repealed by 2.3 million citizens, including 81 percent of Detroit, but the lame-duck Republican legislature turned around and repassed a ballot-proof version. I'm not making this up.

This legislation comes full-blown out of the right-wing think tanks. As the cover of *Time* magazine put it over an image of the Detroit skyline: "Is Your City Next?" They were referring to municipal bankruptcy, but it applies equally to emergency management. Most of my adult life I've lived under Phil Berrigan's adage, "If voting could change anything, they'd make it illegal." Now here I am resisting the big assault on local democracy.

Race and Devastation

How is this happening? Because so far it's being done almost entirely in African American cities. In fact, at this point every major black city in the state but one is under emergency managers. Over half the African American population of the state of Michigan is under nonelected governments. And three-quarters of the black elected officials in Michigan have been replaced by this process. Even if many of the managers are black, as in Detroit, the exercise is fundamentally racist. Constitutional and Voting Rights Act lawsuits have been filed in federal court, but as of this writing they are stayed from going forward.

When one of the Detroit dailies publishes an editorial titled, "Can Detroit Govern Itself?" decoding the subtext is simple: "Can black people rule themselves?" White folks outstate shake their heads and shrug indifference. Problem is, once the mechanisms are perfected and the precedents are set, emergency management will be coming to a white city near you.

Even many black folks in Detroit, steeped in news mainly from our broadcast media, buy into the view. This black majority city just elected its first white mayor in nearly fifty years. He lived all that time in Livonia, known as "the whitest city in America"; moved into Detroit last year too late to be properly on the primary ballot, but won by a landslide as a write-in candidate. Running as an outsider with connections to turn things around, he won the final election with so much corporate money he didn't know where to put it all.

Detroit's financial crisis has structural causes to be sure, and no surprise that race is a factor there as well. With de-industrialization, job flight and capital flight have long eroded the tax base. In the last decade over a quarter million auto-related jobs have disappeared from the metro area. But beginning in the 50s, white flight decimated the city's population. A million people left. Even before the foreclosure crisis nearly one-third of the housing stock had been lost to flight. Detroit has gone from being the city with the highest rate of home-ownership in the nation, to the city with the highest foreclosure rate. As elsewhere, predatory mortgages were heavily targeted toward black neighborhoods, which contributes to losing another quarter of the population in just the last decade.

Also, by state decree, folks in the suburbs working in Detroit do not have their city taxes taken out by employers. They stiff the city to the tune of $140 million a year. Cash flow is affected. The corporations in Detroit also stiff the city on taxes and fees. City Councilwoman JoAnn Watson estimates the amount in arrears to be some $800 million. One noteworthy tax scoff is the owner of the Tigers and the Red Wings, who owes tens of millions by himself. But he's getting a bond measure to build a new hockey rink and is being given the land to boot. Emergency Management makes that work.

Oh the contradictions of my life. Here I am a lifelong, conscientious war tax resister bemoaning tax refusers (though neither conscientious nor honorable). I've always paid local taxes, but now even I think, "Taxation without representation?"

Disaster Capitalism

We are at a moment when late capitalism, reaching certain limits, may be seen turning inward to devour basic institutions like public education and now municipalities. What's been done globally is coming home.

If Detroit were an indebted third-world nation, what is being imposed on us (privatization of assets and services, deregulation, and austerity budgets) would be called "structural adjustment." The economists out of the University of Chicago who hatched this formula decades ago discovered that the quickest way to impose it was in the wake of a natural disaster (tsunami, earthquake, hurricane). Devastation is opportunity. Then it dawned on them that disasters could also be created. Think of Detroit as New Orleans with a different kind of storm.

In Detroit public education under emergency management is being dismantled and replaced with for-profit cyber-school charters. Private security roams downtown looking like cops; their surveillance cameras feed a wall of monitors not at police headquarters, but in a corporate office. The mayor wants a big downtown firm to serve as the "law department." The bus system and lighting are in private hands, as is the Health Department. A few weeks ago the Worker soup kitchen at St. Peter's got our first visit from Not the Health Department. We knew the old inspector by name and face. The new contractor thinks we are a restaurant. New sinks have gone in—one just inside the kitchen door so guests can wash their hands before crossing the threshold to use the phone.

Detroit does have a cash flow crisis, roughly $200 million per year. But that has also been partly manufactured. Governor Snyder, with help from his Republican legislature, has worsened the crisis under review by cutting $67 million in state revenue sharing with the city. Last year Detroiters passed a bond measure of $137 million to address cash flow but while he was weighing whether Detroit was in crisis, the governor held the moneys in escrow. The city unions negotiated with the mayor a package that would have saved Detroit over $100 million, but the governor effectively prevented it from coming to the Council for approval.

Which leads to the moneylenders, as Peter Maurin would say. He would be amazed, well, perhaps not, at the extent to which debt is aggressively marketed to students, homeowners, consumers, institutions, and, yes, municipalities.

In Detroit, the same banks (Bank of America to name one) that have been "devouring widow's houses," eating out housing stock with predatory loans from below, have managed predatory loans from above as well. I won't try to explain "interest rate swaps" here, but suffice it to say that at a time when banks get their money at near zero interest, Detroit is paying the banks at a rate of 6 percent or more. As insiders to the bubble and crash, they knew the day was coming and were even able to manipulate the international base rate, so the decks were stacked.

Couldn't we get out of this deal? Or some of it? The city could seek charges of criminal fraud (like Oakland did). Or an honest bankruptcy could reduce or renegotiate it. But instead the Emergency Manager has put forward a criminal alternative: borrow $350 million from Barclay's of London; use $250m of that to buy Bank of America out of the deal (they've already gotten $800m); the other hundred million is roughly the cost of legal fees for the bankruptcy. What would Barclay's get from the deal? If it goes through, Detroit is on the hook for the $350 million and interest (20 percent of the city budget for the next six years) and they get first dibs on major city assets to be sold, like the Water Department that serves the three-county urban sprawl, or tracts of land, perhaps even the city's jewel of an island park so long coveted by developers. And then, As Glenn Ford notes: "To ensure that the city can never escape the clutches of capital, the contract would allow Barclay's to immediately declare Detroit in default if Emergency Financial Manager rule is ended for any reason—that is, the corporate plan calls for the permanent cessation of democracy in Detroit."

Detroit Has Not Declared Bankruptcy

Make no mistake. Though they are referred to in court and the media as "the city," it is the Governor and the EM who have filed for bankruptcy. When a city files, the judge puts a stay on any suits against the city. However, in this case he has put a stay on the constitutional and Voting Rights Act challenges to the state's Emergency Management law in federal court. The logic is this: first we'll do the bankruptcy, then they can figure out if the EM had the legal standing to even file it.

If the city filed for bankruptcy, and was arguing in its own interest, the banks and the pensioners and the unions would all be on a level playing field. Instead the banks have been dealt with up front, offered eighty cents on the dollar. The city pensioners were offered ten cents. Pensions are actually protected by the state constitution, but the judge has ruled that is trumped by U.S. corporate law.

Though he's running the entire city, Emergency Manager, Kevyn Orr, is a bankruptcy lawyer. He oversaw Chrysler's Chapter 11. Back-channel emails uncovered last summer show him being courted before the Financial Emergency was even ruled. He expressed concern that it appears the EM law was written expressly for bankruptcy. But he took the job. He resigned as a partner of Jones Day, third-largest law firm in the world, among whose primary clients are, you guessed it, Bank of America/Merrill-Lynch—bigger clients for them than the City of Detroit. Just days before Orr's appointment was announced, Jones Day was named by the city as the law firm to restructure the city's debt. Actually to restructure the city. They are now the lawyers in the governor's bankruptcy case. They bill us at $1,000/hour. The firm will make about $100 million.

The Last Vestige of Democracy and Creating Our Own

A local campaign (with a development plan) is named Opportunity Detroit. It sees the city as a housing space, a high-tech corridor, and a destination for sports and entertainment, and that is how the city is being restructured not just financially but spatially. Certain areas, like along the riverfront or major transport spines are being resourced for corporate development, while outlying neighborhoods are having the plug pulled on lights and infrastructure. When the archdiocese was preparing last year for another wave of top-down church closings, the cardinal first met with the mayor to find out which neighborhoods had no future. The foundations and their ancillary nonprofit agencies are in on the mapping (they were recently called into a closed-door meeting with the bankruptcy judge on a similar premise). People lose their homes and neighborhoods not to eminent domain, but simply because the resources—schools, churches, police, fire, lights, and water are being pulled from under them. Land empties and spaces open up. The forested gated communities of the future are being designed.

The neighborhood of my church, St. Peter's, is one being resourced. Hip destination restaurants pop up. Downtown corporations pay employees to move in here. The new streetlights will have surveillance cameras built in and networked. Meanwhile, the Worker soup kitchen is a liability to be closed or harassed out. Our guests are stopped to be frisked, ticketed and criminalized, driven out of town in police cars, suffer violence. They are to make way for opportunity.

More accustomed to arrests at SAC bases, White House gates, or missile factories, my last was in City Council Chambers. It was the morning they ratified the Jones Day contract and also the fiftieth anniversary of Martin Luther King's letter from a Birmingham Jail. We held up the vote. We blocked aisles and sang, "We Shall Not Be Moved." As spectators and speakers joined us the crowd swelled and the harmonies turned rich and deep. But only two of us were arrested. The other, an elected member of the School Board cried, "Shame!" while being hauled away. The police, whose jobs and pensions are on the line, thanked us at the precinct. Come trial, their testimony will be of interest. We have asked for jury trial and it's scheduled for January 27. A jury is the last vestige of democracy in Detroit. We will remind them so. That is, the last vestige other than those we create ourselves, participatory and from below. Everything we do these days must build community and democratic practice.

We know that it is a moment to resist displacement, emergency management, gentrification, corporate occupation. It is also a moment, exiled in our own city, to build and plant and marry. To make real community and practice real democracy. But that's another story to write and to tell.

25

The Dismantling of Public Education: Separate and Unequal (2014)

The Detroit Public Schools are being dismantled by design and effectively looted. Though Detroiters and the elected school board are consistently blamed for their demise, for twelve of the last fifteen years DPS has been under state control.[1]

Mother Helen Moore, an attorney who heads the Education Task Force, has become notorious for her fight on behalf of the schools, and tells the story over and over in community meetings. It's well documented.

When the Detroit schools were first taken over in 1999, enrollment was stable (at 200,000 students), test scores were middle range compared to state averages and rising, an "Afro-centric" curriculum developed by the district over a number of years was in use, there was a $93 million budget surplus, and $1.2 billion from a bond issue intended by residents for building improvements. It was the latter, not any financial emergency, which drew the takeover. Then Governor Engler determined that those improvement dollars should not go to local minority contractors, but to suburban and outstate builders. Follow the money.

---

1. First published in *On the Edge* (Detroit Catholic Worker), Winter 2014.

When control was returned to the board seven years later, the fund deficit was $200 million, enrollment had dropped to 118,000, the curriculum was gone, as was the bond money spent at shamefully inflated prices. One hundred million simply disappeared without audit or indictment. This is the background of emergency management in Detroit.

The elected board was returned to power in early 2006 with the burden of a deficit budget under which they labored for three years, including the 2008 economic collapse caused by the financial industry. The first Emergency Financial Manager, Robert Bobb (not an educator but a developer famous for brokering deals, and supported by Eli Broad if you know what that means), was put in place on the premise of a $135 million budget deficit. When he left, the deficit had ballooned to $327 million and test scores had plummeted to among the worst in the nation. He was paid an annual salary of half a million dollars. Get the drift?

Disaster Capitalism and Public Education

We are at a point in late capitalism where corporations are turning inward to devour other corporations (hostile takeovers), municipalities (as in the Detroit bankruptcy), and basic social institutions (like education—public education in particular).

Globally, the architects of structural adjustment (austerity budgets, deregulation, selling off public assets, and privatization) had discovered that natural disasters afforded the best opportunities for quick takeover. With respect to education, the Katrina flooding is the example of opportunity provided—where New Orleans public education was effectively replaced by a profitable charter system. But they also discovered that disasters could be manufactured as well. We've experienced this in Detroit both as a city and as a school system. Defund. Make it fail or appear so. Take it over.

The Other Emergency Management in Detroit

Because of the bankruptcy recently completed, emergency management as a form of urban fascism is better known at the municipal level in Detroit. However, the Public Schools have been under emergency management now for five years. The destruction and dismantling of that system is what now bodes for the city as a whole.

Though Public Act 436, which allegedly authorizes emergency management, allows that elected bodies taken over and supplanted may vote after eighteen months to put out an EM, the courts have ruled that this means the Governor simply has to install a new and different EM. Emergency Management is a permanent feature of black cities in Michigan.

The elected and unpaid school board, though constantly tarred in the media with corruption or incompetence or simply ignored, has continued to function "in exile" as a body conscientiously accountable to parents, students, and citizens, consistently resisting takeover. (Would that our city council had an ounce of such vision or fiber!) Believe it or not, the State Attorney General sued the district representatives on the board for being elected. Since they were duly seated and sworn in, the maneuver failed. Now a foundation-funded and non-profit-orchestrated campaign seeks to oust them altogether for a structure of "mayoral control."

Emergency management has been the blunt instrument of privatization. More than half the schools in Detroit are charters. Though originally conceived as vehicles for creativity, charters have become a mainstay for union busting and privatization. In the industrial era schools prepared students for work in factory jobs, largely auto in Detroit. Now students are treated as state-funded commodities for extracting profits. The distinction between nonprofit and for-profit charters is all but moot as even most of the former are managed by for-profit contractors. These schools compete with public schools, but have some choice in who they accept and who they don't; and they are not held to the same standards of accountability as public schools for teacher certification or even testing.

In Detroit, headlines recently lamented that DPS had missed the deadline for federal funding of Headstart programs in the public schools. "Bungling black incompetence" is how that was read again in the suburbs—a loss of $4 million. But it was, of course, the Governor's EM who missed the deadline. And not by accident: lo and behold, federal grants now fund Headstart as a privately contracted program in public school spaces.

Though parents were promised that more resources would be driven to the classroom, under Emergency Management administrative costs, actual and percentage-wise, have nearly doubled: from $75 per pupil in 2008 to $143 per student today. Classroom size has taken a similar hit. Next year's budget has proposed the target of thirty-eight students per classroom be expanded to forty-three. With conflicts from such overcrowding, suspensions and expulsions go up; big contracts for restorative justice programs are justified. When a school board member pointed out that there weren't enough chairs in a classroom for that higher number, an administrator replied, "With the absenteeism rate that wouldn't be a problem."

Special schools, even fully funded ones, have simply closed: Oakman Orthopedic (a facility gorgeously built for disabled students—see Kate Levy's film, *Because They Could: The Fight for Oakman School*[2]) and The Day School for the Deaf (similarly equipped) are gone. Such buildings are abandoned or turned over wholesale to profiteers. Catherine Ferguson Academy, a school for pregnant teens and young mothers that had an international reputation for integrated urban agriculture was handed over to a for-profit charter that simply gutted the program. (For a nostalgic look at the school see the film *Grown in Detroit*. It too will break your heart.) The building is now home to a Headstart program run by the sprawling nonprofit, Southwest Solutions.

According to the *Detroit Free Press*, the second EM, Roy Roberts (also not an educator, but a retired auto exec), said he was told when he came that his job was to "blow up the Detroit Public Schools and dismantle it." So far so true.

Racial and Spatial Restructuring

Detroit is being downsized and restructured geographically, as well as financially. The plug is being pulled on certain neighborhoods where poor black folks live. Predatory mortgages, now foreclosed, drive them out. Infrastructure is allowed to fail. Lights go out, fire stations close, cops withdraw. Water is shut off pushing people out; and water bills are attached to tax indebtedness, forcing another round of foreclosures. And yes, schools close in neighborhoods slated to have no living future.

Resources, meanwhile, are going into other neighborhoods close to downtown, along the waterfront, or connected to the pending light rail. There are neighborhoods into which young corporate-type white people are moving exuberantly. It's their generation's turn! These are people generally without children—who don't yet care about schools. Who, without even a second thought, do not care about black children. Their indifference rules the day and the space.

---

2. https://vimeo.com/106652160.

The Educational Achievement ("Apartheid") Authority

"Authorities" are another mechanism for eviscerating, circumventing, and privatizing government. We have many of these para-governmental authorities in the city: the Downtown Development Authority controls funding and land, the Lighting Authority replaces the Lighting Department, the Great Lakes Water Authority essentially takes over the Detroit Water and Sewage Department and will likely hire Evolia, an international water corporation to manage things. For two years we have not had a Health Department, but instead an Institute for Population Health. In like manner the EAA is not even properly an authority, but an inter-local agreement between Eastern Michigan University (where the Governor appoints the university regents) and the Detroit Public Schools (where the Governor appoints the Emergency Manager). Think of it as an agreement between the Governor and the Governor. And call it an authority, a "principality" if you will.

The EAA is supposed to be a statewide school district for failing schools, but all of the schools are in Detroit. The idea was to take those in the lowest-performing bottom 5 percent and turn them around. Two interesting coincidences: 1) almost all the students in failing school district are black and 2) when it came time to transfer the schools from Detroit to the EAA, the criterion seemed to be more a matter of which buildings had been newly renovated. One of the high schools transferred, Mumford, had been virtually rebuilt for $50.5 million. The building went to the EAA, but the reconstruction debt stayed with the DPS and comes out of the per student cost. Can you see how for DPS, those per pupil debt service costs went from $212 in 2008 to $1109 per pupil today? Not having the debt service in the EAA means there is more money per pupil for the private contractors.

Forgive all the numbers, but just a few more. The Chancellor of the EAA makes $325,000 per year (actually her total package approaches nearly half a million). She is new. The previous Chancellor made the same amount, but he was forced to resign under a scandal of corruption, but with a big severance package.

Cyber Curricula

In the era of the Gates Foundation and such, much of the sales and contractual profits to be made in education are technological: hard and soft. EAA students, almost entirely poor and black, have been test subjects for a new computer teaching program called Buzz. It came from Kansas City along with John Covington, first Chancellor of the EAA. At a cost to the district of some $350,000, it is marketed as providing students with an individualized learning experience.[3]

Textbooks left behind in the schools taken over by the EAA were simply thrown in the dumpster. Teachers in such an EAA classroom are no longer teachers—they are facilitators only allowed to help students in using the program before them. One teacher, Brooke Harris at Mumford, was disciplined (she was eventually fired) for attempting to bring books and textbook-related materials into the classroom. "I was told that in the student-centered model, my role as teacher was primarily to supervise students to make sure they were using Buzz."

Speaking out as an EAA teacher is courageous and costly. In the EAA, no union provides protection from retaliation. They tend more often to speak circumspectly, as in these pages, or anonymously and off the record.

Individualized instruction can sound great, but exclusive use of the computer screen is an assault on community-based learning. No give-and-take in group discussion with a teacher.

On its website and in its ads, the EAA touts fantastic progress in bringing a greater percentage of students to proficiency levels in reading and math. And Covington was regularly on the road speaking at conferences to promote and market "the product."

Some of the evidence of shining performance was based on a test internally administered by the EAA. Teachers interviewed by the ACLU reported such pressure to produce positive test results that standard practice included allowing students to retake the test if they didn't do well the first time. Moreover, on the premise of individualized instruction and not wanting to "teach to the test," the EAA attempted to avoid its students even taking the state MEAP tests—even though it was MEAP scores that were used to justify its creation. Teaching to the test is, of course, a bad idea, but you can't have it both ways.

A close reading of MEAP test data released in February, however, shows that the majority of EAA students failed to demonstrate even marginal progress toward proficiency. Consider: 78 percent of students demonstrated no progress toward proficiency or even actual declines in math. The same was true for 58 percent of students in reading. Students who entered the system proficient had even grimmer

---

3. For this and what follows see Curt Gayette, "The EAA Exposed," *Detroit Metro Times*, September 24, 2014.

results—the majority lost ground.[4] This, even though EAA students are held for longer days and year round.

The Buzz program, to be sure, was still being built and improved while it was tested on Detroit students. On a stipend basis, additional curriculum content was added by a team of eight teachers. Half of them were recent college graduates who had not studied to become teachers, had no certification or curriculum design experience, but had been given five weeks of training in the summer before coming to Detroit. They were part of the Teach for America program.

Teach for America

When it opened for business, more than a quarter of the EAA's faculty were Teach for America students. TFA is a controversial nonprofit designed to get new university graduates teaching in low-income urban and rural communities. Participants are encouraged in their college coursework to take education classes and pursue certification, though that is not required and most have not. For those not certified there is the intensive five weeks of training, plus structures of ongoing support, and simultaneous education courses. Military veterans are actively recruited. Participants make a two-year commitment. They come into any given school or district at the entry base salary, but combined with the AmeriCorps program, they receive federal loan forgiveness and vouchers toward further education. If there is a union they are not forbidden to join.

What's the problem? There is a narrative in circulation that bad teachers protected by unions and tenure are the problem. Though originally intended to fill teacher shortages in urban areas, the TFA program actually functions to replace veteran teachers. All teachers in EAA schools were terminated and required to reapply for their positions. More than a quarter of those were filled by TFA instructors fresh out of school. Do the math. There are no unions in EAA schools. The fact that studies are conducted comparing learning at the hands of veteran teachers versus short-term recruits, suggests that replacement is part of the design. The for-profit charters are also full of TFA instructors, as are the public schools. With more of all to come.

---

4. See Dr. Thomas Pedroni, *Detroit News*, April 21, 2014.

Though TFA can be a shortcut into an ongoing teaching career, the two-year commitment, especially for those seeking loan forgiveness, graduate school funds, and resumé experience, means recruits are not committed to a city, a school, or even a teaching vocation. The resignation rate in EAA schools has been extraordinarily high. Add TFA and you have a faculty in perpetual turnover.

African Americans comprise 13 percent of the TFA workforce. If those numbers hold in Detroit, it means students in a city that is 80 percent African American and in a failing school district that is virtually all black are faced with teachers not from their culture, experience, or community. In a city where the young white savior narrative is already running strong, this is yet another version.

Late Breaking: Mayoral Control and New Orleans Complete?

As this issue goes to press there are moves in the lame-duck Republican legislature to abolish the elected school board and put the public schools under direct mayoral control. The current mayor lived his entire life in a northern suburb, literally the whitest city in America. He was "elected" in a corporately funded write-in campaign, winning by a landslide. He was the treasurer of the EAA when an unaccounted "loan" of $12 million was given it from DPS, but claims to be in the dark—to know nothing about it. A decade ago in a ballot measure Detroiters refused to give up the elected board to mayoral control. And more recently the City Council refused to put it again on the ballot. But like Emergency Management, it may simply be imposed. The difference between such a regime and emergency management is not worth talking about—simply more of the same. It's expected that this will pave the way for the entire system to be chartered and union representation ended altogether, bringing the New Orleans-style disaster to completion.

A Dark Time

Though many are celebrating the bankruptcy, its structural adjustment, the giveaways of land and buildings and assets, the development dollars flowing, and the lucrative contracts to be had . . . this is a dark time for Detroit's children, poor and black. They are being pushed down, pushed out, and pipelined toward prison. Sometimes I near despair. Still. There is hope in students who refuse to be so pushed and fight for their own education. There is hope in teachers who love Detroit's young and give themselves for them. There is hope in those who hold the line and struggle on their behalf, in going on record with a history of resistance. There's even hope in naming the darkness . . . and trusting the universe to bend toward light.

26

Her Name Was Charity: The Detroit Water Struggle (2014)

Think of Charity Hicks as the Rosa Parks of the Detroit Water Struggle.[1] She was arrested in Detroit early on May 16 for resisting the shut-off of her own water. The private contractor came early in the morning, but she was up. Since he was hitting a bunch of people on her block, she went door to door rousing people to say: He's coming; fill your tub, fill pots and pans! Then, because she still had two more days to settle her bill, she demanded to see the shut-off order. He had none, only a list of addresses. When the altercation turned physical, she called the police. Let it be said that Charity was a forceful, even, when required, loud black woman. She had a large persona. The white cops who arrived averred that she "needed to be taught a lesson" and instead arrested her. They left her house open and threw her phone and keys on the front lawn. She was essentially disappeared.

Because of the situation in Detroit, arrestees are no longer taken to the precinct. They go directly to a Central Detention Center run by the State of Michigan in a former prison within city boundaries. Still barefoot and bleeding, she was put into a holding area with thirty other

---

1. First published in *The Catholic Worker*, October–November 2014.

women. One toilet. No benches. Find a place on the floor not covered with blood or vomit. It's the weekend, so you'll be arraigned by video before a Court in Romulus.

When her husband returned home and saw the remains of the situation, he began calling local hospitals to try and find her. Eventually, he went to the police station to file a missing person report. They said: We have her.

Visits and bond attempts were turned away. Because she is a diabetic and was going into sugar shock, frantic lawyers were able to get her out on a *habeas corpus* motion. But, truth be told, they had arrested the wrong person. Charity Hicks was a food, water, and environmental justice activist in Detroit. Strong and articulate. A woman not to be messed with.

Two days later, she told this story at St. Peter's Episcopal Church. She urged the gathered activists, in a now-famous phrase, to "wage love" in the water struggle for justice. The occasion was the presence of Nelson and Joyce Johnson, two faith-rooted activists from North Carolina. Nelson had been wounded by Klan members in the 1979 Greensboro Massacre. Since then, they have, among other things, founded the Beloved Community Center and shepherded the first Truth and Reconciliation process on U.S. soil. They were also instrumental in the recent Moral Mondays campaign in which, week after week, groups have been arrested at the State House in Raleigh for resisting the right-wing assault on all social programs and budgets. They were here to discuss the connections between the North Carolina efforts and the struggle in Detroit against Emergency Management.

An Emergency Manager appointed by Governor Snyder (see Jan/Feb 2014) has all the powers of government, and more, in his person: He can write ordinances, repeal laws, fire employees, set budgets, privatize departments, sell city assets, break union contracts, rewrite the city charter, and file for bankruptcy. Or so we are told. The law justifying this was repealed in a ballot measure by Michigan citizens, but the lame-duck Republican legislature repassed a worse version within months. At this point, every black-majority city in the state is under the emergency manager law. Over half the black citizens of Michigan are under nonelected governments. Seventy-five percent of the black elected officials have been replaced by emergency managers. The Detroit Public Schools have been under one for five years and they have been successfully dismantled, privatized, and destroyed à la New Orleans.

Under the Emergency Manager, the Detroit Water and Sewage Department had announced in March that it was beginning to shut off water to anyone more than two months or $150 behind in their bill. One hundred and twenty thousand homes. They were shooting for something like 3,000 shut-offs per week. A couple of years back, $500 million in bond money for infrastructure repairs had been turned over to the banks to buy out the predatory and illegal credit swaps into which the Department had entered. Now, in the effort to privatize Detroit water, poor people were going to have to pay up or be expelled. At the same time, this comported with the reorganizing of Detroit neighborhoods, resourcing some and pulling the plug on others. People not expelled by mortgage and tax foreclosures, or by the disappearance of schools, precincts, and fire stations, could now be sent packing by water shut-offs.

Nelson and Joyce thought something like this might be planned for North Carolina as well. When Nelson heard Charity's story, he said: This is it. In the picture of a child or elder holding a cup at an empty faucet, all the connections can be made. He said, this is the thing that can both deepen and broaden the Detroit movement. He drew a map of campaign on a paper plate. He was prophetic in every sense of the word. What he mapped and foresaw has come to be.

Within the week, Charity was at a conference planned by the People's Water Board in Detroit with Maude Barlowe, a Canadian writer and water activist who had been instrumental in getting the United Nations to declare access to potable water a human right. When she heard Charity's story, she said: This is it. We need to file a complaint with the United Nations. Within weeks, UN representatives had announced that to cut off water to people because they were unable to pay was indeed a violation of basic human rights. That got a lot of international attention and soon, local Detroit papers and TV stations were forced to cover the story themselves.

Charity had been invited to North Carolina to tell the story, but first she went to New York City to speak about the crisis at the Left Forum. While waiting at a bus stop, on her way to speak, she was hit by a car that jumped the curb and struck her down. A hit and run. She was in a coma for weeks. In early July, she crossed over to God and the ancestors.

A group of religious leaders and allies began circulating a letter against the shut-offs and privatization and in support of the People's Affordability Plan of 2005, which would set water prices according to ability to pay. Drawing from interfaith tradition, they said water is a grace, a gift of the Creator, beneath everything. It is the lifeblood of the planet, circulating in river and rain. As a gift of God, it belongs to all creatures equally. In tradition, it is part of the commons for which we are stewards. This view is represented legally in the idea that water is not a utility or a commodity, but a public trust, held for all the people. It is represented in the idea that you can't own a body of water, even if you own the land around it. Any high school kid knows that if you are walking on the beach and someone tells you to get off their property, you step into the water and you're off. It is also represented in the idea that water is a human right—it belongs accessibly to everyone. The faith letter was signed by five bishops and eighty religious leaders in the city, plus many more in the region and nationally. It was hand-delivered to the Water Board, the Detroit City Council, and the shut-off contractor.

Meanwhile, people started protesting every Friday at the Detroit Water Board. They called it Freedom Fridays, echoing the Moral Mondays movement in North Carolina.

In the days that followed Charity's death, a group of ten people decided to take direct action and block the trucks from going out to shut the water off. They went to the gates of Homrich Wrecking, the private contractor with a $5.6 million contract to turn off the water. The company is paid by the shut-off, so they are incentivized to do as many as they can, as fast as they can. We dedicated our action to the memory and spirit of Charity Hicks. For two hours, we blocked the gates. In a very physical confrontation, we were arrested and taken to the Central Detention Facility. So far, this was pretty much how Nelson Johnson had diagrammed it on his paper plate.

The following week, ten more people went back. This time, we blocked the drive and stopped the trucks for seven hours before being arrested. The same day, downtown, more than a thousand people marched from Cobo Hall to Bank of America to City Hall to Hart Plaza to protest the shut-offs. A union, National Nurses United, came forward to support the march and declare the situation in Detroit a public health crisis. When water is shut off, people can't cook, wash, or flush toilets. On top of that, sometimes they lose their children to Protective Services because the situation is made unhealthy and unsafe.

In response, We the People of Detroit set up a hotline for folks who have been shut off to call (844-42WATER) and began to organize stations around the city to provide emergency water and information.

Our church, where the Worker kitchen resides, is one of them. On July 24, the Council of Canadians, led by Maude Barlowe, delivered 300 gallons of water to our water station in an act of solidarity. We stacked the water around our baptismal font at the back of the church and declared it a place of grace. A week later, Keepers of the Mountain in West Virginia (where a chemical spill had left an entire town without water) delivered 1,100 gallons of water. Another, even larger shipment is expected from a UAW local in Chicago. The support is growing.

Hence, the Detroit Emergency Manager has a problem. The Federal Judge in Detroit's bankruptcy called in the Water Board to say, this has become an issue for the bankruptcy trial. (The issue was already deeply embedded.) You're making the city look bad. So the Water Board declared a two-week moratorium on shut-offs. Thereafter, the Emergency Manager announced that he was giving administration of the Water Department over to Detroit's mayor, Mike Duggan. Duggan is white and was "elected" in a landslide of write-in votes. He can't do anything the Emergency Manager doesn't permit, but they work pretty closely together. Think of it as good cop-bad cop. The mayor says that things have been handled badly under the emergency manager, but now we'll do them right. He has a ten-point plan to extend the shut-off moratorium, to give people time to pay up, to hold some informational events, and to crack down on those "stealing" water. There isn't anything in that plan about the $29 million owed by commercial and industrial accounts, and not a word about the Water Affordability Plan.

No one took Nelson's paper plate and followed the design. It's all just happened in a very decentralized and Spirit-led way. Charity Hicks walks among us and we are "waging love." As this is written, the bankruptcy trial is scheduled to begin after Labor Day. More actions are being discerned. The story is not over yet.

Postscript: It's still not over. Since this was written in 2014, two Special Rapporteurs from the United Nations have visited Detroit and declared a violation of the Human Right to Water[2] *(and referred to the truck-blockers as "defenders of Human Rights"). By way of further direct action, four people have been arrested at a Water Board rate increase session; six young people have been removed by police from disrupting the mayor's State of the City Address; police have been called in repeatedly to remove people preventing their own or their neighbor's water shut-offs; two young graffiti artists were charged with*

---

2. http://www.d-rem.org/detroit-minds-dying/.

felonies for painting "Free the Water" on a prominent water tower,; a one-year celebration of the Detroit Bankruptcy featuring the Governor, the Federal Judge, and the Mayor was closed down by vocal protests.

A community-based research group has produced "Mapping the Water Crisis,"[3] aligning shut-offs with race and neighborhoods slated for clearing. In collaboration with Henry Ford Hospital, they have also used emergency room records to document the health consequences in neighborhoods where shut-offs are concentrated. It is estimated that since the initial order by the Emergency Manager, 80,000 shut-offs have occurred. The demolition company, Homrich, Inc., contracted to do those has received $13 million. During that same period, the people of Flint have been poisoned with lead in an action also ordered by an Emergency Manager. A Peoples' Tribunal has been held putting the Governor, the Mayor, and the Emergency Managers on trial for crimes against humanity in Flint and Detroit. Following the verdict, 10,000 Wanted Posters were circulated around the state.

Meanwhile the trial of the Homrich 9, who blocked the water shut-off trucks, is still ongoing. Two of us completed a five-day jury trial, but after closing arguments had been made and the jury instructed, the prosecution came rushing in with a Circuit Court emergency stay pending a mistrial motion.[4] Corporation Counsel for the City of Detroit, the head of the Law Department, had gone to the Judge ex parte (without our knowledge or presence) to secure the order. It took Circuit Court Judge Michael Hathaway ten months to rule on the mistrial and another seven months for the jury to be dismissed. On a ninety-day misdemeanor, with our third District Court Judge, we begin yet another trial in July 2017, three years after the action itself.

---

3. https://wethepeopleofdetroit.com/communityresearch/water/.
4. http://www.d-rem.org/watch-disorder-in-the-court-homrich-9/.

27

Church and the Powers (Church as a Power) (2016)

A Material or Spiritual Reality?

Asked if the church is a spiritual or bodily reality, folks mystified by Walter Wink's claim of an actual spiritual aspect to corporations or institutions barely blink to identify a spiritual dimension to church, either as congregation or denominational structure. In that sense we might be better off beginning rather than ending with reflection on church and the powers.

In fact, Wink found the insights from Revelation 2 (the letters to the angels of the churches) to be useful in understanding the "angels of the nations" as having both personality and vocation[1] and it has been used similarly as a heuristic device to get at the "angel of a city" (see above).

In *Unmasking the Powers*, volume 2 of his powers trilogy, Wink devotes a chapter to answering what might be meant by "the angel of the church at Ephesus."[2] Since the second-person pronouns throughout each letter are singular, and ruling out reference to a bishop or representative, he concludes:

---

1. Walter Wink, *Unmasking the Powers* (Philadelphia: Fortress Press, 1986), 93.
2. Ibid., 69–86.

It would appear that the angel is not something separate from the congregation, but must somehow represent it as a totality. Through the angel, the community seems to step forth as a single collective entity or Gestalt. But the fact that the angel is actually addressed suggests that it is more than a mere personification of the church, but the actual spirituality of the congregation as a single entity. The angel would exist in, with, and under the material expressions of the church's life as its interiority. As the corporate personality or felt sense of the whole, the angel of the church would have no separate existence apart from the people. But the converse would be equally true: the people would have no unity apart from the angel. Angel and people are the inner and outer aspects of one and the same reality.[3]

By outlining the common memo-like structure of the seven letters Wink inferred that the angel had both a vocation (I know this about you . . .), who the church was uttered in the Word of God to be, and a personality (but I have this against you . . .) who the church is in its story of fallenness. Each letter includes an exhortation to repent, to return to its given calling. So the angel embodies, as it were, the church in creation and fall, both what the church is and what it's called to be.

With only a little reflection, preachers understand this instinctively. To prepare a sermon certainly does often involve the individual pastoral needs of particular congregational members, but generally pastors are, in fact, addressing the angel, the essence, the heart of a community, to move it forward into ministry or more fully into its calling. This is to say that the angel is not an agent of change or transformation —that impetus comes from the voice of the Human One or the message of John or the inspired word of the preacher. A church angel is the gyroscopic holder of stability or status quo.[4] Let a new preacher arrive and begin to change leadership only to find that in the manner of a family system, the dysfunctional position is reoccupied by a new person. He or she might move the furniture, or even, God forbid, the flag, only to find everything moved mysteriously back.

I once led a Lenten study with a congregation on the angel of their church. We struggled. They just could not wrap their heads around the idea or quite get it—until they recalled their merger of two congregations into one! It dawned on them that in that moment they weren't just trying to blend leadership personnel, they had been attempting to fuse two angels who were bumping heads and resisting mightily to

3. Ibid., 70.
4. Ibid., 80.

hold their identities. It was a light going on for them. Suddenly they were capable of writing letters to the angel of their congregation (some of which concerned the gifts and wounds of merger).

At about the same time as Wink's book, two related studies appeared. One was James Hopewell's underappreciated book, *Congregations: Stories and Structures*.[5] Using narrative ethnographic techniques of listening for the community's story, Hopewell could get at what he called the "genius" of congregation. He even had a schematology from Greek literature to facilitate interpretation: romantic, tragic, comic, etc. As a pastoral tool it comported well and usefully with Wink's angelic understanding.

The other was Edwin Friedman's more widely read *Generation to Generation*,[6] which brought family process to bear on the congregations of synagogue and church. Here the mechanism of stability and change was approached by perceiving the patterns and systems (functional and dysfunctional) of family/community structure. The people are in the system and the system is in the people. Wink, Hopewell, and Friedman, though writing from different disciplines, are fruitfully read side by side by side.

William Stringfellow more than once addressed his own denomination (he counted himself a "reluctant Episcopalian"). In an article called "On Being Haunted by the Angel of the Church at Sardis" (Rev. 3:2—"I know all your ways; that though you have a name for being alive you are dead"), he was, in effect, writing a letter to the denominational angel of the Episcopal Church USA. It concerned the ordination of women, in particular those who had been "irregularly" ordained virtually as an act of ecclesial disobedience in 1974. If the embeddedness of patriarchy in the structures of the church was to be presumed, he was nevertheless appalled by the spiritual sluggishness of its renunciation. He openly named the Constantinian bondage and investment of the church in the established order—and, in essence, he called it to repent.

On another earlier occasion, he wrote a letter to the East Harlem Protestant Parish.[7] Again, essentially without naming it so, he addressed the Angel of Parish Group Ministry. He wrote mainly in the mode of, "But I have this against you. . . ." It was a letter of resignation,

---

5. James F. Hopewell, *Congregations: Stories and Structures* (Philadelphia: Fortress Press, 1987).
6. Edwin Friedman, *Generation to Generation* (New York: Guilford, 1985).
7. *William Stringfellow: Essential Writings* (Maryknoll, NY: Orbis, 2013), 106–17. Much of the letter was adapted to a passage in *My People is the Enemy* (New York: Holt, Rinehart & Winston, 1964), 85–97. See Bill Wylie-Kellermann, *A Keeper of the Word* (Grand Rapids, MI: Eerdmans, 1994), 130–40.

even if it did appeal for repentance and presumed the vocation of the Parish. The EHPP was the vanguard and flagship of a renewed urban ministry movement in this country in the fifties and sixties, a remarkable and enduring enterprise. Yet Stringfellow's letter conveyed the news that the best we may do is subject to the fall, to idolatry, to inflation and pretention. The parish is become a principality. He saw it indulging a presumption of naming itself, in effect, the "new Jerusalem," of finding its justification in "good works" rather than in the freedom of the gospel. "The sign of dwelling in that freedom in the group ministry will be when all of its members are willing even to give up the group ministry. It is not that it may have ever to actually be given up . . . but it is necessary that there be a full freedom to give it up."[8] In that notion is the seed of an entire ecclesiology.

The Holy Nation, the Exemplary Power

> Let it be said that when I name the church, I do not have in mind some idealized church, or some disembodied or uninstitutionalized church, or just an aggregate of individuals. I mean the church in history, the church constituted and precedented in history at Pentecost, the church that is an organic reality: visible as a community institutionalized as a society. . . . Most concretely I mean the church as the holy nation . . . the church that is the exemplary nation juxtaposed to all the other nations; the church that as a principality and institution transcends the bondage to death in the midst of fallen creation: . . . the church in which the vocation of worship and advocacy signifies the renewed vocation of every creature; the church that anticipates the imminent and prompt redemption of all of life.[9]

Much is implied. Naming the church as the exemplary principality suggests one free from bondage to death, renewed in worship and advocacy.

Let's put it this way: the church as exemplary power means one that remembers its vocation is to praise God and serve human life, indeed all of creation.

A fundamental trait of the fallen principalities is their "ethic of survival." In their anxiety about their mortality and finitude, principalities make their own survival their vocational priority, supplanting their actual vocation to serve creation in their own particular call. In the national security state, survival isn't everything, it's the only thing.

---

8. Ibid., 116.
9. William Stringfellow, *Conscience and Obedience* (Waco, TX: Word, 1977), 102.

In their anxiety about death, the principalities give themselves over to death, to its rule and protection. Because the church is not anxious about its own survival (should it recall that its life is not its own), the church is free to die as institution or community.

Some years ago traveling the States in an anti-war speaking tour, Zen master Thich Nhat Hahn was asked if he'd be willing to sacrifice Buddhism for the sake of peace. Of course, he replied without pausing a heartbeat. I don't need Buddhism to be a Buddhist. But more importantly, if I wasn't willing to sacrifice Buddhism for the sake of peace, I already would have sacrificed Buddhism.

A church that isn't free to die is already dead.

To be sure, there are points in the life of some congregations, perhaps more than claim it, when it is time to tell the story, sing a sweet song, and close the doors. To embrace mortality and freely die. I have, to be sure, seen huddled communities with a death grip on a building (or vice versa) unfree to let go. But the scope of what is being suggested here is far deeper. To be free to die is the freedom to take the big collective and even institutional risk, to bet the farm, to spend the endowment, to take the big leap to begin again, to risk the wrath of the powers, to risk one's good name and reputation, to break the law for the sake of the planet, or to sanctuary immigrants . . . to risk crucifixion. Whatever more. To risk.

In the 1980s something of a renewal movement spread through the churches of North America. It was called the Sanctuary movement and offered protective resistance to refugees and asylum seekers, as many as a million that decade, from the Central American wars sponsored and funded by the United States. The anchors were two congregations, the earliest to declare themselves safe spaces—Southside Presbyterian in Tucson, Arizona and Wellington Avenue UCC in Chicago, but it quickly spread across the country. On the one hand the movement, at some risk, offered hospitality to families being refused asylum or being sought for return home. At the same time it directly opposed U.S. policy, open and covert, which was prosecuting war under the Reagan administration. The churches and their clergy spoke openly, but also provided Salvadoran and Guatemalan refugees a platform and voice in the public debate. In Arizona the Justice department issued a seventy-one-count indictment against sixteen of the religious activists. Though they were denied the necessity defense and were convicted, their trial became essentially an opportunity to indict the administration's proxy and secret wars, and for organizing and expanding the Sanctuary movement.

While these congregations could look to the biblical tradition and even European common law for justification and warrant,[10] their inspiration came from the churches and base communities of Central America, facing daily the risk of disappearance, imprisonment, torture, and death. Bishop Oscar Romero not only opened the cathedral in San Salvador as safe space for the poor, but he turned the pulpit and its weekly radio broadcasts into a source of news naming massacres and disappearances: interceding for the victims, confronting the regime, and calling on the soldiers to lay down their arms. He was assassinated at the altar on March 24, 1980. The Tucson sanctuary was opened on the anniversary of his death.

At Pentecost, in the course of his first sermon Peter says, "let me speak freely unto you" (Acts 2:29 KJV). The decisive Greek word in the text is *parrhesia*, a word that appears only once in Luke but then suddenly flourishes in Acts from the day of Pentecost on.[11] Most often translated as "boldness," or "speaking openly," it seems a mini-Pentecost is packed into the word. Here is a term cunningly lifted from the political lexicon of the Greek city-states. It signified there the right of the citizen to speak fully and freely in the public assembly. It means literally: "the freedom to say all."

---

10. Biblically, the most clearly spelled-out tradition of sanctuary is found in the Torah passages concerning the "cities of refuge" (Exod 21:13-14; Num 35:6-28; Deut 4:41-43; 19:4-13). The six Levitical cities named in Deuteronomy apparently reflect the historical fact that the right of asylum was commonplace at the local altars of Yahweh. When the local shrines were destroyed under the centralized worship of the "deuteronomic reforms," the cities were afforded a special vocation of sanctuary. The residents of these towns were charged with a rigorous task of protection, "lest innocent blood be shed" (Deut 19:10). The asylum was specifically for those accused of manslaughter. By the law and tradition of bloodguilt, the accused were subject to the private justice of vengeance (An eye for an eye . . .). The sanctuary, in the interest of justice, broke the cycle of violence and revenge. At the city gate, a limit was set. The killing stopped there.

    Sanctuary is quite literally a sign and space of nonviolence: check your weapons at the door. Indeed, in the early church, it was the ministry of protection and mediation that by far preceded any public, civil, or imperial acknowledgment of Christian sanctuary. Leaders in the church movement quickly became intermediaries between criminals and those who desired vengeance, and acted as ambassadors of reconciliation and mercy before the throne of justice. Fugitives were protected, slaves interceded for (think of Paul's letter to Philemon on behalf of Onesimus), and debtors sheltered until forgiveness and release were granted. In particular, the growing recognition of the office of bishop as intercessor paved the road to the sanctuary door.

    In common law going back to medieval times, the church was recognized as sanctuary space, and clergy could even accompany fugitives to a boat and safe passage out of the country or the district. From the Levitical cities of refuge to the heyday of sanctuaries in England, sanctuary nonviolence has been neither passive nor sedentary, despite being grounded in the altar. For a fuller account see Bill Wylie-Kellermann, "Sanctuary: The Hospitality of God," *Sojourners*, April 1983.

11. Bill Wylie-Kellermann, *Seasons of Faith and Conscience* (Maryknoll, NY: Orbis, 1991; Eugene, OR: Wipf & Stock, 2008), 202. What follows rehearses a passage of that volume.

However, when exercised by the disciples that freedom has categorically nothing to do with constitutional guarantees, official sanction, or the good graces of the state. It is the evangelical freedom of speech granted to them by the experience of the resurrection. It is the freedom of another citizenship. It is endowed by the Holy Spirit.[12]

In the Acts, nearly every instance of this "boldness" is attended by risk and threat. Often as not the exercise of *parrhesia* "creates" the situation of danger. Consider Peter and John before the Sanhedrin (4:13, 29, 31) or Paul in Damascus (9:27) where "they plotted to kill him," as they did again in Jerusalem (9:29). Paul and Barnabas speak boldly in Antioch (13:46) where "the leading men of the city stirred up persecution against them and drove them out of the district." Likewise in Iconium (14:3) and Ephesus (19:8). Before King Agrippa, after a two-year prison bit, under cross-examination by Festus, Paul speaks freely. The very last word in the book of Acts? *Parrhesia*? It's second to last. In the concluding verse of Acts (28:32) under house arrest in Rome, Paul is still going on about the gospel, talking away, speaking boldly *unhindered*. Nothing, it seems, can shut him up. No surprise that when Paul himself writes from jail he invokes *parrhesia* as courage and boldness to speak even in chains (Eph 6:19–20; Phil 1:12–26; Phlm 8–9).

Not unrelated is another term lifted from the political vocabulary of the Greek city-states: *eklesia*—church. The *eklesia* named the assembly of the citizens of the *polis*, free landed and propertied male. It was a political subversion to appropriate the term for the gathering of women, slaves, and poorfolk. Tell me what *eklesia* looks like; this is what *eklesia* looks like. Not many of them were wise by human standards, few were powerful or of noble birth. For in Christ there is neither male nor female, Jew nor Greek, slave nor free, but all are one. In the *eklesia* of Christ the divisions and hierarchies of wealth, culture, and patriarchy do not reign. The community is not occupied by these powers of empire.

Just so, to be *eklesia*, to be church as exemplary power in this present moment is to be freed of white supremacy, patriarchy, idolatrous patriotism, homophobia, heterocentrism, mammon, militarism, consumer materialism, all the divisions and ideologies of domination.

---

12. See Stanley B. Morrow, *Speaking the Word Fearlessly* (New York: Paulist, 1982).

Church as Fallen Power

But in fact . . . these are the very powers that have insinuated themselves into the structures and fabric of our churches. It's an empirical measure of the fall.

Consider white supremacy alone. The commonplace that eleven a.m. Sunday morning is the most segregated hour of the week remains truer than ever. One of the essays above details the aggressive demonic and spiritual power of white racism and its structural methods. And it suggests ways the demon might be exorcized.

In his Letter from a Birmingham Jail, Dr. King has every right to be amazed and brokenhearted that the church failed to undertake that work of "prayer and fasting" or come to the aid and support of the struggle in Birmingham and beyond. "Who are these people? Who is their god?" Why do they fail to risk in the name of the gospel and its freedom.

In Detroit the mainline churches were fully implicated in the ravages done the city and its economy by white flight. Postwar the denominational church plants and start-ups were already social infrastructure for suburbanization. The wholesale moves of the churches, often in conversation with the realtors and developers engineering white flight through blockbusting, functioned with the economic mechanisms. They didn't simply follow their parishioners, accommodating them with a shorter driving distance. Often as not, they anchored development and identified new neighborhoods to be filled.

Now, as Detroit's footprint is being reconfigured and downsized as it were (a logical consequence of devastation by white flight, job flight, capital fight), the churches figure again in the racial reorganization. Before the last round of church closings, the archbishop sat down for a private meeting with the mayor, presumably to hear and coordinate which neighborhoods had no future. Which were slated for "green space" and "blue space," from which poor and black people would necessarily be expelled. The mechanisms of their removal? Mortgage foreclosures, tax foreclosures, water shut-offs, pulling of infrastructure like bus lines, police and fire stations, the closure of public schools, and yes, the closing of churches.

Though it may take the superficial disguise, this is the very opposite of the church's freedom to die, to risk itself for the life of the poor, the life of creation. It smacks of the fear of death and that anxiety about survival which supplants the vocation to praise God and serve human life.

A church not anxious about its survival? Mainline denominations and congregations crunch the numbers, both membership and budget, wring their hands, and calculate the trended dates of their demise. Taking the cross from the altar and bringing in the couches, megachurch models proliferate. Evangelism ceases to concern a call to discipleship. It's little more than a desperate effort to stem the bleeding. I see it in my own beloved church.

The conversion of Constantine to Christianity in the fourth century, or better the conversion of the church to Roman Empire, marks a kind of watershed in the story of church and the powers. From the standpoint of bold speaking, the establishment of Christianity as imperial religion signifies a moment where free speech is less guaranteed by the Spirit than by the State (and thereby silence is purchased). In a simple sense, church mimicked empire in wealth, hierarchy, even violence—imperial war was explained and justified. Before Constantine one couldn't be a Christian and serve in the Roman army (the allegiances were in conflict); after Constantine one couldn't be in the Roman army and not be a Christian (the allegiances were conflated and confused). From the standpoint of survival and the freedom to die, the sanction and protection of empire rendered a community less beholden to God than to the emperor and his minions.

Stringfellow makes much of the acquiescence and political silence of churches, purchased by the economic rewards of the tax privilege that has enabled the accrual of enormous "unseemly" wealth, the management and maintenance of which is an overwhelming preoccupation. In the seventies he urged a remedy:

> I cannot imagine any other way, at this point, to free the church to recover its vocation as the exemplary principality or holy nation than by notorious acts of disavowal of this traffic with political authority. The churches in America need to divest property, not hoard it any longer, and as part of that I urge renunciation of the tax privilege so that the churches could be freed to practice tax resistance. If that portends direct conflict with political authority and involves such risks as official confiscation of church properties—which it does—then my only response it that it promises a way of consolidating losses.[13]

---

13. Stringfellow, *Conscience and Obedience*, 104.

For nearly three decades I have taught adjunct in an urban ministry training program for seminarians, including much of the material in this book. The project survived theological changes and financial crises, occupying the interstitial spaces between seminaries and connecting students with churches, city neighborhoods, and the streets as a context of ministry and theological reflection. It was a unique program in seminary education. For ten years I even directed one of its programs, supporting during that time the development of an African-centered project of MDiv study.

As it happened, by a complicated legal arrangement this para-institution came to be owner of the building in which it operated. When it was subsequently sold, several million dollars came to the organization and were placed into a foundation making grants to seminary programs, including this one—devoted to urban pastoral education. With a change in organizational leadership the urban ministry program became increasingly interfaith in character—needless to say, an important aspect of urban work in the present era. But then the seminary programs began to wither; enrollment weakened, but so had recruitment. One by one they were shut down and staff released. In the name of boldness, a new program of interfaith immersion studies around the world was hatched (apparently with the foundation moneys to sustain it in the near term).

This happens simultaneous with the inauguration of a new political regime which by all appearances is organizing an assault on poor and working communities, on black bodies, black communities, on immigrant populations, on urban public education, on indigenous peoples and their sovereign claims, on healthcare for the poorest and most vulnerable, on regulations of environmental justice, indeed on the planet itself. The program is dismantled at the very moment that churches and pastors, not only but especially urban ones, need training in resistance to these assaults, need resources to be spaces of freedom and safety for those under attack. But the resources in question will be devoted instead to interfaith global tourism.

Was the old model simply not workable any longer? Some believed that. Did the seminaries, as the board was told, just not want any more of these classes? Did the board, as the seminaries were told, simply want to end the program? Was it finally time, after forty years, for the old para-institution to die and be reconfigured for another's vocation? Or was it done in, back-door style, by the speculative wealth in the bank? Just too tempting and seductive a pot? Did the capital cast its spell and come for the remains of the gospel? Was the angel of the operation too weakened to hold its center? Such is the fate of churchly institutions in era of the fall.

Justification and Redemption

The Constantinian collusion of the church has involved its seduction to the trappings of capital and empire, but also the sanction and theological justification of imperial design. The divine right of kings may be first and foremost, but quick behind is the Doctrine of Discovery, which in turn lies beneath Manifest Destiny, indigenous genocide, the Monroe Doctrine, and all the dirty wars of Central and Latin America. The Doctrine issued in 1493 as a Papal Bull declared that, by God's ordination, Catholic kings had legal dominion over any lands the eye of European explorers fell upon, anywhere they set a foot. It worked the same way for Anglican and Protestant settlers as well. Conquest and military intervention simply followed.

There was great disappointment in the fall of 2015 when Pope Francis in his address to the U.S. Congress, for all its strength, failed to name and denounce the Doctrine and call for repentance.

A year later over 500 ecumenical clergy (one for each year of colonial occupation since the promulgation of the doctrine) were invited by the Standing Rock Sioux Tribe to come to the Oceti Sakowin camp to publicly renounce and ceremonially burn a copy of the Doctrine.[14] The camp itself was a word and example to the churches. A prayer encampment of nearly 10,000 "water protectors" had been set up to block and resist the Dakota Access Pipeline, what the Sioux people called the Black Snake carrying the crude oil of fracking. It was tearing up sacred sites of battleground and burial, and jeopardizing drinking water for the Tribe and all their relations downstream, by running under the Missouri River. They were acutely aware of what fracking means for climate change and planetary degradation. With only prayers, ceremony, bodies, and signs, they faced off with heavily militarized police forces—armored vehicles, attack dogs, water cannons, concussion grenades, rubber-coated bullets, and tear gas. In a certain sense the clergy were invited to glimpse what church could be.

Think again of the Sanctuary movement renewing a longstanding vocation of church and simultaneously renewing its resistance to

---

14. Denise Griebler, "Strange Liberators," *Radical Discipleship*, March 12, 2017. https://radicaldiscipleship.net/2017/03/12/strange-liberators/ (accessed March 12, 2017).

empire and violence. Think of the church putting its "body" on the line, blocking the way. At this writing, in early 2017, there is a revival of the U.S. Sanctuary movement specifically with respect to immigrants and undocumented people. Policies of the Trump administration target these. Churches and houses of worship (Jewish and Muslim) are stepping up. In Detroit seven congregations have declared themselves. At the public announcement, one of the pastors proclaimed, "We will not stand idly by while injustice occurs. . . . We have a message today for Donald Trump: If you want these families you're gonna have to come through us." [15]

Given the times, should houses of worship, churches, and faith communities be thinking of themselves even more broadly as cultural safe houses? Yes for homeless and immigrants, refugees and undocumented, but even for community and culture themselves. For art, theater, poetry, more.

Mapping and Rebuking the Powers

Every Good Friday in Detroit for nearly forty years, beginning from St. Peter's Episcopal, the church I now serve as pastor-in-charge, we walk the streets of our neighborhood, the streets of the city, carrying a cross and marking with prayer and recollection the sites where Christ can be recognized as crucified today. It is our version of the traditional stations of the cross. During Lent we gather to consider the where's and how's—it is a simple work of discernment. To be sure, we are recalling street corners where acts of violence may have occurred, but in a deep sense we are discerning the presence and location of the principalities in our own parish neighborhood. We are virtually mapping where the powers have a foot on the ground in our midst. We are reading the city as a principalities text. During Lent we take the time to write the meditations and reflections to be read in Passion Week. The traditional way of the cross become a ritual of publicly exposing the powers. At the jail, or the bank, or the federal building the powers are addressed—after the fashion of the Ephesians call: that now through the church the wisdom and power of God might be made known to the principalities and powers in high places (Eph 3:11).

Perhaps it's time that churches should enact an Easter equivalent.

---

15. Niraj Warikoo, "9 Churches in Mich. Declare That They Are Sanctuaries for Immigrants," *Detroit Free Press*, March 14, 2017. http://www.freep.com/story/news/local/michigan/2017/03/14/michigan-church-synogogue-immigrant-sanctuaries/99177278/ (accessed March 14, 2017).

Stations of the resurrection. A similar mapping of signs and locations could be done—recognizing sites where freedom from the reach and rule of the principalities, indeed the power of death itself might be seen. Carry the rolled-up garments to the prisoner-run bakery, the people's theater, the gorgeous graffiti with meaning and content, the community garden, the independent free school network, the restorative justice center, a movement newspaper surviving on a thread, the community museum and its oral memory, more. Sing and rejoice. "The truth is Christ has been raised from the dead, the first fruits of those who have died . . . after he has destroyed every ruler and every authority and power. For he must reign until he has put all his enemies under his feet. The last enemy to be destroyed is death" (1 Cor 15:20, 24–26).

28

Trump Powers: Principalities and the President (2017)

> And don't speak too soon,
> for the wheel's still in spin
> and there's no telling who that it's namin'
> for the loser now will be later to win ...
>
> —Bob Dylan

A prophet's warning. To write about the principalities in this present moment, just weeks since the inauguration of the Trump regime in January 2017, is to risk speaking too soon. By the time these reflections see the light of print, impeachment proceedings may be launched, or a nonviolent groundswell of resistance may have brought the president to the brink of resignation, or yet perhaps an iron fist is holding collapse at bay with the "brink" and the "launch" being war, God forbid—even nuclear, or maybe Mother Earth has reached her limit and thrown the planet in deeper turmoil, nor would I rule out some other intervention, unforeseen and virtually miraculous. Such are the times—apocalyptic and spinningly unpredictable.

Trump as Principality

Still there are some things that might be said even now concerning how a theology of the powers might offer insight. Insofar as the "ruler," the *archon* (see above, pages 56–61, the list of created powers in the Colossians 1 hymn) may be defined as the ruler-in-office, the agent-in-role, the President as principality is this fusion of person and institution. In biblical reflection at the beginning of this book, it was asked whether the person takes possession of the presidency or the presidency takes possession of the person. One version of that question wondered aloud whether the gravity and responsibility of the office might sober and change the person Donald Trump, making him, in effect, more presidential. So far, except for demonstrating the capacity to constrain himself sufficiently to read from a teleprompter in an address to Congress, that variety of possession has not proven true. Another version, based on his erratic behavior, even diagnosed from afar by members of the therapeutic community, worries over the consequence of personality infused with the inflation of power (a personal pathology to which Twitter seems remarkably suited). Is he possessed by the office as a vortex through which information and power run? Not in a conventional sense. He doesn't read or sit still for policy or intelligence briefings, and his isolation renders him to a certain degree muted to such. Yet he has brought other substantial powers and forces into the White House. A list of Wall Street and billionaire cabinet choices comes to mind. And, above all, strategic forces of the "alt-right," in the guise of Steve Bannon. It is reported that Trump was angered "that he was not fully briefed on details of the executive order he signed giving his chief strategist a seat on the National Security Council...."[1] And those may yet form him more than can be presently known.

In a number of senses, Trump comes to the office already a full-blown principality. Inauguration, in his case, was a ritual not so much of powerly fusion, as powerly collusion. Let us allow William Stringfellow to be our guide and lens. When he made his earliest list of the principalities, Stringfellow included "images" alongside institutions and ideologies. His simple examples included Marilyn Monroe and Adolf Hitler. The image, he wrote, "is a genuine idol, an entity bearing the

---

1. Glenn Thrush and Maggie Haberman, "Trump and Staff Rethink Tactics After Stumbles," *New York Times*, February 6, 2017, A1.

same name and likeness as the person, with an existence, character, and power quite distinguishable from the person who bore the name."

> In any case, the form of principality identifiable as the public image bearing the name of a person exists independently of that person (though the person may be wholly dependent upon the principality). The form is distinguishable from the person, lies beyond control, and is in conflict with the person until the person surrenders life in one fashion or another to the principality. The principality requires not only recognition and adulation as an idol from movie fans or voters or the public but also demands that the person of the same name give up his or her life as a person to the service and homage of the image. And when that surrender is made, the person in fact dies, though not yet physically. For at that point one is literally possessed by one's own image. The demand, then, made in the conflict between the principality and the personality is one in which the whole life of the person is surrendered to the principality and is given over to the worship of the image.[2]

We are talking here about the cult of celebrity, a form of idolatry, inflated and magnified by corporate and now social media. Image is the power onto which alienated meaning is projected, even by the self.

Donald Trump was clear, almost immediately, that the inauguration ceremony was not so much for him a moment of sacred state covenant or constitutional submission, but of public adulation and comparative crowd-size about which he was sorely anxious. By the following day he was in a Twitter and surrogate war with the press, marshaling the support of "alternative facts" that it was the largest crowd ever to attend the ceremony.

All indications are that he is obsessed with his own media coverage, even reading the *New York Times* and following cable news stations at all hours, which he then denigrates and refutes in day-by-day tweet rants.

A campaign necessarily encourages and inflates image—it may even be thought a measure of alienated spiritual formation for the position. But in Trump's case there were early assessments that his campaign was not so much a serious run, as yet another starring role for his public image, another shot in the ratings war. Predictions were that he would pull out when things got serious, but when his image did well, instead of withdrawing, he got hooked.

---

2. William Stringfellow, *Free in Obedience* (New York: Seabury, 1964), 55.

The image has a life of its own. Think of it as even capable of effecting self-interested policy decisions. In the Trump presidency these early decisions appear to be instant policymaking by Twitter impulse—but it goes far deeper than that. Stringfellow puts it like this in the extreme example:

> Once in a while the public image of a person becomes much more than just an idol, becomes a principality of such magnitude that the image is comparable to an institutional or ideological principality. . . . [I]t may well be that long before his actual suicide the person named Hitler had been wholly obliterated by the principality named Hitler; that the person had indeed been possessed by a demon of that name; and that the devastation and massacre wrought in the name of Hitler was not the work of just some dark genius of the man, nor even of the man's insanity or gross criminality, but of the awesome demonic power that possessed him.[3]

Trump is an image, but also a brand and an economic empire, and so comes to the presidency as a walking principality in more than one sense. As image, he may exaggerate his wealth in claiming a net worth of $10 billion. Financial journalists place it somewhere between $3 and 4 billion, but only tax returns would reveal honest numbers, and those Trump continues to withhold. Of the Trump Organization's over five hundred holdings, 364 bear the Trump name and so its brand. *Fortune* magazine calculated that the campaign itself increased the value of the Trump Organization's holdings and the brand.

At a press conference outlining plans to deal with the conflicts of interests such assets bear, his attorney described the Organization: "As you know, the business empire built by president-elect Trump over the years is massive. . . ." Yet, Trump has eschewed the ordinary legal mechanisms for separating from his office the power and confusion of such assets: divestment, disclosure, blind trust. Instead, members of his family will take on management and decision-making for the duration. The massive business empire is still in the house.

Geographically, it's an expansive web of companies, hotels and apartments, golf courses, real estate holdings, and just "deals" for the Trump name and brand, most substantially in North America, but also, according to his filing with the Federal Election Commission, ventures in Asia, the Middle East, Europe, the Caribbean, and Latin America. Since the election certain of his national operations—in China, the Philippines, Turkey, Saudi Arabia, and of course Russia —have already

---

3. Ibid., 54–55.

become publicly notorious in connection with state phone calls, tweets, and policy directives.

In 1974, when William Stringfellow wrote *An Ethic for Christians and Other Aliens in a Strange Land*, he mused that if there was a hierarchy of powers, the state was preeminent among them. Later, however, almost immediately, he began to wonder aloud if the commercial principalities had not in fact superseded the state as the prevailing and preeminent powers, rivaling and usurping the state's authority and decision-making. Think not only of the Trump empire, but consider the cabinet now gathering around him. In an early take, Naomi Klein makes a related point.

> Let's be clear: this is not a peaceful transition of power. It's a corporate takeover. The interests have long-since paid off both major parties to do their bidding and have decided they are tired of playing the game.... So now they are cutting out the middleman and doing what every top dog does when they want something done right—they are doing it themselves.... After decades of privatizing the state in bits and pieces, they decided to just go for the government itself. Neoliberalism's final frontier. That's why Trump and his appointees are laughing at the feeble objections over conflict of interest—the whole thing is a conflict of interest, that's the point.[4]

Consider: Exxon Mobil for Secretary of State; Goldman Sachs for Department of Treasury; Rothschild, Inc., for Commerce Department. Go on down the list. Jeff Sessions, who praised the Klan and thought the NAACP and ACLU "un-American" in their civil rights work, for Department of Justice; Michael Flynn for National Security Advisor, who resigned after twenty-four days for intervening, between election and inauguration, in the U.S. Russian sanctions and lying about his action; for Housing and Urban Development, Ben Carson, a neurosurgeon qualified by growing up poor in Detroit, who first declined the job because he felt he had "no government experience" and had "never run a federal agency"; for Department of Energy, former Texas Governor Rick Perry, who ran for president on a platform of closing the agency down and who was surprised to learn (what he had previously not known) that one of the Department's primary responsibilities is to design and manage the U.S. stockpile of nuclear weapons; a career military man, "Mad Dog" Mattis, to oversee the Pentagon and what will

---

4. Naomi Klein, "Trump's Crony Cabinet May Look Strong, but They Are Scared," *The Nation*, January 26, 2017.

surely be a vastly expanded military budget; Scott Pruitt, who denies climate change science, for the Environmental Protection Agency; and for Department of Education, Betsy DeVos, of Michigan, whose only experience regarding public education is funding and lobbying for its systematic destruction and privatization. Conflicts of interest? Let Stringfellow fathom it:

> The scene of turmoil and confusion associated with the demonic powers becomes acute when it is recognized that these are rival, competitive powers despite the fact that, at times, they seem to confront human life as compatible or collaborating powers. All alliances among the principalities ... are transient and expedient.... These relationships ... are more intricate, more complicated, more ambiguous, more tense, more hectic than words can describe. The milieu of the powers and principalities *is* chaos.[5]

Welcome to Detroit

Here in Detroit we have, in recent years, suffered through state-imposed Emergency Management where all the powers of government and more were vested in one man. He, not the city of Detroit, declared bankruptcy, a mechanism for rapid gutting of pensions, for paying off the banks for their predatory municipal loans, for selling and privatizing assets. The first white mayor in four decades was elected in a landslide as a "write-in," in an election overseen by the same clerk who rendered 60 percent of Detroit votes unrecountable in the recent presidential election. The mayor and EM have overseen the downsizing of the city's footprint, expelling poor black and brown people from neighborhoods without futures—by means of water shut-offs, foreclosures, infrastructure removal, school closings and the like, all the while shifting resources to make the new city attractive and "safe" for white people. Public education has been gutted, looted, and dismantled by state control of the schools (for fifteen of the last eighteen years, including the immediate eight years prior also under emergency management). More than one hundred Detroit schools have been closed in the last eight years, with a free-fire zone for charters replacing them in the creation of a racial apartheid district of permanent failure. If Detroiters recoil at the configuration of powers gathered in the Trump administration, it is because we have seen the future up close—and it's deadly. We are also steeled for resistance.

---

5. William Stringfellow, *An Ethic for Christians and Other Aliens in a Strange Land* (Waco, TX: Word, 1973), 89, 94.

As the Detroit connection to the Trump administration, Betsy DeVos bears lingering over. She is the spokesperson and face of another billionaire family financial empire whose capital was amassed through a combination of auto parts manufacturing, the network marketing scheme of Amway, and the privatized mercenary army known among other names as Blackwater. Her husband has run unsuccessfully four times for governor, but the DeVos achievement has been in outright purchase of the state legislature, seat by seat, vote by vote, including the passage of a bill doubling the limit for campaign contributions, which itself was secured at a cost of some $300,000 in contributions. With that purchasing power, caps have been lifted from charters in Detroit, an ostensibly statewide failing school district was created (but which, all black, operates only in Detroit), the elected school board has been suppressed and replaced, public entities have been gagged from talking to constituents about local ballot measures. Along with the Governor and with support of the mayor, DeVos money has been the moving force behind the dismantling of public education in the black cities of Michigan, Detroit first and foremost among them.

In a nutshell, under direct state control, schools once middle range in statewide test scores have been turned into "failing schools," a relatively new term in education. Once wrecked, the schools are then ordered closed while removing caps and accountability for charters. That's the plan now elevated to national policy.

As the *New York Times* put it on the day of her confirmation (in a tie vote broken by the Vice President):

> Ms. DeVos is the perfect cabinet member for a president determined to appoint officials eager to destroy the agencies they run and weigh the fate of policies and programs based on ideological considerations. She has never run, taught, or sent a child to an American public school, and her confirmation hearings laid bare her ignorance of education policy and scorn for public education itself. She has donated millions to, and helped direct, groups that want to replace traditional public schools with charter schools and convert taxpayer dollars into vouchers to help parents send children to private and religious schools.[6]

A Spirit Unleashed

Abraham Lincoln, in his first inaugural address, called on Americans to

---

6. The Editorial Board, "Betsy DeVos Teaches the Value of Ignorance," February 8, 2017, A24.

summon "the better angels of our nature." Donald Trump's candidacy, and so far his presidency, has been Lincoln's exhortation in reverse.[7]

—Bret Stephens, Foreign Affairs correspondent
for the *Wall Street Journal*

Proximate to the discernment of signs is the discernment of spirits. This gift enables the people of God to distinguish and recognize, identify and expose, report and rebuke the power of death incarnate in nations and institutions or other creatures, or possessing persons, while they also affirm the Word of God incarnate in all of life, exemplified preeminently in Jesus Christ.[8]

—William Stringfellow

Who would have imagined that the most immediate and caustic outcome of the 2016 presidential campaign, actually culminated and triggered by the election itself, would be the unleashing of a spirit of domination? Ground level and street level. The worst impulses of human beings, however suppressed, were conjured, summoned, and granted a free rein. Fear, hatred, contempt, all were sent on newly appointed errands, house to house. White supremacy is back like guns in an open-carry state. Misogyny is a legitimate political position. Homophobia a heroic stance.

Hate crimes spiked in the days immediately following the election, many perpetuated by persons openly employing Trump's name or campaign slogans.[9]

The sales of confederate flags, briefly stigmatized in the wake of the Charleston church massacre, soar again during the campaign as people fly them from trucks and homes and businesses.

Hate fires against mosques and synagogues ignite and spread.

In the cafeteria, middle-school students in a Detroit suburb begin to chant, "Build the Wall! Build the Wall!"

Two men from India are shot, one fatally, in a bar—mistaken for Muslims.

Online troll storms foul response spaces with hate language.

A woman on the law faculty of Georgetown University was targeted after posting online a column that imagined a worst-case scenario: What if the President, in an erratic move, made to invade or bomb

---

7. Bret Stephens, "Daniel Pearl Memorial Lecture at the University of California," http://time.com/4675860/donald-trump-fake-news-attacks/ (accessed March 3, 2017).
8. Stringfellow, *An Ethic*, 139.
9. https://www.forbes.com/sites/niallmccarthy/2016/11/30/report-trumps-election-led-to-a-surge-in-hate-crime-infographic/#61dd5c972cf5 (accessed February 26, 2017).

a country; might senior military officials simply tell the president, "No, sir, we are not doing that"? When Breitbart News posted the column under the headline, "Ex-Obama Official Suggests 'Military Coup' Against Trump," and it went viral among the alt-right, her inbox and phone were flooded with a huge variety of death threats and all manner of curses, particularly misogynist and racist.[10] Such mass attacks can be spontaneous or organized and orchestrated.

Stringfellow numbers "cursing" among the tactics of the principalities. It is a stratagem fueled by such spirits. "The demonic powers curse human beings who resist them. I mean the term *curse* quite literally as a condemnation to death, as damnation. In earlier times, American Indians were cursed as savages in order to rationalize genocide. Somewhat similarly, chattel slavery involved cursing blacks as humanly inferior."[11]

Whole groups and classes of people are cursed and marked for fear. In keeping with his campaign threats and promises, the two most palpable enactments in these early weeks of the Trump administration have been the travel ban against seven Muslim-majority countries and the broadening acceleration of pick-up and deportation of undocumented immigrants, specifically Mexican and Meso-American. Because of his campaign threats, including the projection of a Muslim registry, it is neither spurious nor disingenuous to call the former a "Muslim Ban."

Upon the signing of Trump's executive order halting travel and immigration from the seven Middle Eastern countries in February 2017, not only did ordinary people appear at airports and refuse to leave until detainees were allowed in, but a Federal court order was issued halting its implementation. Initially, though chaotic, it appeared that Homeland Security and Customs officials might simply continue to act on executive order, provoking, in effect, an immediate constitutional crisis. Would the president and the executive branch honor the restraining power of the courts? For a moment it seemed not. So it was a major political and legal concession to the Constitution when the Attorney General's office appealed the ruling to the Ninth Circuit, rather than simply cursing and ignoring the "so-called judge" (a presidential tweet) of the lower court, whose ruling was, in fact, sustained.

As to the undocumented, "Which part of illegal don't people under-

---

10. http://www.breitbart.com/big-government/2017/02/02/ex-obama-official-suggests-military-coup-trump/ (accessed February 26, 2017).
11. Stringfellow, *An Ethic*, 103.

stand?" asks an ICE agent in Arizona. The administration speaks openly of "taking the shackles off" ICE and border patrol agents, who in turn report how quickly "a new atmosphere has taken hold" in their agencies. Gone is the prioritization of arresting and deporting firstly those who have committed serious crimes. In the new order, to be undocumented is to be a criminal. In Virginia, agents wait outside a church to arrest immigrants who have gone inside to stay warm.[12] Everywhere is declared unsafe. The president describes an ICE raid as a military operation, engendering panic and terror among Mexican families and communities in much the same way that the Klan did in the Jim Crow south. It keeps entire communities passive and quieted, vulnerable to isolation, wage theft, even sex trafficking. On the other hand, its impact can be the very opposite of that publicly intended: driving communities underground into the darkness of criminalization and even crime.

A similar free rein is being granted to local police forces. The Attorney General says they will no longer be monitored by the Federal Government in the effort to reduce killings at the hands of law enforcement. Such constraints only reduce effectiveness, he says. Profiles and cursing tweets may proliferate. Black and brown bodies will feel the heat.

Water Protectors at Standing Rock Camp have faced heavily militarized police on the premise that they are dangerous. People with ties to the camp are approached by the FBI joint *terrorism* taskforce.[13] After months of military-style police activity, the camp is closed down in a sweep following Executive Orders pushing the Dakota Pipeline forward.

Among specific curses of the present moment is "enemy of the people." The phrase, freighted with history going back to the French Revolution but most vivid as a Stalinist condemnation, has been directed by Trump against mainstream and established media such as the *New York Times* and CNN.[14]

America First! Make America Great Again! Such nationalism is less a policy (even if it might translate into moves on NAFTA or the Trans-Pacific Partnership trade deals) than it is a driving ideological spirit that has been invoked and claimed by the Trump regime. Stringfellow

---

12. "Agents Discover New Freedom on Deportations," *New York Times*, February 26, 2017, A1.
13. https://www.theguardian.com/us-news/2017/feb/10/standing-rock-fbi-investigation-dakota-access (accessed March 10, 2017).
14. "Trump Embraces 'Enemy of the People,' a Phrase with a Fraught History," *New York Times*, February 27, 2017, A1.

warns that nation and state, though distinct principalities, are merged in authoritarian governments. In totalitarian regimes, he writes:

> any substantive distinction between the principality of the nation and the principality of the State is lost. The ethos of the nation is absorbed into the apparatus of authority. Or, to put it a bit differently, the spirit and tradition of the nation are abolished by the administration of the State or displaced by a fabricated version of tradition furnished by the State. For all practical purposes, in a totalitarianism, the nation and the State become merged.[15]

Trump Theology: The Devotion of National Populism

Among the very first executive actions taken by President Trump was to declare his inauguration a "National Day of Patriotic Devotion."[16] It was the invocation of a call to worship. Consider this from his inaugural address: "At the bedrock of our politics will be total allegiance to the United States of America, and through our loyalty to our country we will rediscover our loyalty to one another. When you open your heart to patriotism, there is no room for prejudice." To Christians in particular, who declare their total, complete, and final allegiance to God alone (as evidenced and declared in baptism) but also to many others, this will be a troublesome suggestion signifying idolatry outright. "Opening your heart" to the saving power of patriotism is a conspicuous and mocking appropriation of evangelical faith. Patriotism's power to banish and renounce prejudice sounds a bitter irony to those who by it are banned, criminalized, expelled, and consigned even to death.

Another inaugural line related to that: "It's time to remember that old wisdom our soldiers will never forget, that whether we are black or brown or white, we all bleed the same red blood of patriots." Telling. Take that in with a close reading. Just when it sounds like this will be about common humanity, the blood is the blood of *patriots*. That, in many respects, is the hermeneutical key to understanding the constant refrain of "the People" in this inaugural address. It is a day of peaceful transfer of power "back to you, the people." "You came by the tens of millions to become part of this historic movement, the likes of which the world has never seen." It's your celebration. Once again "our gov-

---

15. *Ethic*, 109–10.
16. https://www.federalregister.gov/documents/2017/01/24/2017-01798/national-day-of-patriotic-devotion (accessed February 27, 2017).

ernment is controlled by the people." "January 20, 2017 will be remembered as the day the people became rulers of this nation again."[17]

In the name of unity (even invoking Psalm 133), the president indulges a clear division on the basis of moral and patriotic purity. "The people" are the patriots, the tens of millions who joined his movement, the forgotten he summoned and remembers. They have enemies at hand and indeed, his enemies are become their own—as in "the enemy of the people." This is a conscious, well-tutored, theological, and rhetorical move. It's been noted that when he announced his candidacy, Trump used first-person singular pronouns 256 times in the speech. I am, I will, I do. Me. My. Mine. In his inaugural speech, he used those words only three times.[18] He had not in actuality become less messianic, but his messianism has been rooted, indeed merged, with his devoted and righteous base.

Stringfellow (in the time of Reagan's American exceptionalism) named the "myth of the justified nation." Trump's theology frames justification, mediated by the nation and its leader, as conferred upon "the patriotic people." People publicly shamed and constrained in white racism are suddenly made righteous, justified, and freed. Folks angry at being unemployed and silenced are affirmed in righteous indignation. Men insecure in their sexual superiority are reassured in their identity and emboldened. Fears, instead of being faced, are fed, fanned, and justified. This justification of the People goes hand in hand with the unleashing of the dominating spirit. Notably, it is the offer of salvation without repentance.

In a biblical view, or so Stringfellow names it, the problem hinges essentially on the issue of repentance.

> Topically, repentance is *not* about forswearing wickedness as such; repentance concerns the confession of vanity. For America—for any nation at any time—*repentance means confessing blasphemy*. Blasphemy occurs in the existence and conduct of a nation whenever there is such profound and sustained confusion as to the nation's character, place, capabilities, and destiny that the vocation of the Word of God is preempted or usurped. Thus the very presumption of the righteousness of the American cause as a nation *is* blasphemy.[19]

---

17. All quotations from "Trump's Full Inauguration Speech Transcript, Annotated," https://www.washingtonpost.com/news/the-fix/wp/2017/01/20/donald-trumps-full-inauguration-speech-transcript-annotated/?utm_term=.59042f6d4772 (accessed February 27, 2017).
18. https://www.theatlantic.com/international/archive/2017/02/what-is-populist-trump/516525/ (accessed February 27, 2017).

Donald Trump may be a nominal Presbyterian, but he confesses to not believing in confession. Nor does he repent. When he makes mistakes, he has commented that he does not ask forgiveness or even "bring God into that picture." "I drink my little wine and eat my little cracker,"[20] but that's about it. Repentance on the scale of a nation or a people? Hardly a thought.

In all fairness, Trump's theological mentors, or more properly his pastors, have been thin on the gospel. As a teenager he was pastored by no less than Norman Vincent Peale, whose "Power of Positive Thinking" is hardly a call to discipleship, more akin to a cult of optimistic denial.[21] He was once married at Marble Collegiate Church in New York by Peale, who also officiated there at the burial of his parents. More recently his spiritual advisor has been Paula White, a megachurch pastor from Florida who also preaches a relentlessly upbeat version of "prosperity theology." She prayed a lavish blessing on him at the inauguration.

Theological Responses

There have already been a handful of biblical and theological responses to President Trump. A short list deserves mention.

I. *Christianity Today*, the flagship of evangelical journalism, weighed in theologically during the campaign in a rare public confrontation on the gospel as they saw it. Andy Crouch, executive editor, penned the article, "Speak Truth to Trump." Noting caution in electoral neutrality, naming the difficulty of the choice faced by Christians, and sufficiently excoriating Hillary Clinton, he went on, triggered by the revelations of Trump's "crude boasting about sexual conquest—indeed, sexual assault."

> To indulge in sexual immorality is to make oneself and one's desires an idol. That Trump has been, his whole adult life, an idolater of this sort, and a singularly unrepentant one, should have been clear to everyone. And therefore it is completely consistent that Trump is an idolater in many other ways. He has given no evidence of humility or dependence on others, let alone on God his Maker and Judge. He wantonly celebrates strongmen and takes every opportunity to humiliate and demean the vul-

---

19. William Stringfellow, *The Politics of Spirituality* (Philadelphia: Westminster, 1984; Eugene, OR: Wipf & Stock, 2006), 62–63.
20. http://www.cnn.com/2016/10/21/politics/trump-religion-gospel/ (accessed February 28, 2017).
21. Stringfellow has written about Peale in various places, but suffice to recall Adlai Stevenson's famous quip, "I find St. Paul appealing and St. Peale appalling."

nerable. He shows no curiosity or capacity to learn. He is, in short, the very embodiment of what the Bible calls a fool.[22]

Acknowledging that most Christians who support Trump do so in a "reluctant strategic calculation," based on the president's authority to appoint members of the Supreme Court, he went on, "But there is a point at which strategy becomes its own form of idolatry . . . when we betray our deepest values in pursuit of earthly influence. And because such strategy requires capitulating to idols and princes and denying the true God, it ultimately fails."[23]

II. On January 31, 2017, just eleven days after the inauguration, the Council of Bishops of the African Methodist Episcopal Church issued a letter calling on the denomination's membership to do all they can to "thwart what are clearly demonic acts" of the Trump administration, which they numbered in detail. Among them, appointing Steve Bannon, who has written racist rants against minorities and Jews as his chief Strategist, appointing Alabama Senator Jeff Sessions, with a history of racial indifference, as Attorney General, seeking to repeal and replace the ACA, issuing executive orders that restrict immigration from predominantly Muslim countries, beginning construction of a border wall with Mexico, supporting the Keystone and Dakota Pipelines, the practical denial of climate change. . . .[24]

Are these indeed demonic acts that must be resisted by those who "wrestle not against flesh and blood, but against . . . the rulers of the darkness of this present age, against spiritual wickedness in high places"? Among the churches they lead and address is Mother Emanuel AME in Charleston, S.C., where members of a Bible-study group were murdered point blank by a young white supremacist barely a year ago. Wrestling indeed.

William Stringfellow, who himself wrestled long and hard with these rulers and authorities, may shed some light.

> If the powers and principalities be legion, so are the means by which they assault, captivate, enslave, and dominate human beings. Yet all of the demonic claims against human life—for all their number and variegation and in spite of their dynamic qualities and even though they sponsor chaos—have a common denominator. Typically, each and every strata-

---

22. http://www.christianitytoday.com/ct/2016/october-web-only/speak-truth-to-trump.html (accessed February 28, 2017).
23. Ibid.
24. https://www.ame-church.com/wp-content/uploads/2017/01/Episcopal-Statement-Council-of-Bishops-re-Trump-Actions.pdf (accessed February 28, 2017).

gem and resort of the principalities seeks the death of the specific faculties of rational and moral comprehension which specially distinguish human beings from all other creatures. Whatever form or appearance it may take, demonic aggression always aims at the immobilization or surrender or destruction of the mind and at the neutralization or abandonment or demoralization of the conscience. In the Fall, the purpose and effort of every principality is the dehumanization of human life, *categorically*.[25]

If so, to me the bishops seem theologically adept and on target. Not even speaking too soon.

III. On February 25, 2017, faculty members of Princeton Theological Seminary signed and released a statement, "In Defense of Christian Faith and a Democratic Future." Signed by thirty-three of the current forty full-time faculty, plus twelve Emeriti Scholars and five adjuncts, it reads in part:

> We, the undersigned, believe that because God is sovereign over all creation and because all human beings are embraced by God's all-encompassing grace, the god of Donald Trump's "America first" nationalism is not the God revealed in our scriptures. Regardless of our specific political persuasions we agree that the attitudes fostered by this nationalism are inconsistent with Christian values of welcoming the stranger as if we were welcoming Christ, of seeking to distinguish truth from deception and conceit, and of believing that no institution or government can demand the kind of loyalty that belongs only to God.
>
> We also believe that the policies and approach embraced by the Trump administration run counter to democratic values, as executive orders and members of the new administration's cabinet often seek to demonize Islam, foster white supremacy, compromise the rule of law and intimidate judges, undermine the empowerment of women, ignore the destruction of the environment, promote homophobia, unleash unfounded fears of crime that worsen the "law and order" abuses of police and security forces.[26]

It also included a section confessing complicity in the sinful entanglements that have created this political and social crisis. "Not all of us have taken a firm and vocal enough stance against what Martin Luther

---

25. Stringfellow, *An Ethic*, 97.
26. http://www.ptsem.edu/news/faculty-statement (accessed February 28, 2017). See also Mark Lewis Taylor, http://marklewistaylor.net/blog/princeton-seminary-faculty-members-on-trump-presidency/ (accessed February 28, 2017).

King Jr. called the 'giant triplets' of violence in the United States: racism, extreme materialism, and militarism."

IV. The Matthew 25 Pledge is extreme in its simplicity. Named for the passage that enjoins welcoming the stranger, feeding the hungry, visiting the prisoner—because in this way one will serve Christ in the least of these our brothers and sisters—it is broad in its organizing reach. "I pledge to defend and protect the vulnerable in the name of Jesus." Circulated and propagated by a coalition of groups, from *Sojourners* to denominational Social Justice Offices to the Franciscans and Jesus Revolutionaries, it functions as a theological statement directed at policies that assault and demean. It covers actions of sanctuary, direct accompaniment, intervention, visitation, and more as a simple biblical statement to which many can subscribe and commit their names publicly.

V. During the campaign, the voice of Pope Francis was a spiritually judicious gospel commentator on issues raised by Donald Trump. Though he would not generally speak of him by name, often his comments, especially on walls, immigration, or Islamophobia, would be coincident with remarks of Mr. Trump. So, in a catechesis on "welcoming the stranger" at his general audience just weeks before the election, he could be indirect and still be very pointed:

> Unfortunately, today's context of economic crisis prompts the emergence of an attitude of closure and not of welcome. In some parts of the world, walls and barriers are appearing. Sometimes it seems that the silent work of many men and women who, in different ways, strive to help and assist refugees and migrants is overshadowed by the noise of others who give voice to an instinctive selfishness. Closure is not a solution, rather it ends up encouraging criminal trafficking. The only path to a solution is solidarity.[27] (Oct. 26, 2016)

On the day of the inauguration Francis gave a long interview to the Spanish paper *El País*, in which he responded to a question about Trump that he didn't want to ever judge people prematurely. "We will see what he does." It was an appeal for the specific and concrete. Later in the interview he was asked about populism both with respect to Trump and pending European elections. His answer included these comments.

Hitler didn't steal power, his people voted for him, and then he destroyed

---

27. Thomas Reece, "Pope Francis on Trump's Executive Orders?" February 3, 2017, https://www.ncronline.org/blogs/ncr-today/pope-francis-trumps-executive-orders (accessed February 28, 2017).

his people. That is the risk. In times of crisis we lack judgment, and that is a constant reference for me. Let's look for a savior who gives us back our identity and let us defend ourselves with walls, barbed-wire, whatever, from other people who may rob us of our identity. And that is a very serious thing. That is why I always try to say: talk among yourselves, talk to one another. But the case of Germany in 1933 is typical, a people who were immersed in a crisis, who were searching for their identity until this charismatic leader came and promised to give their identity back, and he gave them a distorted identity, and we all know what happened.[28]

That same day Francis's direct communication with the President greeted him with a word of intercession and an urging to justice:

At a time when our human family is beset by grave humanitarian crises demanding far-sighted and united political responses, I pray that your decisions will be guided by the rich spiritual and ethical values that have shaped the history of the American people and your nation's commitment to the advancement of human dignity and freedom worldwide.... Under your leadership, may America's stature continue to be measured above all by its concern for the poor, the outcast and those in need who, like Lazarus, stand before our door.[29]

Praying for the President

First of all, then, I urge that supplications, prayers, intercessions, and thanksgivings be made for everyone, for kings and all who are in high positions, so that we may lead a quiet and peaceable life in all godliness and dignity. (1 Tim 2:1–2)

There were six prayers at the Inauguration of the President. Such blessings can prove interesting. One, offered by Cardinal Timothy Dolan of New York, was from the Book of Wisdom and was a prayer upon "us" all to be granted wisdom as servants of God. What would be unexpected to many listeners was the feminine of the Sophia being called down.

[S]end her forth from your holy heavens. From your glorious throne, dispatch her that she may be with us and work with us, that we may grasp

---

28. Antonio Cano, *El País*, January 22, 2017, http://elpais.com/elpais/2017/01/21/inenglish/1485026427_223988.html (accessed February 28, 2017). Interesting note: two extreme-right publications picked up on the alternative quotes, *Breitbart* on "Wait and See," *Infowars* on the "Pope comparing Trump to Hitler."
29. http://en.radiovaticana.va/news/2017/01/20/pope_francis_sends_good_wishes_to_us_president_donald_trump/1287205# (accessed March 13, 2017).

what is pleasing to you. For she knows and understands all things and will guide us prudently in our affairs and safeguard us by her glory.

Another, brought by Rev. Samuel Rodriguez, was stunning in a different way. He read the Beatitudes from Matthew's Sermon on the Mount literally as a blessing prayer. So . . . for peacemakers, for those hungering and thirsting for justice, for those reviled and persecuted for righteousness' sake. The Word hung in the air. Yet who among us might imagine themselves qualified for those blessed promises? And then sadly, as if unable to resist, the reading was extended all the way to the City on a Hill—the image grasped in U.S. history to justify and bless manifest destiny and empire. Flipping the scripture.

Because praying for the President, be it laying hands on him in a sanctuary, offering the invocation at a political rally or official event, even naming him from the pulpit in intercessions, can function as endorsement, such prayer is fraught with ambiguity and concern.

Consequently, in the days leading up to the inauguration, Presiding Bishop Michael Curry (the first African American to lead the Episcopal Church USA) issued a statement regarding such prayers. To be sure, the Anglican tradition is the one in which the AME bishops are rooted but which goes back to the English national church essentially created by Henry VIII. Anglicans are deeply rooted in the compromises of church-state, even Constantinian, arrangements. Still:

> This practice of praying for leaders is deep in our biblical and Anglican/Episcopalian traditions. Psalm 72 prays that the ancient Israelite king might rule in the ways of God's justice, defending "the cause of the poor," bringing "deliverance to the needy." 1 Timothy 2:1–2 encourages followers of Jesus to pray earnestly for those in leadership, that they may lead in ways that serve the common good. Even in the most extreme case, Jesus himself said, while dying on the cross, "Father forgive them; for they do not know what they are doing," was praying for Pontius Pilate, the Governor of Rome who ordered his execution, and for all who were complicit in it. . . . Prayer is not a simplistic cheer or declaration of support. Prayers of lament cry out in pain and cry for justice. Prayer can celebrate. Prayer can also ask God to intervene and change the course of history, to change someone's mind, or his or her heart. When we pray for our enemies, we may find that we are simultaneously emboldened to stand for justice while we are also less able to demonize another human being.[30]

---

30. http://www.episcopalchurch.org/posts/publicaffairs/statement-episcopal-church-presiding-bishop-curry-regarding-prayers-president (accessed February 28, 2017).

Putting a fine point on the latter, William Stringfellow prayed a prayer of exorcism, indeed using the form of an ancient liturgy, for the sake of a president on the very night before his inauguration. This was not a demonization, in fact quite the opposite. I allow his account at length and in detail.

> I remember vividly, participating, on the evening before the second inauguration of Richard Nixon, in public worship, where the open invitation focused upon the president and his captivations with arbitrary power and interminable war. When my turn came to speak that night, I invoked one of the church's ancient prayers of exorcism on behalf of Richard Nixon then discernibly possessed by the power of death in these definite ways. The intercession was for the restoration of *his* humanity: for his release: for his healing. I did this with some trepidation, though, I trust, also with due humility, because the crisis for the nation had exceeded official crime and unconstitutionality, as far as I understood, and at that point also involved how this person—the emperor himself—had become victim—perchance the most pathetic and dehumanized victim of all in the whole ordeal of America signified by the Vietnam war. So I said this prayer, which originated in the church's experience in such matters long ago, on behalf of the humanity of Mr. Nixon. The congregation, about a thousand were present, returned "Amen!" and then again "Amen!" and then, as if to make it perfectly clear that the prayer was *their* own prayer, they all stood and the "Amen!" was transposed into a thunderous ovation. "Bless those who persecute you; bless and do not curse them" (Romans 12:14). That measures the outreach of the advocacy of the biblical witness.[31]

Note that the fundamental intent is pastoral care and concern, the humanity of the person to be healed, even freed, from possession by nation, office, power. But note honestly as well that Stringfellow took quiet satisfaction when the administration began to unravel in the scandals of Watergate and its aftermath. He fervently believed in the efficaciousness of prayer for kings and emperors.

Truth, Babel, Troll Storms, and the Principality of Social Media

It was utterly comprehensible, when Trump's Media Advisor, Kellyanne Conway, seemed to invent on the spot in a TV interview the

---

31. William Stringfellow, *Conscience and Obedience* (Waco, TX: Word, 1977), 98–99. I have in my possession the copy of the liturgy used by Stringfellow on this occasion and others.

term "alternative facts" to cover and label outright lies of the administration, that sales of George Orwell's dystopian book, *1984*, should spike across the country.[32] The assault on truth was being taken to such a new extreme, that handles to grasp it were urgent and few. Stringfellow, himself with Orwell in hand, might once again be counted among them.

Here he names among the strategies of demonic powers:

> (1) The Denial of Truth – A rudimentary claim with which the principalities confront and subvert persons is that truth in the sense of eventful and factual matter does not exist. In the place of truth and appropriating the name of truth are data engineered and manufactured, programmed and propagated by the principality. The truth is usurped and displaced by a self-serving version of events or facts, with whatever selectivity, distortion, falsehood, manipulation, exaggeration, evasion, concoction necessary to maintain the image or enhance the survival or multiply the coercive capacities of the principality. Instead of truth as that [which] may be disclosed empirically, the principality furnishes a story fabricated and prefabricated to suit institutional or ideological or similar vested interests (Rev 18:23, 20:3, 10).
>
> 2) Doublespeak and Overtalk – The preemption of truth with prefabricated, fictionalized versions of facts and events and the usurpation of truth by propaganda and official lies are stratagems of the demonic powers much facilitated by other language contortions or abuses which the principalities and authorities foster. These include heavy euphemism and coded phrases, the inversion of definitions, jargon, hyperbole, misnomer, slogan, argot, shibboleth, cliché. The powers enthrall, delude, and enslave human beings by estopping comprehension with "doublespeak," as Orwell named it.[33]

As Stringfellow demonstrates, this is not unprecedented in American political administrations, but the open attack on truth itself, on the social agreement as to what might even constitute a fact, is outrageously bald-faced and blunt.

Fabrication, exaggeration, and disinformation virtually characterized the Trump campaign. In the days immediately following the inauguration, the battle with the press corps focused on the size of the crowd, with false claims and even fictional subway ridership numbers,

---

32. Charles J. Sykes, "Why Nobody Cares the President Is Lying," *New York Times*, February 5, 2017, SR1. Dictionary look-ups for "fact" also spiked. https://www.merriam-webster.com/news-trend-watch/conway-alternative-facts-20170122 (accessed March 4, 2017).
33. Stringfellow, *An Ethic*, 98, 100.

but broadened to include claims post-facto that three million "illegal aliens" voted in the election. When pressed on that by Bill O'Reilly, whether he had facts or data to back that up, the president replied, "Many people have come out to say that I'm right."[34] He or surrogates can stir fears by fabricating or implying massacres in Bowling Green or even Sweden. His press secretary can lecture and excoriate the White House press corps and then circumvent critical media coverage by simply tweeting it directly to 25 million followers. Trump can label critical or unwelcome coverage as "fake news," flipping a term that arises specifically from the domain of social media—and a variety of false information that substantially drove his campaign.

The enormous difference from the time of Stringfellow's lucid utterance is the presence of social media and the Internet itself as a principality of scale on the social scene. In the face of corporate media, controlled by centralized and powerful state and establishment interests, social media holds the opportunity and possibility to subvert and go 'round. We have seen its usefulness here in Detroit where the corporate press, including even public radio and TV, has been in the hands of illegitimate, yet established political authority. Facebook and email, with known and trusted sources, have been places one could go for actual news and analysis of ongoing events.

The Internet and personal or hand-held computers have been touted virtually as countercultural centrifugal tools, decentralizing and democratizing media. They have been credited with movement building in Arab Spring and elsewhere. As the media of choice for a new generation, first Facebook and then Twitter were credited with bringing young people into the political process by Barack Obama, the first social media president.

And yet, as all such structures, they are utterly fallen, ultimately dehumanizing, and in Stringfellow's definition, demonic.

When a group of young people gathered in Detroit last year to reflect on social media as a principality, the first expression of dehumanization they named concerned the character of its addictive mechanisms. It was noticed that the structures of the medium were designed to induce compulsion. It was recognized as ubiquitous distraction from the sacred realities of family, relationship, community. (There is research noting that opioid use among teenagers has dropped precisely in accord with the rise of cell phone technology.[35]) People had

---

34. Stephens, "Daniel Pearl Memorial Lecture at the University of California."

begun undertaking Facebook fasts as a spiritual discipline to break the bondage in which it held their time and attention. There was also a discussion about the way social media and search engines affect the way our minds work, our capacity to think critically—click-by-click decision-making that gathers information a mile wide and an inch deep. The reduction of literacy from book or essay to sound bite to meme to tweet. But more.

In the realms of Facebook and even search-enginery, there is virtually a "fake news" industry. The creation of memes and links to completely and intentionally false stories, particularly political ones during campaign season, is financially incentivized through advertising by the click. Fake news that goes viral can generate thousands of dollars. But in the underworld of social media there are darker motives for such things. Some are generated by nihilistic "trolls" who delight in stirring things up for ironic kicks and watching the effect, just because they can. Such are one with the sadistic pleasures of online trolling. But this nihilism bleeds over into a calculated political motivation, of course. Such hoaxes are cranked out by hyper-partisan blogs. And when fake news stories are picked up and shared by political personalities, say, associated with a campaign, it gives the share a validation boost.[36] Add the likes of "bots" (fake identities and accounts) and you have viral acceleration.

In the final three months of the presidential campaign, the twenty top-performing fake election news stories generated more Facebook engagement than the twenty best-performing election stories from major news sources. All but three of the hoaxes overtly favored Trump.[37] Need it be noted that the so-called "alt-right" is synonymous not just with social media savvy, but being virtually an online movement. Among other things, they generate blogging and extremist news sites where hoaxes and fake news are often posted. At writing, the President is caught in an unsupportable public tweet scandal, based on a fabricated claim, reposted on Breitbart, that President Obama ordered Trump Tower phones wiretapped during the campaign. Direc-

---

35. Matt Richtel, "Are Teenagers Replacing Drug Use with Smart Phones?" *New York Times*, March 14, 2017, D1.
36. Abby Ohlheiser, "This is how Facebook's fake-news writers make money," *The Washington Post, the Intersect*, https://www.washingtonpost.com/news/the-intersect/wp/2016/11/18/this-is-how-the-internets-fake-news-writers-make-money/?utm_term=.3c830f3cc92e (accessed February 27, 2017).
37. Craig Silverman, *BuzzFeed* November 16, 2016, https://www.buzzfeed.com/craigsilverman/viral-fake-election-news-outperformed-real-news-on-facebook?utm_term=.skAdq0Vxn#.vcp21LGPY (accessed March 3, 2017).

tors of both the FBI and NSA have vigorously denied the claim. His press secretary and inner circle are declining to provide alternative facts in this matter.[38] The President is captive in his own fake news loop.

But more. On Facebook, of course, people sort themselves by friends into small communities of generally like-minded engagement. However, structured into the functions of the medium are algorithms, interactive mathematical software processes that communicate with one another and in turn shape our interactions, present us choices. They track our "likes," for example, and prioritize or filter what we see, giving us more of what we like. In effect, they take on a life of their own and become agents determining important aspects of our social reality.[39] Social world-makers, if you like. Algorithms link and enlarge those communities into enclaves or "filter bubbles"[40] where information and opinion loop and circulate. Pour in fake news and you have a large, confidently misinformed body. Fake news playing to those who "like" fake news. It's the conversational core of a political base, as it were.

If Kennedy was the first television president, and Obama the first social media president, Trump may be not just the first Twitter president, but the first algorithmic president.

Facebook thereby is engaged in a massive project of surveillance and data collection—posts, likes, shares, recommendations. That information is for sale as a marketing database. Link it with searches, reward card, and credit purchases, and you begin to have what's referred to as Big Data. Robert Mercer, the little-known U.S. software billionaire who (in line with the Citizen's United unlimited cash support ruling) threw his support to the Trump campaign in the eleventh hour, bringing along Steve Bannon and Kellyanne Conway, was also the largest investor in Cambridge Analytica, a sophisticated marketing company that has been quick to take credit for Brexit (the campaign to vote Britain out of the European Union) and the Trump victory. Based upon an online personality typology, they claim to micro-target political ads and information to individual users based not on broad demographics

---

38. Glenn Thrush and Maggie Haberman, "Trump Aides Address His Wiretap Claims: 'That's Above My Pay Grade,'" https://www.nytimes.com/2017/03/07/us/politics/trump-wiretap-claim-obama.html? (accessed March 7, 2017).
39. Massimo Mazotti, "Algorithmic Life," *Los Angeles Review of Books*, January 22, 2017, https://lareviewofbooks.org/article/algorithmic-life/ (accessed February 26, 2017).
40. Since the election there is a burgeoning industry of software solutions for breaking out of our filter bubbles. Amanda Hess, "Having Built Our Bubbles, Sites Sell a Way Out," *New York Times*, March 4, 2015, A1.

like race, geography, or gender, but on individual psychographic personality types and preferences garnered from Big Data and revealing[41] "hidden voter trends and behavioral triggers." Their claim is that data science is about to reshape marketing and that they are on the cusp of something enormous. Others, including some Trump aides, suggest their role in the campaign is exaggerated by the company for its own marketing purposes.[42]

William Stringfellow, as we have seen, is also remarkably prescient in seeing and anticipating these matters:

> It will suffice here to say that Nixon and Kissinger are no ordinary scoundrels. The public evidence (spare us, Lord, the private intelligence) is of two men so obsessed with their own vanity—in the sense that the Bible so often mentions vanity—that the obsession has become idolatrous, and everything else is pre-empted by it. But how, then, have either of them retained public credibility for so long? The answer is that each has succeeded in shifting credibility from a connection with truth to a dependence upon marketing technics. The shift is from that which is credible because it derives somehow from the truth, to that which is credible because people can be coerced, induced, conditioned, or programmed to believe it whether or not it has any significant relationship with the truth.[43]

Though he never fully developed the idea, he also spoke of technology in a way that thoroughly anticipated the principality of social media:

> Americans have never been regarded as ideologically sophisticated anyway, but now technology has practically displaced the political function of ideology. . . . Political authority in America has little need to launch indoctrination or practice much ideological manipulation because the available means, furnished by technology, of transmitting information have transfixing capabilities to paralyze human comprehension. Even the truth can be dispatched in the American technocracy with such acceleration and redundancy that it estops human beings from hearing or understanding it. Or, as another instance, how can the right of privacy be safeguarded and honored in a society where technology has made surveillance, both private and public, cheap and accessible to virtually any institution or

41. Hannes Grassegger and Mikael Krogerus, "The Data That Turned the World Upside Down," *Motherboard* https://motherboard.vice.com/en_us/article/how-our-likes-helped-trump-win (accessed February 18, 2017).
42. Nicholas Confessore and Danny Hakim, "Bold Promises Fade to Doubts for a Trump-Linked Data Firm," *New York Times*, March 6, 2017, A1.
43. William Stringfellow, "High Crimes and Misdemeanors: The Macabre Era of Kissinger and Nixon," *Sojourners*, January 1984, 13.

person? Does not the technical capability for ubiquitous surveillance of citizens in itself render a constitutional right of privacy quaint? Related to the displacement of ideology by technology has been the transplantation in America of the long entrenched commercial ethic into politics. Not only surveillance but secrecy, manipulation, fabrication, fraud, espionage—all familiar in business practice for generations—have now become politically commonplace.[44]

Yet more. Of course, surveillance of the web and social media is not only for marketing, even marketing cum political targeting, but outright political surveillance as in the National Security Agency. Those wise to or concerned about the surveillance aspect of the Internet and social media have turned to encryption programs (first developed by the U.S. Navy) to render identities anonymous and messaging unreadable. This cyberspace is sometimes called the dark net and operates in the portion of the Web not indexed by search engines. This is where hackers, WikiLeaks, and whistleblowers find anonymous freedom to operate. It is also employed for weapons purchase, illegal pornography, abuse, drugs, finance operations, fraud crime, chat, and extremism. The latter is said to include ISIS recruiters, but also trolls of the alt-right. "Take no part in the unfruitful works of darkness, but instead expose them. For it is shameful even to mention what such people do secretly" (Eph 5:11–12).

This is a rabbit hole I forbear to climb much further down. Suffice it to say that this is the domain of the "trolls." They are active in the web from unreachable anonymity. Hoaxes and fake news are only one tactic of assaulting legitimate users. Smart at starting online fights and flame wars, they create rolling walls of digital chaos and delight in it. They wound, insult, harass, anger, ever eager to ruin lives in the real world while remaining untouched in their own. Featuring themselves as ironic and iconoclastic, they live in a culture that claims to have no principles, only attacking the principles, sacred beliefs, and ideologies of others, perhaps political correctness above all. But, in fact, this is to say they have a point of view, a proto-politics of sorts—yes, misogynist and racist—which the alt-right clan has courted and cultivated in the recent campaign. Klan, in fact, is not beside the point—digital anonymity is very like the hood of the night rider. And by it a group or political force slips the grip of public accountability. Yet even so, now they've been brought above ground, given visibility and credence.

---

44. William Stringfellow, "Does America Need a Barmen Declaration?" *Christianity and Crisis*, December 24, 1973, 274–76.

Irony against irony, Donald Trump is not computer savvy, doesn't even have one on his desk. He's never trusted them. Doesn't "do the email."[45] He had to be talked into an iPhone by his secretary and fell in love with Twitter, which he plays like a troll—recirculating fake news, posting personal attacks, spurring political panic by announcement, terrorizing the vulnerable, taking contradictory positions, leaving a wake of chaos. Without having been formed in its ethos, his own life history has simply made him shameless, beyond shame; he functions as America's "Troll-in-Chief." And operates like he was raised in the dark.[46]

A friend of mine went in to poke around, particularly among the alt-right chat spaces, and found it spiritually debilitating, an exhausting assault on the soul. Such is white supremacy and misogyny, openly claimed. Displayed was an energy that was vitriolic, vulgar, and violent, but also thick with detached and calculated cruelty. There were key words for which they searched, like "alternative" and "community," and lists of countercultural organizations—art, politics, community-building, culture—targeted for organized "troll storms" and real-world disruption. Some projects on the list had already been successfully terminated. The assault on community and culture is one with the assault on truth.

Truth Warriors and the Renewal of Vocation

The *New York Times* has begun to sell truth. Advertisements come to my email. You can read them in print. You can see them on TV: "The truth is hard. The truth is hard to find. The Truth is hard to know. The truth is more important than ever." (Even "The truth is, alternative facts are lies.") Though I myself have railed against the paper and know it needs to be read critically as liberal or neoliberal corporate media, I'm actually thinking of getting a real-world paper subscription. The truth is, I've relied on it as a paper of record in the writing of this chapter.

Will the attacks on journalistic integrity, on mainstream news as fake news, on the media as the "enemy of the people," actually prompt a yearning within the fourth estate for the renewal of the journalistic vocation? There's some evidence.

The *Wall Street Journal* also has a perspective that needs to be read,

---

45. Jeremy Diamond, "Trump the computer and email skeptic-in-chief," CNN, http://www.cnn.com/2016/12/29/politics/donald-trump-computers-internet-email/ (accessed March 11, 2017).
46. For the best short and lucid article on the connection of Trump with trolldom, see Amanda Hess, "Click Bait," *The New York Times Magazine*, March 5, 2017, 11–13.

even deconstructed, critically. So, in February, when Bret Stephens, who writes a foreign affairs column for the paper, gave the Daniel Pearl Memorial Lecture at UCLA, it was striking that his talk was a lucid critique of the newly incumbent regime.[47] Pearl was a journalist disappeared in Pakistan while on assignment in 2002. Stephens named and listed the journalists who had been killed in the subsequent fifteen years, suggesting a costly vocation, and proposing they were all to be honored in his remarks.

> We honor the central idea of journalism—the conviction, as my old boss Peter Kann once said, "that facts are facts; that they are ascertainable through honest, open-minded and diligent reporting; that truth is attainable by laying fact upon fact, much like the construction of a cathedral; and that truth is not merely in the eye of the beholder." And we honor the responsibility to separate truth from falsehood, which is never more important than when powerful people insist that falsehoods are truths, or that there is no such thing as truth to begin with. So that's the business we're in: the business of journalism. Or, as the 45th president of the United States likes to call us, the "disgusting and corrupt media."[48]

I do pray in this present situation for the renewal of investigative journalism as a sometimes-risky calling and rigorous vocation. (And I can give thanks that such exist in Detroit.) Yet even more, I pray just now for the renewal of all vocations, personally and politically. What does that mean or look like?

One glimpse comes from a famous little logion of Howard Thurman's, "Don't ask what the world needs. Ask what makes you come alive, and go do it. Because what the world needs is people who have come alive."[49]

Along the same lines, Stringfellow regarded vocation as distinct from career, that each human being is called to be fully who they are uttered in the Word of God to be. In effect, to be fully and freely human. Come alive, as it were. In that sense, his ethics were vocational: to live humanly in whatever circumstance or history one might be found. So, for example, he was struck how resistance in the Nazi era consisted of day-to-day small actions that in and of themselves seemed all but hopeless—too weak and temporary, haphazard, and trivial to be effective. And yet people persisted, even at great risk. He concluded "that

---

47. Stephens, "Daniel Pearl Memorial Lecture at the University of California."
48. Ibid.
49. Howard Thurman Center for Common Ground, Boston University, https://www.bu.edu/thurman/about/history/ (accessed March 11, 2017).

the act of resistance to the power of death incarnate in Nazism was the only means of retaining sanity and conscience. In the circumstances of the Nazi tyranny, *resistance became the only human way to live.*"[50] For him, living humanly in the Word of God is the vocational ethic. Put broadly as a call to faith:

> In the face of death, live humanly. In the middle of chaos, celebrate the Word. Amidst babel, I repeat, speak the truth. Confront the noise and verbiage and falsehood of death with the truth and potency and efficacy of the Word of God. Know the word, teach the Word, nurture the Word, preach the Word, defend the Word, incarnate the Word, do the Word, live the Word. And more than that, in the Word of God, expose death and all death's works and wiles, rebuke lies, cast out demons, exorcise, cleanse the possessed, raise those who are dead in mind and conscience.[51]

That is the sense in which I pray for the renewal of vocation among us now. Prayer, by the way, is itself a substantial and significant practice of resistance when the domination of these principalities is taken into account. A friend of mine, Rose Marie Berger, writes that prayer "helps decolonize your mind."[52] It combats the assaultive spirits so unleashed. It confronts the powers out there and the powers that have gotten in our heads and hearts. Whether one is oppressed or privileged, structures and spirits like white supremacy, patriarchy, domination are within us, embedded invisibly in our psyches. Name them and pray them out.

This calls to mind some simple suggestions, other spiritual practices for resistance and transformation. I aspire to them myself.

Intercede. Bonhoeffer wrote that intercession is to feel another's sin or need so deeply that we pray their prayer, in their stead, for their sake—as if it were our own. Intercession in this sense is as much a form of solidarity as it is of advocacy. This applies to persons, collectives, creatures, even creation itself.

Speak. Audre Lorde says that our silences won't save us, won't protect us. Break the silence of the night. Speak from the heart of who you are in complete honesty and even confession. Speak to community. Speak to the powers.

---

50. Stringfellow, *An Ethic*, 119.
51. *Ibid.*, 142–43.
52. Rose Marie Berger, "Welcome to the Resistance. Here's Your Survival Guide," 02-01-2017, https://sojo.net/articles/welcome-resistance-heres-your-survival-guide (accessed March 12, 2017). My own list is riffing on hers.

Get trained in nonviolent direct action, in rapid-response intervention, in accompaniment, in violence de-escalation.

Organize and undertake nonviolent direct action, rapid-response interventions, and accompaniment. You know where they're needed.

Fast. Some spirits can only be cast out by prayer and fasting. Fasting is a primary expression of noncooperation and resistance. Fast privately to purify and free yourself from bondage and renew your relationship to all of creation. Fast as a public ritual of solidarity on behalf of those targeted and violated. Fast from food. Fast from gas or electricity. Fast from the Internet. Fast from any form of compulsive consumption.

Related: *go feral.* This is a practice learned from the fallow years of jubilee and Sabbath. Many these days are being tutored by the edge of the Wild.

Nurture community. When so much is under assault, it may actually be the most important thing of all to do. In congregations, movements, on the block, in action affinity groups, households. Work at it. Community is hard work. Sometimes it is harder to love one another in community than it is to love your enemies. Have a dining room table, keep it clear, host guests and break bread. Build community for its own sake. Build community to act as one in the works of resistance and transformation.

Offer gratitude. Community runs on gratitude. Thank people. Make a list of your own gratitudes as a spiritual practice. Include them in your prayers.

Contemplate. Pay attention. Focus your mind and heart on who and what is right before you. Open your eyes, your ears, your senses, your mind. Notice the gift beneath everything. Daniel Berrigan said contemplation was the one thing the Powers That Be can't commodify or co-opt.

Confess your fears—to your closest community. Fears kept inside rule us and hold us; they end up being at the service of the powers. Sometimes fears name the very things we are being called to do. Fears confessed can be at the service of conscience and the spirit.

Count your gifts, personal and communal. Take stock of what resources you have. Know what you can offer and also what your limits might be. Though to be honest, sometimes you start a work trusting on faith that the gifts will come.

Practice hospitality. In home and community. Do so quietly for those threatened with violence or deportation. Make safe spaces for the homeless. Declare sanctuary publicly as a congregation; go on record.

Be ready to take the heat. Count the cost. Be disabused of naïveté. Know that if you stand somewhere for real, the trolls or the authorities may come for you, as they've come for others.

Read the scriptures, together and alone. Read them critically, yes, but always in the end read them engaged with your life and spirit. Read them for what lights up and what calls to you. Read them to remember the big story of which we are part, the conversation that we join. Read them to recall where we come from (we'll never know where we're going if we don't). Read them to recognize and unmask the powers. Read them in order to recognize the Word active and militant now and in this world. Reading them is a primary, practical tactic of resistance.

Read. In a world saturated with images and tweets, read essays beginning to end. Read books. Read poetry and novels. Read analysis of the present crisis. Read movement history. Read children's books to children you love. Tutor. Honor libraries by use. Practice literacy also as resistance.

Make culture. Write. Perform poetry—free verse, hip hop. Paint and draw by hand. On paper or on walls. Make liturgy as art. Publish a paper, a newsletter. Open and protect safe spaces for music, for theater, for storytelling (art is targeted and under attack as well). Learn the healing arts of your ancestors (the memory is not that far back).

Rest. This is another practice related to biblical Sabbath, the seventh year, the seventh day. Don't make an idol of self-care, also easily done, but you neglect it at the peril of movement and community. Any number of the practices urged here require slowing down and sitting still. Dreams and healing come in sleep. Letting go in rest and sleep is a way of trusting the world to God.

Re-member. Put the news, in the dailies or social media, in the context of the larger story, lest today's news be nothing more than tomorrow's cold omelet. Honor and recall movement history. Biblical history. Learn from them. At every gathering summon the ancestors and saints to be present and alive in our midst.

Bless. Bless and do not curse, even those who curse you.

Judge not. At least don't waste your time critiquing what every other faith or movement group is doing wrong. Work together with whomever good faith and conscience will allow. You don't have to like everyone to treat them with respect. Practice basic nonviolence.

Oh, yeah. *Practice nonviolence. Practice. Practice. Practice.*

Honor the truth. Tell the truth. Teach the truth. Live the truth.

Appendix I:
Thinking Biblically and Theologically about a Particular Power:
An Inventory of Provoking Questions

The following questions should prove helpful as guidelines for reflection. Not all may apply to a given power or your experience of it, but they may stimulate thinking.

Creatureliness: Defining a Principality

Of what variety is it?

William Stringfellow thought in terms of institutions, ideologies, and images. John Yoder's categories are: religious structures, intellectual structures (-ologies and -isms), moral structures (codes, customs), and political structures (tyrant, market, school, courts, nation, etc.).

Does it have a "seat" of institutional power and continuity? Where is it located? Does it have a realm, a territory, a sphere of influence? Is that dominion expanding? Does it have a ruler, a person with vested office? What are its material manifestations, the rituals, symbols, and images by which its power is maintained?

Does it have a discernible spirit? an invisible aspect? a characteristic ethos? Do you recognize its "interiority"? Are people conscious or unconscious of that spirit?

What is the vocation of this power? What is its creaturely purpose, its original and best intention? How, in particular, is it called to praise God and serve human life? Who, in particular, is it called to serve? To what is it held accountable in the judgment of God?

Fallenness

Do you see where that vocation has been confused, twisted, distorted? How has an ethic of survival supplanted its calling? How does it reflect an "inverse dominion"? How do human beings make an idol of it? In what ways may it be said to usurp the place of God? Do people find meaning, identity, justification in connection with the power? How are their identities absorbed, confused, distorted? What sacrifices does it demand? In what ways are people conformed, seduced, possessed, hardened, blinded, tyrannized, or otherwise captured into its service? Are they dehumanized in other ways?

Who are the victims of this power—either by outright suffering or by demoralization?

In relation to other powers: How is it allied, bolstered, limited, or rivaled by other principalities? How may it be said to serve death?

Living Humanly in the Sovereignty of God

Where do you see the power unmasked and disarmed? How are its illusions, lies, and deceptions exposed? Do you know instances of human freedom in relation to it? Think of, for example, creative nonconformity, drawing a limit, resistance, refusal to be seduced, steadfast endurance, open confrontation and combat, freedom to act and serve nevertheless, conversion, escape, and such. What tactics can you imagine for living humanly in the face of it? How is the sovereignty of God displayed here and now in relation to this power? What would render it accountable to human life?

What is the work of the church in relation to this power? How might the "manifold wisdom of God" (Ephesians 3) be made known to it? What would it mean for this power to be redeemed? Can you envision its repentance—the renewal and restoration of its vocation?

Appendix II:
Theological Exegesis of the Neighborhood

Name the powers at work in the neighborhood, the parochial domain, of your own ministry. Be clear about the boundaries of the neighborhood you are considering. Identify structures and/or spirits that occupy, impinge upon, reside within, or otherwise have a grip on the community. Stringfellow's elemental categories are: institutions, ideologies, and images. Anabaptist theologian John Howard Yoder suggests another set of types: religious structures, intellectual structures (-ologies and -isms), moral structures (codes, customs), and political structures (tyrant, market, school, courts, the state, etc.).

You may want to begin or end with an attentive and alert neighborhood walk. Toward your naming and social mapping, interview three people who have history there and are currently active in community work or ministry. Listen for theology, but don't let theology get in the way. You ought to be able to get at some basics even without laying out a powers theology or analysis. Simply ask what are the forces at work? What are the structural players? What institutions, what corporate organizations of power, even what physical structures, call the tune and shape life in the area where you minister? Don't forget to move toward the spiritual dimension. Ask about the spirit of the forces, the ethos of the neighborhood, the spiritual struggles of the people. The "Inventory of Provoking Questions" ought to be more than useful in preparing your own questions.

1. *Write a brief paragraph on each Power.* This cannot be a thorough social analysis or theological discernment, but it should provide suggestive

handles, avenues, and openings on which such analyses could proceed. If you name certain powers, as you inevitably must, which are larger than the community and have their seats/centers outside of the neighborhood? Be concrete about how it connects, where it hits the ground in your parish turf. Identify those who are disabled or dehumanized by the powers. With which powers is your congregation or ministry directly (or indirectly) engaged? Is that ministry conscious of this engagement?

2. *"Map" the Principalities.* Try to draw or schematize the players in a kind of visual map or model that gives a sense of their relationship to one another and the community. This is not a street map, but a relational one. Which most affect people's lives? Which have larger influence and dominion? Which are in collusion with one another? Which are in competition or conflict? Which impact the life of your congregation?

Appendix III:
The Angel of a Congregation: Possible Elements of a Continuing Discernment Process

(After the work of Walter Wink)

1. *Gather a core group* of people representative of the congregation including pastor and staff who are prepared to commit a weekend, or better, a series of weekly sessions to a focused process of collective discernment. (The suggestions that follow may be done in a variety of formats.)

2. *Begin with the Bible study* we began together. *Revelation 1:9-20:* Who is the figure of One like a Human Being? What is the *meaning* of each characteristic? What is his relationship to the churches? Also *Revelation 2:1-7, 8-11* (or any of the other letters in chapters 2 and 3): What is the angel of the church? Why does the letter address the angel? Does *your* congregation have a particular and unique personality? Outline the structure of the letters. Notice the recurring pattern. What does the structure of the letter say about the nature of the angel? (Recall our conversation about vocation and fallen character.)

Ways to begin getting at the angel of your congregation:

3. *Church story and history.* Reconstruct collectively a history of your congregation. Use a timeline or list it out on newsprint. This is not compiling a history of pastorates (unless a particular preacher con-

ferred his or her own personality on the church). What were the decisive moments that shaped and defined the identity of the congregation? What outside influences imposed a particular character? Where did the church discover its vocation? Who is the keeper of the story? (Even if this person has no formal position, they are likely a powerful person especially in maintaining the identity of the congregation (perhaps in maintaining, as well, the status quo).

4. *Recall how the biblical saga* shaped and defines the community of faith. If you were to locate your congregation in a period of Israel's history (broadly recounted: Call, Slavery, Liberation, Wilderness wanderings, Period of tribal confederation in Canaan, Established monarchy and prophetic response, Judgment of destruction, Babylonian exile, Restoration and return, Resistance to imperial occupation, etc.), is there a moment that resonates with your own as a church? Are there particular biblical texts from that historical period that address or nourish you here and now?

5. *Structural considerations.* If the angel is the interiority, the "within" of a church, its genius or spirituality or corporate personality, then the outer manifestations of a church ought to point to its inner identity. What are some visible attributes that suggest the angel of your church? List on newsprint. What do these attributes (architecture, age or racial makeup, organizational structure, etc.) reveal about the angel's personality? If you were going to listen for the voice of the angel, where (in the building or elsewhere) would you sit?

6. *Bible Study: Luke 13:34-35 and Luke 19:42-44.* To simply start with the pronouns again: In Luke 19 all of these are second person singular (12x in 3 vv.). Whom is Jesus addressing? Once again, can a collectivity know? See? Can Jerusalem choose? Why does Jesus weep? Is it for the individuals, the "children"? Or does he love Jerusalem whole? What do you imagine he loves about it? What is his true longing for the city? The name of Jerusalem, according to tradition, means "foundation of peace." Is it true to its name? True to its vocation? (Who named your congregation? By what authority? Does that name in any way reveal or mask its true vocation before God and humanity?) Where does Jesus stand to address Jerusalem? Jesus says this is a "time of visitation," a *kairos* moment. (*Kairos* is a Greek word for time as a ripeness or fullness. It's come to mean a decisive opportunity, a moment of choice put by God.) Is the judgment and its instrument fixed? Could the city make a

choice that might alter its history, its fate in the judgment and mercy of God?

Has your congregation ever faced a *kairos* moment? Is it facing one at the present time?

7. *One person to lead others in guided meditation* (modeled on Revelation 1-2): breathing and relaxation; go in your mind to the "place" where you would listen/look for "angel of church"; notice sounds, smells, any people present, etc.; turn to see One like a Human Being ("the Son of Man") as described in 9-20; fall on your face as though dead (what do you need to die to in order to hear the Word?); rise and listen to the word for your congregation ("Say to the Angel of _____"); turn again—where are you? same place? changed? how? take it in; now turn to see the angel of the church—feelings/color? shape? human form?; ask, "Who are you? and What are you saying in this moment?"; convey the Word from the Human One; return to your place.

8. *"Right brain" exercise:* Without speaking, take up paper and pens and begin to draw images out of your meditation. Or: take up clay and begin work it; think with your hands; form the "angel"; this needn't be artistic or creative; share the results in group conversation.

9. *A writing exercise* to be done individually. A letter from the "Son of Man" to your congregation using the Revelation 2 format.

To the angel of _____:

From the One who (*characteristic of the Human One*):

I know your works, that you (*works or characteristics of the congregation that convey or point to its vocation before God*):

But I have this against you (*ways in which that calling is distorted, or transformation is resisted, or the church falls short, etc.*):

(An exhortation—imperatives that the congregation needs to undertake to fulfill its calling now)

(Blessing and promise)

Those who have ears let them hear what the Spirit is saying to the church...

Where will you stand to listen? (You may in reality want to situate yourself in a particular place in the church.)

10. *Bring these "letters,"* admittedly subjective, back to the group. Perhaps they might be shared in the context of a group liturgy. Together they represent a kind of collective discernment. They might also be used in morning worship as a word to the whole congregation.

11. *Concluding discussion:* How do these readings of the congregation, its potentiality, its vocation, its identity in calling and fallenness alter the direction of your church and its ministries in this moment of its history?

Additional Resources:
Walter Wink, "The Angels of the Churches," in *Unmasking the Powers* (Philadelphia: Fortress Press, 1986).
James Hopewell, *Congregation: Stories and Structures* (Philadelphia: Fortress Press, 1987).
Edwin H. Friedman, *Generation to Generation: Family Process in Church and Synagogue* (New York: Guilford, 1985).

Appendix IV

Questions for use with *Poletown Lives* (film produced by George Corsetti and Jeanie Wylie; Information Factory, 3512 Courville, Detroit, MI 48224):

1. What image from the film remains most vividly with you?
2. Can you generate a list of identifiable principalities at work in the film?
3. To what extent are they in rivalry and conflict? in coalition and collusion?
4. G.M. President James McDonald makes a slip of the tongue: "Well, would you like Detroit to be in General Motors . . . ?" Is that what he really means? Which is more powerful?
5. There is a long street discussion about the media. Is it a distinct power? What is its vocation, its first and best purpose? What is their actual role in the Poletown story?
6. In the funeral sermon, the preacher says, "He tried to slow and stay the heavy hand of corporate, materialistic, economonistic objectives masking themselves as the common good." How do the powers mask themselves?
7. Paul blames the "gods of this world" for causing a kind of blindness. Walter Wink speaks of the domination systems' "delusional apparatus." What illusions do the Poletown residents suffer? Of what illusions do they become free? How so?
8. The Police Commander is asked: "You don't see yourself as serving any particular master?" Is that an inappropriate question? Who or what interests are the police serving? Are they aware of that or blind to it? In this situation, is the law itself a master or a servant? Of whom?

9. What do you make of the public destruction of the GM car? Is it mere ventilation and vengeance? Compare Jeremiah's act of smashing an earthenware pot to declare judgment against Israel (Jer 19:1–13). Is this a fair comparison?
10. How is prayer portrayed in the film?
11. A Korean seminarian viewing the film spoke of the shanty towns surrounding Seoul. When they spring up, the first institutions to arrive are the churches. But when it is announced that they are to be bulldozed, the churches are the first to pull up stakes and leave. How do you see the church in the film? Does it address, rebuke, or confront the powers? How does it conform to and abet the powers? Can the church itself be said to have the aspect of a principality?
12. Councilman Ken Cockerel speaks of Poletown as a "dramatic example of the power, the raw, naked power of government in coalition with multinational corporations." Colossians says that in the cross, Christ "disarmed the principalities and powers and made a public example of them, triumphing over them." How does the cross expose the powers? How does it triumph over them?
13. It is sometimes said that the principalities rule by the power of despair. What does that mean? Where is despair at work in this struggle? Where is hope at work? How does hope break the powers-that-be?
14. By their title, the filmmakers have consciously or unconsciously evoked "resurrection" as a theme in the film. What image does that convey? What form does the freedom of the resurrection take? Do you see the film as ultimately despairing or hopeful?

Index of Names and Subjects

addictive society/system, 117 118, 150; adrenaline, 181; chemical, consumables and process, 118, 139, 144, 196; church as, 121; debt addiction 114; economics of, 180; in family systems, 118, 126, 129, 145; and the Garasene demoniac, 119; and patriarchy, 118; and social media, 279

African Methodist Episcopal Church, bishops' pastoral letter on the demonic, 272; Mother Emanuel AME Charleston, 272

alt-right, and Ku Klux Klan, 283; death threats, 266; misogyny and racism, 283; and social media, 280; spiritually debilitating, 284; and troll hoaxes, 280. *See also* Bannon, Steve; Conway, Kellyanne; Mercer, Robert

anarchism, 22, 53; in anarcho-primitivism, 46

angel, xvi, 38, 143; as actual spirituality, 245, 246; of *Angelus Novus*, by Paul Klee, xviii; of annunciation, xvi; as "better angels" (Abraham Lincoln), 265; of churches, 24, 32, 246, 293; of cities, xix, 20, 85; discernment of, 90, 293–96; of Detroit, 87; of Washington DC, xvii; of East Harlem Protestant Parish, 247; fallen, xvi, xix, 80, 101; as genius, 247; of history, xviii; of Jerusalem, 89; of nations, xxix, 10, 24, 52, 87; of law, 100; letters to in Revelation 1 and 2, 87, 246, 295; of nature, 32; of Rome, 90, 102; of urban ministry school, 255. *See also* Satan

apocalyptic, 6n9, 149, 259; defined, 207

Archdiocese of Detroit, 155, 252

Arab community, Detroit, 90, 214

architecture, 294; social, 169; urban 207

Arendt, Hannah, xviiin8

arson, 93

authorities/powers/*exousiai*, xvi, 8, 59–60, 68, 102, 136, 140, 212, 213, 233, 272, 287; defined sociologically, 58, 86; destroyed, 257; disarmed, 65, 67; imperial, 53; legitimated, 53, 60; limited, 73

authorities, municipal, 233; Downtown Development Authority,

299

233; Educational Achievement Authority (EAA), 233–36; Great Lakes Water Authority (GLWA), 233; Lighting 233

Beast, of Revelation, 23, 100, 102, 103. 145, 177, 200; and the Dragon, 102; identified by Marx, 140
Babel, tower city, 88, 92, 95; confusion of language, 9n18, 277, 286; as verbal tactic of the powers, 21
banks, 87, 992, 224, 225, 241, 254, 264; Bank of America, 224, 242; Barclay's, 225; and financial industry, 114, 221; Goldman Sachs, 263; vocation of, 34, 63, 137–38; World, 188. *See also* redlining
Bannon, Steve, 260, 281. *See also* alt-right; Cambridge Analytica; Conway, Kellyane; Mercer, Robert
baptism, xix, 12, 1, 18, 32, 68, 79, 171–72; and exorcism, 5; as final allegiance, 269; and gift of water, 243
barbed wire, 71–79, 74, 80, 82; as darkness, 75; and extermination camps, xvii; as idol, 73; and modernity, 71n3; as principality, 71; as seal of death, 71, 274
Barlowe, Maude, 241, 243; and Council of Canadians, 243
Barot, Madeleine, 5
Barth, Karl, xxix, 9, 10, 11, 24, 34, 57, 173; in East Harlem, 11
Belgrave, Bishop of Norway, 5

Beloved Community, as church and movement, xix, xxv, 53, 191, 240
Benjamin, Walter, xviii, xx
Belle Isle, 90, 95
Berger, Rose Marie, xviii, xiiifn6, 286, 286n52
Berrigan Daniel, xvii, xix; arrest on Block Island, 15; and Bonhoeffer, 39; his eulogy for Stringfellow, 42; and freedom of resurrection, 43; as guest and friend, 43; as host, 77; and hospice chaplaincy, 41–42; as mentor, xxxi; and the Plowshares Eight, 41; poems, 38, 40–41; as prisoner, 44; underground, 14, 39; and underground seminary, 39, 40. *See also* Catonsville Nine; Plowshares actions
Berrigan, Phillip, 33; on conscience embodied, 33; on voting, 222. *See also* Catonsville Nine; Plowshares actions
Berry, Wendell, 189. *See also* National Security Strategy
Bethge, Eberhard, 39
The Bible in Human Transformation (1973), 8fn14, 30, 33; as hermeneutical exorcism, 8. *See also* Wink, Walter
Bing, Mayor David, 252
blasphemy, 3; corporate, 161; national, 270; presidential, 202
blockbusting, 252
Block Island, cottage, 37
blood, 49, 199; of Abel, 88, 196; of the cross, 54, 61, 65; of a female god, 47; in the foundation, 193; of the innocents, 80; of martyrs, 38; of a murdered god, 47, 53; of

patriots, 269; of prisoners, 40; of slaves, 193
Bobb, EFM Robert, 230
Boggs, Grace Lee, 151, 153
Bonhoeffer, Dietrich, xx, 9, 39; and church resistance, 39; execution at Flossenberg Prison, 39; on Finkenwalde underground seminary, 39; on intercession, 286; as martyr, 38; on power of darkness, 9. *See also* Bethge, Eberhard; Marsh, Charles
Broad, Eli, 230
Brown vs. Kansas Board of Education, 153
Bush, George W., 49, 214; and blasphemy, 202; doctrine of preemptive war, 189; draft articles of impeachment, 214n4; legal justification of war, 215; legitimated by war-making, 215; "shock and awe," 200. *See also* myth of redemptive violence; war
Bush, George H. W., 116; and new world order, 49

Caird, G. B., 101; and biblical history of Satan's fall, 100
Caligula, Roman Emperor, 103
Camus, Albert, 38, 41
capitalism and capital, 140; assault on family, 131; consumer, 164; disaster, 223; global, 161; and Nixon's reply, 131; personified in fetishism, 140; and Protestant work ethic, 163; and slavery, 195; and vocation of unions, 162
casinos, 85–86
Cass Corridor, 90

Catholic Worker, 37, 42, 77, 172, 221, 239; Detroit, 199n1, 229; Los Angeles, 199n1
Catonsville Nine, xxix, 37, 39, 41, 43, 77; trial of, 13. *See also* Berrigan, Daniel; and Berrigan, Phillip
Central Intelligence Agency (CIA), xvii, 115, 210
Christ: allegiance to, 12; and antichrist, 140; body of, 171; confronting the powers, 12; in creation hymn, 54, 55; crucified, 41, 99, 120; epiphany of, 82; exemplifying the Word, 3; and human unity, 12, 169; as image of God, 64; as light, 76; Lordship of, 5, 10, 64; love of, 148; as new creation, 68; powers created in and through, 61, 135; realm of, 68; risen, 79, 81, 84, 161; unmasking powers, 102, 160; in whom death fails, 14. *See also* Jesus; *Sophia*/wisdom
Church: in bondage to the powers, 208, 247, 252, 254; as exemplary principality, 248, 251; as *ekklesia*, 251; as fallen power, xix, 161, 247; free to die, 9, 248; as free from powers, 251; as holy nation, 248; and spiritual dimension, 245–46; vocation of, 246, 248; and white supremacy, 198, 252. *See also* angels, of churches; confessing church struggle; Constantinian arrangement; doctrine of discovery; *parrhesia*/bold speaking; sanctuary

301

Church and State (1939), 10. *See also* Barth, Karl

churches, 180; Central United Methodist, 73; church closings, 226; Episcopal, 83, 267; Methodist, 57, 83, 157, 198; of Revelation 1 and 2, 246; Riverside Church, 17, 57; and white flight, 252. *See also* St. Peter's Episcopal Church

climate change: denial, 267, 272; as wrath of creation, 207. *See also* Standing Rock Sioux

Clinical Pastoral Education, 147

Clinton, Hillary, 271

Columbus, Christopher, and slave triangle, 194

commodity fetishism, 140. *See also* Marx, Karl

Cone, James, 198n13

confessing church struggle, 9, 39. *See also* Barth, Karl; Bonhoeffer, Dietrich; Niemoeller, Martin

Congregation: Stories and Structures (1987), 247. *See also* Hopewell, James

conscientious objection, 122

conspiracy: of authorities, 9, 112, 114, 117; charges, 210

Constantine, Emperor, 7, 253

Constantinian arrangement, xix, 6, 8, 208, 247, 255, 276; and hermeneutics, 65

Coontz, Stephanie, 127n4, 130, 131

corporations, 6, 94, 96, 136, 151, 155, 298; and contempt for community, 160, 188; and corporate charter, 153, 187, 195; and corporate culture, 137; escaping accountability, 161, 187, 188; and their ethic of infinite growth, 190; gone underground, 112; history of, 157, 186–87; and human accountability, 157, 160, 187–88; and new international law, 188; as "persons," 136, 153, 179, 187; and vocation renewed, 160. *See also* Emergency Management

Covington, John, 234

crack cocaine, xvii; marches, xxxiii, 123; market, 94, 95, 118; and neighborhood clearing, 114. *See also* drugs

creation hymn of Colossians 1, 19, 20, 54–65, 260; as foundation-shaking, 54; and image of God, 64–65; and powers as creatures, 55; its theological movement, 61; as "tool" of social analysis, 56–61. *See also* authorities; dominions; rulers; *Sophia*/Wisdom; Thrones

creation spirituality, 53

cross, xxxi, 12, 218; as disarming the powers, 65–68, 298; as hope, 68; as nonviolence, 17, 35, 74; praying forgiveness from, 276; as reconciling powers and all things, 54, 61; removing from church, 253; stations of, xxxiii, 82, 256; as triumph imperial liturgy, 66–67; way of, 74

cry, 88, 160, 194, 196

Curry, Bishop Michael, 276

Dachau, concentration camp, 72

Dalai Lama, xix

Daily Death Toll Project, 30

dark net, 283; and spiritual assault, 284
Dark Alliance: The CIA, the Contras, and the Crack Cocaine Explosion (1998), xviin4
Dawn, Marva, 10n19
Day, Dorothy, 41, 77
demonic powers, 88, 100, 102, 106, 113, 116, 138 168, 173, 264, 278, 279; aggressions of, 145, 169, 212, 252, 267, 272; and death as social purpose, 13; and inverse dominion, 63; possession by, 59, 74, 100, 262, 286; in views of Stringfellow vs. Wink, 26n56. *See also* African Methodist Episcopal Church
demons, xv, xxxiv, 9, 20, 120, 121, 132, 240, 286; and demonizing, 123; of white supremacy, xix, xxxiv, 165, 167, 169, 252, 262. *See also* exorcism
Detroit, 202, 225–56, 230, 236, 240, 243, 244, 264; and bankruptcy, 222, 225–26, 230, 236, 240, 243, 244, 264; as Black majority city, xxxi, 89, 222, 240; as *de troit* ("the straits"), 90; geographically and racially restructured, 226, 232, 264; and home-owning, 223; as Motor City, 94; as "Murder City," 88; newspaper strike, xxxiii, 34, 63, 151–55. *See also* Detroit Public Schools; Emergency Management
Detroit Public Schools: *Because They Could: The Fight for Oakman School,* film, 234; dismantling of, 229–37; elected board, 227, 229, 231, 232, 236, 265; board in exile, 231; *Grown in Detroit*, film, 232; and mayoral control, 236, New Orleans model, 236. *See also* Emergency Management; DeVos, Betsy; Teach for America
Detroit Rebellion of 1967, xxix, 89, 206
Detroit Renaissance Center, 91, 92
Detroit Water and Sewage Department, 233, 241. *See also* Detroit Water Struggle; water
Detroit Water Struggle, 239–44
DeVos, Betsy, 263–65
discernment: of actions, xxxiii, 75, 78, 83, 243; of powers, xx, xxix, 34, 135, 145, 163, 356; of signs, 266; of spirits, 3, 32, 89, 94, 95, 122, 141, 266, 289, 293–96. *See also* spiritual practices
doctrine of discovery, 255
domination system, 16, 185, 219; and delusional apparatus, 297; as movement parlance, 34n3, 35; and nuclear weapons, 71; and power of death, 25, 139
dominion, 56, 58, 135; 43; inverse, 62–62, 64, 88, 163, 290; *kyriotes*, 58; not had by death, xix; and power of the air, 25; as realm or territory, 58, 86, 89, 148, 178, 255, 289, 292. *See also* creation hymn of Colossians 1
drugs, 283, xvii–xviii; and addictive system, xxxiv, 117–19; and CIA, 115; as economic entity, 87, 94, 112, 114; and neighborhood clearing, 114; as a power, xvii, xxiii, 96, 111, 112, 113, 114, 121; and prayer, 121; and racism,

303

116–17; and scapegoating, 119–20; as spirit, 113
Duggan, Mayor Michael, 243
Durkheim, Emile, 176
Dylan, Bob, 259

East Harlem, 11, 13; and grace of resurrection, 146; and powers, xxix, 4, 145, 146
East Harlem Protestant Parish, 247; angel of the group ministry, 247
economics: casino, 85; of commercial principalities, 130, 131, 135–41, 161, 186, 262; consumer, 131, 180, 183; disaster, 23–24; drug, xvii, 87, 94, 112, 114; global, 185–98; jubilee, 163; slave, 191–98; of solidarity, 274; of violence, 194
Eisler, Riane, 48n7, 49
Elliot, T. S., 32
Ellul, Jacques, xxix, 9, 10n19, 34, 92; and angel of the city, 85, 87–88; and the fall, 21–23, 25; and hope of freedom, 23; and money as a power, 140–41; and powers as creatures, 19–20, 22; and Stringfellow, 18–19, 20, 21; and technology as a power, 105–7
Elmwood Cemetery, 91
Emergency Management, 29, 34, 221–27; and bankruptcy, 222, 223, 225; defined, 221–22, 248; law repealed, 222; and participatory democracy, 227; and privatization, 231; and race, 222–23; and schools, 29, 227, 229–37, 230; as urban fascism, 221; and water 6, 34, 241, 243–44; and white racism, 233,

236, 240, 264. *See also* Detroit, bankruptcy; Detroit Public Schools; Detroit Water Struggle
empire, xiv, 54, 158, 188, 206, 208, 211, 251, 261–63; and church, 253, 255–56, 275; colonization of the mind, 119, 286; and counter liturgies, 50–56, 64–68; and imperial liturgies, 47–50, 177; and media, 110; and scripture 6–7; U.S., 188. *See also* Constantinian arrangement
Engaging the Powers (1992), 24. *See also* Wink, Walter
Engler, Governor John, 229
Enuma Elish, 47–50, 53
An Ethic for Christians and Other Aliens in a Strange Land (1973), 6, 8, 9, 14, 15, 17, 18, 20, 21, 22, 44, 57, 59, 65, 99. *See also* Stringfellow, William
ethics: commercial, 282; consumption, 131, 132, 163; of freedom, 13, 23, 26; incarnational, 23; improvisational, 23, 191; of the resurrection, 23; sacramental, 12, 23; social, xxix, 4, 34; spiritual practice as, 286; survival, 190, 248, 290; theological, 11, 20, 27; of unfinite growth, 189–90; vocational, 285; Wesleyan, 194; work, 57
The Ethics of Freedom (1976), 20, 42, 105. *See also* Ellul, Jacques
Eucharist, 80, 81, 140, 177
exorcism, xxix, xxxiv, 121, 165–72, 171, 251, 286; ancient rite of, 4, 276; as element of baptism, 5, 172; hermeneutical, 6, 8, 33; poem, 37; political, xxix, 4, 13,

41, 119; as a prayer for the president, 276; and prayer warriors, 123; public, 8, 95, 121, 75

Faith and Resistance retreats, 82
Fall, xvi, xvii, 7, 10, 26, 88, 140, 144, 163, 207, 212, 254, 272, 290; as alienation, 21, 61, 174; as anxiety about death, 64, 186, 248; as distorted vocation, xvii, 34, 87, 138, 146, 152, 161, 162, 174, 178, 246; as "dysfunctionality," 127; as inverse dominion, 62; as necessity, 23; as rise of civilization, 49; of Satan, 101; transcending, 3, 248. *See also* demonic
family: in addiction and system theory, xxxiv, 118, 121, 126–27, 129–30, 145, 246; beset by the powers, 125; as form of resistance, 51, 134, 132; as local, 185; as principality, 125–26; as unit of consumption, 130–31
Fellowship of Reconciliation, 31
fetishism, 140
Field of Dreams, film, 175
Finkenwalde, underground seminary, 39
Foreign Intelligence Surveillance Act (FISA), 214
Foreman, James, 31; and the Black Manifesto, 31
Ford, Glenn, 225
foreclosures, and racial clearing, 283, 241, 252, 264
Francis, Pope of Rome, 274–75; addressing Congress, 255; and Donald Trump, 274; *El Pais* interview, 274–75; on populism and Hitler, 274; on praying for the president, 275
Friedman, Edwin, 127, 247

Galilee, 89; over-fishing, 159
Gandhi, Mohandas, xxxiii, 26, 76, 93, 200
Gates Foundation, and cyber curricula, 233
General Motors, 94, 136, 137, 297. *See also* Poletown
Generation to Generation (1985), 127n2, 247, 296. *See also* Friedman, Edwin
giant triplets of racism/materialism/militarism, 17, 30, 273; as principalities, 15
Girard, Rene, 119. *See also* scapegoat
globalization, corporate, 64, 87, 137, 185; assault on community, 187; and community as a response, 190–91; defined, 185; and Mammon, 190; and September 11, 186
God, 197, 202, 271; allegiance to alone, 269; creativity of, 51, 52, 53, 100; hospitality of, 250n10; image of, 53, 64; incarnation of, 21, 81, 191, 203; judgment of, xvi, 20, 23, 64, 87, 137, 193, 196, 199, 200, 202, 271, 290, 208; nonviolence of, 65–68, 124; sovereignty of, 73, 83, 94, 207, 273; vocation to praise, 7, 34, 56, 62, 63, 89, 100, 134, 162, 174, 182, 190, 248, 253, 290; Word of, 3, 7, 42, 51, 246, 266, 285, 286, 290; rest of, 46; wrath of, 205–8

Greensboro Community Truth and Reconciliation Project, 34n3, 240
Griebler, Denise, 255n14
Guild for Psychological Studies, 30, 31
Gumbleton, Bishop Thomas, 155

Hampton, Fred, 38
Harris Brooke, 234
Harry Potter, films, xxxiii, 217–220; and his signature charm *Expelliarmus*, 218
Harry Potter and the Deathly Hallows, film, 217; book, 218. See also Rowling, J.K.
Harvard, 57, 157; Divinity School, 7; School of Business, 7, 135
Henry Ford Hospital, water health study, 244
Herrada Elena, 227. See also Detroit School Board in exile
Heschel, Abraham, 165
Hicks Charity, 239–44; arrested, 239; and "Wage Love," 240, 243
Hiroshima, 41, 42, 49, 109, 200
Hitler, Adolf, 108, 260, 263, 274, 275, 275n28
Homo Ludens (1950), 174, 175n4. See also Huzinga, Johan
Homrich 9, 242, 244, 244n4
Homrich Wrecking Inc., 242, 244
Hoover, J. Edgar, 16, 39, 212
hope, xx, xxxii, 12, 14, 17, 21, 26, 29, 43, 68, 78, 81, 83, 87, 96, 123, 132, 163, 166, 171, 172, 190, 236–37, 298; and hopelessness or despair, 12, 23, 29, 68, 81, 113, 117, 121, 123, 132, 163, 166, 167, 171, 189, 200, 203, 236, 285, 298

Hopewell, James, 247, 296
Horsley, Richard, 159
hospital, 143, 145, 202, 244; as principality, 43, 63, 137, 143, 146, 147, 249, 250n10
hospitality, xix, xxix, xxxiv, 43, 77, 90
House, Gloria Aneb, 93n2
Howes, Elizabeth Boyden, 31
Hughes, Langston, 17
human being, 8, 19, 35, 68, 125, 134, 170, 293; as image of God, 53, 64
The Human Being (2002), 32, 53n18. See also Wink, Walter
Hurricane Katrina, 205–8, 230; and impeachment, 210; wrath of, 207
Hussein, Saddam, 49, 107, 201
Huzinga, Johan, 174, 175n4

images, as principalities, 11, 60, 91, 103, 105, 110, 129–31, 139, 178, 260–62, 289, 291
Immigration and Customs Enforcement (ICE), 267; and the Ku Klux Klan, 268
impeachment, 17, 259; articles of for George W. Bush, 209–15, 214n4
imperial liturgies, 47–48, 65–68, 177
inauguration, presidential, 59; of Donald Trump, 60, 254, 259, 261, 269, 274–75; prayers, 271, 275–76, of Richard Nixon, 277
indigenous peoples, 174
Intifada, 51
Iran-Contra, xvii, 115

Jackson, Phil, 176
jails and prisons: Birmingham,

INDEX OF NAMES AND SUBJECTS

Alabama, 67, 226, 252; Danbury Correctional, 37, 40, 44; Detroit Central Detention, 239, 242. *See also* Paul, as prisoner

Jesus: and the bank, 33; confronting the city, 89, 206, 294; crucified, 25, 64, 99; discerning the angel of Jerusalem, 89; and economy, 159, 160n3; and his family, 129, 134; and Mammon, 139–40; name of, 273; and "the other side," 171–72; and politics of healing, 120–21, 144, 147–48; and the powers, 12, 13, 63, 65, 101, 120, 138, 171; resisting violence and empire, 31; and resurrection freedom, 14, 68, 203; story hijacked, 219, 220; and surveillance, 211–12; on trial, 25

Jesus' Third Way (1987), 31. *See also* Wink, Walter

Johnson, Nelson and Joyce, xiv, 240, 241; and Greensboro Massacre, 240; and Greensboro organizing, 191; and Moral Mondays Movement, 240

Jones-Day law firm, 226

Jordon, Michael, 178; as image and idol, 178; as principality, 179

Josephus, 66

The Joy of Sports (1993), 176. *See also* Novak, Michael

Jung, Karl, 24, 32

jury, last vestige of democracy, 227

Just Jesus, My Struggle to Become Human (2014), 30, 35. *See also* Wink, Walter

justification, 25, 88, 101, 130, 131, 163, 168, 178, 248, 270, 290; in faith and freedom, 23, 68, 182

kairos, 89, 294–95. *See also Seasons of Faith and Conscience*

Kasemann, Ernst, 68

Keepers of the Mountain West Virginia, 243

Kelsey, George, 168; as professor to Martin Luther King Jr., 168

King, Martin Luther, Jr., xxix, 11; assassination, 15; "Beyond Vietnam: Breaking the Silence," xxix, 15n32; and the FBI, 212; and the giant triplets as powers, xxix, 15, 273; "Letter from a Birmingham Jail," 67, 226; and vocation of agony, 16; and workers, 157

Kissinger, Henry, 108, 201, 282

Korten, David, 186, 186n2, 190

Ku Klux Klan, 263; dark net-like, 283; and Greensboro Massacre, 240, and ICE, 268

land: and eminent domain, 226; urban clearing, 114, 244

law, xv, 15, 66, 73, 99; above the (lawless authority), 102, 160, 187–88, 201–2, 214, 215; aggressions of, 99; "Black laws," 170; and Emergency Management, 222, 225–26, 240; as Levitical purity code, 169; vocation of, 100

legitimation, 7, 48, 279; and military action, 201; presidential, 59–61, 200–201

A Letter to the Vietnamese, 40, 41n6. *See also* Berrigan, Daniel

Levy, Kate, 232

liturgical action, xxxiii, 4, 13, 31, 41,

307

46, 49, 65–68, 71, 76–81, 83, 95–96, 140
Liuzzo, Viola, 38
Lowery, Joseph, 158

Malcolm X, 14
Mammon, 137, 139–40, 161, 189–90
Manning, Donte, xviii
"Mapping the Water Crisis" (2016), 244
Marsh, Charles, 39
Marshall Thurgood, 118
Matthew 25 Pledge, 273
Matthiesen, Bishop Leroy, 75
Marx, Karl, xxxiv, 105, 138, 176, 181; and fetishism, 140
The Matrix, film, 220
Maurin, Peter, 221, 224
McAlister, Elizabeth, 37
The Meaning of the City (1970), 18, 20, 21, 22, 85, 87. See also Ellul, Jacques
media, Detroit, xxxiii, 75, 116, 151–55, 196, 222, 261, 268, 277–79, 288, 297; *Cable News Network,* 268; *Christianity Today,* 271–72; *Detroit Free Press,* 151, 232; *Detroit News,* 63, 151, 155; *Detroit Sunday Journal,* 154; *New York Times,* 151, 155, 206, 261, 265, 268, 284; social, 261, 277–84; *Wall Street Journal,* 265, 284
Mercer, Robert, software billionaire, 281; and the Trump campaign, 281. See also Bannon, Steve; Cambridge Analytica; Conway, Kellyanne
Methodism, xv, 57, 73, 83, 194–98, 271; and slavery, 198
middle passage, 132, 192, 194, 197

Miller, Alice, 127
Milosz, Czeslaw, xix
miracle, 31
money, 193–94, 196, 221; as a principality, xix, xxxii, 57, 106, 140–41, 159, 172, 189, 241, 254, 264; and moneylenders, 221, 224. See also banks; fetishism; Mammon
Money and Power (1984), 140n2. See also Ellul, Jacques
Monroe, Marilyn, 260
Moore, Helen, 229
Moral Monday's Movement, 240, 242
Myers, Ched, 54, 65, 163n3, 171
myth, 49, 88; of domination, 25, 176; of a justified nation, 270; of nuclearism, 48n5, 49; of objectivism, 8, 25; of origins, 46–54, 67; of redemptive violence, xxxiv, 34n3, 35, 49; and resistance, 50–54; technological, 22

Naming the Powers (1984), 24, 25, 34, 56, 113. See also Wink, Walter
nations, 3, 5–6, 17–18, 63, 102; angels of, xxix, 87; as servants of God, 33, 102
National Conference on Religion and Race 1963, 11, 165
National Security Agency (NSA), 57, 214, 280
National Security Strategy, 189. See also Berry, Wendell
Nazism, xxix, 5, 32, 34, 39, 121, 285
neoliberalism, 263. See also structural adjustment
Nevada Desert Experience, 82
New Orleans, 207, 223, 230, 237, 240

INDEX OF NAMES AND SUBJECTS

Nicaragua, xvii, 115
Niemoeller, Martin, 5
Nightingale, Florence, 63, 137, 146
Nixon, Richard, 108, 130, 181; exorcism of, 4, 277; and Henry Kissinger, 282; and pastoral care, 277; and reduction of truth to marketing and credibility, 282
nonviolence, xxxii–xxxiii, 16, 17, 18, 24, 31, 35, 51, 67, 76; as antiwar movement, 14, 16, 39, 249; as direct action, xxxiii, 30, 31, 123, 286; as freedom struggle, 14, 16, 165, 167; Gandhian, 200; gospel, 162; as resistance movements, 83; training for, 210, 286; and truth, 200. *See also* Berrigan; Catonsville Nine; Homrich 9; liturgical action; Martin Luther King Jr.; Plowshares; sanctuary
North American Free Trade Agreement (NAFTA), 161, 187, 268
Novak, Michael, 176, 176n6
nuclear weapons, 106, 263; arms race, xxxi, 58–59, 73, 81; and nuclearism, xxii, 48n5, 107, 121; resistance, 34, 73, 75, 76, 78–84. *See also* Hiroshima; Plowshares; war

Obama, Barack, 60, 266, 279, 280, 281
Oppenheimer, Robert, 74–75
Opportunity Detroit, 226
Orr, Kevyn, 225
Orwell, George, and Orwellian, 110, 277; the assault on truth, 278

parrhesia/bold speaking, 250–51, 250n10, 251n12
patriarchy, 2, 48, 53, 55, 121, 128, 129, 249, 251. *See also* Eisler, Riane
Paul, 250n10; and justification, 68, 130, 168; and the law, 100–102, 168, 169; and the powers, 7, 102, 129; as prisoner, xvi, 54, 54n20, 55, 121, 169, 170, 251; speaking boldly, 251
Peace is the Way (2000), 35. *See also* Wink, Walter
Peale, Norman Vincent, pastor to Donald Trump, 271
Pentagon, xxix, 13, 57, 74, 83, 108–9, 113, 115–16, 200
Peoples' Water Affordability Plan of 2005, 241, 243. *See also* water
Pinkney, Reverend Edward, xiv
Plowshares actions, 41, 82
Poletown, 93; arson in, 93; documentary, 297–98, 94n2
possession, 5, 7, 58, 74, 102, 107, 197, 260
prayer and the powers, xvii, xvi, 5, 34n35, 41, 73–75, 81–83, 95, 123–24, 140, 144, 158, 167
The Presence of the Kingdom (1967), 19, 20. *See also* Ellul, Jacques
Principalities and Powers: and the assault on truth, 109, 168, 199–200, 277–79, 282, 284; as beyond human accountability, 13, 62, 63–64, 149, 153, 157, 160–61, 182, 186–88, 191, 201–2, 283, 290; as biblical language, xxix, 7–8, 15, 57, 136; as creatures, 19–20, 34, 45, 52, 55, 61–63, 137, 138; and demonic

aggressions, xxxiv, 6, 9, 14–15, 59, 116, 138, 144, 146, 168–69, 267, 272; and their ethic of survival, 64, 189–90, 248, 252, 290; and the exemplary powers, 141, 248–51; as exposed or unmasked, xxxiv, 3, 8, 31, 52, 56, 67, 75, 120, 122, 177, 207, 290, 298; as legion, 57, 119–21; and mapping, 291–92, 256; and pastoral care, xxxiv, 3, 5, 112, 143–48, 157, 277; and the preeminent power, 71, 188, 263; in rivalry and collusion, 113–17, 119, 189, 264, 297; as separating us from God, 143, 144; their tactics and strategies, 21, 267, 283; victims of, 14–15, 59, 82, 91, 121, 144, 168, 177, 196, 250, 277; as visible/invisible (interior/exterior, inner/outer, heavenly/earthly), xxix, 25–26, 35, 56, 57, 100, 122, 136–37, 163, 169, 190–91, 245–46, 289; their varieties, 289; as having vocation, xvii, 7, 20, 34, 61–64, 87, 132, 137–38, 141, 146–47, 153–54, 160–63, 182, 183, 246–51, 284, 290, 293–94; and the work of the church, 35, 141, 162–64, 191, 248, 253, 255, 290

The Principalities and Powers (1956), 101n2. *See also* Caird, G.B.

Protestant work ethic, 57, 131, 163

Race Matters (1993), 132. *See also* West, Cornell

racism, xxxiv, 6, 11–12, 132–33, 155, 165, 250, 270; as a principality, 11–12, 15–17, 116, 165–72. *See also* giant triplets

Readers United (RU), 152–55

Reagan, Ronald, xvii, 128, 201, 270

redlining and restrictive covenants, 170

resurrection, 43, 146, 298; breaking the power of death, 14, 199, 203, 257; breaking of the "seal," 79; and Easter Vigil Liturgy, 78–81; as ethic, 23; as freedom, 14, 43–44, 68, 251; "stations" of, 257. *See also* resistance

Rivera, Diego, 90

resistance, xxxii, 9–10, 39–40, 46, 83, 132, 134, 189–92; liturgy of, 50–54, 78, 83; as the way to live humanly, 5–6, 86–88, 203, 285–86, 290

Ricoeur, Paul, 48

Roberts, EM Roy, 232

Romero, Bishop Oscar, 250

Rowling, J.K., 217; and the commercial powers, 218; and the Oxford Inklings, 217

Ruether, Rosemary, 134

ruler, xvi, xxxiii, 10, 25, 58–59, 65, 99–100, 117, 260, 269–70, 289; *arche/archon*, 58–59, 260

St. Peter's Episcopal Church, 226, 224, 240; and Good Friday public stations of the cross, 256; as water distribution station, 243

sanctuary, 73, 287; current revival, 255, 256; movement in the 1980's, 42, 50, 249

Satan, 24–25, 79, 100; as "adversary," 101; as agent provocateur, 101; as the Dragon, 102; as

310

executioner, 101: as a parable of the fall, 100–102; as the power of death, 5, 101; prosecutor in heavenly court, 101
scapegoating, 119–20, 132. *See also* Girard, Rene
Schools in Detroit: Catherine Ferguson Academy 232; charter, 231; Cooley High School, 206; Day School for the Deaf, 232; Oakman Orthopedic, 232
schools of theology, xxv, 30, 32, 33, 135–36, 231; Auburn Seminary, 24; Finkenwalde, 39; Princeton Theological Seminary, 273; underground seminary, 13n29, 39, 40; Union Theological Seminary, xxx, 9, 40; urban ministry, 254–55; Word and World, 205n1
Seasons of Faith and Conscience; Reflections on Liturgical Direct Action (1992, 2008), xxxii, 71, 105, 250n11. *See also* Wylie-Kellermann, Bill
A Second Birthday (1970), 146. *See also* Stringfellow, William.
secrecy, 74, 76, 209, 282
September 11/Twin Towers, 60, 200–201, 202, 206, 215
Sessions, Jeff, 263; and Ku Klux Klan, 263
Shaef, Anne Wilson, 117n7
Silberman, Neil, 159
Snyder Governor Rick, 224, 240
social media, 277–84; and addictive mechanisms, 279; and algorithmic enclaves, 281; and Big Data, 281; as centrifically democratizing, 279; and fake news or hoaxes 280; as principality, 277–84; and surveillance, 283; and trolls, 280, 283. *See also* alt-right; dark net
Sojourners, xvii
Sophia/Wisdom, 55, 275
Sorrow Built a Bridge (1989), 41. *See also* Berrigan, Daniel
Southern Christian Leadership Council (SCLC), 158; motto, 167
Spirit of Detroit, 92; sculpture, 91
spiritual disciplines and practices, 35, 90, 95–96, 182–83, 206, 286; discernment, 3, 137, 163, 167, 176, 256. *See also* prayer and the powers
sports, as imperial liturgy, 177; as play and praise, 174; as a principality, 139, 173–83; as religion, 175
Standing Rock Sioux, 255
state, 7, 10–14, 44, 48, 53, 102–3, 186, 248, 250, 251, 263. *See also* Constantinian arrangement
Stations of the Cross, 256. *See also* cross, stations of the resurrection
Stephens, Bret, 265, 284–85
Stringfellow William: on the aggressions of the powers, 99, 212, 267, 272; and Anthony Towne, 4, 14, 37; on the assault on truth, 278, 282; on the authority of humanity, 62; on baptism, 12, 171; and Barth, 9–11, 57, 173; and Berrigan, 13, 37, 40, 41, 42; as biblical theologian, 4; on blasphemy, 270; on commercial athletics, 173; on creatureliness of the powers, 45; on the demonic, 63; on discern-

ment, 3, 145, 266; on displacement of ideology by technology, 282; in East Harlem, 4, 13; ecclesiology, 141, 247, 253; and Ellul, 18–23; on the ethic of survival, 139; eulogy for, 42–43; as exorcist, 4–5, 276; on friendship, 43; at Harvard, 35–36; in illness, xxviii, 145; on image as a power, 261, 262; as indicted felon, 15; on leaders as victims, 59; on living humanly, 286; and Martin Luther King Jr., 11, 17, 165; as mentor, xxxi, 3–4, 206; on the power of death, 14; on the powers in rivalry and collusion, 264; on racism, 12, 166; on resurrection, 43–44, 146; on the scope and number of the powers, 57; on state absorbing nation, 268; in theological conversation, 3–27; his theological method, 22; as theological reviver of the principalities, 7; on the undoing of creation, 63; on the vocation of the powers, 88, 160; on the weather, 207; and Wink, 23, 24, 25, 34, 186; and World Student Christian Movement, 5; on the Wrath, 205

structural adjustment, 224

surveillance, xix, 116, 209–15; Jesus and, 211–13; Martin Luther King and, 212; normalized as commercial, 213; as pretention to divine omniscience, 213; and social media, 281, 283; as spiritual assault, 212; technology of, 116, 213, 224, 226, 282, 283; as unconstitutional, 209, 210, 214, 282. *See also* Foreign Intelligence Surveillance Act (FISA), National Security Agency (NSA)

The Symbolism of Evil (1967), 48. *See also* Ricoeur, Paul

tax resistance, 203, 211, 223, 253

Teach for America, 235–36

The Technological Society (1954), 21, 87. *See also* Ellul, Jacques

The Technological System (1980), 22n48. *See also* Ellul, Jacques

technology: as autonomous power, xxix, 22, 51, 105, 106, 107; and education, 233; as means, 107; military, 13, 59, 105, 107–9; as replacing ideology, 110, 281; as sacred realm, 106; and social media, 281, 283; and surveillance, 116, 213, 224, 226, 282, 283; and technocracy, 13, 21, 282

terrorism, state, 201

Thoughts on Slavery, 193, 196. *See also* Wesley, John

Tiamat, as god, 47

Thich Nhat Hahn, 249; and the sacrifice of Buddhism, 249

throne, 47, 52, 86, 275; *thronos*, 57–58

torture, 65

Towne, Anthony, 4, 14, 18, 37, 43, 44

Trible, Phyllis, 128

Trump, Donald, era of, xxxiv, 259; administration as a collusion of powers, 264; as biblical "fool" and idolater, 271; as brand principality, 262; church challenges to, 256, 271, 272, 273, 274–75; as economic empire, 262–63; as image principality, 261–62; and islamophobia, 267; possessed by office, 260; prayers for, 275–76; and social media, 279–84; and the theology of national populism, 269–71; as Troll-in-chief, 283; unleashing a spirit of domination, 265–69

truth, 271, 273, 264–65, 286, 288; and "alternative facts," fake news, and hoaxes, 261, 277, 279–81, 283; assault on, 277, 278, 282, 284

unions, 11, 51, 152, 224, 225, 235; AFL-CIO, 152; AFSME sanitation workers, 157; and the church, 155, 157–64; and community struggle, 153–54, 191; Council of Newspaper Unions, 155; National Nurses United, 242; as principalities, 161; Teamsters Union, 157; United Auto Workers (UAW), 161; United Mine Workers, 155

United Nations, 241; Special Rapporteurs on Water and Housing, 243; and water as a human right, 241

Unmasking the Powers (1986), 24. *See also* Wink Walter

"The Uses of Money," sermon, 194. *See also* Wesley, John

Vance Security, 154

vocation, 16, 100; of a power, 34, 152; of a newspaper, 152

Voldemort, 218–20

wall of hostility, 169, and "the other side," 171

war, xxxii, 6, 17, 29, 42, 60, 66, 115, 220, 252, 253, 259, 277; in Afghanistan, 115, 215; in Central America, 115, 249, 255; Cold, 108, 115; crimes, 201; on drugs, 115, 122; in the Gulf, 49, 106–8; in Iraq, 49, 199–201, 210; nuclear, 81, 108, 138, 259; in Panama, 116; preemptive, 189; on terror, 201, 207; in Southeast Asia, 11, 13, 16–17, 30, 109–10, 181, 277; theology of, 48, 49; and "war powers," 116, 215; World War II, 9, 11, 108, 109. *See also* tax resistance

water: affordability, 241; and climate change, 149, 207; and Detroit struggle, 239–44; direct actions, 242, 243, 244; as human right, 242; protectors, 255, 268; and public health, 42, 149, 244; as public trust, 242; as sacred gift, 242; shut-offs, 6, 232, 243, 244, 264; shut-off moratorium, 243. *See also* Charity Hicks; Detroit Peoples' Water Board; Henry Ford Hospital health study; Homrich 9; "Mapping the Water Crisis"; Peoples Water Affordability Plan of 2005

Watson, JoAnn, minister and councilwoman, 223

We Die Before We Live (1980), 42. *See also* Berrigan, Daniel

We the People of Detroit, 242. *See also* Henry Ford Hospital health study; "Mapping the Water Crisis"

weather and the sovereignty of God, 207
Weber, Peter, 73
Wesley, John, 193–98; and abolitionist movement, 197; and William Wilberforce, 197
West, Cornell, 132
When Corporations Rule the World, (1996), 186n2. *See also* Korten, David
Where the Water Goes Around, xxxii. *See also* Wylie-Kellermann, Bill
white flight, 223; and block busting, 170, 206; and churches, 252; as organized and engineered xix, 170
White, Lynn, 46
White, Paula, 271
wilderness, 50, 218, 294
Wink, Walter: and the angels of the churches, 246, 293–96; bad career move, 33; as baptized in the spirit, 31; and the church's task, 64; on Constantine, 7; his critique of biblical objectivism, 33; and the domination system, 139, 185, 297; and economics, 185; and Elizabeth Bowden Howes, 31; as exegete, 35–36; and James Foreman, 31; and June Keener Wink, 30, 31, 32, 33, 36; on hermeneutical exorcism, 8; on human being, 35–36; and integral (spiritual/material) worldview, 26, 32, 35, 56, 113, 136, 166, 245, 293–96; and language for the powers, 34–35, 57–61, 86–87; and Martin Luther King Jr., 30; as mentor, 32; and the myth of redemptive violence, 47, 49, 219; his pedagogy and hermeneutics, 33–34, 36; powers trilogy, 23; and Riane Eisler, 49; as scholar-activist, 29, 31; and the Sermon on the Mount, 33; and Stringfellow, 4, 9, 24, 34, 160, 185; and theology of nonviolence, 24, 35
World Student Christian Federation, 19; Oslo gathering (1947), 19
wrath of God, 205–8; as insurrection, 206
Wylie-Kellermann, Bill, xvii, xv, xx
Wylie-Kellermann, Lydia, 209, 210

Yoder, John Howard, 11n25
Young Mayor Coleman Alexander, 86

www.ingramcontent.com/pod-product-compliance
Lightning Source LLC
Chambersburg PA
CBHW071147070526
44584CB00019B/2700